Having witnessed many efforts at school improvement in Birmingham and London in particular, I just wish we had had available this latest volume from Deb McGregor and Linet Arthur. Every new school leader obtaining a copy and all those wanting to extend their confident competence and understanding will bless the day that the authors put this invaluable and readable volume together.

Sir Tim Brighouse, *British Educator, Former Schools Commissioner for London*

Leading schools can be challenging, collegial, creative and confounding – sometimes all in the same day! This book synthesises an impressive range of evidence and theory across a broad range of areas, providing an excellent handbook for practitioners and students of contemporary school leadership. In addition, it brings the research to life through a variety of examples and quotes drawn from national and international contexts, including the authors' own work and experience of working with school leaders in England.

Professor Toby Greany, *Professor of Education and Convener of the Centre for Research in Education Leadership and Management, University of Nottingham*

Drawing on a wide range of research evidence and the authors' many years of experience of teaching and studying what works in the world of successful school leadership (and what doesn't!), this timely and comprehensive book provides new and refreshing insights into the field. As such, it should prove an invaluable resource for scholars, policymakers, and practitioners, especially those aspiring to lead and colleagues who are already in middle and senior school leadership positions.

Professor Alan Floyd, *Institute of Education, University of Reading*

This book is a must for all aspiring head teachers. It provides a broad spectrum of the work on the subject. I particularly enjoyed the chapter on School Culture and Improvement. Overall, it is a great resource to 'dip into' when needed.

Tony Wilmot, *Head teacher, Secondary 11–16 School*

This book is a great source of information for head teachers. I wish I'd had it to read before teaching the NPQH and NPQs. The chapter on retention and recruitment is particularly useful.

Duncan Birds, *Head teacher, Primary 3–11 School*

This book was an incredibly interesting read. I found it useful as I move into headship. Not only have I found some great advice and guidance I have also found comfort in some of the stories and examples that have shown me that I'm not failing so early in the job but am just on the journey that so many other heads and schools have been, and are on.

Neal Critchley, *Associate Head teacher, Secondary 11–18 School*

What Works in School Leadership?

The key purpose of school leadership is to improve learning. *What Works in School Leadership?* examines research evidence and leadership models that focus on learning and provides resources that will help readers to understand their school's culture and develop strategies to change and improve their schools. It introduces and explains contemporary research, leadership theories and real-world examples to identify what works (and doesn't work) in school leadership.

Recognising that leadership occurs at all levels in schools, this book addresses factors that underpin successful distributed, middle and team leadership. Chapters identify how leaders can effectively recruit, retain and motivate their staff, as well as the ways in which professional development can be supported. Key aspects of inclusive leadership that address diversity and equity are also considered in depth.

Each school is unique and there is no magic formula that will guarantee instant results in every school; with this in mind, *What Works in School Leadership?* provides readers with a range of research evidence and resources to enable them to select strategies that will create a positive learning environment for staff and pupils at their own school.

This is essential reading for school leaders, those aspiring to leadership and anyone studying or researching school leadership.

Linet Arthur has extensive experience in educational leadership. This includes teaching courses on educational leadership and management to hundreds of students (at MA and doctoral levels). She has also undertaken research, training and consultancy in educational leadership for schools, local authorities and government departments in the UK and internationally.

Debra McGregor works at Oxford Brookes University. She has worked in education for nearly 40 years. She has taught in primary and secondary schools and various university settings in the UK, Europe and the USA. She has published many papers and books concerned with teaching and learning, the performing arts, cognitive development, the nature of creativity, school leadership and close to practice research.

What Works in School Leadership?

Making Evidence-Informed Choices

Linet Arthur and Debra McGregor

LONDON AND NEW YORK

Designed cover image: © Getty Images

First edition published 2025
by Routledge
4 Park Square, Milton Park, Abingdon, Oxon, OX14 4RN

and by Routledge
605 Third Avenue, New York, NY 10158

Routledge is an imprint of the Taylor & Francis Group, an informa business

© 2025 Linet Arthur and Debra McGregor

The right of Linet Arthur and Debra McGregor to be identified as authors of this work has been asserted in accordance with sections 77 and 78 of the Copyright, Designs and Patents Act 1988.

All rights reserved. No part of this book may be reprinted or reproduced or utilised in any form or by any electronic, mechanical, or other means, now known or hereafter invented, including photocopying and recording, or in any information storage or retrieval system, without permission in writing from the publishers.

Trademark notice: Product or corporate names may be trademarks or registered trademarks, and are used only for identification and explanation without intent to infringe.

British Library Cataloguing-in-Publication Data
A catalogue record for this book is available from the British Library

Library of Congress Cataloging-in-Publication Data
Names: Arthur, Linet, 1956- author. | McGregor, Debra, author.
Title: What works in school leadership? : making evidence-informed choices / Linet Arthur and Debra McGregor.
Description: First edition. | Abingdon, Oxon ; New York, NY : Routledge, 2025. | Includes bibliographical references and index. |
Identifiers: LCCN 2024022300 (print) | LCCN 2024022301 (ebook) | ISBN 9780367202712 (hardback) | ISBN 9780367202729 (paperback) | ISBN 9780429260612 (ebook)
Subjects: LCSH: Educational leadership--Research. | School management and organization. | School improvement programs. | Classroom environment.
Classification: LCC LB2806 .A645 2025 (print) | LCC LB2806 (ebook) | DDC 371.2--dc23/eng/20240713
LC record available at https://lccn.loc.gov/2024022300
LC ebook record available at https://lccn.loc.gov/2024022301

ISBN: 978-0-367-20271-2 (hbk)
ISBN: 978-0-367-20272-9 (pbk)
ISBN: 978-0-429-26061-2 (ebk)

DOI: 10.4324/9780429260612

Typeset in Melior
by SPi Technologies India Pvt Ltd (Straive)

This book is dedicated to all school leaders, their staff and students who have participated in educational research; without them this book would not have been possible.

In memory of Sir Tim Brighouse, an inspiring educational leader.

Contents

List of illustrations	xiv
Preface	xviii
Foreword	xxiii

1 Introduction — 1
- Introduction: what is the nature of leadership? — 1
- What is the English context? — 3
- What are the main aspects of school leadership? — 4
- What are instructional, distributed and transformational leadership approaches? — 5
- What is considered in this book? — 6
- References — 9

2 Leading learning — 11
- Introduction — 11
- What does leadership concerned with learning look like? — 12
- How do domains of leadership practice connect with learning? — 12
- What makes a difference in school leadership? — 14
- What does effective leadership influencing learning look like? — 14
- What are the characteristics of effective school leaders? — 15
- How is leadership for learning understood and enacted? — 17
- How is leadership of learning understood and enacted? — 20
  - School leaders matter: How and why? — 21
- How do action learning sets (ALSs) become a collaborative forum for leaders to discuss, plan, enact and review leadership practice? — 22
- How is learning-centred leadership understood and enacted? — 30
  - Data and leading improvement — 30
  - Practices and leading improvement — 32
  - Setting directions — 32
  - Building relations and developing people — 33
  - Developing the organisation to support desired practices — 34
  - Improving the teaching programme — 35
- Conclusion — 35
- Note — 43
- References — 43

3	School culture and improvement	46
	Introduction	46
	What does 'culture' mean?	47
	What are the key aspects of culture?	48
	Culture is shared	48
	Culture is seen and unseen	49
	History plays a part in culture	50
	How to clarify cultural characteristics?	51
	How do national cultures impact on schools?	54
	How to surface cultural assumptions?	56
	What is the difference between culture and subculture?	57
	Is there a link between school culture and school improvement?	59
	What are the differences between primary and secondary schools' culture?	64
	How can school leaders influence culture?	64
	Conclusion	67
	References	74
4	Leading change	77
	Introduction	77
	What are the key challenges of educational change?	79
	Definition of change	79
	Success and failure in educational change	81
	What are the challenges of national policy change?	81
	What are the challenges facing school leaders in managing change?	83
	What are the challenges for middle leaders?	85
	What are the challenges for teachers?	85
	What are the challenges relating to parents?	86
	What are the challenges relating to students?	88
	What are the challenges relating to resources?	89
	What are the challenges relating to the school context?	89
	How do teachers respond to change?	91
	What tends to be teachers' initial response to change?	92
	What are the likely emotional reactions of teachers to change?	93
	How far do teachers' attitudes towards change depend on agency and identity?	95
	What makes a positive difference to teachers' responses to change?	96
	What are the different theories and models of educational change?	96
	How to establish vision/aims/goals?	100
	How to identify 'change agents'?	103
	How to communicate with participants and take action?	103
	How to address barriers to change, including the need for training and development	104
	How to monitor results and celebrate success, bearing in mind accountability?	106
	How to maintain progress and create sustainability through cultural change?	107
	Conclusion	110
	Note	117
	References	118

5	The empowered and/or squeezed middle	123
	Introduction	123
	What is the difference between distributed and middle leadership?	124
	Distributed leadership defined	125
	Middle leadership defined	125
	Why has distributed leadership become such a popular concept?	126
	Problems with distributed leadership	128
	Why are middle leaders so important?	131
	What do middle leaders do?	132
	Teaching and learning	132
	Managing relationships and supporting collaborative professionalism	133
	Professional development	133
	Administration	135
	How are middle leaders squeezed?	136
	How do middle leaders create effective teams?	138
	What are the key theories about teams?	139
	Stages of team development	139
	Team roles	141
	Task, team and individual	143
	What is the difference between effective and ineffective teams?	143
	What are the obstacles to team effectiveness?	146
	Conclusion	146
	Notes	150
	References	150
6	Leading professional development	156
	Introduction	156
	What does professional development mean?	157
	Professionalism	157
	Performativity and professionalism	158
	Definitions of professional development	158
	What are the key theories about learning and professional development?	159
	Adult learning approaches	160
	Reflective practice	161
	Enquiry-based professional development	164
	Communities of practice	166
	Learning organisations and professional learning communities	168
	Collaborative approaches	171
	Coaching and mentoring	171
	What is the role of induction in professional development?	176
	What are the key Influences on teachers' professional development?	178
	What can work in professional development for teachers?	179
	Critique of what works	180
	Guidelines for PD	181
	What can work in school leadership development?	182
	National versus local systems of school leadership development	183
	School leaders' learning needs	183

Effective school leadership preparation	184
National Professional Qualification for Headship	184
How should professional development of teachers and leaders be evaluated?	185
Conclusion	188
References	194

7 Recruitment and retention of staff: leadership implications — 202
- Introduction — 202
- How do teacher supply and demand differ? — 203
  - Supply — 203
  - Demand — 204
- What should be considered in teacher and headteacher recruitment? — 205
  - Recruitment and retention of headteachers — 206
- What does teacher turnover mean? — 208
  - Teacher turnover in high-need schools — 208
  - Costs and benefits of teacher turnover — 209
  - Training and teacher turnover — 210
- What makes teachers leave? — 210
  - Workload — 210
  - Stress — 211
  - Pupil behaviour — 212
  - School leadership and professional support — 213
  - Resilience — 215
  - Autonomy, agency and performativity — 217
- What are the solutions to recruitment and retention? — 218
- Conclusion — 220
- References — 222

8 Motivating teachers — 226
- Introduction — 226
- What is intrinsic and extrinsic motivation? — 227
- What is self-determination theory? — 228
- What is self-efficacy theory? — 230
- How to build motivation through community and agency? — 232
- What is Herzberg's motivation-hygiene theory/two factor theory? — 233
- What is achievement goal theory? — 235
- What are the shortcomings of motivation theories? — 237
- Conclusion — 238
- References — 247

9 Leading more inclusively: addressing diversity and equity — 251
- Introduction — 251
- What are the key terms linked to diversity and equity? — 252
- What is the role of school leaders in managing inclusion? — 254
  - Use of data to address inequalities — 255
  - Organisational and community approaches — 257
- How does social justice relate to diversity? — 258
  - Challenges of addressing social justice — 259
  - Action for social justice — 261

How can school leaders address different aspects of diversity?	261
Disability and inclusion	261
Race	262
Gender	265
LGBTQ+	267
What can work in managing diversity and creating equitable schools?	269
How to embrace diversity?	270
Conclusion	272
References	280
10 Conclusion: Reflecting on school leadership	**284**
Introduction	284
School leadership: evidence of what can work in turbulent times	285
Reference	289
Glossary	290
Index	294

Illustrations

Figures

3.1	The cultural iceberg	50
3.2	The cultural web	52
3.3	School culture, effectiveness and improvement	59
5.1	Team function impact matrix	144
6.1	Kolb's experiential learning cycle	160
6.2	The process of reflective teaching	161
6.3	Action research spiral	165
8.1	Relationally locating teacher and learner agency to indicate structural and others' influences	233

Tables

2.1	List of practices within the four domains that successful leaders engage in	12
2.2	A list of the ten key characteristics of successful leadership that have been mapped onto the four domains of effective leaders' practices	17
2.3	Summary of the range of 'concerns' and leadership 'actions' planned that resulted in raised attainment	27
4.1	Models of educational change	98
5.1	Leadership functions in the transition and action phases of teamwork	141
5.2	Promotion and inhibition of effectiveness of SLTs, based on Wallace	145
6.1	Questions that assist the process of developing reflective practice	162
6.2	Senge's five disciplines and how they apply to schools	169
6.3	Impact of coaching	174
6.4	Standards and skills in the DfE Early Career Framework	177
8.1	Herzberg et al.'s motivation and hygiene factors	234
8.2	Extracts from Butler's Goal Orientations for Teaching	237

Boxes

1.1	Advert for Assistant Headteacher, 2023	1
1.2	School leaders: pressure within the system	4
1.3	Headteachers describe their work	4
2.1	A case of developing leadership skills across a school	19
2.2	A primary school headteacher's strategy for maintaining an Ofsted rating of 'Outstanding' for more than ten years	21
2.3	Action learning sets focusing on potential leadership actions to improve learning	23
2.4	A focus on teacher assistant (TA) professional development	25
2.5	Illustrating the use of data to improve student learning	31
2.6	Looking at data to inform how to improve boys' attainment in writing	31
2.7	Questions for reflection and action	36
3.1	Values and vision (Hallinger and Heck, 2003, p. 221)	48
3.2	Example of a school's past history influencing the present culture	51
3.3	Teachers talking about their school's culture	52
3.4	Cultural web of an academy	53
3.5	Understanding cultural expectations	57
3.6	Student views of school culture	58
3.7	Educational culture statements: what is characteristic of the school	61
3.8	Links between school culture and improvement	63
3.9	Reflections on a beneficial school culture	64
3.10	Symbols of cultural leadership	65
3.11	Actions arising from the assessment of a school's culture	66
3.12	Questions for reflection and action	68
4.1	Some of the many policy changes in schools in England since 2005	77
4.2	First-order and second-order change in two schools	80
4.3	Putting policy into practice: the case of formative assessment	82
4.4	Principals' experience of teacher resistance	84
4.5	School case studies of leading change: The Wroxham School	87
4.6	Superheads: a policy mistake?	90
4.7	Teachers' justifications for not changing	92
4.8	Leading change: Burlington Danes	101
4.9	Building change into school structures	108
4.10	Leading change: Manning School	108
4.11	How to make change fail/What NOT to do if initiating change	111
4.12	Questions for reflection and action	112
5.1	The leadership vs management debate	124
5.2	Experiences of distributed leadership	127
5.3	Two examples of distributed leadership in large, inner-city primary schools	127
5.4	Appointing staff	133
5.5	Professional development for middle leaders: action learning sets	135
5.6	Benefits of teamwork	139
5.7	Questions for reflection and action	148

6.1	Models of teacher professionalism	158
6.2	Examples of reflective PD activities in schools	163
6.3	Example of collaborative enquiry: Teacher Peer Excellence Groups	166
6.4	Example of teacher community of practice: TeachMeet	167
6.5	Example of PLCs: teacher learning communities	170
6.6	Examples of collaborative PD: lesson study and collegial visits	172
6.7	Examples of coaching and mentoring: the GROW approach and the Classroom Assessment Scoring System	175
6.8	Example of a Local Education Authority induction programme for new headteachers	178
6.9	Guidelines for PD activities	181
6.10	Example of measuring the impact of professional development (personal communication)	187
6.11	Questions for reflection and action	189
7.1	Recommended recruitment practices (Podolsky et al., 2019)	205
7.2	School case study: succession planning	207
7.3	Headteachers talking about the impact of the cost of living	208
7.4	Teachers talking about workload	211
7.5	Teachers talking about stress	212
7.6	Headteacher and teachers talking about the demands and rewards relating to pupils	213
7.7	Teachers talking about support	214
7.8	Headteachers talking about support services	215
7.9	Headteacher and teachers talking about resilience	216
7.10	Teacher and headteacher talking about accountability	218
7.11	Headteachers talking about 'growing your own'	220
7.12	Questions for reflection and action	220
8.1	Extrinsic factor: COVID-19	227
8.2	Extrinsic factor: teachers' pay	228
8.3	Lack of self-determination in a US school	229
8.4	Unjustified self-efficacy	232
8.5	Teachers talking about motivation factors	235
8.6	Questions for reflection and action	238
9.1	Developing more inclusive policy and practice	254
9.2	The dangers of stereotyping	256
9.3	Social justice and distributed leadership in Ireland	258
9.4	Social justice and improving student achievement in the USA	260
9.5	Case study: BME teacher segregation in the USA	264
9.6	Gender issues for special educational needs coordinators (SENCos)	266
9.7	A case of developing international links to address diversity	270
9.8	The impact of leadership courses for under-represented groups	272
9.9	Questions for reflection and action	273
10.1	Excerpt from headteacher job description	284
10.2	Leading change in a large primary school	286

Appendices

2.1	A unified model of effective leader practices	37
2.2	Introducing action learning sets	38
2.3	Framing and using action learning sets	40
2.4	Engaging in dilemmas about the nature of education provided by the school	41
3.1	Questions to help identify a school culture	68
3.2	Educational culture statements: what is characteristic of the school?	68
3.3	Questionnaire to assess the school's culture (based on Hargreaves, 1999 and Cheng Yin Cheong, 2000)	70
3.4	Questionnaire to assess the school's culture (based on MacBeath, 1998)	71
3.5	Questionnaire to assess the school's culture (based on Zhu et al.'s 2014)	72
4.1	Values and aims of schools in different Ofsted categories	112
4.2	Surfacing your educational values	114
4.3	Preparedness for change and improvement	115
4.4	Characteristics of effective change leaders	117
5.1	Key tasks in curriculum leadership	148
5.2	Running effective meetings	149
5.3	Addressing problems in teamwork	150
6.1	Professional learning community development profile	190
6.2	The GROW model. Possible questions	190
6.3	Evaluation questionnaires	192
7.1	Thinking about interviews	221
8.1	Tschannen-Moran and Woolfolk Hoy's Teachers' Sense of Efficacy Scale	239
8.2	Bandura's Self-Efficacy Scale	242
8.3	Janke et al.'s goal orientation questionnaire	246
9.1	Critical reflection prompts	274
9.2	Equity audit	275
9.3	Key activities of school leaders in managing diversity	277
9.4	Data collection for organisational readiness	279
9.5	The school for equity	279

Preface

This book has emerged as a result of the two authors engaging in many research projects with schools, teachers and headteachers from around the country and internationally. We have been privileged to witness inspiring and outstanding practices across both primary and secondary schools. School leadership has been key to the success of the schools we have encountered.

This book aims to offer an evidence-informed text that will be useful for school leaders, those aspiring to leadership and anyone studying or researching school leadership. There are a range of different leadership approaches and practices that are described and reviewed. We consider ways school leaders can excel while collaborating with and motivating their staff to create a culture of learning for students and teachers whilst embracing innovation. Throughout, we offer up-to-date perspectives of school leadership and research evidence with an appropriate critique, alongside real-life case studies or vignettes and tried-and-tested activities to support improvement that could be carried out in any school.

We hope that the book will enable school leaders to assess the evidence and make informed choices about what will work in their schools, because we recognise that there is no magic formula that will ensure success in every school. Even the best and most up-to-date evidence from research only shows what has worked in the past, in a particular set of circumstances and not what will necessarily work in the future (Biesta, 2007). In addition, it is important that school leaders are clear about what they value in education because there is no point in identifying what works if it does not achieve their aims.

The book draws on the experience and expertise of the authors developed during the teaching (of master's and doctoral students for over a decade) and the leading of educational projects and research directly related to school leadership and management. Many direct quotations from heads and teachers themselves are drawn from two particular research projects in which the authors have recently been directly involved: Leadership for Learning and the Teacher Retention Research project. These are described in the following sections.

Leadership for Learning project

The Leadership for Learning project (Menter and McGregor 2015; McGregor and Browne 2016) involved 12 Oxford City schools and over 60 primary school headteachers and middle leaders. Oxford City Council had recognised that, in order to address the problem of growing youth unemployment, academic achievement was vital to improve potential employment opportunities. In looking at the results of the schools in Oxford there was notable 'below the floor' (below the national average) attainment in English and mathematics. So the Leadership for Learning project was designed to redress this surprising lack of academic achievement in Oxford city.

The project involved senior and middle leaders engaging in a two-year programme that provided expert input in the form of whole day workshops once a term; regular evening seminars; in-school action learning set meetings (explained further in Chapter 2, 'Leading Learning') each term and bespoke headteacher coaching (discussed further in Chapter 6, 'Developing appropriate professional capital'). The research element involved termly scrutiny of external data, for example, the percentage of pupils achieving level 4 or above in English and mathematics and the percentage making expected progress in English and mathematics. The Ofsted reports for each school were also examined for gradings and commentary on leadership of teaching and learning. Throughout the two years, field notes from workshops were collated; questionnaires were collected form all participants on a termly basis; transcriptions and outputs from the action learning sets (of both middle and senior leaders) and six headteacher hour-long interviews were carried out after the project was completed. It is not clear why some schools appeared to have benefited more than others, but those that committed more fully appeared to reshape organisationally into more distributed leadership models, with middle leaders taking more responsibility within their school, as well as becoming more accountable for successful learning. There was also significant uplift in Key Stage 1 and 2 performance in literacy and numeracy in some participant schools (see Glossary). Some schools also notably improved their Ofsted grade by the end of the programme.

Interestingly, as is discussed throughout this book, the progress of the project was hindered by continuing changes of teaching staff within the schools. At one extreme, in one primary school, there was a 75% change in staffing over one summer break! The staffing 'churn' was also reflected in the -movement of headteachers over the duration of the project. Only two of the 12 schools retained the same head throughout the two-year period. The impact of staffing churn on school leadership and improvement is discussed further in Chapter 7, 'Recruitment and Retention'.

Teacher Retention project

The Teacher Retention Research project (Arthur and Bradley, 2023) aimed to investigate the reasons why teachers choose to remain working in challenging schools.

The research used a case-study design, comprising in-depth interviews with headteachers and teachers at nine schools in England, a secondary and two primaries in each of three different locations: an inner city, in which there are large areas of deprivation, a Shire County, where pockets of poverty exist among areas of relative affluence, and a coastal town in which underinvestment and industrial decline pose a number of challenges. Schools were selected based on the proportion of pupils eligible for free school meals as a proxy measure of poverty. The findings indicated that the following factors were critical in retaining teachers:

- Positive relationships with the pupils
- Sense of social justice
- Collegial support
- Resilience
- Recognition – being valued by leaders and colleagues
- Enjoyment of the challenge
- Supportive leadership
- Professional development.

Accountability measures, pupil behaviour and, to some extent, workload were factors that the participants found more challenging. Workload was not considered a reason for resigning, however – several of the teachers said that their own perfectionism and commitment were partly responsible for the level of their workload. Participants in the study gave permission for extracts from the interviews to be used in publications. Consequently there are many quotations from the interviews in this book; they serve to illustrate not only the nature of leadership practice, but also how theories can be applied (or drawn from) to highlight how the reality of school leadership might be explained and made more explicit for would-be leaders as well as experienced heads to inform their thinking or indeed particular courses of action.

National Professional Qualifications

Many readers of this book will be interested in how the material relates to the National Professional Qualifications (NPQs) relating to leadership. It should be apparent that the areas addressed across the ten chapters in this book are comprehensive. Some of the chapters map directly to the NPQ framework (DfE 2020), for example, 'School Culture' is discussed in Chapter 3, 'School cultures and improvement'; 'Teaching' and 'Curriculum and Assessment' are particularly considered as part of 'Leading learning' in Chapter 2; 'Additional and Special Educational Needs and Disabilities' are addressed in Chapter 9, which provides clarity on 'Leading more inclusively by addressing diversity and equity'. 'Professional Development' is also discussed at length in 'Developing appropriate professional capital for challenging times'. Other aspects of the NPQ framework are considered across the chapters; for example, 'Organisational Management' is mentioned throughout the book, but particularly in Chapter 5, 'The empowered and/or squeezed middle'. Given that the Universities Council for the Education of Teachers criticised the narrowness of research evidence underpinning the NPQs (UCET, 2022), this book provides a rich source of information in which a wide range of research evidence is analysed and critiqued.

Purpose of this book

Besides focusing on key issues and areas of concern regarding the leadership of schools, the text also presents relevant and recent research studies. Frequently in our work with heads, they explain how they would like to know what 'research says' about an issue they are concerned with or about. We hope that the research evidence which is presented and critically analysed here will address this need. The extensive bibliography offers an in-depth and wide-reaching scope of literature that is useful for any aspiring school leader, middle leader or senior leader. It is intended that readers can 'dip into' areas covered by the book that they wish to know more about. It will also be useful for trainers and organisations developing and delivering NPQs. Besides informing and supporting those directly involved with school leadership, the book offers a broad and comprehensive discussion of recent and relevant subject matter to which any master's or doctoral students can refer.

In order to translate theory into practice, the appendices to each chapter provide questionnaires, activities and thought-provoking questions that address the main themes of this book: leadership of learning; school culture and improvement; the nature and impact of change; middle leadership; professional development; recruitment and retention of staff; teacher motivation and issues of diversity and inclusion.

We truly hope that this book provides helpful, explanatory evidence to support and even inspire all of those involved in leading our schools today.

Linet Arthur and Deb McGregor

References

Arthur, L. and Bradley, S. (2023). Teacher retention in challenging schools: Please don't say goodbye! *Teachers and Teaching*, vol. 29, no. 7–8, pp. 1–19. DOI: 10.1080/13540602.2023.2201423

Biesta, G. (2007). Why 'what works' won't work: Evidence-based practice and the democratic deficit in educational research. *Educational Theory*, vol. 57, no. 1, pp. 1–22.

DfE (2020) National professional Qualification: Headship Framework. Available at https://assets.publishing.service.gov.uk/government/uploads/system/uploads/attachment_data/file/1125999/NPQ_Headship_FINAL_Ref.pdf

McGregor, D. and Browne, L. (2016) Review of the Impact of Oxford City Council's Education Attainment Programme (2012 – 2014) Oxford City Council. Available at https://www.oxford.gov.uk Accessed 1 May 2023.

Menter, I. and McGregor, D. (2015) Leadership for Learning 2012 – 2014. Evaluation Report. Oxford City Council. Available at https://www.oxford.gov.uk Accessed 1 May 23.

UCET (Universities' Council for the Education of Teachers) (2022). Golden thread or gilded cage? An analysis of Department for Education support for the continuing professional development of teachers. https://www.ucet.ac.uk/downloads/14605%2DGilded%2DCage%2DUCET%2DCPD%2Dposition%2Dpaper%2D%28full%2Dversion%29.pdf. Accessed 5 October 23.

Foreword

During the first two decades of the 21st century, the focus on educational leadership strengthened enormously. While this was true in many countries around the world, in the UK and especially in England, this was emphasised through the establishment and subsequent activities of the National College for School Leadership (NCSL). While this was very much a 'New Labour' institution and was later abandoned by Conservative-led governments, nevertheless it had a very significant influence on educational practices across schools in England. The idea that the success of a school was dependent on the quality of its leadership became almost a commonplace, to some extent subsuming the earlier mantra that the quality of a school is dependent on the quality of the teaching in that school. Of course, in reality, both leadership and the quality of teaching are fundamental to the success of all educational establishments. To some extent that combination is recognised in the phrase 'Leadership for Learning'. This was the title of a professional development programme initiated by Oxford City Council in 2012. The authors of this book, Linet Arthur and Deb McGregor, were both centrally involved in the development and implementation of that programme and I had the pleasure of working with them on it. What is reported and discussed in this book emerges in part from that programme but also from other work carried out by the authors, as well as significant analysis of the scholarship around educational leadership (which has burgeoned over these years).

What Arthur and McGregor achieve in this important new contribution is a very well-balanced and well-grounded account of both the complexities and the significance of leadership in educational settings. Among the critical points they make are that educational leadership is not the sole prerogative of those who are formally in leadership positions, such as headship; it is a matter, indeed a responsibility, for all educational staff. Leadership matters in the classroom, in the individual relationships with children, as well as in the overall structure and organisation of the school. Next, they successfully critique the idea of the 'leader as hero', the idea which it must be said did emerge partly out of the NCSL discourse. While we can all recognise the exceptional qualities of some leaders – in politics as well as in education – we can also identify major flaws and weaknesses in some 'strong' or 'charismatic' leaders – again in politics as well as in education. Effective leadership requires humility as well as confidence, sensitivity as well as decisiveness. And furthermore, as we see in this book, context is all important. What works well in one school setting may not work in another place (as the very title of the book suggests).

It is my belief that a careful reading of this book will provide fresh and critical insight for readers to the contemporary challenges of leadership for education professionals wherever they are working and in whatever kind of educational setting they are in. What shines through most powerfully is the authors' commitment to ensuring that those children who are living and learning in the most challenging situations and may be facing the possibility of educational disadvantage should benefit from being taught by teachers and other professionals who are capable of working together to lead those children to the best possible outcomes.

Ian Menter
Emeritus Professor of Teacher Education, University of Oxford

Introduction

Introduction: what is the nature of leadership?

In 2023, the headteacher of an outstanding secondary school that serves a challenging, inner-city catchment area, posted an advert for a new assistant headteacher. However, the advert was swiftly withdrawn after provoking a Twitter [now 'X'] storm about the requirements for the post. Extracts from the advert, quoted later in *The Guardian* (Weale, 2023), the *Sheffield Wire* (Barron, 2023) and the ITVX website (ITVX, 2023) are in Box 1.1.

> **BOX 1.1 ADVERT FOR ASSISTANT HEADTEACHER, 2023**
>
> The candidate will 'ooze leadership' and be 'a great orator', someone who 'handles authority well, is willing to hold the line and lead with bravery'.
>
> (Weale, 2023, n.p.)
>
> We want someone who rolls up their sleeves, a doer and a grafter. Not just a visionary, but someone who also walks the hard yards.
>
> (Weale, 2023, n.p.)
>
> We want a like-minded individual who will work ridiculously hard to deliver for our pupils. When I state ridiculously hard, I mean it. Are you ok with the team contacting you in the evening? Meeting in holidays and being prepared to do detentions on a Saturday morning? Can you cope with huge demands throughout the day, which include teaching a high load, managing pastoral issues and being on alert from 7 a.m. through until 6 p.m., once we have walked the pupils safely down the road and finished detentions?
>
> (Barron, 2023, n.p., Weale, 2023, n.p.)

DOI: 10.4324/9780429260612-1

2 Introduction

> High energy and sacrifice are required to excel in this position.... We cannot carry anyone; we need a commitment from our assistant headteacher to stay until the job is done.
>
> (ITVX, 2023, n.p.)

Comments on Twitter [now 'X'] after the advert appeared suggested that these high expectations were the reason why teachers are leaving schools in England. The advert also prompted concerns in the press about the well-being of senior school leaders (Weale, 2023). It later featured in a blog post on the British Educational Research Association website, in which Hughes et al. (2023) argued that, despite the criticisms, the advert presented an honest account of the intensified work of school leaders. They further commented:

> professional knowledge no longer focuses on educational values, research, debate and judgement about the curriculum, pedagogy and assessment, but concerns process and outcome delivery.
>
> (Hughes et al., 2023, n.p.)

The school that posted the advert was operating in an educational system that valued its performance-driven culture. The 2023 Ofsted report of the school judged the leadership and management to be outstanding:

> Leaders' ambitious vision for the school has been realised. The headteacher and senior leaders have created an exceptional learning environment, where staff and pupils can flourish. Staff morale is high. They are proud to work at the school.
>
> (Ofsted, 2023, p. 3)

The advert and the responses to it are indicative of the current state of school leadership in England. Perhaps the most striking aspect is the sheer relentless pressure for those in senior leadership positions. The education system has been undergoing continuous turbulence for many years and there has been a constant flux of new policies for leaders and teachers to adopt (see Chapter 4 for a summary of major changes). The national system is influenced by government ministers and also by international comparisons. These add to the pressure to raise standards and meet targets (DfE, 2022), with a knock-on effect on school leaders and teachers.

This book explores the changing nature of school leadership in England, using national and international research to identify, as far as possible, what could work in particular circumstances and what has not worked in certain situations. We recognise, however, that it is difficult to make sweeping generalisations about what is effective in education because the context of each school is unique in terms of social and economic catchment area, history, culture, governorship and staffing, pupils and parents, resources, infrastructure and policies. Moreover, schools operate within national systems of education which are different for every country. Identifying what could work depends on the evidence available through research, the professional knowledge of teachers and leaders and the goals of education, some of which are determined by government policy. Rather than taking a directive and prescriptive approach, our aim is to enable leaders and those who aspire to leadership to make professional decisions based on the best available evidence. School leaders are best placed to take into account the context of their school and the constraints of educational policy and practice in their particular country.

The following section outlines key aspects of the English educational system to enable readers from inside and outside England to make informed assessments about how school leadership works in this country.

What is the English context?

In England, the structures within the system have recently changed. The headteacher of an individual school or academy may now be operating within a multi-cademy trust (MAT) or a federation of schools, or they may still be part of a local education authority (LEA). Within some MATs, headteachers have been found to lack autonomy because of the hierarchical structures in place and the constraints of the MAT's policy agenda (Thompson et al., 2020). The same may be true of schools in federations or LEAs. Some schools share an executive headteacher, repositioning leaders of individual schools to operate more like deputy headteachers, working under and reporting to the executive head. Some schools may be in a state of limbo because they have been put in the Ofsted inspection category of 'Inadequate', which means that they are obliged to become a sponsored academy (part of a MAT), but they may not be able to find a MAT willing to include them. Thus the current school system is fragmented nationally. This has impacted on local schools, their interactions with local communities and neighbouring schools, and on the role of the head.

Mirroring the changes in school structures, there is also a range of models of school/academy governing bodies, with differing levels of community and parental involvement and power. In particular, local school governing bodies in MATs may have few decision-making powers (Gibson and Outhwaite, 2022).

Meanwhile, schools are still, in 2024, experiencing the impact of the COVID pandemic, with the need to address a major deficit in children's learning (Betthäuser et al., 2023) resulting from the months of lockdown – a task which will take some years to resolve. At the same time, school leaders are under pressure to demonstrate improvements in student achievement despite reduced budgets and recent strikes by teaching staff. Headteachers, while experiencing a high level of autonomy, also have to contend with a punitive system of high-stakes accountability and external evaluation. The competing and often contradictory demands on them are summarised in Box 1.2.

> **BOX 1.2 SCHOOL LEADERS: PRESSURE WITHIN THE SYSTEM**
>
> School autonomy policies have placed huge power in the hands of, and pressure on the shoulders of, school leaders. They sit at the fulcrum of high-autonomy – high-accountability systems.... Thus they should: exercise their autonomy to innovate in response to parental and other stakeholder needs, whilst at the same time meeting centrally prescribed targets and requirements; improve literacy and numeracy scores every year, whilst maintaining a broad and balanced curriculum; close attainment gaps, while pushing the brightest and the best; and collaborate with their peers to develop teachers' skills and capacity, while competing to ensure that their schools move up the local status hierarchy.
>
> (Greany and Earley, 2022, pp. 5–6)

What are the main aspects of school leadership?

The assistant headteacher advert illustrates the balance school leaders need to maintain between the heroic and the prosaic, charisma and hard work, vision and action (Hargreaves et al., 2014). Applicants for the post needed the eloquence to put across a clear vision, while at the same time being able to 'walk the talk'. Achieving this balance requires a broad range of skills, summarised in the Head Teacher Standards (DfE, 2020). These encompass school culture, teaching, curriculum and assessment, behaviour, special educational needs, professional development, organisational management, continuous school improvement, working in partnership, governance and accountability. Headteachers also need to be able to juggle numerous demands, to deal with unpredictability and to manage conflict. Perhaps it is not surprising that leadership vacancies in England have been 'rocketing' (Bernades et al., 2023). Yet despite all the pressure, many headteachers love their job. In Box 1.3, headteachers describe why they find headship so satisfying.

> **BOX 1.3 HEADTEACHERS DESCRIBE THEIR WORK**
>
> To be a headteacher is the best job in the world! Being entrusted with the opportunity to work alongside and lead a team of dedicated professionals in our school community is an absolute privilege. As a team, we all have the same focus and drive to ensure that the children in school have an exceptional experience both academically and personally. We will do whatever it takes to ensure that children feel happy, safe, and fulfilled in school. We know that when children feel like this, with great teaching, they will thrive academically. Our children deserve the very best and we strive to give them that. It is an absolute joy to see how the children develop and flourish as young people whilst at our school. No two days as a headteacher are the same but it is incredibly rewarding!

> (Headteacher of large primary school: over 800 pupils, aged 5–11; 40% eligible for free school meals; Ofsted rated Outstanding)
>
> You go into teaching as a vocation to make a difference by improving children's lives and life chances and by guiding them to become well-rounded individuals. As a headteacher you hold the key position in a school to mould this, creating strong links with the community and doing all that you can to cater for the needs of those in your care. You have a tremendous opportunity to lead the shaping of the ethos of the school, generating a pride in it from all stakeholders. You also have the privilege of leading the professional development of those working in school to further improve pupils' life chances. To see staff develop and move on in their careers is extremely rewarding. (Former headteacher of relatively large primary school: over 300 pupils, aged 5–11; 5% eligible for free school meals, 15% pupils related to service personnel; Ofsted rated Good)

The assistant headteacher advert also points to a particular leadership approach preferred in that school: authoritative and top down. Directive leadership such as this is no longer popular in England, where schools have more of a focus on democratic communities (Gumus et al., 2018), although it may be the most appropriate approach for schools in challenging circumstances. Headteachers are now encouraged to exercise power *with* others, in a cooperative spirit, rather than using power *over* others to dominate the staff (Woods, 2016).

The leadership approach of a headteacher is important in determining how they interact with staff and students and there is evidence that some approaches are more likely to improve student achievement. While there are many possible leadership styles or approaches, there are three that are important in the current research literature: instructional, distributed and transformational leadership. These are discussed later in the book and are described briefly in the following section.

What are instructional, distributed and transformational leadership approaches?

Instructional leadership, sometimes referred to as leadership for learning, focuses primarily on teaching and learning. It involves a school vision with clear learning goals and the development of a learning community (Shaked et al., 2018). Instructional leaders maintain their identity as teachers and participate actively in the classroom, modelling effective teaching to support learning and evaluating lessons in order to encourage quality practices (Murphy et al., 2016). They organise meaningful professional development for teachers and ensure that data is used for instructional decision-making (Shaked et al., 2018). Instructional leadership has been shown to improve student achievement (Shatzer et al., 2014) but Shaked (2020) suggests this may be at the expense of social justice. In Chapter 2 of this book, instructional leadership and leadership for learning are considered in more detail.

Distributed leadership has been a popular approach for several decades, partly because headship has become too complex for one person to be able to do alone. Leadership is distributed when it is dispersed throughout the school rather than remaining solely with the headteacher (Harris, 2010). It can empower staff, giving them a sense of ownership which enhances their motivation (Hartley, 2010; Day, 2009). However, it may be difficult to distinguish between distributing leadership and delegation. Also, headteachers may be reluctant to distribute leadership in a high-stakes accountability culture (Hughes et al., 2023). Distributed leadership is discussed in more detail in Chapter 5, 'The empowered and/or squeezed middle'.

Transformational leadership originated in the business sector but has since become popular in education. Transformational leaders create a shared vision and empower others (Cummings, 2008). Often charismatic, they inspire teachers to embrace their vision and values (Shatzer et al., 2014). They address individual needs, develop their staff and may redesign the school (Leithwood and Jantzi, 2006). They are 'enthusiasts, forecasters and cheerleaders' (Woods and MacFarlane, 2022, p. 65). Transformational (or inspirational) leadership was identified as one of the 'nine pillars of greatness' by the programme directors of the London Leadership Strategy (Woods, MacFarlane and McBeath, 2018).

Although it is useful to recognise different styles and models of school leadership, in practice most headteachers use a variety of approaches to lead, not just one. Many adopt different approaches depending on the situation and the school context (Bush and Glover, 2014). One headteacher described this as a metaphorical 'wardrobe' and, a little like dressing for the day depending on the weather, she would adopt an appropriate leadership approach for the particular circumstances she encountered. She explained, 'You have to deal with a myriad of issues in a variety of ways often knowing that what you say will be significant and stay with that person for a long time' (Personal communication, 2023). Research evidence also indicates that leaders change their usual approach as they gain experience, for example, moving from being more directive to more collaborative (Day, 2009).

What is considered in this book?

We hope that this collection of chapters highlights concerns that will be both informative and useful for readers looking for evidence about what can work (and what may not) in school leadership. Key recurrent themes, issues and concerns for leaders inform the book chapters as follows:

Chapter 2: Leading learning

This chapter discusses how leaders of schools who are 'committed to transforming life chances of their pupils' (Waters, 2013, p. 293) go about doing so. There is discussion of the different ways that leadership approaches can support and improve learning. The three models of leadership considered in particular in this chapter are: Leadership for learning (Leithwood et al., 2020); Leadership of learning (Earley and Greany, 2022) and Learning-centred leadership (Southworth, 2009, Earley, 2013).

Chapter 3: School culture and improvement

This chapter considers the way that a school's culture influences staff and students, and is, in turn, influenced by them. Key aspects of a culture such as values, vision, beliefs, organisation, artefacts, routines, historical influences and national policy are each considered to examine how they affect the ethos and successful running of a school. Research examining the cultures of effective and improving schools is also discussed. The chapter also explores ways in which school leaders can assess and enhance their school's culture. Various metaphors are used to illustrate how the nature of a school's culture is complex, but nurturing it appropriately can really make a difference.

Chapter 4: Leading change

This chapter discusses a comprehensive range of internal and external factors that require different approaches to leading change. Evidence of different ways that headteachers have led their schools through changing circumstances is illustrated by vignettes and summaries describing alternative practices and approaches. There is also discussion about why some approaches were successful and others were not.

Chapter 5: The empowered and/or squeezed middle

This chapter discusses the contrasts between distributed and middle leadership. Evidence indicating which factors can affect the success (or not) of distributed and middle leadership is reviewed and critiqued. Theories and practices in leading teams are considered.

Chapter 6: Leading professional development

Headteachers recognise that professional development of their staff is key to improving many aspects of running a school, the quality of teaching and consequently successful learning and academic achievement of the pupils. However, there is no one best way to support professional development of staff. There are a multitude of approaches, some that have substantial evidence to vindicate them. The extent to which different approaches are more or less effective is discussed in this chapter.

Chapter 7: Recruitment and retention of staff: leadership implications

This chapter discusses the relatively under-researched area of recruitment and retention in schools. The multiple factors that affect staffing in schools generally as well as those in deprived areas and in challenging circumstances are also considered. There are detailed quotations from teachers and headteachers that demonstrate the complexity of hiring and retaining quality staff. There is also consideration of practical approaches that leaders could employ to address recruitment and retention issues.

Chapter 8: Motivating teachers

This chapter discusses a range of different motivation theories and how they apply to schools. It considers how school leaders can encourage and empower teachers, offer career opportunities and professional development, support collaborative activities and recognise staff achievements.

Chapter 9: Leading more inclusively: addressing diversity and equity

Leadership that addresses diversity and is inclusive can be challenging. It requires sensitivity to lead inclusively, but it can result in a vibrant, exciting, dynamic and successful school. This chapter discusses the educational challenges related to inclusivity, the role of school leaders in managing diversity, social justice, different aspects of diversity (race, gender, LGBTQ, disability), relevant theories and what can work in relation to leading a thriving and inclusive school.

Chapter 10: Conclusion: reflecting on school leadership

This chapter synthesises the evidence from this book about how school leaders can improve their schools.

In each chapter, we review the research evidence critically, recognising that what works in one school in a particular set of circumstances may not work in another. As Sanderson (2003, p. 341) argues, for teachers and leaders, the question is 'not simply "what is effective" but rather, more broadly it is, "what is appropriate for these children in these circumstances".' In weighing up the research evidence, school leaders need to combine effective professional judgement with moral wisdom. This indicates that an additional key consideration for leaders is the potential educational value of their choices (Biesta, 2007).

This book contains chapters written to address key aspects of school leadership that enable headteachers and those aspiring to lead to make an informed assessment of research evidence to decide what could work more effectively in their school. Those who are studying or researching school leadership will gain an in-depth understanding of the field. The book is not simply about the latest research in schools, but also the application of theories and evidence, using case studies and vignettes of real-life experience. Each chapter offers practical activities, including short questionnaires, that school leaders could use not only to develop their knowledge about their school, but also to work collaboratively within their community to extend the professional expertise of others. While we may not be able to state conclusively what will work in every school, we hope that this book will provide an invaluable source of information to assist school leaders in identifying what could work for them.

References

Barron, J. (2023). "You will be wedded to it": Sheffield school goes viral for controversial job advert. *Sheffield Wire*, 20 February 2023.

Bernades, E., Thomson, P. and Greany, T. (2023). Headteacher recruitment crisis: 5 tips for action. *TES*, 9 June 2023. https://www.tes.com/magazine/leadership/staff-management/headteacher-recruitment-crisis-applications. Accessed 3 September 23.

Betthäuser, B.A., Bach-Mortensen, A.M. and Engzell, P. (2023). A systematic review and meta-analysis of the evidence on learning during the COVID-19 pandemic. *Nature Human Behaviour*, vol. 7, pp. 375–385.

Biesta, G. (2007). Why 'what works' won't work: Evidence based practice and the democratic deficit in educational research. *Educational Theory*, vol. 57, no. 1, pp. 1–22.

Bush, T. and Glover, D. (2014). School leadership models: What do we know? *School Leadership and Management*, vol. 34, no. 5, pp. 553–571.

Cummings, A. (2008). *Only Connect: Using a Critical Incident Tool to Develop Multi-Agency Collaboration in Two Children's Centres*. Nottingham: NCSL.

Day, C. (2009). Capacity building through layered leadership: Sustaining the turnaround. In A. Harris (ed). *Distributed Leadership*. Dordrecht: Springer, pp. 121–137.

DfE (Department for Education) (2020). *Headteachers' Standards 2020*. London: DfE. https://www.gov.uk/government/publications/national-standards-of-excellence-for-headteachers/headteachers-standards-2020. Accessed 2 September 23.

DfE (2022). *School Leadership in England 2010 to 2020 – Characteristics and Trends – Addendum*. London: Department for Education.

Earley, P. (2013). *Exploring the School Leadership Landscape: Changing Demands, Changing Realities*. London: Bloomsbury.

Earley, P. and Greany, T. (2022). Postscript: The future of leadership. In T. Greany and P. Earley (eds). *School Leadership and Education System Reform*. London: Bloomsbury, pp. 273–279.

Gibson, M. and Outhwaite, D. (2022). MATification: Plurality, turbulence and effective school governance in England. *Management in Education*, vol. 36, no. 1, pp. 42–46.

Greany, T. and Earley, P. (eds). (2022). *School Leadership and Education System Reform*. London: Bloomsbury Publishing.

Gumus, S., Bellibas, M., Esen, M. and Gumus, E. (2018). A systematic review of studies on leadership models in educational research from 1980 to 2014. *Educational Management Administration and Leadership*, vol. 46, no. 1, pp. 25–48.

Hargreaves, A., Boyle, A. and Harris, A. (2014). *Uplifting Leadership: How Organizations, Teams, and Communities Raise Performance*. San Francisco, CA: Jossey-Bass.

Harris, A. (2010). Distributed leadership: Current evidence and future directions. In T. Bush, L. Bell, and D. Middlewood (eds). *The Principles of Educational Leadership and Management*. London: Sage, pp. 55–69.

Hartley, D. (2010). Paradigms: How far does research in distributed leadership 'Stretch'? *Educational Management, Administration and Leadership*, vol. 38, no. 3, pp. 271–285.

Hughes, B., Courtney, S., Armstrong, P., Gunter, H., Gardner-McTaggart, A., Heffernan, A., Innes, M. and Skerritt, C. (2023). *What Schools Want: Recruiting Senior Leaders in England*. https://www.bera.ac.uk/blog/what-schools-want-recruiting-senior-leaders-in-england. Accessed 2 September 23.

ITVX (2023). Job advert for assistant head disappears after backlash. Job advert for assistant head at Sheffield's Mercia School disappears after backlash | ITV News Calendar 20 February 2023.

Leithwood, K., Harris, A. and Hopkins, D. (2020). Seven strong claims about successful school leadership revisited. *School Leadership and Management*, vol. 40, no. 1, pp. 5–22. DOI: 10.1080/13632434.2019.1596077

Leithwood, K. and Jantzi, D. (2006). Transformational school leadership for large-scale reform: Effects on students, teachers, and their classroom practices. *School Effectiveness and School Improvement*, vol. 17, no. 2, pp. 201–227.

Murphy, J., Neumerski, C.M., Goldring, E., Grissom, J. and Porter, A. (2016). Bottling fog? The quest for instructional management. *Cambridge Journal of Education*, vol. 46, no. 4, pp. 455–471.

Sanderson, I. (2003). Is it 'What Works' that matters? Evaluation and evidence-based policy making. *Research Papers in Education*, vol. 18, no. 4, pp. 331–347.

Shaked, H., Glanz, J. and Gross, Z. (2018). Gender differences in instructional leadership: How male and female principals perform their instructional leadership role. *School Leadership & Management*, vol. 38, no. 4, pp. 417–434. DOI: 10.1080/13632434.2018.1427569

Shaked, H. (2020). Social justice leadership, instructional leadership, and the goals of schooling. *International Journal of Educational Management*, vol. 34, no. 1, pp. 81–95.

Shatzer, R., Caldarella, P., Hallam, P. and Brown, B. (2014). Comparing the effects of instructional and transformational leadership on student achievement: Implications for practice. *Educational Management, Administration and Leadership*, vol. 42, no. 4, pp. 445–459.

Southworth, G. (2009). Learning-centred leadership. In B. Davies (ed). *The Essentials of School Leadership*, 2nd edition. London: Sage.

Thompson, G., Lingard, B and Ball, S. (2020). 'Indentured autonomy': Headteachers and academisation policy in Northern England. *Journal of Educational Administration and History*, vol. 53, nos. 3–4, pp. 215–232.

Waters, M. (2013). *Thinking Allowed on Schooling*. Carmarthen: Independent Thinking Press.

Weale, S. (2023). Sheffield school criticised for saying job applicants must be 'wedded' to role. *The Guardian*, 20 February 2023. https://www.theguardian.com/education/2023/feb/20/sheffield-school-criticised-for-saying-job-applicants-must-be-wedded-to-role. Accessed 2 September 23.

Woods, D. and MacFarlane, R. (2022). What makes a great school now? In T. Greany and P. Earley (eds). *School Leadership and Education System Reform*, 2nd edition. London: Bloomsbury Academic, pp. 61–70.

Woods, D., MacFarlane, R. and McBeath, D. (2018). *The Nine Pillars of Great Schools*. Woodbridge: John Catt Educational.

Woods, P. (2016). Authority, power and distributed leadership. *Management in Education*, vol. 30, no. 4, pp. 155–160.

2 Leading learning

Introduction

Learning is the core purpose of any school, so effective leadership of, and for, learning is crucial. As discussed throughout this book, there are many models and conceptualisations of school leadership. In fact, Greany and Earley (2022, p. 82) indicate that that there are 65 different classification systems for leadership and over 300 definitions of leadership. There are also many research studies that indicate how, in a variety of ways, leadership can influence student outcomes (Day et al., 2011, Leithwood et al., 2008, 2020).

As Caldwell (2014) suggests, although we know much about the nature of leadership and the characteristics of successful leaders, it is not possible to generalise specific strategies that should be adopted to ensure success for *all* schools, at *all* times, in *all* settings. In fact, he draws from the studies presented in Day and Gurr (2014) to suggest that it is good judgement, even wisdom, possibly artistry and certainly sheer hard work that is likely to bring about success as a school leader. However, what is of direct importance for *all* headteachers are the practices of leadership that are concerned with generating an effective learning community for all students to succeed in their academic achievements, that is, 'to create the conditions for people to thrive, individually and collectively and achieve significant goals' (Pendleton and Furnham, 2012, p. 2).

The ways in which headteachers adopt and prioritise various leadership practices that influence and shape how school learning may be affected are generally thought about in three particular ways. These three perspectives of leadership directly concerning learning considered in this chapter are:

 i. Leadership for learning;
 ii. Leadership of learning;
 iii. Learning-centred leadership.

What does leadership concerned with learning look like?

Within each of these three previously introduced conceptions, the actions or practices of the headteachers may differ somewhat. However, embraced within these three perspectives are practices that emphasise different aspects of leadership, summarised later in Table 2.1 and explained further in the following text.

Leadership *for* learning, for example, embraces practices that create and maintain a conducive environment for effective learning, prioritising the vision and culture of the organisation. This also involves facilitating best practices that can enhance student learning outcomes. This approach resonates with 'distributed leadership' (Greany and Earley, 2022, p. 82) where responsibility for generating the ethos and implementing school goals is shared amongst leaders, teachers, students and other stakeholders.

Leadership *of* learning recognises leaders' involvement in curricular development as well as their influence on processes of teaching, learning and assessment. Arguably this approach could involve a 'combination of pedagogic and transformational leadership' (Robinson, 2011; Day and Sammons, 2013 cited in Greany and Earley, 2022, p. 85).

Learning-centred leadership (Southworth, 2009; Earley, 2013), which holds learners and teachers as central, has evolved from the 'Instructional Leadership' (Day and Gurr, 2014, p. 147) model. Southworth (2004, 2009) developed a model of learning-centred leadership that acknowledged the value of modelling, monitoring and dialogue that underpinned teachers' learning and informed their actions in classrooms that could then improve student learning. In addition, West-Burnham (2005) suggests how mentoring with coaching offers a significant strategy for leaders to support the development of colleagues in learning-centred leadership.

Although quite nuanced, each of the three leadership approaches can impact student outcomes in somewhat varied ways. To contrast the nature of these three approaches it is useful to consider different dimensions or domains of leadership practice. Identifying these key domains and associated aspects of practice that characterise different forms of leadership, it becomes clearer how an assemblage of different kinds of activity comprises different leadership approaches. These are discussed further in the following.

How do domains of leadership practice connect with learning?

Two large scale studies, one carried out over five years (Leithwood and Louis, 2012) and another over three years (Day et al., 2011), have contributed to suggestions about 'domains' of related practices that successful school leaders engage in. Leithwood and Louis (2012), looking across 180 elementary, middle and secondary schools in nine different states in the USA, collated evidence about the ways that successful leadership influenced the quality of teaching and learning. They highlighted how 'collective leadership' that involved all the teachers in the school was more influential on student achievement than individual leadership. They also provided evidence that school leaders primarily impacted on student achievement through their influence on teachers' motivation and working conditions. The influence of leaders on teachers' knowledge and skills, though, had less impact on student achievement. Louis and Wahlstrom (2012, p. 25) highlighted further how 'leadership practices targeted directly at improving instruction (teaching) have significant effects on teachers' working relationships and indirectly on student achievement'. This is because 'effective leadership strengthens the professional community' and generates an 'environment within which teachers work together to improve their practice and improve student learning' (Louis and Wahlstrom, 2012, p. 25).

Day et al. (2011) report on a three-year, extensive national research project involving primary and secondary headteachers in England designed to look at the impact of leadership on pupil outcomes (IMPACT). In order to participate, the schools involved in the study all had to demonstrate improved pupil attainment over a three-year consecutive period. The findings of this project identified how all leaders were 'sensitive' (p. 17) to the features of the school and wider environment that could make a difference to the quality of schooling for the pupils. They found that leaders adapted, combined or amassed from four 'core [domains of] practice'.

Like Leithwood and Louis (2012), the evidence suggests that successful schools are led by headteachers who adopted practices from several identifiable domains. These 'core practices' are specific kinds of leadership activities that successful leaders appear to carry out in most contexts (Day et al., 2011, p. 18). The domains of 'core practices' include:

- *Setting directions*: providing a vision and goals for the school

- *Building relationships and developing people*: supporting the staff responsible for the running of a school

- *Developing the organisation to support desired practices*: generating structures and processes that create and support the school community

- *Improving the teaching and learning program*: making sure successful curricular, instructional and assessment processes are in place.

Further details of the ways that different practices comprise the four 'domains' are listed in Table 2.1.

What makes a difference in school leadership?

In an insightful review of empirical studies 12 years apart, Leithwood et al. (2008, 2020) substantiate seven strong claims about successful school leadership. The claims that they present are supported 'in varying amounts of quite robust empirical evidence' and are summarised as such to 'provide a synthesis' of the evidence (Leithwood et al. 2020, p. 5). They include the following:

1. School leadership has a significant effect on features of the school organisation which positively influences the quality of teaching and learning. While moderate in size, this leadership effect is vital to the success of most school improvement efforts;

2. Almost all successful leaders draw on the same repertoire of basic leadership practices;

3. The ways in which leaders apply these basic leadership practices – not the practices themselves – demonstrate responsiveness to, rather than dictation by, the contexts in which they work;

4. School leadership improves teaching and learning, indirectly and most powerfully, by improving the status of significant key classroom and school conditions and by encouraging parent/child interactions in the home that further enhance student success at school;

5. School leadership can have an especially positive influence on school and students when it is distributed;

6. Some patterns of distribution are more effective than others;

7. While further research is required, a well-defined set of cognitive, social and psychological 'personal leadership resources' show promise of explaining a high proportion of variation in the practices enacted by school leaders.

Within this chapter these claims suggesting how the nature of leadership can influence teaching and student achievement are considered further.

What does effective leadership influencing learning look like?

It is important to consider the evidence relating to the seven claims about school leadership. The first claim, in 2008, that school leadership is second only to classroom teaching as an influence on pupil learning, was primarily supported by case studies of exceptionally performing schools (Reitzug and Patterson 1998 cited in Leithwood et al., 2008, p. 28) and comparing high- and low-performing schools (Mortimore, 1993 cited in Leithwood et al., 2008, p. 28). Much additional evidence from large-scale studies assessing the impact of leadership was drawn from studies reviewed by Hallinger and Heck (1998), for example, to suggest that leadership effects are 'small but educationally significant' (Leithwood et al., 2008, p. 28). More recently several studies, including Chapman et al.'s (2015) work, offered significant evidence that factors 'outside of school' could also account for significant variation in pupils' academic progress.

The second claim that 'Almost all successful leaders draw on the same repertoire of basic leadership practices' (see Table 2.1) was originally synthesised from school and non-school evidence that suggested what kinds of activities leaders engaged in to accomplish organisational goals (Leithwood et al., 2008, p. 29). However, since 2008, the two large-scale empirical studies (Leithwood and Louis, 2012; Day et al., 2011) introduced earlier detail the impact of different kinds of leadership practices on student achievement, whilst others (Hitt and Tucker, 2016; Leithwood, Sun and Pollock, 2017) have carried out reviews of work assessing how leadership influences learning. These practices are summarised in Table 2.1.

The third claim about school leaders being responsive to rather than constrained by their school context (Leithwood et al., 2020, p. 9) is substantiated through discussion about the ways in which core practices would be enacted differently if a school were judged to be 'outstanding' or 'requires improvement', that is, in different stages of special measures. For example, 'Building vision and setting directions' for an outstanding school might involve extending the extra-curricular provision or further developing the professional development programme for qualified staff. For a school that requires improvement there would need to be clear, short-term priorities for a school in early crisis, but these would inevitably change to become more long term once the 'turnaround' was achieved.

The fourth claim addressing how school leaders improve teaching and learning indirectly and most powerfully through their influence on staff, was originally supported by justifications that headteachers can affect 'working conditions' and 'motivation' (Leithwood et al., 2008, p. 33). Since 2008, more evidence has emerged suggesting a wide range of ways that headteachers could mediate staff and influence wider family influences to improve pupils' learning (Sebastion, Huang, and Allensworth, 2017 cited in Leithwood et al., 2020, p. 11).

Chapter 5 considers the nature and impact of distributed leadership further (claims five and six) and Chapter 9 discusses personal traits (related to claim seven) and equity in more depth. In this chapter it is primarily the first four claims that impact on the relationship between leadership and attainment outcomes that are considered in more depth.

What are the characteristics of effective school leaders?

A useful review of the international literature (Day and Sammons, 2013, p. 5) identifies ten key characteristics stated to be important in leadership, that is, to

Table 2.1 List of practices within the four domains that successful leaders engage in (Leithwood et al., 2020)

Domains of practice	Specific dimensions of leadership practice
Set Directions	Build a shared vision
	Identify specific, shared, short-term goals
	Create high-performance expectations
	Communicate the vision and goals
Build Relationships and Develop People	Stimulate growth in the professional capacities of staff
	Provide support and demonstrate consideration for individual staff members
	Model the school's values and practices
	Build trusting relationships with and among staff, students and parents
	Establish productive working relationships with teacher federation representatives
Develop the Organisation to Support Desired Practices	Build collaborative culture and distribute leadership
	Structure the organisation to facilitate collaboration
	Build productive relationships with families and communities
	Connect the school to its wider environment
	Maintain a safe and healthy school environment
	Allocate resources in support of the school's vision and goals
Improve the teaching [instructional] programme	Staff the instructional programme
	Provide instructional support
	Monitor student learning and school improvement progress
	Buffer staff from distractions to their instructional work

'do things right'. In looking at the features of leadership across 14 countries, Day and Sammons (2013, p. 18) indicate that 'it is striking that the values, aspirations, qualities, achievements and ways of enacting, achieving and sustain success are similar across all countries and all school phases'. However, they did find variations were evident when new-in-post principals had inherited long-term problems and alternate strategies were adopted to generate different conditions for improvement.

Arguably the ten features of 'doing things right' (Day and Sammons, 2013, p. 5 as cited in Greany and Earley, 2022, p. 117) could be 'mapped' onto the domains of practice (see Table 2.2).

Table 2.2 A list of the ten key characteristics of successful leadership (Day and Sammons, 2013) that have been mapped onto the four domains (Day et al., 2011; Leithwood et al., 2020) of effective leaders' practices

Characteristics of effective leadership	Mapped onto the four domains
Providing vision	Setting directions
Developing through consultation, a common purpose	Setting directions
Facilitating the achievement of organisational goals and fostering high performance expectations	Setting directions
Having a future orientation	Setting directions
Supporting the school as a lively educational place	Building relationships and developing people
Linking resource to outcomes	Developing the organisation to support desired practices
Working creatively and empowering others	Building relationships and developing people
Responding to diverse needs and situations	Developing the organisation to support desired practices
Providing educational entrepreneurship	Developing the organisation to support desired practices / Improving the teaching and learning programme
Ensuring that the curriculum and processes related to it are contemporary and relevant	Improving the teaching and learning programme

How is leadership for learning understood and enacted?

In 2020, as explained earlier, Leithwood et al. revisited new evidence that had emerged within the last 12 years, to re-consider whether or not the original claim that leadership affects pupil learning was supported or refuted. Previously, studies of the impact of leadership on learning only took account of factors 'within the school's walls' (Leithwood et al., 2020, p. 6). However, more evidence has recently accrued which demonstrates that pupils' cognitive, social and emotional development is influenced by variables other than school leadership, such as the socio-economic context of the family (Domina et al., 2018); parental involvement (Jeynes, 2011) and the nature of dialogue between home and school (Goodall (2018). There is also a 'much larger corpus of high-quality quantitative evidence' (Leithwood et al., 2020, p. 6) demonstrating the nature of indirect contributions of school leadership to pupils' learning. This includes a three-year study observing and analysing leaders' practices on student achievement (Grissom, Loeb and Master, 2013).

In examining critical features of leadership in school districts in Canada where achievement of students was high, Leithwood (2012) was able to identify what made a difference. These features included a shared vision, coherence in teaching, professional development for teachers, deliberate and consistent use of multiple sources of evidence, alignment of budget structure and use with the shared educational vision, commitment to leadership development, policy-oriented board of trustees and productive working relationships with staff and other stakeholders.

Hallinger and Heck (2010) carried out empirical analysis over four years of the impact of collaborative leadership in 198 primary schools across the USA. They looked at the different ways that teams of school leaders (discussed further in Chapter 5) worked together to improve student learning. They looked at four different models of leadership and found the most significant impact on academic improvement was a reciprocal approach involving teachers and leaders collaborating to influence student learning.

Hitt and Tucker (2016) reviewed 56 research studies in an attempt to identify leadership practices affecting student learning and attainment. They found that in addition to the four aforementioned domains (Table 2.1) securing accountability was important. They also found seven more dimensions of leadership practice potentially impacting on student learning, but to differing extents. In short, their synthesis offers a framework of discrete, research-based practices that can be drawn on to inform development of future leaders and 'serve as a tool for self-assessment' (see Appendix 2.1). They do admit, though, that 'curriculum, instruction and formative and summative assessment' stand to be strengthened and that although 'high-quality teachers' remain the best resource for promoting student learning, it is 'talented leaders who can take student success to scale' (p.563).

There are therefore several studies that evidence how important collaboration between leaders and teachers is to improving learning outcomes. Distributed leadership (Leithwood et al., 2020, p. 13) can particularly influence student outcomes, however, it does depend on the 'decision making' of those enacting leadership. The following vignettes illustrate the differing ways that salient information or data has been considered by leaders to inform their decision-making about 'actions' to be taken or the practices to be adopted. What is also clear in each case is the way in which the 'practices' listed in Table 2.1 are not necessarily identifiable as discrete approaches. What is often apparent is the presence of each domain, but the ways in which the practices are integrated or combined to constitute a particular leader's approach differs.

This vignette [in Box 2.1] demonstrates how different domains of leadership are more or less prominent in particular strategies that headteachers develop and enact. In this school, the headteacher set a clear direction, developed the staff,

Leading learning 19

> **BOX 2.1 A CASE OF DEVELOPING LEADERSHIP SKILLS ACROSS A SCHOOL**
>
> In this case, a headteacher of an Oxford school (inspected and judged to be Satisfactory in 2010) was approaching retirement. The context of an ever-changing pupil population and expensive living costs presented a challenging situation for the leadership of the school. The Ofsted report indicated that both the achievement of pupils and the quality of teaching needed to be improved.
>
> In preparing for leadership succession, knowing that there would likely be very few applications, the senior leadership team (SLT) decided to initiate a project planning team (PPT) approach. That is, they decided to focus on developing the leadership capabilities of the deputy head and the middle leaders. The SLT adopted a variety of strategies, including appointing someone with temporary responsibility to work with the SLT to lead, monitor and evaluate the school's new curricular initiatives for numeracy and literacy. A key tactic in their succession planning was to involve middle leaders in promoting the PPT approach, which included all teaching and learning staff engaging with a change team that was focused on mathematics, early years or quality teaching. Within these teams all members would take responsibility for some elements of the PPT's work, for example, monitoring staff implementation through learning walks; administering questionnaires to staff and children about their views of the initiatives; supporting peer-peer observation of more experienced teachers; revising materials to better 'fit' the context of the school's population. Within a year there was an improvement in learning, especially writing, numeracy and reading, and the school had increased leadership capacity in preparation for the departure of the headteacher.

created a structure (the project planning teams) and improved the teaching and learning programme (in relation to mathematics, early years and quality teaching).

While the checklist of practices presented in Table 2.1 and the Unifying framework offered in Appendix 2.1 identify key activities of effective leaders, they do not tell the whole story. There has to be a balance between these activities. The checklist does not indicate what proportion of time should be spent on each practice, nor does it provide much detail about how the activities might be enacted or, indeed, when. The way in which an activity is undertaken may determine whether or not it is successful. A headteacher might, for example, believe that they are distributing leadership, but the staff may interpret their actions as 'dumping' or 'delegating'. It may also be more challenging or difficult in some schools to carry out the activities. For example, headteachers may not be able to collaborate effectively if their staff are mainly early career teachers (ECTs) or inexperienced, while some teachers may resist collaboration because they have family or caring commitments and cannot take on any extra work. In some cases, leaders may not have sufficient funds to carry out their preferred activities. Whilst all leaders might aspire to allocate resources to support the shared vision of school, in the current financial climate, their options to do so may be greatly constrained. As a result, although the checklist can provide a useful framework, individual school leaders still need to make their own decisions in relation to each of these activities within the context of their school.

How is leadership of learning understood and enacted?

There is a persisting concern about leadership of learning, as Earley and Greany (2022) note. They warn about leaders who are focused on improving attainment to the extent that learning is shaped by the 'narrowly defined standards-based curriculum'. Such schools risk becoming 'examination factories' where 'teaching is to the test' (Earley and Greany, 2022, p. 275), that is, training pupils how to pass national assessments through repeated drill and practice. This may have unintended consequences as Watkins (2010) notes, 'A focus on learning can enhance performance whereas a focus on performance (alone) can depress performance' (Watkins, 2010, p. 4).

MacBeath and Dempster (2008) argue that leading learning entails the constant endeavour to sustain teachers' engagement and stimulate the desire to learn, which requires qualities of insight and connoisseurship. They discuss learning leadership and the type of environment that may be more promising for the future that could promote leadership of learning. In promoting this approach, they present five principles:

1. A focus on learning
2. Creating conditions favourable to learning
3. Dialogue
4. Sharing leadership through structures and procedures supporting participation
5. A shared sense of accountability.

They also suggest how, in informal learning environments, it is the young people who potentially can take up the leadership of learning. This, however, disrupts long-established perspectives that school has long been thought of as the place of learning with the role of the pedagogue almost universally accepted as that of the adult teacher. Arguably, they suggest, the explicit 'leadership' plainly visible in the hierarchy of the school can be in tension with more implicit, dispersed and shared endeavours which may be more appropriate in the 21st-century classroom. In discussing how learning is best led in times of change, they argue that the five principles could underpin collaborative leadership of learning communities extending across boundaries and beyond schools.

School leaders matter: how and why?

Branch et al. (2013) reported that it is possible for effective school leaders to raise students' attainment by between two and seven months of learning in a single school year. However, they also noted that the reverse was possible: students' achievement could be lowered by similar amounts. As Earley (2013) explains, teachers can have a direct impact on all the pupils in their classroom, however, school leadership can affect all students in a given school.

Earley (2016) goes on to highlight that the nature and demands of educational policies potentially disrupt the focus of school leaders from teaching and learning and student improvement. Teachers are expected to mobilise a set of targeted activities that will maximise student performance in national assessments (Ball et al., 2012). That is, they are expected to adhere to enacting policy that prescribes and also 'constrains' how success in learning is measured. School leaders have to translate educational policy to shape practice in the classroom and enact practices that direct what teachers should do (Ball et al., 2012). School leaders are therefore responsible for interpreting and managing the translation of policies into 'actions' that their school community adopts.

Policy can generate the school 'pressure cooker' culture (Ball et al., 2012) within which teachers are policy actors. However, a 'thoughtful' curriculum or one that 'celebrates creativity' can facilitate schools concentrating on teaching and learning rather than attainment or high stakes assessment. As indicated earlier, Watkins (2010) suggests that those focused on teaching and learning rather than purely academic outcomes are more likely to be successful. In Box 2.2 the headteacher of an Ofsted-rated 'Outstanding' school for more than 10 years shares some of her strategies to maintain the high standards required for inspection.

> **BOX 2.2 A PRIMARY SCHOOL HEADTEACHER'S STRATEGY FOR MAINTAINING AN OFSTED RATING OF 'OUTSTANDING' FOR MORE THAN TEN YEARS**
>
> We have consistently maintained our key principle of exceptional teaching and learning for the pupils. However, we have also commissioned external professionals to review different aspects of our school to ensure that we remain 'at the top of our game.'
>
> Last year we had a full school review carried out by an Ofsted inspector, using the new framework. This year we have had external reviews carried out of our Early Years Foundation Stage (EYFS), our approach to using the Pupil Premium and its Impact and another scrutiny of our Safeguarding. These have all been carried out by different people who are experts in these areas. Any details that need addressing are immediately put into an action plan and are included in the school improvement process/monitoring.
>
> The school has an exceptionally strong reputation in the local community. Fellow professionals know that we operate at a high level here and if you can 'cut it' at this school then you are an outstanding practitioner!

> Our school is located in a pocket of deprivation in the north of the city – our number of Pupil Premium pupils is currently 46% so we have a significant number of disadvantaged children. So the offer that we have here is not just about teaching and learning for pupils, but as equally important is their personal development and ensuring that their basic needs are met (they feel safe, are happy, fed, cared for and have the basics for accessing the curriculum – PE kit, etc.).
>
> All of our staff go 'above and beyond' for the children in these aspects.
>
> The school is not for every teacher and some professionals find the pursuit of providing an exceptional experience (both in their learning and personal development) for our pupils to be too difficult. We provide outstanding weekly professional development for staff that is directly linked to our school improvement priorities. We provide excellent support and coaching for ECTs, middle leaders and senior leaders.
>
> The help and support is there – we just need staff to 'buy in' to our culture and we will give them the rest!
>
> (Headteacher of an Outstanding School, since 2012).

In strategizing, as Earley (2013) suggests, to go beyond the narrow standards-based perspective of teaching and learning, a wide range of pedagogic practices may be adopted. In a city-wide project (Menter and McGregor, 2015; McGregor and Browne, 2016), a cohort of schools worked together to address the lack of improved attainment through a careful focus on leadership of learning. Instead of concentrating purely on development of leadership practices, this project aimed to raise attainment through:

i. improving leaders' confidence to lead learning (particularly for middle leaders);

ii. supporting leaders using [different forms of] data in a more focused way;

iii. increasing collaboration and networking between schools in the area, and

iv. increasing engagement with pupils' families.

The professional development provided for the leaders employed various activities including seminars, workshops and action learning sets (ALSs) to facilitate these four (i–iv) aims. What became evident within this project was that collaboration predominated, not only between participating schools, but also within each school community too.

How do action learning sets (ALSs) become a collaborative forum for leaders to discuss, plan, enact and review leadership practice?

Action learning sets were devised to take place (Menter and McGregor, 2015) in each of the Oxford City project schools. Each ALS involved a group of six or seven middle/senior leaders from across the city meeting together (either after the school day or during the afternoon) to review and disseminate each individual's or a whole school's progress. The intention of the ALSs was to provide the opportunity for participants to consider what was of highest concern for them as leaders, and to draw on the content, research and advice offered at the seminars and workshops to identify how to address the challenges that faced them. There were six meetings organised for each learning set over the year, each lasting for about two hours. See Appendix 2.2 for details about how to run an ALS.

The wide range of foci for ALSs (Box 2.3) reflects the extent to which the senior and middle leaders understood how many influences or practices (Table 2.1) could affect improvement in attainment.

BOX 2.3 ACTION LEARNING SETS FOCUSING ON POTENTIAL LEADERSHIP ACTIONS TO IMPROVE LEARNING

The following list provides a rich series of approaches that emerged from the action learning sets (Appendix 2.2). These were devised by the leaders of the Oxford City schools, to raise the attainment of their students. Any individual school could adopt and adapt any one of these strategies to address their particular areas of concern or practices to be developed. The shared communications and discussions between and within the ALS members facilitated adoption of a range of activities that directly or indirectly related to improving student achievement and/or attainment.

Focusing on assessment for learning (AfL) included identifying and action planning where it could be used more (e.g., mini plenaries; peer marking etc.); engaging in video recording to collect good exemplars of using AfL; developing better consistency with AfL practices; disseminating good practice for Newly Qualified Teachers (NQTs) and/or Early Career Teachers (ECTs).

Focusing on mentoring and professional development included becoming more cyclical in implementing development of a 'plan → do → review' approach that informed mentoring of NQT/ECTs; applying theory (e.g., Positive Mindsets) to inform practice; sharing success criteria for APP and differentiated learning; adopting appraisal for support staff; adopting a lesson-study approach with new staff; engaging in more regular learning walks; paired teaching and coaching alongside teachers requiring improvement; orienting peer observations to develop practice, not assess; promoting more open dialogue about teaching and learning generally; regularly video recording happenings (with a purpose) to provide in-school CPD material; encouraging teachers to engage in cross year group observations (and writing of follow-up discussion) of teaching (e.g., Y2 & Y6 teachers).

Focusing on data and academic performance analysis, including looking at data regularly (e.g., Y1 Phonics performance; % level 4 in reading, writing and mathematics; % making expected progress in reading, writing and mathematics) to gauge progress;

> developing simple processes to analyse data and consider 'what could be done'; meeting more regularly to consider [progress/changes in] data especially within lessons; more day-to-day discussion that consider, 'What can I do that makes a difference?'

Hargreaves and Shirley (2018) reflect on achievement in Ontario, Canada. Ontario has started to move from an 'Age of Achievement and Effort' to the 'Age of Learning, Well-being and Identity'. Until 2014, its policy priority was improving student achievement. Ontario proclaimed that it would 'reach every student' through 'three core priorities' of 'going deeper on literacy and numeracy', 'reducing the gap in achievement for those groups of students who, for whatever reason, need extra help', and increasing 'public confidence in publicly funded education' (Hargreaves and Shirley, 2018, p.5). A large-scale educational reform at this time was driven by four compelling questions.

1. How are we doing?
2. How do we know?
3. How can we improve?
4. How can this benefit everyone?

Hargreaves and Shirley (2018) described this period as the Age of Achievement and Effort. It raised expectations and improved results, especially for some students whose challenges were not well captured by aggregated data. However, the increased expectations in the Age of Achievement and Effort also incurred problems. It led some educators to concentrate more on students' deficits rather than their assets. Teachers complained of a narrowed curriculum. They reported that the system's push to ensure students reached appropriate proficiency levels created pressure on teachers to give most attention to students who were just short of the point of proficiency, 'at the expense of helping other struggling students who could not yield such immediate gains in terms of proficiency scores' (p.5).

This echoes closely the situation with schools in England focusing more on students who were performing at the GCSE border of 4/3 (with 4 being a 'pass') rather than others who might have needed more help performing at level 1 or 2. Hargreaves and Shirley (2018) highlight how there are now more pressing concerns with the mental health of young people, harmful effects of digital technologies and a surge in transient refugee populations which need to be taken into account when considering the nature of education required in schools today. These kinds of issues have informed Ontario's awareness of moving to the second age, 'The Age of Learning, Well-being and Identity' (p.5) which resonates with current concerns in England. Questions for this age include (p.6)

1. How can we promote student learning and attend to their well-being at the same time?

2. How can students succeed academically and also thrive as human beings?

3. How can our schools recognise, include, bring together and build young people's identities in a world where acknowledgement and inclusion of people's identities is now seen as indispensable to equity?

The rich diversity of foci and potential leadership actions of the action learning sets in Box 2.3 were each intended to improve pupil attainment. The following case study suggests how one very successful school recognised that teaching assistants (TAs), as valuable members of the wider teaching team, were not supported as well as they could be. The headteacher realised that, through professional development, support and specific guidance, TAs, as well as classroom teachers, could better help learners to achieve.

BOX 2.4: A FOCUS ON TEACHER ASSISTANT (TA) PROFESSIONAL DEVELOPMENT

The headteacher of a school in special measures [in 2011 it was Graded 4, deemed inadequate], changed many aspects of the culture and organisation, so that within four years he had turned it around so it became 'Good'.

Describing some of the changes in an interview the head outlined what he did to bring about this improvement:

> I think it is [...] not about leadership alone; it is where the school is. So when you come into a school that is in special measures you are very focused and you haven't got time to fail [...] you have to be very clear about what needs to be done very quickly [...] and you need to work out which members of the team are able.

Initially he focused on working with his senior leadership team to devise a 'raising achievement plan'. Then he worked with the SLT to gradually devolve much more leadership and responsibility for achievement to middle leaders. Next, with the SLT, he focused on supporting teachers 'taking responsibility for their own classrooms and really being their own leaders in their own classrooms'. Then the SLT turned to TAs and development of their own practices, so that they too became leaders of learning and were accountable and responsible for each of the students they supported.

Previously the TAs were generally expected to use their common sense to know what to do. So the SLT worked with a designated middle leader, who built on the successful professional development of teachers to also provide TAs with bespoke targets and support. The middle leader and TAs worked together to develop standards for classroom assistants that were directly relevant to supporting teachers, learners and learning within the school. Development of the TAs' skills was audited. There was also arranged cover for development time involving the TAs in performance reviews.

> The TAs reported feeling more valued by the school and their motivation increased. There was more effective use of TA skills. All TAs now have personal development plans.
>
> The TA standards have been developed and shared with other schools to inform and scaffold support for their development. As a result of this focused initiative the 2015 Ofsted report for the school involved stated that, 'teachers and TAs use subject specific language consistently. This extends pupils' confidence in the use of language and particularly well supports their good progress in mathematics and writing'. It also recognised that, 'Teaching assistants work effectively alongside teachers to support individuals and groups of pupils. They help pupils to concentrate and tackle tasks in the most appropriate way for them, such as by using information and communication technology'.

In terms of leadership practices demonstrated in Box 2.4, there was a shared vision developed across the SLT and middle leaders to improve the effectiveness of TAs' support both in the classroom and around the school. Previously they had been left to their own devices. The collaborative generation of a set of 'standards', actions or roles they were expected to engage in and take responsibility for provided clarity around the high expectations for their performance. Their assistance was needed to help the school emerge from its 'Inadequate' inspection rating. The involvement of SLT, middle leaders and the TAs themselves to articulate, apply and assess the successful use of the 'standards' built effective relationships between leaders at all levels. The school SLT ensured that the project was given appropriate status through the ways that time and resources were made available for staff to work on the 'standards' and processes to support and monitor TAs' progression in achieving them. This demonstrated how the organisation changed its ways of working to support a desired practice. Excerpts from the Ofsted inspection report as quoted in Box 2.4 evidence how this initiative impacted on pupils' attainment and academic performance throughout the school. Clearly most of the domains and leadership practices presented in Table 2.1 were implemented (consciously or not) to really make a difference to this particular school and students' academic performance.

The following outline demonstrates the concerns, actions and impact that an initiative or project focused on developing middle leadership (see Chapter 5) designed to improve pupils' attainment might promote. Table 2.3 presents a summary of evidence about the ways that some of the Oxford City schools (Menter and McGregor, 2015), each with significant challenges regarding their student intake (many with high numbers of pupils eligible for free school meals and English as a Second Language), strategised through a middle leaders' ALS to promote in-school changes that they planned would initiate and support developments underpinning improvements in pupil attainment. The leadership actions ranged from new original approaches borne out of the termly seminars or workshops provided for leaders in the city schools project (Menter and McGregor, 2015) or revisiting and revising previous practices to more closely align with mediating and supporting leadership capabilities; encouraging collaboration across the school/s; increasing engagement

Leading learning 27

Table 2.3 Summary of the range of 'concerns' and leadership 'actions' planned that resulted in raised attainment

ALS middle leader member	Issue/concern voiced by middle leader	Specific action taken by middle leader	Impact that promoted attainment
1	Early Years (EYS) need to improve in speaking and listening. School decided to address questioning to attend to Ofsted concerns.	Find out/observe which teachers employ good questioning in their teaching. Review lesson planning (and questioning within that too) to elicit what constitutes good practice.	Modelling and exemplifying good practice (in questioning, in both planning and practice). Developing colour-coded kit to guide teachers to help with using Blooms taxonomy (so they could quickly recognise how to ask easier or more challenging questions).
2	Need to improve writing across the school.	Developed guided and shared writing tasks. Invited external expert review.	Realised the need to focus on spelling and grammar progression throughout the school. Activated Learning Walks to review writing. Provided coaching to support writing for new members of staff. Encouraged storytelling.
4	Increasing level 4 achievement by end of year 6.	Celebrate achievements in writing, especially when children reach level 4. Develop a storytelling approach to embrace the whole school curriculum (particularly art, geography, science, literacy etc. through stories).	The new curriculum has provided a fresh opportunity to redevelop teaching and learning. Storytelling has resulted in an instant impact on writing!

(Continued)

Table 2.3 (Continued)

ALS middle leader member	Issue/concern voiced by middle leader	Specific action taken by middle leader	Impact that promoted attainment
5	To improve outcomes in writing to improve Literacy Early Years Foundation Stage Prime (EYFSP) results.	Improve resourcing outdoors for stimulus opportunities through boys' writing project. More links were made with construction, vehicles and the wooded area (boat and investigations/sensory). Developed writing 'tool kits' and clipboards for shared writing with all adults praising boys' efforts in particular. Targeted efforts to support boys' engagement with writing. AfL focused on those children not accessing writing resources has made a significant contribution to raising outcomes. Continued development of physical writing competencies and skills through activities designed to develop both fine and gross motor skills and co-ordination. These include Write Dance, Dough disco and finger gym etc. in a well-resourced garden.	EYFSP Good Level of Development (GLD) 2014 shows that children have made good progress with an improved outcome from the previous year's GLD.

| 6 | Reviewing the experience of pupil premium (disadvantaged) children to improve their transition through year groups. | Surveys to teachers through email that reviewed half-day visits for Y6 to secondary school. Reviewed other schools' approaches. Interviewed children to see what they think. | In term 6 devised a whole school topic – Alice in Wonderland, where pupils spent time in their old and new classes. Pupils met new secondary teachers. Teachers focused on getting to know their pupil premium children at the beginning of the new school year to ensure they made appropriate progress. Completed the project with a Mad Hatter's Tea Party where pupils wore the hats they had made with their new teacher and celebrated together. The transition project was successful in helping the teachers and children feel more confident with their new classes. |

with pupils' families; improving student attainment and thinking about sustainability (from a staffing and change perspective).

How is learning-centered leadership understood and enacted?

As discussed earlier, learning-centred leadership evolved from instructional leadership and, like other models introduced in Chapter 1, it can be comprised of various practices outlined in Table 2.1. A key focus for learning-centred leadership is, of course, the use of varied strategies and practices that directly improve teaching and learning in the classroom.

Leaders needing to improve the academic performance of students in their schools will likely adopt practices that are both 'transformational' (introduced in Chapter 1) and 'learning-centred'. As Brown et al. (2022, p. 117) suggest, this will involve 'effective development of, engaging in and sharing of evidence-informed effective practice'.

Data and leading improvement

There have been many calls for teachers to use different forms of data to reform their practice or, indeed, for educational leaders to make decisions drawing on evidence derived from students' academic performance in schools and other measures of impact (Connolly et al., 2018). Collins and Coleman (2022, p. 20) describe this is as 'the rise of evidence' in response to policy calls related to the need for 'evidence-informed' policy and practice in schools. However, this differs somewhat to 'evidence use' in policy and practice. In their review, Rickinson et al. (2017) suggest a distinction between *what* and *how* evidence is used to inform development of policy. What is considered as informative evidence and the way it is interpreted and applied may differ between schools. Collins and Coleman (2022) continue to consider a dichotomy of ways that evidence is thought about in schools and propose that it may be used for *accountability* as well as *improvement*.

The increasing autonomy of schools since the introduction of the Academies Act (2010) has meant that a wide variation of practices (Greany, 2015) has emerged as schools decide how to implement policies to succeed in an increasingly competitive landscape. Using school data to inform the development of policy and practice (Supovitz, 2015) has been shown to be challenging because readily available information may not be the most suitable to enable the resolution of specific problems.

In the Oxford City project the leadership practices identified in each school demonstrate a plethora of ways that they used different forms of 'data' to inform or assess development/s needed. In the case described in Box 2.5, an ALS focused on tracking underperforming pupils, using data to address gaps in attainment. This case (Box 2.5) illustrates how specific leadership actions impact on improving attainment.

BOX 2.5 ILLUSTRATING THE USE OF DATA TO IMPROVE STUDENT LEARNING

One middle leader in the ALS focused on how to ensure that data were used more purposefully. The action taken was to have more focused communications with teachers about the progress of their pupils, setting more specific targets for them and working on strategies to help them achieve their targets. Subsequently attention was focused on pupils who were making little or no progress. These actions resulted in the development of new procedures for using data to narrow the gap in attainment and achievement. The resultant impact demonstrated how well the new procedures worked. The children were assessed every six weeks. Progress was measured against a baseline and average point score as it was hard to measure progress across a relatively short period (4–6 weeks). There was an 'amber' designation for children just below expected targets. At pupil progress meetings children were placed in different categories, used for planning lessons. A 'vulnerable Venn' diagram was used to plot results. The resultant impact demonstrated that the new procedures worked well.

The need at another school in the ALS to track children who were not meeting expectations was addressed by training the staff in using a pupil target tracker. The middle leader started by using data in their own classroom to identify effective/ineffective interventions. A grid was developed to show where children were in relation to their targets. The middle leader encouraged the teachers to learn how to analyse electronic data. These actions resulted in the development of a bespoke data system to assess and discuss pupil progress. Data were used to prepare lessons for teaching classes.

As can be seen from the vignettes (in Boxes 2.1 to 2.5) considered thus far, different forms of data can be used in various ways to inform the focus, nature and impact of different leadership practices. In this next case the 'vision' to improve boys' writing led to a variety of actions promoted by the middle leader responsible.

BOX 2.6 LOOKING AT DATA TO INFORM HOW TO IMPROVE BOYS' ATTAINMENT IN WRITING

The various 'actions' set in play by the middle leader responsible included raising aspirations of the boys; exploring what boys do in response to the tasks set; reviewing the nature of the tasks set to assess appropriateness in content (e.g., nature, cars, football) and also the type of writing required (texts, letters, newspaper articles, etc.).

The approach to collecting data also included setting up an action research project; tracking a group of boys; monitoring their choices of tasks in class; looking at the impact on boys' writing of different tasks; considering progress in relation to the baseline data.

A team was set up to steer, action and monitor the project looking at the teaching influence on boys' responses to writing tasks.

> A creative approach was adopted to track six boys, who collated a photo diary (deemed easy and fun to complete). The variety of activities chosen by the boys was noted, and the depth of engagement and deeper concentration for longer periods was also collated. The boys also provided their reflections on the writing activities.
>
> The project then developed AfL strategies to raise further the quality outcomes of pupils' writing, specifically with a view to increase motivation through targeted praise and reward.
>
> The outcomes of this project resulted in a higher proportion of boys achieving level 4 in their writing in year 6.

Practices and leading improvement

Geijsel et al. (1999) report on a large-scale Dutch innovation examining the impact of transformational leadership. In the qualitative aspect of their research they found that 'vision, individual consideration and intellectual stimulation' (p. 309) were key dimensions in changing teachers' practice. These elements have also been evidenced in the Oxford City project (Menter and McGregor, 2015). Vision, for example, is demonstrated by the way the headteacher planned for his succession in Box 2.1. Individualised consideration of TA development is evident in Box 2.4. Intellectual stimulation is demonstrable in a range of activities, particularly including NQTs and ECTs in Box 2.3.

As can be inferred from reflection on the case studies, improvement in attainment requires leadership that engages in all the practices identified in Table 2.1:

1. Setting Directions

2. Building relationships and developing people

3. Developing the organisation to support desired practices

4. Improving the teaching programme

These are considered in more detail in the following section in relation to the Oxford City project.

Setting directions

Ensuring a school is clear about its shared vision and aims involves good communication, awareness and empathy of others' viewpoints. As one headteacher in the Oxford City project (McGregor and Browne, 2016, p. 35) said,

> I think because when you first start to lead something you think it might be relatively easy but then of course when you come to an issue you then

sometimes have to change your style of leadership and how you communicate [... you should] not presume that you have been understood.

The involvement of all leaders (senior and middle) is important in agreeing a school's priorities. The vision and aims need to be kept 'front and centre' (Webster, 2022, p. 128) and present in the minds of staff. As a headteacher who improved the school's Ofsted grade to 'Good' stated, 'What has really helped is the attitude of our staff, who really want to be better teachers and make a difference' (McGregor and Browne, 2016 p. 36).

An example of an activity that could be used (and adapted) to engage groups of teachers in discussing and coming to an agreement about their beliefs regarding the nature of education is included in Appendix 2.4. Considering arguments about different ways that the school should support effective learning could prepare staff for a fresh 'vision' of the education their school could offer.

In various cases outlined in this chapter, data of differing forms has influenced leaders' decisions about the nature and/or focus of their school aims or intentions about ways to improve pupils' academic performance. More discussion about creating a shared vision is in Chapter 4.

Building relations and developing people

This domain of practice can be implemented in varied ways. As one headteacher (of a successful school) reported, "the SLT supported TAs looking at developing their own practices [....], they became their own leaders. So you move from a top down approach into a bit of versatility to be able to allow ... people [... autonomy ...] to fail sometimes and learn from their mistakes and take risks" (McGregor and Browne, 2016 p.35).

Webster (2022, p. 128) notes how involving TAs in leading learning may require a phased approach:

i. Creating a climate for change;

ii. Engaging and enabling staff;

iii. Implementing and sustaining change.

Leading and supporting these kinds of steps in the process of 'change' can be challenging. However, working with others within the school, and/or collaborating across senior or middle leadership teams through the ALSs mentioned earlier (Menter and McGregor, 2015) and engaging in dialogue about potential possibilities with other schools can offer evidence of effective ways to navigate development of this kind. Networks that developed across Oxford City, for example, offered a way of validating potential ideas or even exploring others' experiences. As one headteacher shared, the ALS provides, an ideas sounding board and [for] a development of a policy and plan it's still the best thing. The opportunity for discussions with other headteachers, in a similar position, offers ways of checking out the feasibility of new ideas and possible projects or developments.

The networks developed across the participating schools, see Rincon-Gillardo (2020) for further discussion, enabled recognition of sources of local expertise or experience that could inform research and evaluative processes focused on educational improvement.

Developing the organisation to support desired practices

The recognition that professional space is needed for leadership teams to discuss, deliberate and decide what to do to improve the student's academic performance may be facilitated, as one headteacher (McGregor and Browne, 2016, p. 35) described, 'we've given our SLT [...] a lot of management time, a lot more than other schools, so they get one day a week completely for management which for middle leaders in a school this size is a lot' (headteacher of an Ofsted-rated Good school). Other schools realised that staff need to be freed up from teaching commitments to support staff development, for example, by having a non-teaching Deputy (McGregor and Browne, 2016).

The approach to leadership within the Oxford City project schools generally became much more *distributed* amongst both senior staff and middle leaders. With collaboration between leaders, distributed leadership developed from the previously more prevalent directive or authoritarian forms. As Leithwood et al. (2020, p. 7) evidence, distributed leadership is a practice that 'supports building organisational conditions that foster high quality teaching and generate improvement in learner outcomes'.

In the Oxford City project, staff working together within schools developed leadership teams for a range of purposes and began to use them in a way that modelled the application of ALSs within the school. For example, one particular school developed 'change teams' based on the ALS approach. These teams were comprised of a senior leader in the school, as well as more junior teaching and support staff. These teams were responsible for leading and developing new initiatives throughout the school. One successful example of this was the introduction of a storytelling approach within a school (requiring fresh curricular and teaching materials to be developed throughout each year group and across all the subject areas).

Within schools, senior leaders from the Oxford City project realised how regularly creating space for staff to discuss, plan and consider (drawing on evidence to support potential projects or innovations in school) is more likely to succeed, rather than headteachers making isolated or individual decisions about new developments within the schools. Across the city, one head echoed others' views about the impact of the project, saying 'partnership I feel at the moment is really strengthening, and ... it has promoted school-to-school support and the sense of sharing. We are serving the same community and actually there's so much more that we can do together' (McGregor and Browne, 2016, p. 38).

Improving the teaching programme

Headteachers and middle leaders recognise how looking at evidence can i.) inform what might and can be done to improve pupils' attainment; and ii.) provide data that supports (or not) what has been done. The latter is deemed 'evidence for accountability' (Collins and Coleman, 2022, p. 23). As such, a new in-post head said that she had developed an appreciation 'that everyone must have that understanding within the school and that dissemination of the understanding will take a period of time, say up to 2–3 years' (McGregor and Browne, 2016, p.38).

Recognising the value of evidence from academic performance data is invaluable to inform classroom teachers how they might direct and invest their energy and focus to help specific children (or cohorts) to make progress in particular directions. This has meant some schools now collect more data than is nationally required, even up to 'four times a year [...] because we want to have the conversation'. Data-informed conversations help to finely tune the actions of the teachers, ensuring the best possible performance is reached in 'term 5 because that is when the data has got to be in' (headteacher from a 'Good' school, McGregor and Browne, 2016, p. 39).

Sometimes headteachers know what they want to do, but they cannot find the evidence to back up their ideas. In these cases, effective working relationships with other heads offers the opportunity to discuss with them what they have done and to share 'what they have learnt'. Talking to other headteachers about how they have initiated change, what they have learned from doing it (i.e., how they know it worked) is a form of evidence-based decision-making that school leaders recognise they can use 'to develop themselves' (headteacher from a 'Good' school, McGregor and Browne, 2016, p. 39). This is also known as a 'self-improving school-led school system' (Earley and Greany, 2022, p. 277).

Conclusion

What has been considered in this chapter are the ways that the key domains of practice (summarised in Table 2.1: Setting directions; Building relationships and developing people; Developing the organisation to support desired practices and Improving the teaching programme or approach) have been integrated or combined in varied ways to catalyse improved attainment (and achievement) of pupils across many schools.

The varied ways that the four domains of practices are emphasised shapes the extent to which models of leadership concerned with learning (Earley, 2022) are enacted. There may be more or less focus on leadership for learning (Leithwood & Lewis, 2012) that orchestrates an appropriate and supportive school culture for improved achievement; or, learning-centred leadership (Southworth, 2009; Earley, 2013), focused entirely on leadership strategies that directly impact on pupils' learning.

What is clear, though, is that data-driven or evidence-informed decision-making by senior and/or middle leaders in schools is key to impacting upon, and influencing the ways that leaders' domains of practice are played out or enacted in schools. Leadership practices, informed by evidence, can then positively and sustainably impact upon teaching and learning.

> **BOX 2.7 QUESTIONS FOR REFLECTION AND ACTION**
>
> - Which leadership practices have been successfully enacted by your school?
> - Which 'domains' and associated practices still need addressing (and should be noted within the school action plan)?
> - What areas of leadership for learning would you use action learning sets to address?
> - How (and whom) would you involve in these action learning sets?
> - Who would you involve in discussions about the nature of education in your school?

Appendix 2.1 A unified model of effective leader practices. (After Sebring et al., 2006; Murphy et al., 2006; Leithwood, 2012, cited in Hitt and Tucker, 2016, p. 543, that could serve as a tool for 'self-assessment'.)

Domains and dimensions	In place: Yes/No	Action plan to address: Yes/No
Establishing and conveying the vision • Creating, articulating and stewarding shared mission and vision • Implementing vision by setting goals and performance expectations • Modelling aspirational and ethical practices • Communicating broadly the state of the vision • Promoting use of data for continued improvement • Tending to external accountability		
Facilitating a high-quality learning experience for students • Maintaining safety and orderliness • Personalising the environment to reflect students' backgrounds • Developing and monitoring curricular programmes • Developing and monitoring instructional (teaching) programme/s • Developing and monitoring assessment programme/s		
Building professional capacity • Selecting for the right fit • Providing individualised consideration • Building trusting relationships • Providing opportunities to learn for whole faculty, including leaders • Supporting, buffering and recognising staff • Engendering responsibility for promoting learning • Creating communities of practice		

(Continued)

Domains and dimensions	In place: Yes/No	Action plan to address: Yes/No
Creating a supportive organisation for learning • Acquiring and allocating resources strategically for mission and vision • Considering context to maximise organisational functioning • Building collaborative processes for decision-making • Sharing and distributing leadership • Tending to and building diversity • Maintaining ambitious and high expectations and standards • Strengthening and optimising school culture		
Connecting with external partners • Building productive relationships with families and external partners in the community • Engaging families and community in collaborative processes to strengthen student learning • Anchoring schools in the community		

Appendix 2.2 Introducing action learning sets

How will we work together?

1. Tick the five statements that are most important to you as we work together.
2. Discuss these with a partner and finally agree together as a group the key parameters of our working relationship

To make the most of our meetings I would like us to:	Personal Rank	Pairs decision	Final agreed working contract
respect the professional expertise of all our members			
listen actively			
not interrupt one another			
understand the different contexts in which we work			
stay focused on our objectives			

(Continued)

To make the most of our meetings I would like us to:	Personal Rank	Pairs decision	Final agreed working contract
value all contributions equally			
focus on making a difference and not on accepting the status quo			
seek to understand and to be understood			
evaluate ideas and make constructive criticisms			
monitor participation: encourage everyone to contribute equally			
agree on the confidential nature of our discussions and maintain that confidentiality throughout			
Start and finish on time			
Others?			

The role of the facilitator

The facilitator is part of the action learning set; their role is to:

- Support the group to set up ways of working and implement those, including keeping time
- facilitate learning by questioning, challenging, prompting and supporting – in face-to-face sessions and online
- provide resources that can stimulate, challenge and extend learning
- support in understanding how best to undertake school-based exploration of issues and how to gather evidence
- help draw together conclusions and help participants to determine changes in leadership practice
- take notes of agreed actions for each participant
- review regularly the way in which the action learning set is working, ensuring participants are happy with the process
- monitor progress and report back to the core team

Appendix 2.3 Framing and using action learning sets

Action Learning Set – first meeting

- Introductions (school, role and what would like to achieve from the action learning set (intervention)
- Explain how the action learning set will work. Participants commit to 'taking action' between learning set meetings and report back on progress. Participants should encourage and challenge each other to make the meetings worthwhile.
- Audit to be completed (How will we work together?) and then discussed in pairs to consider rankings. Whole group discussion to agree working contract, i.e.: retain confidentiality.
- Participants share their key leadership challenge. Others ask questions for clarification and to explore potential influences.
- Each participant to articulate:
  - Specific challenge to improving student achievement you're concerned with;
  - What information is needed to appreciate the nature and extent of the challenge;
  - What previous actions have been undertaken [and relative success];
  - What issues are you anticipating in tackling the challenge;
  - What action/s will you commit to undertaking before the next ALS meeting [encouragement to gather baseline data against which impact of future actions can be measured].
- Agree future meetings date/location [rotating around the schools].
- Once 'actions' for each participant agreed, review the success of the meeting to consider adjustments to the ground rules (as listed in Appendix 2.2 & 2.3).
- Facilitator to produce:
  - accounts of variations in leadership practice/s for others to learn from
  - accounts of measures of impact to demonstrate how leaders are engaging others in ways of changing practice
  - case studies informed by the ALS approach exploring leadership challenges, i.e. the process so that it can be adopted as a tool for others to use when undertaking school-based enquiry/action research
- Facilitator to administer [including collating notes] and support coordination of meetings

Key foci of ALS discussions

i. Issue/concern voiced by ALS participant

ii. Specific action taken by ALS participant

iii. Impact of specific actions ALS participant took

iv. Which of these aspects[1] of the outcomes does the impact relate to (and how)?

- ○ Active collaboration
- ○ Reflection for action
- ○ Developing sustainability
- ○ Raising attainment
- ○ Increased engagement with families

The second meeting (and ongoing subsequent meetings)

Preparation for reflections:

- what I did
- what happened
- what was different from what I expected
- what I have learned
- what is the issue now
- what action should I take next
- what I would like in terms of challenge and support.

See also Appendix 2.2: How to set-up and focus discussions for an ALS.

Appendix 2.4 Engaging in dilemmas about the nature of education provided by the school (from Berlak, A and Berlak, H. (1981) "The dilemma language" in Dilemmas of Schooling: teaching and social change London: Methuen)

The following statements offer suggestions about polarised views related to education and learning. These statements could be adopted/adapted for professional development with teachers. The purpose could be rethinking the school vision for the pupils or considering more widely about behaviour policy or even education beyond the school gates.

The control dilemmas (pp 136–144)

Whole child versus child as student (realms)

On the one hand, looking at a whole range of realms of the child's development (i.e. taking responsibility for the child's aesthetic, intellectual, physical, social-emotional and moral development), and on the other hand, focusing on the child as student (i.e. taking responsibility for a narrow range of school subjects, focusing primarily on intellectual and cognitive development).

Teacher versus child control (time)

On the one hand, the teacher controlling all aspects of the child's use of time, from when they begin an activity to the duration of the activity to the ending of the activity; on the other hand, the child controlling their use of time.

Teacher versus child control (operations)

The extent to which teachers try to control children's behaviour when undertaking aspects of the curriculum (e.g. allowing children to choose from a wide range of options), or, conversely, dictating exactly what the children will do.

Teacher versus child control (standards)

The extent to which teachers set and monitor the standards of students' performance.

The curriculum dilemmas (pp 144–156)

Personal knowledge versus public knowledge

The extent to which teachers relate what they teach to the personal knowledge of the child. Public knowledge can be seen as the traditions of knowledge which have stood the test of time. Personal knowledge implies a view that knowledge is only worthwhile if it relates to the knower.

Knowledge as content versus knowledge as process

The extent to which knowledge is viewed as facts, theories or generalisations rather than a process of thinking, reasoning or testing.

Knowledge as given versus knowledge as problematical

The extent to which knowledge is seen as objective truth, rather than constructed, provisional or tentative, subject to political, cultural and social influences.

Intrinsic versus extrinsic motivation

The position that the impetus for learning comes – and should come – from within, versus the position that action from the teacher is required for learning to be initiated and sustained (e.g., by giving rewards, punishments etc.)

Note

1 Constructive use of evidence [that Oxford project was concerned with].

References

Ball, S.J. Maguire, M. and Braun, A. (2012). *How Schools Do Policy*. London: Routledge.

Branch, G.F., Rivkin, S.G. and Hanushek, E.A. (2013). School leaders matter: Measuring the impact of effective principals. *Winter*, vol. 13, no. 1, pp. 62–69.

Brown, C., Stoll, L. and Godfrey, D. (2022). Leading for innovation and evidence-informed practice. In T. Greany and P. Earley (eds). *School Leadership and Education System Reform*. London: Bloomsbury, pp. 113–121.

Caldwell, B. (2014). Foreword. In C. Day and D. Gurr (eds). *Leading Schools Successfully: Stories from the Field*. London: Routledge.

Chapman, C., Muijs, D., Reynolds, D., Sammons, P. and Teddlie, C. (eds). (2015). *The Routledge International Handbook of Educational Effectiveness and Improvement: Research, Policy, and Practice*. New York, NY: Routledge.

Collins, K. and Coleman, R. (2022). Evidence-informed policy and practice. In T. Greany and P. Earley (eds). *School Leadership and Education System Reform*. London: Bloomsbury.

Connolly, P., Keenan, C. and Urbanska, K. (2018) The trials of evidence-based practice in education: A systematic review of randomised controlled trials in education research 1980–2016. *Educational Research*, vol. 60, no. 3, pp. 276–291.

Day, C. and Sammons, P. (2013). *Successful Leadership: A review of the International Literature*. Reading: CfBT Education Trust.

Day, C., Sammons, P., Leithwood, K., Harris, A., Hopkins, D., Gu, Q., Brown, E. and Ahtaridou, E. (2011). *Successful School Leadership: Linking with Learning and Achievement*. London: Open University Press.

Day, C. and Gurr, D. (eds). (2014). *Leading School Successfully. Stories from the Field*. London: Routledge.

Domina, T., Pharris-Ciurej, B., Penner, A., Penner, E., Brummet, Q., Porter, S. and Sanabria, T. (2018). Is free and reduced-price lunch a valid measure of educational disadvantage?. *Educational Researcher*, vol. 47, no. 9, pp. 539–555.

Earley, P. (2013). *Exploring the School Leadership Landscape: Changing Demands*. London: Changing Realities Bloomsbury.

Earley, P. (2016). Global trends and challenges for school leaders: Keeping the focus on learning. *Journal of Educational, Cultural and Psychological Studies*, vol. 14, pp. 21–33.

Earley, P. (2022). Conceptions of leadership and leading the learning. In T. Greany and P. Earley (eds). *School Leadership and Education System Reform*. London: Bloomsbury.

Earley, P. and Greany, T. (2022). Postscript: The future of Leadership. In T. Greany and P. Earley (eds). *School Leadership and Education System Reform*. London: Bloomsbury.

Geijsel, F., Sleegers, P. and van den Berg, R. (1999). Transformational leadership and the implementation of large-scale innovation programs. *Journal of Educational Administration*, vol. 37, no. 4, pp. 309–328. DOI: 10.1108/09578239910285561

Greany, T. (2015) How can evidence inform teaching and decision making across 21,000 autonomous schools?: Learning from the journey in England. In C. Brown (ed) *Leading the Use of Research and Evidence in Schools*. London: Institute of Education Press, pp. 11–19.

Greany, T. and Earley, P. (eds). (2022). *School Leadership and Education System Reform*. London: Bloomsbury.

Grissom, J.A., Loeb, S. and Master, B. (2013). Effective instructional time use for school leaders. *Educational Researcher*, vol. 42, pp. 433–444.

Goodall, J. (2018). A toolkit for parental engagement: From project to process. *School Leadership and Management*, vol. 38, no. 2, pp. 222–238.

Hallinger, P. and Heck, R. (1998). Exploring the principal's contribution to school effectiveness: 1980–1995. *School Effectiveness and School Improvement*, vol. 9, pp. 157–191.

Hallinger, P. and Heck, R. (2010). Collaborative leadership and school improvement: Understanding the impact on school capacity and student learning. *School Leadership and Management*, vol. 30, no. 2, pp. 95–110.

Hargreaves, A. and Shirley, D. (2018). Executive summary. Leading from the Middle: Spreading learning, well-being, and identity across Ontario. Council of Ontario Directors of Education Report. Code Consortium, Leadership and Innovation. https://ccsli.ca/downloads/2018-Leading_From_the_Middle_Final-EN.pdf

Hitt, D. and Tucker, P. (2016). Systematic review of key leader practices found to influence student achievement: A unified framework. *Review of Educational Research*, vol. 86, no. 2, pp. 531–569.

Jeynes, W. (2011). *Parental Involvement and Academic Success*. New York, NY: Routledge.

Leithwood, K. and Louis, K.S. (2012). *Linking Leadership to Student Learning*. San Francisco, CA: Jossey-Bass.

Leithwood, K., Harris, A. and Hopkins, D. (2008) Seven strong claims about successful school leadership, *School Leadership and Management*, vol. 28, no. 1, pp. 27–42.

Leithwood, K. Harris, A. and Hopkins, D. (2020). Seven strong claims about successful school leadership revisited. *School Leadership & Management*, vol. 40, no. 1, pp. 5–22. DOI: 10.1080/13632434.2019.1596077

Leithwood, K., Sun, J. and Pollock, K. (eds). (2017). *How School Leadership Influences Student Learning: The Four Paths*. The Netherlands: Springer.

Louis, K.S. and Wahlstrom, K. (2012). Shared and instructional leadership: When principals and teachers successful lead together. In K. Leithwood and K. Seashore Louis (eds). *Linking Leadership to Student Learning*. San Francisco, CA: JosseyBass, pp. 25–41.

MacBeath, J. (2013). Learning in a world of change [chapter 3 in Leadership for 21st Century learning]. OECD. Available at https://read.oecd-ilibrary.org/education/leadership-for-21st-century-learning/leading-learning-in-a-world-of-change_9789264205406-5-en#page1. Accessed 3 April 2023.

MacBeath, J. and N. Dempster (eds). (2008) *Connecting Leadership and Learning: Principles for Practice*. London: Routledge.

McGregor, D. and Browne, L. (2016). Review of the Impact of Oxford City Council's Education Attainment Programme (2012–2014) Oxford City Council. Available at https://www.oxford.gov.uk. Accessed 1 May 2023.

Menter, I. and McGregor, D. (2015). Leadership for Learning 2012–2014. Evaluation Report. Oxford City Council. Available at https://www.oxford.gov.uk. Accessed 1 May 2023.

Mortimore, P. (1993). School effectiveness and the management of effective learning and teaching. *School Effectiveness and School Improvement*, vol. 4, no. 4, pp. 290–310.

Murphy, J., Elliot, S.N., Goldring, E. and Porter, A.C. (2006). *Learning-centered Leadership: A Conceptual Foundation*. New York, NY: Wallace Foundation.

Pendleton, D. and Furnham, A. (2012). *Leadership: All You Need to Know*. London: Palgrave MacMillan.

Reitzug, U. and Patterson, J. (1998). 'I'm not going to lose you!': Empowerment through caring in an urban principal's practice with pupils. *Urban Education*, vol. 33, no. 2, pp. 150–181.

Rickinson, M., de Bruin, K., Walsh, L. and Hall, M. (2017). What can evidence-use in practice learn from evidence-use in policy? *Educational Research*, vol. 59, no. 2, 173–189.

Rincon-Gallardo, S. (2020). Leading school networks to liberate learning: Three leadership roles. *School Leadership & Management*, vol. 40, nos. 2–3, pp. 146–162. DOI: 10.1080/13632434.2019.1702015.

Robinson, V. (2011). *Student-centred Leadership*. San Francisco: Jossey Bass.

Sebastion, J., Huang, H. and Allensworth, E.. (2017). Examining Integrated Leadership Systems in high schools: Connecting principal and teacher leadership to organizational processes and student outcomes. *School Effectiveness and School Improvement* vol. 28, no. 3, pp. 463–488.

Sebring, P.B., Allensworth, E., Bryk, A.S., Easton, J.Q. and Luppescu, S. (2006). *The Essential Supports for School Improvement*. Chicago, IL: Consortium on Chicago School Research.

Southworth, G. (2004). Learning-centred leadership In B. Davies (ed). *The Essentials of School Leadership*. London: SAGE.

Southworth, G. (2009). Learning-centred leadership In B. Davies (ed). *The Essentials of School Leadership. 2E*. London: SAGE.

Supovitz, J. (2015). Teacher data use for improving teaching and learning. In C. Brown (ed). *Leading the Use of Research and Evidence in Schools*. London: IOE Press, pp. 117–125.

Waters, M. (2013). *Thinking Allowed on Schooling*. Carmarthen: Wales. Independent Thinking Press.

Watkins, C. (2010). *Research Matters: Learning, Performance and Improvement*. https://www.ioe.ac.uk/about/documents/Watkins_10_Lng_Perf_Imp_ev.pdf

Webster, R. (2022). Leadership for Inclusion. In T. Greany and P. Earley (eds). *School Leadership and Education System Reform*. London: Bloomsbury.

West-Burnham, J. (2005). Leadership for personalisation. In J. West-Burnham and M. Coates (eds). *Personalised Learning: Transforming Education for Every Child*. Stafford: Network Education Press.

3 School culture and improvement

Introduction

> I cannot explain what it is that makes our school feel like a comfortable jumper, but it seems to have an impact on the staff.... The way everybody is so friendly and supportive to each other is as good now as it was 20 years ago.
> (Primary School teacher, coastal school,
> Teacher Retention Research Project)

This teacher's description of her school demonstrates both the importance of school culture and the difficulty in pinpointing exactly what it is. The feeling of 'a comfortable jumper' encapsulates what attracted her to the school and kept her there for over 20 years, but she finds it difficult to identify what has fashioned that sense of warmth and comfort.

It is school culture that helps to create the atmosphere that nurtures teachers. They may describe their school culture as 'a positive feel', 'family', 'ethos of togetherness', 'a shared journey' (Teacher Retention Research project). As well as enabling teachers to feel at ease, school culture is crucial to generate a positive context to improve teaching and learning, for both teachers and students (Ishimaru and Galloway, 2014).

The importance of school culture has long been recognised. Back in 1985, an article entitled 'Good seeds grow in strong cultures' advocated a focus on positive 'cultural norms' including collegiality, high expectations, trust, support, appreciation and honest communication (Saphier and King, 1985). Since then, a broad consensus has developed about the centrality of cultural leadership in school improvement (Leithwood et al., 2020). This is because culture pervades everything in a school: the way people behave and dress, the kind of conversations they have, the level of collaboration between staff and how teachers and students feel about learning (Deal and Peterson, 2016). Recognising the 'thisness' of a school, which encapsulates its community and values, is vital when planning change (Giles and Bills, 2017).

The difficulty in describing the 'thisness' of a school reflects the complex nature of school culture, however. What feels like a comfortable jumper to one teacher may seem like a straitjacket to another. Some important aspects of culture, such as values and beliefs, are invisible, which challenges leaders to identify and engage with them. Furthermore, school cultures are in 'continuous flux' (Walker and Riordan, 2010, p. 60). This exacerbates issues leaders face when trying to understand their school's culture.

This chapter aims to unravel the cultural 'jumper' of a school in order to identify what it is and how school leaders can 'knit together' a positive school culture. Many aspects of school culture are considered: the impact of different cultures; the links between school culture and school improvement; differences between primary and secondary school culture; and the role of school leaders in developing a positive culture. Accompanying questionnaires in the appendices are designed to help school leaders assess their school's culture.

What does 'culture' mean?

In order to discuss school culture, a clear definition is helpful. There are numerous alternative definitions and the word 'culture' is often used interchangeably with climate, atmosphere, tone, ethos and character (Prosser, 1999). Schein's (1985) definition is still widely cited: that culture is the shared basic assumptions learned by a group while solving problems. Schein (1985) suggested that culture comprises:

- artefacts (which are visible)

- beliefs and values (which are not visible but can be brought into being through discussion or questionnaires or articulated as policy intentions)

- basic assumptions (which are invisible, unconscious, taken-for-granted beliefs, so not easily accessible)

Essentially culture is 'the way we do things around here' (Garratt, 1991, p. 317). In relation to staff, it includes their feelings about the school, the way things are done, rituals, symbols and historical ways of working. It has aspects that are visible and invisible, shared and challenged, messy and dynamic, and it has multiple layers (individual, organisational, national). As Brighouse and Woods (2013, p. 28) state:

> [Culture] manifests itself in customs, rituals, symbols, stories, language and norms of behaviour. Where a school has a positive culture, established norms of behaviour are taken for granted, as unspoken rules, and the ethos is implicit, embedded, shared by everyone. There is a compelling and inclusive moral purpose driving the school forward on equity, social justice and unshakeable principles.

For the purposes of this chapter, we are defining 'school culture' as the shared values, beliefs and assumptions within the community at the school and the way in which these are reflected in practice. These different aspects of culture are considered in more detail in the next section.

What are the key aspects of culture?

School cultures are shared, both seen and unseen, changeable and historic. These different elements are discussed next.

Culture is shared

School cultures are, by their nature, collective. Although one person (such as the headteacher) may influence a school's culture, it is not possible to have a one-person organisational culture. For a culture to develop, there has to be a shared understanding and commitment to it, building a consensus about what is important (Sailes, 2008). Communities of teachers and students contribute to and are influenced by the culture (Zhu et al., 2014).

School cultures are based on shared values (Prosser, 1999, p. 8), although individuals' values and beliefs about learning may differ depending on, for example, their gender, ethnicity, class, education, religion, political and professional views. These produce a 'mosaic of organisational realities' (Morgan, 1997, p. 137). The school's culture helps to create a pattern from the mosaic which encompasses the key values shared by most staff. Box 3.1 provides questions which might help to articulate staff values and vision.

> **BOX 3.1 VALUES AND VISION (HALLINGER AND HECK, 2003, P. 221)**
>
> Hallinger and Heck (2003, p. 221) suggest asking the following questions to ascertain the values and personal vision of teachers:
>
> 1. In what kind of school would you wish to teach?
> 2. What brought you into education in the first place?
> 3. What are the elements of the school that you would want your own children to attend?
> 4. What would the school environment in which you would most like to work look like, feel like and sound like?
> 5. If your school/college/educational organisation were threatened, what would be the last things that you would be willing to give up?
> 6. On what issues would you make your last stand?

There is an emotional aspect to culture. It is about feelings (such as the 'comfortable jumper'), because beliefs and values are inevitably attached to emotion. Staff who are happy with the culture may demonstrate ways of being and interacting to ensure the feeling of the 'comfortable jumper' is maintained.

Culture is seen and unseen

An important aspect of school culture is that much of it is invisible: it is about 'how organisations work when no one is looking' (Morgan, 1997, p. 145). Anthony (1994, p. 52) suggested that it is in the nature of culture to be 'unperceived by those who share it and difficult to penetrate by those who do not'. People's experience of culture has been compared to that of a fish, which is unaware that it is swimming in water (Bourdieu and Wacquant, 1992). A fish or an individual removed from their immediate environment or assumed culture would be like a 'fish out of water'. New staff may initially notice the ethos of a school until they, too, become absorbed and their 'total immersion in the culture has them swimming in a similar manner' (Giles and Bills, 2017, p. 123). This image of a fish illustrates culture's 'taken for granted' nature, but for those entering the water who are not fish, the community can be difficult to access.

The visible and invisible aspects of culture can be illustrated by the metaphor of an iceberg – see Figure 3.1. 'The way we say we get things done' is above the water and 'the way we really get things done (and why we do them)' lies hidden below the surface (Hall, 1981). Visible, above-the-waterline features, such as the school's prospectus, pupil behaviour, classroom layout and departmental structures may not be an accurate reflection of the school's underlying culture (Prosser, 1999). Sometimes it is the invisible elements of the cultural iceberg – beliefs, assumptions, attitudes, feelings, values – that wreck efforts to change and improve a school.

Culture has also been compared to an onion (Hofstede, 2020), with layers of visibility that gradually diminish, starting with symbols (such as school logos and uniforms) as the outer layer, followed by heroes (those who influence others, including staff and students), meetings and celebrations (such as school assemblies). The innermost, hidden layer is where shared values are found.

While helpful in making sense of culture's complexity, one problem with the metaphors of icebergs and onions is the portrayal of it as essentially static. The same is true for the suggestion that culture is a form of 'social glue' (Brighouse and Woods, 2013) which holds together staff communities. Research evidence indicates that, on the contrary, culture is changeable (Hollingworth et al., 2018) – this is a source of hope for leaders who want to make improvements to their school.

Although what you see in a school may not reflect all the invisible aspects of culture, it offers an impression through 'enactments' (Morris et al., 2020). These may include the school vision statement; assessment strategies; what staff wear; how teachers speak to students; what appears (or does not appear) on the school noticeboard; the decor and even display cabinets in the school reception area.

50 School culture and improvement

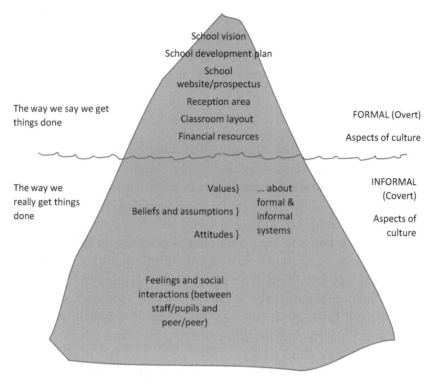

Figure 3.1 The cultural iceberg
(Based on Herman, 1971)

Culture is evident in professional relationships, organisational structures and learning opportunities (MacGilchrist et al., 1995).

Symbols are an important aspect of culture, they are 'rich in meaning' and consolidate shared understandings (Alvesson, 2013, p. 5). Perhaps it is no coincidence that newly formed academies have often changed the uniform of the previous school (Davies, 2015), providing a visible signal indicating a shift in culture.

History plays a part in culture

Cultures are historically imbued (Dimmock and Walker, 2005). They are shaped by the past experiences of current staff and students and even storied narratives of past events. Traditions and rituals are part of the culture (Sailes, 2008), which may explain why some school cultures can be resistant to imposed change. Much of the research on school communities has been 'snapshot,' describing a particular time, rather than longitudinal studies which investigate cultural changes over a period. The historical development of school cultures is under-researched. Historical aspects of culture can come to the fore unexpectedly when changes are made, however, as in the example in Box 3.2.

BOX 3.2 EXAMPLE OF A SCHOOL'S PAST HISTORY INFLUENCING THE PRESENT CULTURE

A new primary school headteacher arranged for the names of past prefects and head girls and boys to be sanded off a wooden pillar in the assembly hall over the summer holidays. The names dated from many years previously when the school had been a secondary modern, so this action seemed perfectly reasonable in asserting the culture of the primary school. However, some of the primary school's teaching assistants were shocked when they saw what had happened. In some cases their own or their siblings' names had been on the list, or they knew other people whose names were there. Memories of the previous school formed part of their identity and connection with the primary school. For them, it was an element of the school's cultural history. The headteacher's action was interpreted by these staff as high-handed and insensitive. It set up conflictual relationships between the headteacher and staff from the outset.

How to clarify cultural characteristics?

Cultures have been described as 'fuzzy' (Dimmock and Walker, 2005, p. 53) and 'ambiguous' (Alvesson, 2013, p. 204), partly because of the multiple interpretations within different staff groups, as in the case of the erased names. Culture tends to be naturally dynamic (Hollingworth et al., 2018), constructed by a school's stakeholders and the communities it serves (Nahbani et al., 2012), with changes occurring as shared meanings develop. Thus, school cultures can be seen as 'living systems' (Giles and Bills, 2017, p. 123).

In order to clarify the nature of organisational cultures, Deal and Kennedy (1982) identified the following elements:

- shared values and beliefs: what people believe is important and the values of the organisation
- heroes and heroines: role models and mentors
- rituals and ceremonies: common practices, celebrations, rites of passage
- stories: shared anecdotes and humour, myths and history
- informal network of cultural players: including storytellers, gossips, spies, the guardians of cultural values.

These different characteristics have been used as the basis for a series of questions which might help a headteacher and staff to identify their school culture (see Appendix 3.1). These cultural elements are also illustrated in Box 3.3, Teachers talking about their school's culture.

> **BOX 3.3 TEACHERS TALKING ABOUT THEIR SCHOOL'S CULTURE**
>
> I think there's just a real sense of "we're all in it together". (Teacher, inner-city primary school)
>
> I think we create a feeling of family. ... Every time there's a new member of staff it feels like our family's getting bigger. (Teacher, inner-city primary school)
>
> There's a real culture in this school, people making the effort to say thank you to you and to make you feel valued and appreciated, and it seems like such a small thing when you say it, but actually it's huge; it really is huge, because it's such a tough job, and to do it with no thanks is hard work!. (Teacher, inner-city secondary school)
>
> (Teacher Retention Research Project)

Johnson et al. (2012) built on Deal and Kennedy's (1982) elements to develop a 'cultural web' which includes additional aspects of an organisation, such as power structures, control systems and organisational structures. The cultural web is often displayed as interconnecting circles, at the centre of which is the 'paradigm' of the taken-for-granted assumptions shared by members of an organisation (see Figure 3.2).

The different elements of the cultural web (Johnson et al., 2012) are as follows:

- stories: shared by members to illustrate important events and characters in the organisation's history, exemplifying what is important in the present

Figure 3.2 The Cultural Web
(Johnson et al., 2012)

- symbols: objects, events or acts that create meaning, such as what appears in a school's display cabinet, or even whether a school has a display cabinet
- power structures: the way in which power is distributed to individuals to enable them to persuade or coerce others to undertake certain actions
- organisational structures: the roles, responsibilities and reporting relationships, often presented in the form of an 'organogram' showing line management responsibilities in a school
- control systems: the ways in which people are monitored and supported, including measurements and rewards
- rituals and routines: rituals are special events that highlight what is important, such as prize-giving days, while routines are the [daily] way people behave
- the [cultural] paradigm: comprises the overall norms, values and assumptions of the organization.

Box 3.4 provides a case study of an academy where the culture was analysed in relation to Johnson et al.'s (2012) cultural web.

BOX 3.4 CULTURAL WEB OF AN ACADEMY

This case study focused on an academy with 1200 pupils aged 11 to 18. About two-fifths of the students were eligible for the pupil premium (an indicator of poverty). The research methods included questionnaires (to 73 staff with no responsibility), focus groups (for 31 staff with management responsibility) and interviews (with 14 members of the senior leadership team). The findings were summarised in relation to each element of the cultural web:

Stories: these focused on major changes that had occurred, including the change to an academy, new headteacher and deputies, changes in staffing and a deterioration in staff morale

Symbols: these included parking, the front offices, staff titles, new branding for the academy and a more corporate environment

Power structures: these incorporated a large senior leadership team and a sense of more autocratic leadership

Organisational structures: these were regarded as hierarchical and top heavy with a prohibition on informal work (such as additional channels of communication)

Control systems: these comprised the performance management system and methods of staff assessment, and the rewards offered to students and staff (financial)

> *Rituals and routines:* these comprised staff promotions, socialisation and training
>
> *Central paradigm:* this was student-centric with a strong focus on student progress and student rewards, an emphasis on staff conformity and top-down leadership.
>
> The researcher identified a number of ways to address problems that he had identified in the Academy's culture, for example, encouraging alternative staff views (to reduce the pressure to conform), praising staff (to improve morale), introducing team-building activities (to encourage staff socialisation), distributing leadership (to shift from a top-down culture) and appointing two vice principals (to move away from the totalitarian control of the only vice-principal).
>
> (Morris, 2020)

One criticism of both Johnson and Scholes' (2012) and Deal and Kennedy's (1982) cultural characteristics is that they seem to be based on an assumption that culture is mainly created internally. But the external forces of national cultures and government policies (including accountability measures) affect school cultures. A research study comparing schools in Belgium and China found, perhaps not surprisingly, that the cultural differences between Chinese schools and Flemish schools were greater than 'within-culture' differences between schools in the same country (Zhu et al., 2014). This reflected how national culture influences school cultures. A more detailed review of the impact of national cultures is provided in the next section.

How do national cultures impact on schools?

Understanding the impact on school communities of broader, local and national cultural dimensions is important, particularly when engaging with parents who experienced school in a different country. Their expectations of 'the way we do things around here' may be at variance with the school culture. The same is true for leaders of intercultural teams, who may find that staff have different expectations about the design of classrooms, student behaviour, how teachers teach, relationships with managers and different levels of openness, particularly in relation to self-disclosure and privacy (Walker and Riordan, 2010).

A key contributor to current theories about national cultures is a Dutch researcher, Geert Hofstede, who identified a number of characteristics or 'dimensions' of national cultures. His original study was undertaken when he was working in personnel research at IBM. He conducted an employee opinion survey in 40 countries, with more than 100,000 responses. The survey focused on values and included questions about what staff valued in a manager, what caused them to feel stress, and the importance to them of other people, salary and prestige. From this and other data, Hofstede (1980) identified four cultural dimensions where staff from the same country appeared to share similar values:

1. Power distance: the preference for hierarchical (high power distance) or more egalitarian (low power distance) relations between manager and staff – this cultural dimension could apply to relations between school leaders and staff or between parents and teachers.

2. Uncertainty avoidance: whether ambiguity is embraced or seen as stressful (which can mean an abundance of rules in order to avoid uncertainty) – this cultural dimension could apply to parental concerns about school rules.

3. Individualism-collectivism: the extent to which people want to fulfil their own ambitions or to support their family or community – this cultural dimension could apply to teachers' attitudes towards promotion.

4. Masculinity-femininity: how far trust and interpersonal relationships are valued compared to salary and prestige. There were no questions about gender roles in the survey, but men consistently scored higher in relation to salary and prestige than women. This cultural dimension could apply to staff perceptions of school leadership.

Two further dimensions were later added to the original four, the first in collaboration with Michael Harris Bond, and the second in collaboration with Michael Minkov (see Hofstede et al., 2010):

5. Long-term–short-term orientation: clinging to tradition (short-term) or being willing to accommodate change (long-term). This dimension applies to staff attitudes to change.

6. Indulgence–restraint: the extent to which people are encouraged to express their feelings and desires (indulgence) or to restrain that expression (restraint). This dimension applies to understandings of professionalism in schools.

In relation to Hofstede's (2010) six dimensions, the UK scores relatively low for power distance (preferring egalitarian relationships between leaders and staff); relatively high for individualism (people put their own needs above those of their community); is fairly 'masculine' (valuing competition, achievement and success), low in uncertainty avoidance (able to tolerate ambiguity and an unknown future); is neutral in relation to time orientation, because both tradition and short-term rewards are valued; and is relatively indulgent in expressing feelings (despite the idea of the 'stiff upper lip') (Hofstede, 2010).

There is a danger, however, in attributing national or regional cultural characteristics to a particular person. Cultural stereotypes do not take into account the many variations and subcultures within one nation. In the UK, for example, Scotland, Wales and Northern Ireland have distinctive cultures, as do individual cities. Cultures differ in the north and south of the country, in the countryside or by the coast compared to cities and in relation to working, middle- and upper-class norms. Culture may also differ depending on religious beliefs and ethnicity.

Hofstede et al. (2010) were aware that the original questionnaire was designed by 'westerners' and did not include a full range of cultural dimensions – hence the addition of the long-term–short-term orientation to take into account the fast-growing economies of the east. But the term 'Western culture' is also problematic, implying that diverse countries such as the Netherlands, the USA or UK have the same culture, when in fact they are very different (Cheng Yin Cheong, 2000).

Other criticisms of Hofstede's (1980, 2010) research are:

- the original research is dated – the surveys took place in 1968 and 1972, long before the Berlin wall came down; national cultures have changed since then

- it was based on standardised questionnaires, which do not take contextual complexity into account; in addition, people from the same country did not necessarily all agree in Hofstede's original surveys (Jepson, 2009)

- IBM had its own corporate identity and within IBM, only marketing plus service personnel were present in all the 40 countries, so the comparisons between countries were based on data from this limited selection of employees, which could have influenced the results

- there is a danger of losing a wider perspective when 'putting culture into neat, sometimes unconnected, little boxes' (Tayeb, 2001, p. 93)

Nevertheless, Hofstede's (1980, 2010) theorisation may help to create a better understanding of the values and expectations of people from different cultures, whether teachers, students or parents, and this is important in a multicultural society. It should not, however, be used as the basis for stereotyping national characteristics; as Cheng Yin Cheong (2000, p. 215) notes: 'Even within one society, cultural profiles may vary across the classroom, school, community and society levels, depending on complex human, historical and contingent conditions.' Cheng Yin Cheong (2000) argues that, for this reason, educational achievement should not be attributed to cultural differences: societal cultures are too diverse, with a wide spectrum of subcultures, to be able to generalise about links between home culture and educational outcomes.

How to surface cultural assumptions?

It is important for headteachers working with culturally diverse staff to be aware of their own cultural assumptions. Walker and Riordan (2010, p. 54) call this 'cultural positioning'. They suggest leaders reflect on their expectations of teachers and the extent to which these are culturally determined. They offer the questions in Box 3.5 as a means of developing an understanding of the cultural assumptions of staff.

> **BOX 3.5 UNDERSTANDING CULTURAL EXPECTATIONS**
>
> Possible questions to discuss with staff:
>
> - Who speaks for the school?
> - Who makes the decisions in the school? (And who should make the decisions?)
> - What motivates teachers to work and to collaborate with each other?
> - What forms the basis for relationships?
> - How are students best disciplined?
> - What is the meaning of responsibility?
> - Are performance management systems applied uniformly to all staff or adapted to individual circumstances?
> - How are people judged?
> - Are directives from the principal followed or circumvented?
> - What gets noticed in the school?
> - Are individual teachers or groups named and recognised in the school?
>   (Walker and Riordan, 2010, pp. 57–8, based on Lustig and Koester, 2006)

A greater knowledge of national cultures can foster improved relationships between staff, parents and students, but care is required to avoid oversimplified stereotypes. Understanding of, and empathy for, other cultures are needed rather than judgement and negativity.

What is the difference between culture and subculture?

It is rare for any complex organisation, such as a school, to have a single culture. There are more often multiple subcultures which contribute to or resist the overarching organisational culture (Stoll, 1999). For example, the cultures of teachers, leaders, departments, support staff, year groups and parents can all be elements of the overarching school culture (Stoll, 1999). In secondary schools, 'balkanisation' can occur when subject departments build up strong subcultures which cut them off from the rest of the school (Hargreaves, 1994). There may also be countercultures among disenchanted staff and pupils.

One difference between the overall culture of a school and its various subcultures is that the former tends to develop from consensus and shared values, while subcultures represent diversity and, potentially, conflict. Dimmock and Walker (2005) suggest that schools could be placed on a culture continuum with homogeneous (shared, all-encompassing) at one end and heterogeneous (diverse, fragmented) at the other. Homogeneous cultures may be reflected in classrooms, representing 'a strong sharing of norms and values between students and teachers' (Cheng Yin Cheong, 2000, p. 212). Heterogeneous cultures, with multiple subcultures, may result in confusion and contradiction (Wallace et al., 2011), although there can also be a strength in cultural diversity. Ideally the culture of a school system should be 'more than the sum of its parts' (Giles and Bills, 2017, p. 123).

Although there has been more research on staff compared to pupils, the student culture makes an important contribution to the nature of a school (Stoll, 1999) and represents one of its subcultures. In secondary schools particularly, where students' adolescent identities shift and mature, there is the potential for clashes between staff and pupils' values (Stoll, 1999). Typical examples of this collision of cultures are arguments about school uniform, attendance and behaviour. In MacBeath's (2008, p. 140) research interviews with 12 headteachers, two described an 'anti-achievement' student culture in which students 'are quite interested but they mustn't show it.' The headteachers' response was to create an atmosphere where pupils felt safe and supported, to involve students actively in improving the school's learning environment and to reach out to the parent community. Box 3.6 summarises a research study on students' views of their school's culture.

BOX 3.6 STUDENT VIEWS OF SCHOOL CULTURE

Bell and Kent's (2010) case study research took an unusual approach in asking sixth formers about their views of the school culture. The research comprised four elements: semi-structured interviews with a sample of sixth formers (four from year 12 and four from year 13); a questionnaire completed by 240 students, half from each year group; an observation of informal student behaviour during a lunch hour; and interviews with the current headteacher and his predecessor. The researchers found, in their case study grammar school, that academic values were strong, together with a positive attitude to work. There was social pressure to conform to these values. The heroes tended to be students who succeeded academically or in sport. The head of sixth form and heads of department influenced the student culture. Subcultures appeared to form around expressions of social identity, rather than as a resistance to the mainstream. Changes in society had influenced attitudes to homosexuality and gender in the school culture, while working in part-time jobs provided an alternative culture for some sixth formers. Students questioned whether any one person had a dominant influence on culture: 'Interview responses suggest that while students do not discount the role of the headteacher, they perceive a richer and more complex collaboration of "different people and voices", who influence the culture of a school'.

(Bell and Kent, 2010, p. 25)

Bell and Kent's (2010) study has a number of limitations: it focuses on a particular type of school (a grammar) and data from only two year groups within the school (years 12 and 13). Their findings demonstrate, however, the multiple influences on school culture: headteacher, head of year, departmental heads, teachers, students and from outside the school, including students' workplaces and society more generally.

Is there a link between school culture and school improvement?

Culture is such an important, prevailing aspect of any school that, unsurprisingly, there have been attempts to identify what kind might lead to school effectiveness and improvement. Stoll and Fink (1996) developed a typology of school cultures, based on whether a school was effective (defined as one in which pupils make more progress than expected) or ineffective, and whether it was improving (defined as undertaking concurrent strategies to enhance pupil outcomes) or declining. This has the benefit of suggesting how a school's performance is considered over a period of years, rather than a 'snapshot' which might not be representative. Figure 3.3 summarises the typology.

Stoll and Fink (1996) identified five types of school cultures. 'Moving' schools are effective and improving, focused on clear goals and with the skills to get there. 'Cruising' schools are effective but declining, with reasonable pupil progress due to parental support. Those schools are marking time rather than preparing their pupils for a changing world. 'Struggling' schools are ineffective but improving, in that their current levels of achievement are too low but are on an upward trajectory. They are willing to try anything that will make a difference and recognise that change is necessary. 'Sinking' schools are ineffective and declining, with a culture of isolation, blame and loss of faith, often in areas with high social and economic needs. In the middle are 'strolling' schools which are neither effective nor ineffective and improving too slowly to keep pace with change, sometimes with ill-defined and

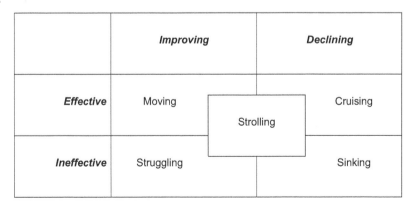

Figure 3.3 School culture, effectiveness and improvement
(Stoll and Fink, 1996, p. 85)

conflicting aims. Stoll and Fink (1996) suggest that 'cruising' schools tend to be in areas of high socioeconomic status where pupils do well with little support from the school. Conversely, 'sinking' schools are usually in areas of poverty where teachers' expectations may be low, pupils challenging and parents difficult but undemanding.

Identifying where a school fits in this typology could be useful for choosing priorities when initiating change. However, adopting appropriate measures of effectiveness and improvement is problematic. Increasingly, a school's effectiveness is quantified by pupils' performance in external assessments. This is evident from Ofsted reports which judge a school to be good in every category except 'Outcomes for pupils', but deems it 'Requires Improvement'. Even if external assessments are contextualised in order not to disadvantage schools whose pupils arrive with low levels of attainment, they remain a blunt instrument in relation to school culture. For example, there might be a dip in a school's results one year, moving the school from effective to ineffective and from improving to declining, but the culture may not have changed significantly during that period.

Perhaps more helpful are Stoll and Fink's (1996) 'norms' in the cultures of improving schools, based on their own research and their understanding of the literature. These norms represent underlying values and shared assumptions, focusing on 'fundamental issues of how people relate to and value each other' (Stoll and Fink, 1996, p. 92) and are summarised as follows:

1. Shared goals: 'we know where we're going'
2. Responsibility for success: 'we cannot fail'
3. Collegiality: 'we're in this together'
4. Continuous improvement 'we can get better'
5. Lifelong learning: 'learning is for everyone'
6. Risk taking: 'we learn by trying something new'
7. Support: 'there's always someone there to help'
8. Mutual respect: 'everyone has something to offer'
9. Openness: 'we can discuss our differences'
10. Celebration and humour: 'we can feel good about ourselves'

While Stoll and Fink's (1996) typology and norms could help schools to identify their own culture, they were not based on research which focused specifically on school culture. A more unusual but systematic study (Hobby, 2004), carried out by the Hay Group, set out to analyse the cultures that were typical in effective and ineffective schools. First, the research team generated (from existing research) 30 statements that were designed to capture characteristic values and beliefs in schools. See Box 3.7 for some examples of the statements, and Appendix 3.2 for the full list.

BOX 3.7 EDUCATIONAL CULTURE STATEMENTS: WHAT IS CHARACTERISTIC OF THE SCHOOL

The following are some examples of the statements about educational culture which formed the basis of Hobby's (2004) research.

1. Measuring and monitoring targets
2. Raising capability – helping people learn – laying foundations for later success
3. Respecting authority – providing direction
4. Taking initiative and responsibility – participation at every level – healthy dissent
5. The school comes first – no one is bigger than the school – doing what is expected of you
6. People come first – everyone can make a contribution and deserves control over their own destiny

In Hobby's (2004) study, 134 schools undertook a 'card sort' exercise in which groups of staff from the same school worked together to organise the 30 statements (each one written on a separate card) into a diamond pattern. The cards most characteristic of their school were placed at the top and those least representative at the bottom. The senior leaders group worked together so that they could not influence the views of the rest of the staff. The groups noted the number and position of each card in the diamond and the results were sent to the Hay Group. The activity was then run a second time to find out staff views about the characteristics of an ideal school. These results were also recorded and sent to the Hay Group. In all, over 4000 school staff participated in the research. Most of the schools were secondary (62%) and located in urban areas (49%).

Across all the schools, the most common characteristics were:

- 'Measuring and monitoring targets and test results'
- 'Raising capability – helping people learn – laying foundations for later success'
- 'Focusing on the value added – holding hope for every student - every gain a victory'.

The least relevant characteristics were:

- 'Investing time with those who can achieve the most'
- 'Preventing mistakes – making sure nobody and nothing slips through – planning for all eventualities'.

In terms of an ideal school, staff valued most the collaborative and nurturing characteristics:

- 'Working together – learning from each other – sharing resources and ideas'
- 'Raising capability – helping people learn – laying foundations for later success'
- 'Creating a pleasant and collegial working environment'

The main purpose of the research was to identify whether there was a particular culture associated with successful schools. For this part of the research, only the secondary schools were included. In order to judge a school's performance, the researchers considered overall attainment (taking the percentage of free school meals into account), the rate of improvement in results over three years and the value added. One interesting finding was that 'Measuring and monitoring targets and test results' was the top characteristic of every school, irrespective of its status, perhaps indicating the extent that national policy impacts on all schools. In terms of statistical significance, the following were more characteristic of high value-added schools:

- High hopes and expectations
- Promoting excellence
- Respecting authority
- School comes first
- Single minded dedication.

The following were more characteristic of low value-added schools:

- Making allowances
- Respecting autonomy
- Warmth and humour
- Admitting mistakes
- People come first.

While offering an interesting contrast, a major problem with any conclusions that result from these findings is that the schools most likely to be in the 'low value-added' category are high-need schools in areas of socio-economic deprivation (van de Grift, 2009). A logical conclusion to Hobby's (2004) findings is that the cultures associated with the worst-performing schools should be abandoned in favour of those of the best-performers. There are, however, some characteristics which may be essential to the needs of staff working at challenging schools, including warmth and humour, being able to admit mistakes and share how they feel. Recognising the importance of individual staff and their contribution may also be vital to retain teachers in such schools. So it may not be appropriate for the leaders of high-need schools to aim to cultivate the same cultural characteristics as schools in less challenging circumstances.

Hobby (2004) acknowledged some further potential flaws in this research study. The diamond exercise was self-administered by the schools so may not have been carried out as the research team intended. The statements may have missed out some key values. The participants were self-selecting so there may have been a bias towards more confident staff/schools. Each of the card statements contained clusters of characteristics, which may have made it difficult for staff to choose a card on which one or two elements might have been characteristic but not the others. Another criticism of Hobby's (2004) findings is that the measurements used to judge whether a school was successful are questionable. Some value-added measures used at the time reflected raw results (Timmermans et al., 2011), thus undermining this as a means of taking into account the factors that may depress results in schools in more challenging areas (such as low attainment on entry).

Despite these criticisms, Hobby's (2004) study remains one of the few that explores school culture in this depth in England. The tools they developed for the research are useful resources for school leaders who wish to analyse their culture with their staff and, potentially, change it (see appendix 3.2). Hobby's (2004) research is, however, rather dated. Box 3.8 gives an example of more recent research into the links between school culture and improvement.

BOX 3.8 LINKS BETWEEN SCHOOL CULTURE AND IMPROVEMENT

Evidence-informed practice is fundamental to school improvement. This was recently investigated (Ion and López Sirvent, 2022) to determine which elements of school culture supported evidence-informed practice. A survey was sent to 462 teachers from 204 primary schools in two Spanish autonomous regions. The findings indicated that the schools with evidence-informed practice have a climate of trust, which encourages teachers to experiment with innovative practices, and to debate decisions and evidence. The school leaders welcomed discussion and reflection on practice as well as innovation and change. The authors conclude that 'schools perceived as open to the use of research evidence are characterized by a culture in which members feel involved and where scientific evidence is part of routine organizational practice'.

(Ion and López Sirvent, 2022, p. 624)

What are the differences between primary and secondary schools' culture?

There appear to be cultural differences between primary and secondary schools. Primary schools act as an extended family whereas secondary schools have a more academic focus linked to subject expertise (Stoll, 1999). Hobby's (2004) research found that the top cultural characteristic in secondary schools was 'Measuring and monitoring targets and test results' while 'Working together – learning from each other – sharing resources and ideas' was the most popular in primary schools. It appears that primary school cultures are more homely and collaborative, whereas secondary schools are more focused on attainment. It is perhaps unlikely that a secondary teacher would describe their school culture as a 'comfortable jumper'.

The age of the pupils may be partly responsible for these differences. Children at primary school do not have the same needs as secondary students and may benefit from a more sympathetic, family atmosphere. They may also be more open to cultural influences from the school. The changes of developing adulthood and puberty may make secondary students more challenging, while the need for them to pass external assessments inevitably affects the school's priorities. Secondary students may also be less willing to conform to the school's culture.

How can school leaders influence culture?

Developing a school's culture is a key task for headteachers because healthy cultures create school communities that make a difference to pupil outcomes (Giles and Bills, 2017). Yet if culture is, by its nature, developed and shared within a school community rather than dictated by a leader, what can one individual do to shape it? An example of the way in which leaders can encourage a pattern that has beneficial effects on learning at the school is described in Box 3.9.

BOX 3.9 REFLECTIONS ON A BENEFICIAL SCHOOL CULTURE

Jonathan Smith, reflecting on a lifetime of teaching, wrote the following:

> You work for a head and for the school if you feel that you, the head and the school are pulling in the same direction. It's a great feeling, a daily encouragement, and this direction does not have to be articulated into a vision statement (about which I'm sceptical) because it can be understood. If the head, the staff and the pupils all feel that they are, broadly speaking, in the same boat, you are in a happy school. As a teacher you feel you are setting the pace and yet, paradoxically, you are being led. In this collaborative atmosphere the creative energy flows and that energy is transferred to the pupils. Teachers then run the extra mile, teachers then

> live in goodwill, and this goodwill encourages individuality and risk-taking and – a sign of a healthy community – can handle dissenting voices.
>
> (Smith, 2001, pp. 208–209)

It is useful for school leaders to develop an awareness of their own cultural assumptions (Giles and Bills, 2017). In order to do this, according to Walker and Riordan (2010), they could consider formative influences on their own views of learning and how they see the position of the leader within the school's culture. They need to think about how they understand and support collective work. They could also review how their actions express their cultural understanding, including humour, metaphors, anecdotes and strategies (see Box 3.10).

In addition to understanding their own cultural background, headteachers need to know their school's culture. Hobby (2004) recommended that school leaders initiate joint exercises with the whole staff to:

1. Look clearly at the internal and external challenges faced by the school

2. Analyse the school's culture, for example, by doing the diamond sort exercise

3. Challenge their aspirations, by identifying the ideal culture staff and leaders would prefer

4. Create an action plan to achieve the ideal culture.

BOX 3.10 SYMBOLS OF CULTURAL LEADERSHIP

Two researchers in Finland (Lahtero and Mika Risku, 2012) set out to describe the leadership culture of a comprehensive school. Their research included interviews with the school leader and teachers, review of the leader's emails to the teachers and observations in the school. They identified four 'categories of symbols' that seemed to characterise the leadership culture: respect, communality, equality and humour. The examples they gave of these different aspects of the culture had been identified by the staff. *Respect* was demonstrated by the principal's promptness at meetings, which meant that staff did not have to wait. *Communality* was evident by noticing staff's 'special days' (such as birthdays). The way the principal dressed demonstrated *equality* because he did not dress more formally than the teachers. In relation to *humour*, the principal was noted for 'stirring up laughter' (Lahtero and Mika Risku, 2012, p. 529). These shared understandings create a 'network of meanings' through which staff interpret what has happened and which then guide their own actions.

One difficulty in changing cultures is that there is no blueprint (Walker and Riordan, 2010). Every school and individual leader is different. However, a research study investigating teacher leadership in Australia, Canada and Colombia (Pineda-Báez et al., 2020) found similar actions were identified across all three countries to change the school culture in order to ensure the success of teacher leadership. These included 'changing mindsets of staff in terms of what counts as quality teaching, changing work practices and relationships, and student engagement' (Pineda-Báez et al., 2020, p. 408).

Appendices 3.3 to 3.5 provide a number of questionnaires which school leaders can use to analyse their school culture. After assessing teacher and leader perspectives, it is important to identify ways in which the culture could be improved. A first step could be to integrate measures of cultural development into the school improvement plan, with a means of evaluating progress. Other actions could include changing visible symbols, such as decor and logos, to align with the school's values, reviewing appropriate rewards and sanctions, or revising organisational structures of the school. Box 3.11 summarises the actions agreed by one school after researching their culture.

BOX 3.11 ACTIONS ARISING FROM THE ASSESSMENT OF A SCHOOL'S CULTURE

This case study focused on a primary school in South Australia with over 300 pupils, serving a significantly disadvantaged community. The researchers were invited to investigate the organisational culture of the school and used 'appreciative enquiry', beginning with questions such as:

- Describe a time when you were most engaged, alive and energised in your work within the school
- What are some of the strengths of the relationships within the school?
- Can you describe a leadership initiative that appears to have strengthened individuals' practice?
- If you had three wishes to improve the health and vitality of the relationships within the school, what would they be?

(Morris et al., 2020, pp. 126–127)

After analysing the data and reporting on the key aspects of the school culture, the researchers identified actions that the school could take to enhance its culture, including

- model the well-being of teachers and students, for example, by using informal and appreciative occasions that recognise effort and achievement, and by allowing time in the busyness of teaching duties to debrief and reflect
- continue the focus of leadership on 'releasing others' strengths'

> - encourage staff to co-construct aspirational statements, for example, by evaluating practices and looking for different ways of engaging individuals
> - explore and articulate a school-wide conceptual framework for pedagogy and curriculum
> - review and enhance the goal of developing students as lifelong learners
> - broaden recognition of leadership roles.
>
> (Morris et al., 2020, pp. 132–135)
>
> These actions were presented to the teachers and leaders at the school and received a strongly positive response (Morris et al., 2020).

Conclusion

Culture is a difficult concept to describe yet it is an essential component of every school. The headteacher's awareness of their own cultural assumptions and the ways their actions may be interpreted by staff (and pupils) are important in ensuring that subliminal messages are in line with the leader's intentions. A number of different theories and models have been presented in this chapter, which alongside the appendices could help leaders to identify and understand key aspects of school culture. By engaging with staff to explore the ideal culture for the school, headteachers can initiate cultural change.

Earlier in the chapter, the metaphors of a cultural iceberg and onion were considered to be inadequate in representing the complexities of school cultures. A third metaphor for culture is a 'fertile garden for school improvement' (Stoll, 1999, p. 46). This recalls the earlier suggestion that 'good seeds grow in strong cultures' (Saphier and King, 1985, p. 67).

The metaphor of a garden (or ecological habitat such as a woodland or pond) encompasses better the different aspects of culture. Flowers, trees, bushes and produce suggest a varied range of visible elements of culture and could be seen as a vision of the future when seeds are planted. Below the surface are roots which help the plants to grow, just as positive values and attitudes support school improvement. The soil enables nurturing of the plants or the opposite, in the same way that relationships can help schools to develop or decline. There is the danger of slugs and insects, which may eat anything that is good, just as adverse influences may damage school cultures. Weeds grow whenever the gardener's eye is taken off the ball. The natural community of a garden, woodland or pond changes with the seasons too, influenced by external elements that a school leader cannot control. However, the school leader has an important role ensuring that culture is 'not simply something that grows weed-like but is created and nurtured' (MacBeath, 2008, p. 141). Stoll (1999) suggests school leaders may need to 'reculture' their garden to improve the school, enabling new ideas to bloom (Box 3.12).

BOX 3.12 QUESTIONS FOR REFLECTION AND ACTION

- How would you and your staff describe the culture of your school?
- What are the key shared values at your school?
- What are your own cultural expectations and those of your staff?
- Where does your school fit in relation to the cultures of improving schools?
- What actions could you take to improve the culture at your school?

Appendix 3.1: Questions to help identify a school culture (Hobby, 2004, p. 10)

These questions could be used in a school to gain an understanding of its culture. The responses could contribute to a staff discussion about culture and how to improve it.

- Your biggest celebration this year – what did you celebrate [and how]?
- The most respected person in the school – what are they respected for [why]?
- Please name:
  - the first thing you notice in the school reception area
  - something that commonly happens in other schools that could never happen in your school
  - the behaviour, in an adult, that is most frowned upon
  - something that people regularly 'get away with' (things you know are wrong but still do – e.g., be late for meetings)
  - something that people worry about a great deal
- Complete the following sentence: 'We will raise standards of achievement most effectively if we focus on …'.

Appendix 3.2: Educational culture statements: what is characteristic of the school? (Hobby, 2004, p. 21)

The following statements could be transferred to individual cards to enable staff members to create a diamond shape, with the statements that are most characteristic of the school at the top and the statements that are most different at the bottom. The diamond starts with one card at the top, then in subsequent rows, two, three, four cards; then two rows of five, then four, three, two, one. This activity can be undertaken individually, in small groups or across the entire staff.

1. Measuring and monitoring targets
2. Raising capability – helping people learn – laying foundations for later success
3. Respecting authority – providing direction
4. Taking initiative and responsibility – participation at every level – healthy dissent
5. The school comes first – no one is bigger than the school – doing what is expected of you
6. People come first – everyone can make a contribution and deserves control over their own destiny
7. Respecting professional autonomy – creating a space to call your own – perfecting your patch
8. Working together – learning from each other – sharing resources and ideas – investing in others
9. Recognising personal circumstances – making allowances – toleration – it's the effort that counts
10. Keeping promises – confronting poor performance – taking ownership
11. Embedding – evaluating – measuring changes and taking stock
12. Experimenting – trying new things – looking to the next big idea
13. Preventing mistakes – making sure nobody and nothing slips through – planning for all eventualities
14. Taking calculated risks for worthwhile goals – try it and see
15. Single-minded dedication – relentless pace
16. Warmth – humour – repartee – feet on the ground
17. Setting achievable goals and realistic expectations – incremental improvements
18. A hunger for improvement – high hopes and expectations
19. Investing time with those who can achieve the most
20. Focusing on the value added – holding hope for every student – every gain a victory
21. Dignity – reserve – respecting privacy – keeping a lid on it – self-control

22. Admitting mistakes – providing challenging feedback – letting people know how you feel
23. Promoting excellence – pushing the boundaries of achievement – world-class
24. Creating opportunities for everyone – widening horizons – fighting injustice
25. Creating a pleasant and collegial working environment
26. Making sacrifices to put students first
27. Mastering your subject – gaining expertise – sharing knowledge
28. Admitting you don't know – listening to dissent – curiosity and humility
29. Keeping up with initiatives – doing what's required – following policy
30. Anticipating initiatives – making them work for us – picking and choosing

Appendix 3.3: Questionnaire to assess the school's culture (based on Hargreaves, 1999 and Cheng Yin Cheong, 2000)

Invite staff to indicate, by circling a number from 1 to 6, where they feel the school is positioned in relation to each of the different cultural aspects.

Warm and friendly	1	2	3	4	5	6	Cool and hostile
High expectations	1	2	3	4	5	6	Low expectations
Professionally rewarding	1	2	3	4	5	6	Professionally unrewarding
Highly achievement-focused	1	2	3	4	5	6	Insufficiently achievement-focused
Strongly led by the SLT	1	2	3	4	5	6	Weakly led by the SLT
Collaborative	1	2	3	4	5	6	Individualistic
Pupil-centred	1	2	3	4	5	6	Teacher-centred
Participative	1	2	3	4	5	6	Centralised
Innovative	1	2	3	4	5	6	Traditional
Flexible	1	2	3	4	5	6	Rule-oriented
Engaged with the community	1	2	3	4	5	6	Isolated from the community
High level of trust							Distrust and suspicion

Appendix 3.4: Questionnaire to assess the school's culture (based on MacBeath, 1998)

Add relevant statements for your own school and invite the staff to indicate how far each cultural 'norm' is present in the school (on the left side), and how important it is for school effectiveness (on the right side).

The school now 1 = strongly agree 2 = agree 3 = uncertain 4 = disagree 5 = strongly disagree						The effective school 1 = crucial 2 = very important 3 = quite important 4 = not very important 5 = not at all important				
1	2	3	4	5	Pupils respect teachers in the school	1	2	3	4	5
1	2	3	4	5	Teachers believe that all children in the school can be successful	1	2	3	4	5
1	2	3	4	5	Teachers regularly discuss ways of improving pupils' learning	1	2	3	4	5
1	2	3	4	5	Teachers regularly observe each other in the classroom and give feedback	1	2	3	4	5
1	2	3	4	5	Standards set for pupils are consistently upheld across the school	1	2	3	4	5
1	2	3	4	5	Teachers share similar beliefs and attitudes about effective learning and teaching	1	2	3	4	5

Appendix 3.5: Questionnaire to assess the school's culture (based on Zhu et al.'s (2014, p. 571) school culture scales)

School culture scales	Extent to which this is evident at this school			
	Not at all	To a limited extent	Fairly widespread	School-wide
Goal orientation				
All teachers work together to accomplish our school goals.				
Our school team is enthusiastic.				
Everybody here walks the same line.				
Teachers support our school goals.				
Not all teachers have the same opinion of what is important for our school.				
Supportive leadership				
The headteacher goes out of his/her way to help teachers.				
The headteacher praises teachers.				
The headteacher explains his/her reason for criticism to teachers.				
The headteacher is available after school to help teachers when assistance is needed.				
The headteacher uses constructive criticism.				
Participative decision-making				
In our school, the headteacher discusses important decisions with the staff members before they are made.				

(Continued)

School culture scales	Extent to which this is evident at this school			
	Not at all	To a limited extent	Fairly widespread	School-wide
In our school, the staff members are involved in the decision-making process, such as giving suggestions for policy proposals.				
In our school, the headteacher stimulates staff members to take the initiative.				
Innovation orientation				
At our school, teachers have a positive attitude towards change.				
At our school, teachers are expected to have an innovative attitude.				
Teachers at our school are expected to try something new in teaching and learning activities.				
At our school, we expect all staff to have a flexible attitude towards change and innovation.				
Formal relationships				
Among colleagues, we work together to find new and different methods for teaching and learning.				
Consulting with colleagues provides a great support for me.				
I work together with colleagues a lot, in order to improve my work.				
My colleagues regularly ask me what I'm currently working on in my class.				

References

Alvesson, M. (2013). *Understanding Organizational Culture*. London: Sage.

Anthony, P. (1994). *Managing Culture*. Buckingham: Open University Press.

Bell, L. and Kent, P. (2010). The cultural jigsaw. A case study exploring the ways in which sixth-form students perceive school culture. *Educational Management Administration and Leadership*, vol. 38, no. 1, pp. 8–32.

Brighouse, T. and Woods, D. (2013). *The A–Z of School Improvement: Principles and Practice*. London: Bloomsbury.

Bourdieu, P. and Wacquant, L. (1992). *An Invitation to Reflexive Sociology*. Chicago: University of Chicago Press.

Cheong, C.Y. (2000). Cultural factors in educational effectiveness: A framework for comparative research. *School Leadership & Management*, vol. 20, no. 2, pp. 207–225.

Davies, E. (2015). Cost of school uniform 2015: Department for Education Research. Report. https://assets.publishing.service.gov.uk/government/uploads/system/uploads/attachment_data/file/436576/RR474_Cost_of_school_uniform.pdf. Accessed 12 January 21.

Deal, D. and Peterson, K. (2016). *Shaping School Culture*, 3rd edition. San Francisco, CA: Jossey-Bass.

Deal, T. and Kennedy, A. (1982). *Corporate Cultures: The Rites and Rituals of Life*. Reading, Mass: AddisonWesley Publishing Company.

Dimmock, C. and Walker, D. (2005). *Educational Leadership: Diversity and Culture*. London: Sage.

Garratt, B. (1991). The cultural contexts. In A. Mumford (ed). *Handbook of Management Development*. Aldershot: Gower.

Giles, D. and Bills, A. (2017). Designing and using an organisational culture inquiry tool to glimpse the relational nature of leadership and organisational culture within a South Australian primary school. *School Leadership & Management*, vol. 37, nos 1–2, pp. 120–140.

Hall, E.T. (1981). *Beyond Culture*. Garden City: Anchor Books.

Hallinger, P. and Heck, R. (2003). Understanding the contribution of leadership to school improvement. In M. Wallace and L. Poulson (eds). *Learning to Read Critically in Educational Leadership and Management*. London: Sage, pp. 215–235.

Hargreaves, A. (1994). *Changing Teachers, Changing Times: Teachers' Work and Culture in the Postmodern Age*. New York: Teachers College Press.

Hargreaves, D. (1999). Helping practitioners explore their school's culture. In J. Prosser (ed). *School Culture*. London: Sage, pp. 48–65.

Herman, S. (1971). What is this thing called organization development? *Personnel Journal*, vol. 50, no. 8, pp. 595–603.

Hobby, R. (2004). *A Culture for Learning*. London: The Hay Group.

Hofstede, G. (1980). *Culture's Consequences*. London: Sage.

Hofstede, G. (2010). *Cultures and Organizations: Software of the Mind: Intercultural Cooperation and its Importance for Survival*. New York: McGrawHill.

Hofstede, G.H., Hofstede, G.J. and Minkov, M. (2010). *Cultures and Organizations: Software of the Mind: International Cooperation and Its Importance for Survival*, Rev. and expanded 3rd edition. New York, NY: McGraw-Hill.

Hofstede, G. (2020). What do we mean by 'culture'? https://news.hofstede-insights.com/news/what-do-we-mean-by-culture. Accessed 19 February 2021.

Hollingworth, L., Olsen, D., Asikin-Garmager, A. and Winn, K. (2018). Initiating conversations and opening doors: How principals establish a positive building culture to sustain school improvement efforts. *Educational Management Administration and Leadership*, vol. 46, no. 6, pp. 1014–1034.

Ion, G. and López Sirvent, E. (2022). Teachers' perception of the characteristics of an evidence-informed school: Initiative, supportive culture, and shared reflection. *School Effectiveness and School Improvement*, vol. 33, no. 4, pp. 610–628. DOI: 10.1080/09243453.2022.2093921.

Ishimaru, A. and Galloway, M. (2014). Beyond individual effectiveness: Conceptualizing organizational leadership for equity. *Leadership and Policy in Schools*, vol. 13, no. 1, pp. 93–146.

Jepson, D. (2009). Studying leadership at cross-country level: A critical analysis. *Leadership*, vol. 5, no. 1, pp. 61–80.

Johnson, G., Whittington, R., Scholes, K., Angwin, D. and Regner, P. (2012). *Fundamentals of Strategy*, 4th edition. Harlow: Pearson Education Ltd.

Lahtero, T.J. and Mika Risku, M. (2012). Symbolic leadership and leadership culture in one unified comprehensive school in Finland. *School Leadership and Management*, vol. 32, no. 5, pp. 523–535.

Leithwood, K., Harris, A. and Hopkins, D. (2020). Seven strong claims about successful school leadership revisited. *School Leadership & Management*, vol. 40, no. 1, pp. 5–22.

Lustig, M. and Koester, J. (2006). *Inter-Cultural Competence: Interpersonal Communication Across Cultures*. Boston: Pearson Education.

MacBeath, J. (1998). The coming of age of school effectiveness. Keynote address, international congress of school effectiveness and improvement, Manchester. In Hargreaves, D. (1999) *Helping practitioners explore their school's culture*. In Prosser, J. (ed) (1999). School culture. London: Sage, pp. 48–65.

MacBeath, J. (2008). Stories of compliance and subversion in a prescriptive policy environment. *Educational Management Administration and Leadership*, vol. 36, no. 1, pp. 123–148.

MacGilchrist, B., Mortimore, P., Savage, J. and Beresford, C. (1995). *Planning Matter: The Impact of Development Planning in Primary Schools*. London: Paul Chapman.

Morgan, G. (1997). *Images of Organization*. Thousand Oaks: Sage.

Morris, J., Lummis, G., Lock, G., Ferguson, C., Hill, S. and Nykiel, A. (2020). The role of leadership in establishing a positive staff culture in secondary school. *Educational Management Administration and Leadership*, vol. 48, no. 5, pp. 802–820.

Morris, J. (2020). Is this the culture of academies? Utilising the cultural web to investigate the organisational culture of an academy case study. *Educational Management Administration and Leadership*, vol. 48, no. 1, pp. 164–185.

Nahbani, M., Busher, H. and Bahous, R. (2012). Cultures of engagement in challenging circumstances: Four Lebanese primary schools in urban Beirut. *School Leadership and Management*, vol. 32, no. 1, pp. 37–55.

Pineda-Báez, C., Bauman, C. and Andrews, D. (2020). Empowering teacher leadership: A cross-country study. *International Journal of Leadership in Education*, vol. 23, no. 4, pp. 388–414. DOI: 10.1080/13603124.2018.1543804.

Prosser, J. (ed) (1999). *School Culture* London: Sage.

Sailes, J. (2008). School culture audits: Making a difference in school improvement plans. *Improving Schools*, vol. 11, no. 1, pp. 74–82.

Saphier, J. and King, M. (1985). Good seeds grow in strong cultures. *Educational Leadership*, vol. 42, no. 6, pp. 67–74.

Schein, E. (1985). *Organizational Culture and Leadership: A Dynamic View*. San Francisco, CA: Jossey-Bass.
Smith, J. (2001). *The Learning Game*. London: Abacus.
Stoll, L. (1999). Black hole or fertile garden for school improvement. In J. Prosser (ed). (1999) *School Culture*. London: Sage, pp. 30–47.
Stoll, L. and Fink, D. (1996). *Changing our Schools*. Buckingham: Open University Press.
Tayeb, M. (2001). Conducting research across cultures: Overcoming drawbacks and obstacles. *International Journal of Cross-Cultural Management*, vol. 1, no. 1, pp. 91–108.
Timmermans, A.C., Doolaard, S. and de Wolf, I. (2011). Conceptual and empirical differences among various value-added models for accountability. *School Effectiveness and School Improvement*, vol. 22, no. 4, pp. 393–413.
van de Grift, W. (2009). Reliability and validity in measuring the value added of schools. *School Effectiveness and School Improvement*, vol. 20, no. 2, pp. 269–285.
Walker, A. and Riordan, G. (2010). Leading collective capacity in culturally diverse schools. *School Leadership and Management*, vol. 30, no. 1, pp. 51–63.
Wallace, M., Tomlinson, M. and O'Reilly, D. (2011). The mediation of acculturation: Orchestrating school leadership development in England. *Educational Management Administration and Leadership*, vol. 39, no. 3, pp. 261–282.
Zhu, C., Devos, G. and Tondeur, J. (2014). Examining school culture in Flemish and Chinese primary schools. *Educational Management Administration and Leadership*, vol. 42, no. 4, pp. 557–575.

Leading change

Introduction

Nearly 20 years ago, concern was expressed about the amount of change in the education system in England: 'Over the past 15 years, teachers have been swamped by innovations' (Fink and Stoll, 2005, p. 19). Yet the experience of being 'swamped' by change still resonates with many school leaders and teachers today. Since 2005 (when this quote appeared), schools in England have faced even more changes to school structures, curricula, assessment, inspection, appraisal and the ways that teachers qualify to become a professional (see Box 4.1).

> **BOX 4.1 SOME OF THE MANY POLICY CHANGES IN SCHOOLS IN ENGLAND SINCE 2005**
>
> ■ *Structural changes* – a rapid shift to academies, particularly in the secondary sector; the development of Multi-Academy Trusts (MATs); a corresponding change in the balance of school oversight powers from local authorities to MATs and national government
>
> ■ *Curriculum changes* – a new national curriculum for primary and secondary schools, followed by a new creative curriculum for primary schools; more demanding, linear subject content in GCSEs and A levels; the phasing out of many vocational BTEC courses
>
> ■ *Assessment changes* – new Early Years baseline assessments and phonics testing in primary schools; the removal of the previous framework of assessment levels in primary education; the introduction of the 'EBacc' (the English Baccalaureate) in secondary schools, which requires students to study a broad range of academic subjects at GCSE; a shift away from continuous assessment back to examinations in GCSEs and grades changing to 9 to 1 to extend the former A* grade; the introduction of A/S level qualifications (first year of A levels), subsequently reduced in importance

DOI: 10.4324/9780429260612-4

- *School evaluation and inspection changes* – the implementation of 'Progress 8', which is a measure of school performance based on the amount of progress pupils make at secondary school instead of the previous measure of the proportion of pupils achieving 5 A* to C grades at GCSE; Ofsted shifted the category of Satisfactory to Requires Improvement (RI), which entails regular monitoring visits from Ofsted and a re-inspection within two years; a fresh inspection framework paid more attention to the processes of learning and eliciting more information about pupils' attitudes and behaviours rather than judging solely on test data

- *Teacher appraisal changes* – teachers' performance is required to be judged against 'Teacher Standards'

- *Teacher training changes* – a shift away from university-based courses towards school-based teacher training, introducing a plethora of routes into becoming a teacher; a new curriculum for initial teacher education (ITE)

- *Impact of Covid-19* – schools were forced to change rapidly during the lockdowns which resulted from the pandemic and are still working to offset the long-term, damaging impact on children's education and socialisation.

Box 4.1 identifies just some of the government reforms to education introduced nationally. Educational change comes from other sources, too, for example, Local Education Authorities or Multi-Academy Trusts (for schools within their control). Headteachers also spearhead their own initiatives in order to make improvements in their schools or to respond to recent research. Teachers, too, may be stimulated by the latest research on learning and teaching, and may also be inspired to make changes in their practice through professional development and on-the-job learning. Fashions for new approaches to teaching and learning (such as 'brain gym') come and go. Not surprisingly, constant change has become a normal part of life in schools. A little like the 'new lamps for old' story of Aladdin, it sometimes appears that change is always seen as 'good' and the previous approaches as 'bad': 'new is always better than old, change better than continuity, innovation better than tradition' (Hotho, 2013, p. 366).

This does not, however, make change any easier for school leaders to implement, particularly when advice and recommendations from researchers in the field are often contradictory. For example, should school leaders have a clear vision and lead from the front (Coates et al., 2015) or develop a shared vision and empower teachers (Liu, 2020)? Dudar (2013) suggests prioritising a clear plan of action at an early stage while, conversely, Fullan (2016, pp. 45–6) recommends 'change by doing rather than change by elaborate planning'. There is advice to engage the staff who are resisting change in order to identify possible weaknesses in what is proposed (Fullan, 2016) and also to ignore the resistors because they sap energy (Everard et al., 2004). In relation to accountability, one view is that this should be shared mutually between leaders and staff (Edwards-Groves et al., 2019), while another is that headteachers are ultimately accountable (Coates et al., 2015). These contradictions in the literature demonstrate the problems for school leaders in developing appropriate strategies to lead change effectively.

Perhaps the greatest dilemma is whether to embark on change in the first place. Much of the literature comments on the over-abundance of change, calling it 'dizzying' (Coates et al., 2015, p. 222), an 'epidemic' or 'tsunami' (Priestley et al., 2011, pp. 266–7), resulting in 'overload' (Fullan, 2016, p. 58) or 'repetitive change injury' (Igoe, 2011, p. 44). On the other hand, change is often desirable and necessary, whether it is to turn around a failing school, to respond to problems within an educational system or to reflect recent developments, such as technological innovation, in an ever-changing world. There may be serendipitous changes to be addressed, too, when old staff leave and new staff arrive, generating unforeseen impact.

How, then, can school leaders ensure successful change, especially when there is an ever-present danger of defeat? In responding to this dilemma, this chapter will address the following questions:

- What are the key challenges of educational change?
- How do teachers respond to change?
- What are the different theories and models informing implementation of (and responses to) change?

The chapter includes a variety of school case studies, illustrating contrasting approaches to turning around failing schools and reflecting on the different styles of leadership in relation to the theories.

What are the key challenges of educational change?

This section considers some of the potential difficulties of change, starting with defining what change means, then looking at success and failure and the various types of challenges for different categories of staff and pupils within schools, before analysing the challenges of resources and context.

Definition of change

In order to consider the challenges of educational change, it is useful to define what it means. Educational change can be large-scale (across a whole system), medium-scale (across a school) and small-scale (in a classroom). Change can be incremental, building on what went before, or 'discontinuous', for example, when educational structures or the whole curriculum changes fundamentally (Nadler and Tushman, 1995). This difference has been called 'first order' and 'second order' change, with

> **BOX 4.2 FIRST-ORDER AND SECOND-ORDER CHANGE IN TWO SCHOOLS**
>
> In some cases, schools determine whether policy change is first order or second order. For example, Braun et al. (2010) described the introduction of the government's personal, learning and thinking skills (PLTS) policy at two different schools. This policy required schools to include team working, independent enquiry, self-management, reflective learning, effective participation and creative thinking in the curriculum. At one school, Campion, a wholesale, second-order change took place with PLTS replacing two weeks of traditional maths lessons every six weeks. At the second school, Atwood, the change was minimal. The school's existing practice was identified as PLTS and three elements of the framework were included in citizenship and humanities lessons, making this a first-order change. The difference between the two schools was that Campion was under more pressure to improve and was more vulnerable to external judgements by Ofsted, whereas Atwood was a 'good' school with less compulsion to make major changes in adopting a new policy.

first order change being a modification or adjustment of existing practice, while second order change means radical reforms such as organisational restructuring or shifts of values, transforming the way problems are solved (Cuban, 1988). See Box 4.2 for an example of the ways first-order and second-order change have been enacted by different schools.

There is obviously a difference between planned change and unplanned change. Responding to national policy, for example, is planned change (Spillane et al., 2012), while a teacher leaving may be unplanned. National policy is also an 'external' influence for change (coming from outside the school), whereas teachers' own innovations can result in 'internal' change. School leaders and teachers feel differently about internally and externally driven change. Perhaps not surprisingly they are generally more positive about self-initiated change than that which is imposed externally (Hargreaves, 2004). Reflecting on the difference between 'top-down' (large-scale, external) change and 'bottom-up' (teacher-initiated) change, Fullan (2016, p. 10) argues that neither works alone. Top-down fails to gain ownership by the teachers, while bottom-up is unpredictable and often unsustainable. Fullan (2016) suggests that both are needed in combination.

Educational change, for the purposes of this chapter, encompasses any new developments taking place in schools, whether planned or unplanned, external or internal, incremental or discontinuous. Educational change in this sense is a process rather than an event (Fullan, 2016). This is because changes in education tend to take time and may not come to a 'clean' conclusion.

Success and failure in educational change

The greatest challenge of educational change appears to be ensuring success, particularly when multiple changes are being implemented at any one time. Terhart (2013, p. 497) argued that, as far as educational reform is concerned, 'we should regard failure as a normal phenomenon'. One problem is that schools have to continue to operate, providing high-quality teaching and learning for their pupils, while also undertaking change. Soini et al. (2016, p. 455) suggest, 'School reforms, no matter how well conceptualised, powerfully sponsored, brilliantly structured or closely audited, often tend to fail in the face of the reality of everyday school life'. Starr (2011, p. 646), too, writes about the 'busy, messy quotidian of expected and unexpected events' in schools which, alongside the range of different stakeholders (including the increasing diversity of pupils) and frequent policy reforms, combine to make 'major change difficult and sometimes impossible to implement'. The unfortunate result of policy failures in education is frustration, disillusionment and a sense of incompetence for all involved, followed by increased cynicism about any future changes (Fullan, 2016). Policymakers, then, need to be aware of the pressures on school leaders and find ways to ensure the successful implementation of evidence-based policies.

Paradoxically, despite the significant changes outlined in schools over the last few decades, much has remained the same. The hierarchical structure of most schools, the division of subjects and departments, the retention of age-related year groups, streaming and setting (Fink and Stoll, 2005) are still recognisable. This indicates, perhaps, aspects of schooling that have stood the test of time, the 'strength of the status quo' (Sarason, 1990, p. 35) and the resilience of traditional aspects of education whatever other external and societal changes take place.

In exploring the challenges of educational change (before looking at possible solutions), this section now turns to consider more specifically national policy, leadership, teachers, parents, pupils, resources and context.

What are the challenges of national policy change?

One key challenge for schools is the way in which change is introduced nationally. When governments make policy decisions affecting education, they often assume schools can respond rapidly. Government ministers work to a political calendar, however, not the school year. Policies are announced to demonstrate momentum, to coincide with the party conference and for the Queen's speech (Hyman, 2005). After moving from 10 Downing Street to work in schools, Hyman (2005, p. 272) observed that this tends to make life harder for those working in schools and constant reforms 'conspired to make the lives of frontline staff more frustrating and more difficult'.

This experience was confirmed by Starr's (2011) three-year research study into the learning needs of school principals which found 'too many externally imposed changes in policy and practice were seen as unnecessary and interfered with school-based change initiatives that were far more important to students, learning and teaching' (Starr, 2011, p. 652). It appears that too much change by national policymakers may be counterproductive, undermining the efforts of the real experts in educational practice, school leaders and teachers.

National policy has been described as a 'game' that headteachers have to play (Barber, 1997; Bottery, 2007; Gunter, 2012). This gives the impression of something relatively light-hearted, but school leaders are held to account for the implementation of national policy, and, in the worst-case scenario, may be sacked for failing to achieve the change required. Rayner's (2014) research explored whether headteachers are able to retain their own values while 'playing the game'. He found that where national policy ran counter to headteachers' values, they prioritised the needs of their school community above that of policy. While Rayner's research was relatively small-scale (based on three headteachers, one from a primary and two from secondary schools), his findings are echoed elsewhere. Coates et al. (2015, p. 223) suggested: 'The fickle nature of recent education policy has served as a reminder to headteachers to focus on meeting the needs of their students, rather than move with the shifting sands of central policy'. This illustrates that policy implementation is a messy process, with policies being interpreted, negotiated and sometimes contested when enacted within schools (Maguire et al., 2015).

Coates et al. (2015) describe national policy as 'shifting sands', but it could also be compared to an ocean liner, slow to change direction even when it is heading the wrong way. Terhart (2013, p. 498) suggests that education reforms seem to 'become unstoppable even if problematic side effects soon become apparent. Too much energy, hope, resources or prestige have been invested'. Terhart (2013) could, perhaps, also have included the time spent on developing national policies, since the planning, development and evaluation of reforms at all levels of an education system can be lengthy processes, which may make rapid adjustments difficult.

It is also the case that once policy is implemented in schools there may be unintended consequences, and the outcomes may not reflect the intentions of the policymakers. Box 4.3 illustrates one example of a school implementing a new assessment strategy with unexpected results.

BOX 4.3 PUTTING POLICY INTO PRACTICE: THE CASE OF FORMATIVE ASSESSMENT

This example focuses on the introduction of formative assessment (that is, monitoring students' learning and providing ongoing feedback) in a school in Wales. Two researchers, Smith and Gorard (2005), were invited to evaluate a small-scale trial of formative assessment in the school. The Year 7 pupils were divided into four mixed-ability teaching groups and, for one year, one group was given detailed formative assessment, but no marks or grades on their work, while the other three groups were treated 'as normal', which meant they were given marks or grades and minimal comments. At the end of the year, the pupils in the 'formative assessment' group performed no better than the other pupils and many said they did not like the approach. They did not always understand the feedback they were given, could not read all their teachers' comments and the feedback did not appear to have enhanced the learning process. Moreover, the lack of grades and marks meant that they could not identify when they were making progress, so the pupils were inadvertently disadvantaged. Smith and Gorard (2005) recognise this was a small study, in one school, without a standardised public test to measure the outcome at the end of the year. Their intention was not, however, to challenge the merits of formative assessment. Instead, the study provides an indication of what can happen when a new innovation is 'rolled out' to schools, without the teachers being given the same level of training, support and attention as those in the original research (in this case, Black and Wiliam's (2003) study of formative assessment in six case study schools). Smith and Gorard's (2005) study provides evidence that the original version of an innovation may not be properly replicated in schools and yield unintended and possibly adverse consequences for pupils.

As Box 4.3 indicates, new approaches may not work as the initiators intended. Unfortunately the feedback mechanisms from schools and academies upwards to the national policymakers do not appear to enable swift and robust communication about the impact of reforms at the 'chalkface' – and it is possible that policymakers may be reluctant to hear messages that their favoured policies are not working. Perhaps an appropriate metaphor for educational reform is a large boulder poised at the top of a mountain, which requires an enormous push to get moving. Once inertia has been overcome, it travels with headlong momentum, striking (and in some cases, destroying) multiple obstacles in its path, with no possibility of sending back information to those who launched it, until it crashes at the bottom, brought to rest on the many reforms that preceded it. To prevent this happening, new policies need to be rigorously trialled, with feedback on their impact (including in relation to equity – see Chapter 9) and appropriate adjustments made. Policymakers also need to provide a clear rationale for change and make efforts to persuade school leaders and staff of its benefits.

What are the challenges facing school leaders in managing change?

In responding to the challenge of national policy changes, a key role for school leaders is to build coherence between external, government reforms and their own school's priorities – in other words, between external and internal change. Researchers in Finland (Soini et al., 2016) investigated the impact of a large-scale school reform and identified the issue of coherence as crucial in their five in-depth school case studies. The principals of these schools used problem-solving, learning-oriented strategies to include staff in the school reform. The researchers conclude that developing coherence is a two-way process between 'translating big ideas into local educational practices' while reconciling specific school priorities with national reforms (Soini et al., 2016, p. 464). This may be difficult, however, because sometimes large-scale reforms counteract individual school changes (for example, national curriculum changes may undermine a school's own curricular development). Also, at times national changes come so thick and fast that dovetailing them with local priorities becomes impossible.

Even if they are committed to developing coherence between national and school policies, headteachers still have to face the challenge of persuading their staff to adopt change. Principals tend to view teacher resistance to change as both inevitable and negative (Starr, 2011), despite the possibility that criticisms might be constructive. Box 4.4 summarises the principals' experiences of teacher resistance from Starr's (2011) research.

> **BOX 4.4 PRINCIPALS' EXPERIENCE OF TEACHER RESISTANCE**
>
> Resistance, as principals discussed it, covered a spectrum of behaviours from the aggressive and violent to the defensive, passive or silent. The most distressing stories concerned illegal activities: one principal received death threats and was living with 24-hour security protection; a few had property vandalised; others experienced professional sabotage (for example, papers stolen or files destroyed). Some stories concerned blows to professional identity, for example, staff in one school delivered a vote of no confidence in the principal to the governing council, while another principal confronted heated delegations of staff and parents demanding reversal of a decision. Most principals had experienced undermining through exclusion…. 'Bad' behaviours included temper tantrums and physical outbursts such as door slamming. Principals also cited behaviours such as 'nit-picking' whereby dissidents try to find fault in words or actions… or facing difficult questions designed to embarrass them in public. Principals reported being the subject of slanderous rumours or disingenuous remarks, experiencing 'back-stabbing', 'white-anting' or receiving anonymous letters and blackmail.
>
> (Starr, 2011, p. 650)

Box 4.4 describes some more extreme examples of staff resistance to change, but even low-level resistance can be demoralising for the leader. It is worth remembering how reluctant people are to change their behaviours in general, even when the outcome may be illness or death. In the recent coronavirus pandemic, it was not until the UK government instituted a legally backed 'lockdown' that people could be persuaded not to socialise. Information about the risk of spreading or dying from the disease was not enough to convince them to forego a visit to the pub, cinema or cafe.

If it is so hard to persuade people to modify their behaviour in extreme circumstances, how much more difficult is the task for school leaders, where change for teachers will inevitably mean more work and often has no guarantee of success?

There has, however, been much research on educational change, and the resulting recommendations about what is likely to improve the chances of achieving change are summarised later in this chapter.

What are the challenges for middle leaders?

Challenges exist at the level of middle leadership, as well as for principals. Middle leaders may have split loyalties, torn between whole school reforms on the one hand, and on the other, loyalty to their departments and colleagues. Edwards-Groves et al.'s (2019) research looked at middle leadership in three case study primary schools in one school district in regional New South Wales, Australia. They found that an important role for the middle leaders was to adapt national changes to the school context (similar to the headteachers in Soini et al.'s (2016) research mentioned earlier). This included longer term professional development for the teachers in order to sustain the change. One of their focus group teacher participants commented, 'Even though it might be the mandatory stuff, Shelly [the middle leader] connects it to us, we can see how it relates to the kids in this disadvantaged community' (Edwards-Groves et al., 2019, p. 329). Edwards-Groves et al. (2019) concluded that middle leaders' 'insider' knowledge of their school's circumstances helped them to navigate change successfully, encouraging their teachers to implement change in a sustainable way. More information about the role of middle leaders can be found in Chapter 5.

What are the challenges for teachers?

Classroom teachers are central to educational change, but it can be a challenge for them to implement it effectively. Some teachers may be reluctant to experiment with new ways of teaching. Changes in teaching practices often require practitioners to bid farewell to tried and tested approaches that represent their own values and understanding of good teaching (Starr, 2011). There is also a danger that teachers only engage superficially, paying lip service to the change rather than implementing it as intended (Fullan, 2016). The example of the introduction of formative assessment in Box 4.3 demonstrates how a superficial approach to engaging with an innovation can be unsuccessful.

Even when teachers want to engage with change, they have to grapple with conflicting policies, a lack of time and resources and a high-stakes culture in which failure is risky (Priestley et al., 2011). How, then, can they be persuaded to take ownership of change? Liu (2020) argues that teachers need to be included in decisions in order to garner their support for the initiative and develop their commitment to it. In his systematic review of research into 'turnaround leadership',

Liu (2020, p. 13) found that it was 'problematic when principals are the main force in the change process while teachers are only partially included'.

Fullan (2016) points out a fundamental difference between school leaders and teachers in relation to change: leaders are more likely to be future oriented, focusing on the potential benefits of change, whereas teachers are more aware of the present, particularly the costs of change in terms of loss of existing routines and additional preparatory and follow-up work. It is undoubtedly the case that some teachers become stressed and anxious as a result of change (Terhart, 2013). In some instances this is met with solutions such as stress management and a focus on well-being (Hargreaves, 1997) to manage the pressure, when perhaps a more appropriate option would be to reduce the number of initiatives undertaken by a school at any one time.

The responses of teachers to change are addressed more fully later in the chapter.

What are the challenges relating to parents?

The challenge to include school stakeholders also relates to parents. Yet, paradoxically, although the involvement of parents has been identified as essential to effectiveness, parents are not often mentioned in the research and literature about how to improve schools (Reck and Reitzung, 2014).

The overall research into parental influence has been summarised as follows: 'The closer the parent is to the education of the child, the greater the impact on child development and educational achievement' (Fullan, 2016, p. 158). Coates et al. (2015, p. 50), too, emphasise that 'parents matter' and argue that engaging parents is vital in improving schools and raising achievement. Bryk and Schneider's (2002) longitudinal research into school reform in 12 Chicago elementary schools found that the school's relationship with parents was an important factor in successful change. They contrasted the schools they described as 'low-trust', where the teachers' perceptions of parents were generally negative (they were critical about the parents' attitudes to education and their lifestyles) with the 'high-trust' schools where teachers reached out to parents, recognised their vulnerabilities and respected their views, whatever their educational background. They argued that teachers and leaders need an empathetic understanding of parents, especially where the parents' backgrounds differ from those of the staff in terms of race, class and education.

Engaging parents in actively supporting changes in schools can be challenging, however. Like other stakeholders, they may have rather traditional (or negative) ideas about education, based on their own school experiences (Stoll and Fink, 1996). Parents may not always agree with the strategies developed by the school leadership team and in some cases have forced out headteachers whose approaches to change they did not like. Gibson and Simon (2020) describe a Catholic primary school in England in which the principal, 'Mary', was hounded out by parents after trying to introduce changes following a poor inspection result. She had only been leading the school for a short time so she had inherited the faults identified by Ofsted from her very popular predecessor. Mary said in a reflective research interview after the event: 'There was a band of parents got together and apparently had meeting after meeting outside of the school to generate the hatred against me' (Gibson and Simon, 2020, p. 36). The governors initially supported her but eventually decided that her position had become untenable and she was forced to leave.

Clearly, it is important for schools to engage with parents when undertaking change. In Dudar's (2013) research, many of the school leaders had included parents in their change 'task force' and valued their participation. The school case studies described in Box 4.5 identify ways in which one of the schools worked with parents and students as it moved from 'inadequate' to 'outstanding'.

> **BOX 4.5 SCHOOL CASE STUDIES OF LEADING CHANGE: THE WROXHAM SCHOOL**
>
> The school studies outlined here and in Box 4.8 later in the chapter are drawn from accounts written by two former headteachers: Dame Sally Coates, former headteacher of Burlington Danes and Dame Alison Peacock, former headteacher of The Wroxham School (Coates et al., 2015; Peacock, 2011). Both schools were in difficult circumstances when the headteacher started (The Wroxham School was in special measures) and in both cases the headteachers were able to transform them into 'outstanding' schools (as judged by Ofsted). Both schools are located in areas of deprivation. Burlington Danes is an inner-city school in London and The Wroxham School is in Potters Bar, Hertfordshire. The schools are not directly comparable, however. They are not only different in school phase and size, but the case studies were written at different times. When Coates took over as headteacher in 2008, Burlington Danes was a secondary academy with around 800 students from ages 11 to 18 and capacity for more. When Peacock arrived as headteacher at The Wroxham School in 2003, it was a primary school with a nursery and approximately 200 pupils aged 3 to 11. What is interesting, however, is that the two leaders had very different approaches to turning the schools around (although there were some common features too) yet both were able to make significant improvements.
>
> Here, the participatory approach to leading change is exemplified by The Wroxham School, including the involvement of pupils. Peacock (2011, p. 31) believed that 'leading a school out of difficulty requires not only hard work but also clarity of vision and a high degree of professional courage'. She wanted to demonstrate that school leadership could be transformative and decided to 'engage the entire community in the process of improvement' (Peacock, 2011, 34).
>
> On her first day at the school, Peacock held a circle meeting with every class, including the teacher, in which she asked them what was good about the school and how to improve the playground. The children contributed their playground ideas to a display board, entitled 'We are a Listening School'. Lottery funding provided the resources to transform the playground, based on the children's suggestions. The Listening School

> display board became a long-term interactive area where children and staff could leave notes on any subject.
>
> In Peacock's first week, she held two meetings for parents and families to present her vision for the school and ask for their feedback. She also held meetings with the classroom support staff, kitchen staff, playground staff and cleaners to open up channels of communication.
>
> Peacock was eager to establish a system of whole-school mixed-age circle meetings to ensure that pupils' voices were heard. This had been successful at her previous school, but she waited until the teachers at The Wroxham School were ready to take it forward, because she did not want them to feel forced into it. The mixed-age meetings started in her second term and lasted for 15 minutes, prior to the morning playtime on Tuesdays. Each group had around 25 children aged 6–11 and was facilitated by a teacher. Peacock provided a planning sheet consisting of a warm-up game, feedback from the previous week's meeting, a theme for discussion, and concluded with a warm-down game. The discussions included everyone, but children were allowed to 'pass' if they did not want to contribute. The circle meeting groups later helped to write the school's mission statement and the words 'team', 'listening', 'supporting each other' and 'doing our best' were repeated in most groups. The circle meetings contributed to and were symbolic of the culture of partnership in the school.
>
> The Wroxham School developed a collaborative approach to curriculum planning, review and assessment, which included the children. The concept of person-centred leadership guided Peacock throughout. Peacock (2011, pp. 38–39) comments: 'Our story of change is about hard work, dedication, clear vision and a passionate belief that we all benefit from genuine participation and voice'.

What are the challenges relating to students?

Students, too, may present challenges when schools change but, like parents, they have been neglected in research (Reck and Reitzung, 2014). There is a danger that students become commodified, represented either by student assessment results (Reck and Reitzung, 2014) or by numbers, in that rising pupil enrolments tend to represent an upward trajectory for the school. Yet students are important stakeholders in changes in education and should be included in discussions about new initiatives in schools (Rudduck, 2007). As Cook-Sather (2002, p. 3) points out: 'there is something fundamentally amiss about building and rebuilding an entire system without consulting at any point those it is ostensibly designed to serve'.

Students can provide fresh perspectives on teaching and learning from the position of an 'expert witness' and it is important to empower them to shape their own education as active citizens (Akshir Ab Kadir, 2019). This needs to be genuine, rather than tokenistic. Different political parties in England have supported the involvement of young people in developments in education (Fielding, 2015).

Yet there are few examples of schools that have become democratic communities, with young people experiencing participatory engagement in decision-making (Fielding, 2013).

The case of The Wroxham School in Box 4.5 indicates how pupils can be involved in turning around a failing school.

What are the challenges relating to resources?

A key challenge for school leaders is the lack of resources to support change. Resources can include funding for teaching materials, IT equipment, buildings and professional development (Peters, 2012; Fullan, 2016; Liu, 2020). Hatch's (2002, p. 629) research, based on conversations with principals, administrators and staff working on improvement programmes in the Bay Area district of California, found that education initiatives often involve 'far more time, effort and resources than some schools have readily available'. If schools are bombarded with one change after another, it becomes hard for them to plan their expenditure as well as professional development for their staff. In addition there may be hidden costs, particularly in sustaining a change after the initial funding has expired. Hatch (2002, p. 630) describes one school leader weighing up the costs and benefits of engaging in a new technology partnership:

> What happens if they come in and work with us for a year ... and put all those computers in? Can it be sustained after that year, or is it going to drain all of our funds to maintain the technology?

The distribution of resources can also be challenging for school leaders during times of change. They have to balance two roles: one as the financial controller, deciding which priorities to fund, and the other as a 'facilitator of shared learning' empowering staff to engage in change (Soini et al., 2016). This creates tension between the headteacher encouraging staff to participate in decision-making while at the same time retaining overall control of the budget.

What are the challenges relating to the school context?

The individual, geographical and social context of schools have an important impact on change. Coates et al. (2015, p. 136) argue that 'schools must fit the contextual challenges in which they operate, rather than stick rigidly to a prescribed formula'. A school's context includes the staff, the neighbourhood, parental expectations, the students, the school ethos and its teaching and learning approaches (Sanders, 2011). It is not just the 'backdrop' for change: 'Context is not a container within which the school is situated. Rather it is a powerful determinant of what can and must be done and in what order' (Sanders, 2011, p. 2).

The size of a school is an important aspect of its context. To function effectively, secondary schools arguably need to be large enough for a sixth form (at least

1400 pupils). For primary schools, it can be advantageous to have a two- to three-form entry because it allows teachers in the same year group to collaborate. Where schools are too small, teachers have to teach multiple subjects, which constrains preparation time, professional development (because this becomes focused on subject areas with which teachers are less familiar) and time for other activities.

The importance of context becomes clear when a headteacher moves to a new school and finds that the strategies that were effective in a previous school do not transfer easily to a different context. The 'superhead' experience in England is an example of this – see Box 4.6.

BOX 4.6 SUPERHEADS: A POLICY MISTAKE?

The idea of 'superheads' was introduced in England in the late 1990s as part of a 'Fresh Start' scheme that enabled experienced, successful headteachers (i.e., superheads) to be parachuted into failing schools, which were closed and then reopened with a different name and leader (Henning, 2016). Unfortunately the implementation of this scheme began with a rocky start: one headteacher refused to take up their appointment while three others resigned within five days (Gillard, 2018).

The first superhead, Torsten Friedag, was appointed to the newly re-opened Islington Arts and Media School in September 1999. Described as 'a charismatic enthusiast', 'gentle giant' and 'genial Berliner' (Spencer, 2001, n.p.), Friedag's progressive '60s-style approach to leadership had made him an outstanding leader at his previous school (Woodward, 2001). His experience at the Islington Arts and Media School, filmed as a television documentary 'Head on the Block', was not a happy one, however, and exemplifies the problem of trying to transfer a successful approach to a different context. Woodward (2001) describes Friedag playing Ringo Starr's 'With a Little Help from My Friends' to pupils at an introductory assembly – to their apparent bafflement. Friedag faced multiple problems when he started at the school: building work was still ongoing, there was no timetable and around 300 of the pupils were very challenging. Within two terms he resigned, after failing to improve attendance or prevent violent behaviour; that year only 5% of pupils attained five A* to Cs at GCSE, making it the 10th worst-performing school in England (Woodward, 2001).

Despite the problems experienced by Friedag and a number of other superheads, the concept of superheads has not yet disappeared from English schools. McInerney (2016) quotes a recent study in which researchers at the Centre for High Performance observed 160 academies over five years, recording pupil, teacher, management and financial performance as well as interviews with headteachers. Twenty-one of the schools had superheads and, interestingly, they used similar strategies to try to boost their school's results. These strategies included:

- excluding badly behaved students (21 out of the 21 superheads)
- focusing on maths and English (21/21)

- moving outstanding teachers to year 11 (20/21)
- persuading parents to home-school low-performing students (19/21)
- not entering low-ability pupils into exams (18/21).

In the short term these schools showed an improvement in results (an average increase of 9%), but after the superheads departed, there was a dip in performance (by 6% on average) and the results only started to advance again after three years. By comparison, the schools that did not have superheads showed better results and more sustainable improvement in the long term.

The introduction of superheads demonstrates the adverse consequences when school leaders apply tried and tested approaches which have previously worked well for them but which do not address the needs of a different school context. Even when superheads appeared to have improved the results of their academies, their strategies were not only morally dubious (for example, persuading parents to home-school low-performing students or not entering them for exams) but proved to be a 'quick fix' which did not ensure improvements in the long term.

Clearly approaches to implement change, like teaching strategies, need to be adapted to fit the particular school context, taking into account the mix of different ages, genders, abilities, ethnicity and social class of students, as well as the staff, parents and locality of the school. The next section looks at teacher responses to change, before moving on to the theories and models of change that might help school leaders to develop appropriate strategies for their own school.

How do teachers respond to change?

As Fullan (1991, p.117) wrote: 'Educational change depends on what teachers do and think – it is as simple and as complex as that'. Thus, understanding how teachers respond to change is essential. It has been noted earlier in the chapter that teachers tend to be rather negative about change, seeing it as involving additional work with often limited rewards. This does not mean teachers are antagonistic to educational reform in general, however. Rather, they seem reluctant to change their own classroom practice (Terhart, 2013). This section looks in more detail at research on how teachers respond to change, addressing the following questions:

- What tends to be teachers' initial response to change?
- What are the likely emotional reactions of teachers to change?
- How far do teachers' attitudes towards change depend on agency and identity?
- What makes a positive difference to teachers' responses to change?

What tends to be teachers' initial response to change?

Although undoubtedly there are teachers who make frequent changes to their practice in order to improve their skills and who welcome the prospect of educational change, it appears they are in a minority (Terhart, 2013). Education reforms may appear to some teachers like an assault on their professional competence and identity (Saunders, 2013). Change invariably means the loss of the status quo, familiar routines and tried-and-tested approaches as well as additional work, so it is perhaps not surprising teachers may not be positive about it. Terhart (2013, p. 488) sets out three questions teachers frequently ask when first confronted with a proposed change:

1. Why change things? Will this help to resolve teaching and learning problems for me?

2. How will that work? Can I adapt the change to meet my students' needs?

3. What is in it for me? How much of my time and energy will it take, and is it worth it?

Terhart's (2013) research was a meta-analysis of studies of change including large-scale surveys, in-depth school case studies and one quasi-experimental study (where one group of teachers was given training in data analysis while the other was not). Most of the research projects found teachers were generally negative about change. Terhart (2013) identified a number of different justifications teachers used to explain why they did not want to change (see Box 4.7). School leaders may find it useful to consider which of their teachers have adopted any of these arguments, as well as whether the arguments resonate with their own views about change.

BOX 4.7 TEACHERS' JUSTIFICATIONS FOR NOT CHANGING

- The 'No Time!' argument: probably every teacher sees the working day as being filled to the brim. It is simply not possible to address or engage with the new given the [pressure] of daily duties.

- The 'I am innocent!' argument: there is no need to change one's own practices. Problems exist, of course, but other people, or groups, or the system, society, etc. are responsible.

- The 'burnt child' argument: past reforms have brought nothing. A lot of time and energy has been invested by many, but in the end nothing has led to improved quality, not even an alleviation of everyday schoolwork and teaching.

> - The 'two worlds' argument: reforms are developed in the boardrooms of administrators, quality managers or educational researchers. However, schools and teachers work in a completely different world; they are the ones who are 'in the firing line' or 'in the trenches', and a lot of things concocted by the higher [echelons] do not work in practice.
> - The 'biographical' argument: it is now the turn for younger colleagues to take over; [we] older ones have had our share of having to experiment with new-fangled ideas. It is of no importance or value to us anymore.
> - The 'lack of personal benefit' argument: there is nothing in it for me, only more work. School reforms only benefit those in school administration, school supervision, ministries, universities and so on.
>
> Terhart (2013, pp. 494–5)

The arguments outlined in Box 4.7 clearly depend on the kind of change that is being proposed, although the 'no time' argument may apply to any change. Such arguments form part and parcel of potential resistance to change by teachers and have been identified in other studies. For example, in Johnson's (2004, p. 282) Australian case study schools, some teachers 'publicly spoke against some aspects of the reforms, invoking common arguments like "we have done this before", "it isn't classroom based or practical" or "the kids and parents don't want this".' In some schools teachers 'grizzled' to parents and colleagues to gain support for opposing the changes. In one school, teachers formed coalitions to challenge and subvert the reforms. In two of the secondary schools, subject and year group leaders defended their subject disciplines and used their expert status to resist restructuring and changes to assessment practices.

Interestingly, in Starr's (2011) research, the way in which teachers reacted to change influenced how the principals perceived them. Where opposition was expressed politely, leaders were more respectful, whereas outright confrontation created hostility from the principal. The leaders were aware that if they themselves openly resisted new educational policies or accountability measures that were imposed on them, it would have a negative outcome. Perhaps they, in turn, applied this to their staff.

What are the likely emotional reactions of teachers to change?

Educational reform efforts tend to focus on changing teachers' behaviours and beliefs and pay less attention to the emotional dimensions of change (Saunders, 2013). The arguments in Box 4.7 indicate a strongly emotional response, particularly if it entails a change to teaching practice (Terhart, 2013). But Terhart (2013) seems to assume teachers are locked into one particular response or attitude to change, whereas it is possible that people's emotions vary at different times.

Vahasantanen (2015) found teachers took different positions towards reform: resistant, inconsistent/ambiguous and approving. In some cases, teachers' positions changed, for example, from being critical to supportive, or initially enthusiastic to disillusioned. Their engagement with reforms varied from active participation to passive accommodation.

Some theories suggest people experience predictable stages of feelings in response to change (for example, Carnall, 2003; Kavanagh and Ashkanasy, 2004; Sitkin and Pablo, 2004). These stages can be broadly summarised as antagonism, adjustment and acceptance. Initially people feel hostile towards the change, greeting it with shock, denial or anxiety. They then gradually adjust to it, recognising its inevitability. Finally, they accept and internalise the change, with a sense of relief and satisfaction.

These theories of change assume participants initially feel negative. However, some staff may see change as an opportunity and feel happy about it (Pritchard and Williamson, 2008). Even if individuals begin by viewing change antagonistically, this stage is considered to be temporary, with people reaching a more positive frame of mind in due course. There is no indication of how long this might take, however, nor what happens if individuals remain negative about the change. Another problem with the theory of predictable stages of response is the assumption that people only have to deal with one major change at a time, but in the fast-moving world of education, it is likely individuals face multiple and frequent initiatives which might mean being at different stages of the process simultaneously. In addition, teachers may not respond emotionally in a linear way, as implied by the models. Saunders (2013, p. 327) found teachers' sensitivities were frequently 'experienced and re-experienced at different stages of the change journey', so that, rather than going through one stage at a time, the teachers exhibited simultaneously a 'combination of concerns, often accompanied by strong positive and negative emotions.'

Saunders' (2013) research aimed to improve understanding of teachers' emotions when implementing new instructional processes. It was based on 27 completed questionnaires and two interviews with vocational education teachers in Western Australia. While the research was small scale, this enabled Saunders to consider the emotional impact of change in depth. She concluded (2013, p. 328):

> In this case, orchestrated rationalistic models of change which assume that change occurs in a series of discrete steps are limiting when considering the emotional landscape of professional change. The reality is that change is played out at the complex and dynamic interface between individual emotions, identities, beliefs and systems, relationships and politics.

Teachers have different emotional responses to internal or self-initiated change compared to externally imposed change, as Hargreaves (2004) found in a research study that drew on 50 teacher interviews in Canada, as well as supplementary focus groups. Hargreaves (2004) concluded teachers were largely positive about self-initiated change and negative about externally mandated change. So far, so predictable, but one interesting discovery he made was that almost half the examples of self-initiated changes described by the teachers had actually been externally mandated originally. It appeared that the teachers had adopted some of the external changes to such an extent that they conceived of them as their own idea. Hargreaves (2004) suggested the source of an innovation is less important than the extent to which school leaders can create teacher ownership of the change.

How far do teachers' attitudes towards change depend on agency and identity?

Teacher agency is linked to ownership, that is, it concerns the extent to which teachers feel a sense of power and self-efficacy in relation to their work. Vahasantanen (2015) investigated the role of teacher agency in relation to change, using five studies based on interviews with 16 vocational teachers, with 14 of these teachers re-interviewed after a year. Vahasantanen (2015) contrasted the teachers' feeling of powerlessness over wider reforms with their strong sense of agency in the classroom, where they were able to make pedagogical decisions. If changes meant that teachers were unable to influence how they carried out their professional duties, this lack of agency caused dissatisfaction and their commitment to work was reduced. Vahasantanen's (2015) research was small-scale, however, and may not be generalisable, but the findings chime with other writers (for example, Fullan, 2016; Terhart, 2013) who emphasise the importance of involving teachers when planning change.

In some cases, educational reforms seem to undermine teachers' agency and identity. Identities depend on personal and biographical influences as well as professional training. All of these aspects affect teachers' responses to change (Fink and Stoll, 2005). Saunders (2013) suggested that changes that force teachers to reflect on and abandon their existing pedagogical approaches challenge their beliefs and values, thus impacting on their sense of identity.

In contrast to teachers feeling undermined and powerless in the face of change, Lukacs and Galluzzo (2014) suggest that teachers can become change agents, who actively drive reforms at work. They describe such teachers as 'not afraid of taking risks, [...] highly motivated and [...] confident in their abilities to pursue solutions to schoolwide change' (Lukacs and Galluzzo, 2014, p. 104). Teacher change agents were able to articulate trends positively to colleagues to gain their commitment. Similarly, Collinson's (2012) research, informed by interviews with exemplary teachers, found that teachers became innovators in order to help students learn and then influenced colleagues to adopt similar positive strategies. Even if they took on leadership roles, their focus was always on learning and supporting students.

One of the difficulties for school leaders is that every teacher is a unique individual and while some teachers may see change as an exciting opportunity to develop their practice, others view change as burdensome and unwelcome. As a result, it is problematic to generalise about how leaders should introduce change, but the next section considers ways in which to help teachers feel more positive.

What makes a positive difference to teachers' responses to change?

A number of measures have been suggested in order to assist teachers to engage positively with large-scale change. One is that leaders need to pay attention to the emotional needs of those involved and support them more effectively – relationships between leaders and teachers need to be collaborative, based on mutual trust and respect (Saunders, 2013). Another is to build time into professional development to allow teachers to discuss any feelings that they might wish to share.

It helps if leaders are aware of, and feel empathy for, the challenges facing teachers in times of reform: 'They are required to assimilate new information and novel educational practices, to negotiate their professional identities, to determine their response to the reform, and to consider their engagement strategies regarding the reform' (Vahasantanen, 2015, p.11). Empowering teachers through participatory processes assists in strengthening teacher agency and protecting their professional identities (Vahasantanen, 2015). Collaboration, dialogue, professional reflections and shared decision-making can all help to encourage trust (Priestley, 2005). School leaders are also encouraged to build positive relationships with teachers and other staff as they plan and implement change.

Teachers' attitudes towards change are influenced by informal social processes as well as their knowledge and understanding of teaching. Whereas a conventional approach to change management is to persuade teachers through rational arguments, it is important to address the emotional and social dimensions of the change, too. To make change work, Li et al. (2021) recommend that middle leaders such as subject department heads or curriculum leaders help to facilitate teachers' receptivity towards initiatives, considering both subject knowledge and an understanding of the social processes involved.

The next section looks at a range of different theories and models of change which focus on the process – although inevitably that includes the people involved too.

What are the different theories and models of educational change?

Alchemists sought to change base metal into gold; the search for a successful recipe for educational change seems equally unattainable. Nevertheless, for failing schools there are preferred models: 'When a school is judged by inspectors as failing there is, currently, a centrally held belief that improvement comes from strict adherence to a set of externally monitored interventions' (Sanders, 2011, p. 31). In the United States, the 'punitive' strategies to turn around failing schools are threefold: replace the principal and institute comprehensive changes; replace at least 50% of the staff; and close the school and then re-open as a new school (Reck and Reitzung, 2014, p. 42).

A number of change models for education have been proposed, from Lewin's (1947) basic, but still often quoted, 'Unfreeze-Change-Refreeze', to Kotter's (2012) eight-step process, which was recommended by the former National College for School Leadership in England. Table 4.1 compares three different models of change: Fullan's guidelines in 2010 and 2016 (the latter in italics); Kotter's (2012) eight steps, and Dudar's (2013) model for rapid change.

There are criticisms of all these models, however. Fullan (2016) makes a number of rather provocative suggestions, perhaps the greatest of which is to avoid too much detailed planning before taking action. This somewhat contradicts his earlier view that 'the main problem is not the absence of innovations but the presence of too many disconnected, episodic, piecemeal, superficially adorned projects' (Fullan, 2001, p. 109). Schools with this approach to change have been dubbed 'Christmas tree' schools, decorated with the ornaments of all the latest ideas (Sebring and Bryk, 2000, p. 442). Fullan's (2016) suggestion of taking action early without systematic strategic planning seems destined to create an incoherent programme of change.

Kotter (2012) re-named his eight steps 'accelerators' to address an earlier criticism that a linear approach to change (first step one, then step two and so on) does not work in the fast-moving world of education – or business, for which the process was originally proposed. Like other change models, Kotter's 'eight steps' is problematic in schools. It focuses on a 'single big opportunity', but schools are often required to implement multiple changes at the same time, or else they are halfway through making one major change when another appears over the horizon. In addition, if change is like 'oil in water' (Netolicky, 2019, p. 157), it is fluid and unpredictable, so linear plans, however carefully conceived, may be overturned.

Dudar's (2013) 'rapid change model' was based on her extensive research in Alberta, Canada, involving a leadership questionnaire completed by 39 school leaders, in-depth interviews with 16 of the questionnaire respondents and, at eight of these schools, focus groups with teachers, students and parents. Her findings were mainly based on the self-reported testimonies of the school leaders who had been identified as having implemented change rapidly (within three years). There is always a danger that leaders will have a more positive view of their performance than others. In addition, the changes the school leaders had implemented varied in complexity, so the model Dudar (2013) developed may not be appropriate for all kinds of change.

The main difficulty with all these models of change, however, is that each school is a unique institution, requiring its own process of change to respond to the particular needs of its context (Fink and Stoll, 2005). There is no 'one best solution'

Table 4.1 Models of educational change

Process	Fullan (2010 and 2016)	Kotter (2012)	Dudar (2013)
Establish vision/aim/ goals	Focus on a small number of ambitious goals Make sure that instruction and student achievement are at the heart of the matter *Define closing the gap as the overarching goal*	Create a sense of urgency around a single big opportunity Form a strategic vision and develop change initiatives designed to capitalise on the big opportunity	Pre-plan to establish the rationale for change, the order and priority of processes and initiate positive relationships with participants Collect data to inform the change agenda (evidence-based decision-making)
Identify change agents	Commit to whole-system reform – 100% of the system involved from day one	Build and maintain a guiding coalition (of volunteers to spearhead the change)	Create a task force charged with the responsibility to support the leadership vision and establish appropriate processes
Communicate with participants and take action	*Recognise that all successful strategies are socially based and action-oriented – change by doing rather than change by elaborate planning*	Communicate the vision and the strategy to create buy-in and attract a growing volunteer army	Maintain regular communication patterns with all stakeholders to motivate participants, share information and provide feedback

Leading change

Address barriers to change, including the need for training and development	Build individual and collective capacity in tandem. Work towards greater social capital as the accelerator of wider and deeper reform *Assume that lack of capacity is the initial problem and then work on it continuously*	Accelerate movement towards the vision and the opportunity by ensuring that the network removes barriers	Address resistance to change, ideally including the disengaged and disenfranchised
Monitor results and celebrate success, bearing in mind accountability	Establish transparency of results and practice as the norm, avoiding heavy-handed accountability *Build internal accountability linked to external accountability*	Celebrate visible, significant short-term wins	Celebrate participants' change efforts and outcomes
Maintain progress and create sustainability through cultural change	Stay the course through continuity of good direction by leveraging leadership *Establish conditions for the evolution of positive pressure*	Sustained acceleration: never give up; keep learning from experience; don't declare victory too soon Institutionalise strategic changes in the culture	Consider and plan for sustainability

(Lukacs and Galluzzo, 2014, p. 104) and, even though Fullan (2008, 2010, 2016) offers guidelines for change, he recommended that school leaders develop their own theory of change, rather than adopt a model designed by someone else (Fullan, 2008).

There may not be a magic formula or 'silver bullet' to manage educational change successfully. However, there are many 'silver bullet-points' about change in the literature. Guiding principles are not intended to be prescriptive or linear but may help school leaders when undertaking change. This is clear in the comparison between the three models in Table 4.1. They each include similar processes or practices:

- establish vision/aim/goals
- identify change agents
- communicate with participants and take action
- address barriers to change
- monitor results and celebrate success
- ensure sustainability.

These are considered in more detail ahead.

How to establish vision/aims/goals?

Vision has been defined as a 'view of a realistic, credible, attractive future for the organization, a condition that is better in some important ways than what now exists' (Bennis and Nanus, 1985, p. 89). As such, it seems to apply more to large-scale changes in schools than to incremental change, for which the terms 'aims' or 'goals' seem more appropriate than 'vision'.

Vision often appears as a first step in change. Ries (2012), for example, had vision as the initial stage in his model of change ('vision, steer, accelerate'), but this was developed for the commercial sector. Fullan (2013) adapted Ries' (2012) three steps in his 'stratosphere agenda', suggesting that change should start with directional vision as the first stage, followed by focused innovation and then consolidation.

A leader's vision can provide an initial inspiration to motivate staff to engage with change (Dudar, 2013). In order to do this, the vision has to be communicated effectively (Burke, 2008) and revisited frequently (Lyng and Mortimer, 2011). In Dudar's (2013, p. 251) research, the leaders identified a 'visionary goal' which determined the changes they adopted and how to implement them. They remained focused on their vision whatever the challenges they faced.

One problem with the issue of vision is that often the leader's vision is considered paramount, which constrains the teachers' influence (Lukacs and Galluzzo, 2014). Enabling staff to shape the school vision with the leader helped to motivate the process of organisational learning in Israeli schools (Kurland et al., 2010). Similarly, in a study of the introduction of co-teaching in New Zealand and Australia, the leaders had not only 'held the vision' but encouraged the development of shared beliefs and ownership of the vision (Mackey et al., 2017, p. 477). The teachers felt empowered by this process. A shared vision is also important in turning around failing schools (Liu, 2020).

It is useful to consider what should underpin a school's vision. Closing the gap between high- and low-performing groups (Fullan, 2016), improved pedagogy (Sanders, 2011) and better student outcomes (Dudar, 2013) are important. It can also include critical inquiry and high academic criteria (Liu, 2020). Building on what the school does well can be as important as identifying which problems to address when developing the vision (Sanders, 2011).

There is a close connection between vision and values, or moral purpose, in schools. Moral purpose is seen by Fullan (2016) as a driving force for successful educational change. In Johnson's (2004) research in five Australian schools, the discussions with focus groups of teachers led him to conclude that change at the schools was driven by a moral commitment to the educational and social well-being of the students: key values were the 'driving force for reform (rather than leader-inspired 'visions of reform')' (Johnson, 2004, p. 267). Appendix 4.1, Values and aims of schools in different Ofsted categories, has some examples of the values and aims of schools. Appendix 4.2, Surfacing your educational values, provides some questions to help establish educational values.

Box 4.8 gives an example of a headteacher taking a top-down approach to creating a vision for a struggling school. This demonstrates that it is possible to change schools successfully without necessarily taking a collaborative approach. This example shows the way in which the headteacher persuaded staff and students to adopt her vision and engage with the changes that she imposed.

This shows that there is not just one way to lead change at a struggling school. Peacock and Coates had completely different approaches. Peacock encouraged

BOX 4.8 LEADING CHANGE: BURLINGTON DANES

Previously, in Box 4.5, The Wroxham School leader's participatory approach to leading change was described. In contrast, Dame Sally Coates, the headteacher at Burlington Danes, adopted a top-down approach. She used her expertise to create a strategic plan for the school and encouraged teachers who were not performing well to leave.

Coates et al.'s (2015, p. 19) view is that 'the leader must lead from the front'. Coates visited Burlington Danes several times before starting there as the headteacher and arrived with a meticulous plan of action. On the first day of her headship, she spoke to the staff about the school's strengths and weaknesses, aiming to demonstrate her confidence in the potential for improvement, as well as stating clear expectations of staff behaviour in terms of dress code, planning, display, attendance, staff briefing, staff bulletins and new systems. When the pupils arrived the next day, she held assemblies with every year group to tell them her plans for the school and identified the benefits of her proposed changes (which included improvements to the playground and the addition of table tennis facilities). She had earlier asked the heads of year to identify the most disruptive pupils and at the end of each assembly she called 15 to 20 students to the front, gave them a letter for their parents and said they would not be allowed back in the school unless their parents came with them to meet her – in order to discuss their child's behaviour at the school. Only one of the students was subsequently excluded.

Coates asked the senior leadership team to comment on the performance of individual teachers and subsequently met with each of the 23 members of staff (out of about 65) who were identified as inadequate. She warned them that she would be monitoring their performance. Twenty-one of the staff resigned that first year; the remaining two left the following year. This mirrors the 'punitive' approach of turnaround schools in the USA, with half the teachers being replaced (Liu, 2020). However, Coates also created a new staffroom and instituted a daily staff briefing, with individual teachers invited to share a moment of reflection. This could include sharing a personal story, inviting everyone to participate in yoga stretches or reading a simple poem. This, alongside professional development, time for marking, planning and collaborating, and occasional treats and benefits, helped to generate a professional culture of goodwill at the school.

The new approach to student behaviour, described by Coates et al. as 'rigorous' (2015, p. 202) included a one-hour same-day detention if students were late for school (even by a few seconds) and lining up in silence in the playground at the start of the day. Detention was, however, accompanied by a conversation with the pupil to discuss how to avoid subsequent detentions. Regular offenders were identified by one of the vice-principals, who liaised with the heads of year to arrange support for those students. Controversially, every half term, students in years 7 to 9 (aged 11 to 14) were rank ordered, based on their performance in assessments in all the 'foundation' subjects. The rank orders were displayed in the school, including hanging from the pillars in the assembly hall. In some cases the length of the list meant that the pupils' names at the bottom of the rank order were scuffed by those passing through. Coates et al. (2015, p. 107) commented:

> On the day they are posted, pupils are very excited: some elated, others crushed with disappointment. We often say that this process mirrors public exams and hold onto the feeling as a reminder of how you either want, or don't want to feel.

Coates was absolutely committed to ensuring that every one of her students achieved the best possible outcome while at Burlington Danes. This not only included a strong focus on learning and teaching, with regular assessments to identify progress (or lack of it), but also opportunities to develop their interests, with a broad range of clubs after school and at lunchtime. The school also held an annual tea dance and 'charity week' and experimented with extending the students 'cultural capital' by taking time out to visit key attractions in London.

participation and collaboration at The Wroxham School, whereas Coates was a top-down leader, inspiring staff and pupils to embrace her vision for the school. While both schools were subsequently judged to be outstanding, after Coates left Burlington Danes, an Ofsted inspection in 2018 judged the school to be 'Requires Improvement', followed by a 2022 inspection which moved the school to 'Good'. The Wroxham School was judged to be outstanding in 2013 (after Peacock had left) but has not had another inspection in the last 10 years.

How to identify 'change agents'?

There are different views about engaging with staff when implementing change. One is to search out those who are enthusiastic about the change to create a change 'task force' that ideally includes parents (Dudar, 2013; Lyng and Mortimer, 2011). In contrast, some leaders identify the anti-change agents or 'toxic staff' – those who are most resistant to change – and encourage them to leave the school (Peters, 2012).

Fullan (2016) takes another position. Rather than creating a task force committed to change, he recommends including everyone in the change effort, including those who are opposed to it. He suggests that all staff should be seen as change agents and that there are many benefits to teamwork: 'All successful change initiatives develop collaboration where there was none before. When relationships develop, trust increases, as do other measures of social capital and social cohesion' (Fullan, 2016, p. 48).

Clearly collaboration is an ideal approach. Fullan (2016) does not, however, explain how leaders deal with staff who do not agree with the proposed changes and who do not accept the leader's reasons for the change. These include teachers who are openly resistant as well as those who pay lip service to the change but do not implement it. There is also a danger that participation in planning as well as implementing change creates additional work for teachers who are already overloaded (Soini et al., 2016). Leaders, it seems, need to take a balanced view about how to engage staff with change, encouraging maximum participation while recognising and accepting that some staff may not be interested. Appendix 4.3, Preparedness for change and improvement, provides an activity to help to identify whether the school staff culture is likely to support change and improvement.

How to communicate with participants and take action?

Open communication is key to enabling failing schools to be turned around (Liu, 2020), but it is hard for schools to develop a perfect system of communication in times of change. If there is too little communication from the leader, staff may feel excluded and ill-prepared. If there is too much communication, staff may feel overwhelmed and anxious. The timing of communication needs to address these issues – ensuring that participants are provided with information that meets their needs when they are ready for it (Dudar, 2013).

Communication includes the way messages are circulated as well as the content within the messages. Leaders in Dudar's (2013, p. 251) study used the following means of communication to ensure rapid change:

- active listening, to detect areas of concern and needs for change
- written documents to communicate the change plan and schedules for the participants
- presentations by the leader and task force to articulate the vision and to provide feedback on ongoing implementation efforts
- one-to-one conversations to encourage resistant individuals
- verbal communication to praise and drive the change plan.

Two-way communication is considered more effective than one-way, because it ensures that the message has been understood, as well as enabling people to feed back their own views (Coleman and Glover, 2010). Dialogue can be a means of co-constructing meaning, thus facilitating ownership and participation of change (Priestley et al., 2011, p. 281). Providing opportunities at a relatively early stage for staff to discuss the proposed plan for change enables feedback from staff and a common perception of the endeavour. An important role for school leaders is to enable 'shared understanding in the professional community' (Soini et al., 2016, p. 460) in order to ensure that change is implemented effectively.

Time pressures may make it difficult, however, for effective two-way communication in large schools. Here, middle leaders can help: 'Middle leaders are able to reframe abstract initiatives and policies and articulate them in relation to locally realised practices in real terms' (Edwards-Groves et al., 2019, p. 331). In other words, middle leaders can translate school-wide changes into what will work within their own department or key stage.

The change plan typically includes participants' roles, the process for enacting change, key performance indicators and required resources. In terms of the process, principals implementing large-scale change in Finland reported 'taking small steps simultaneously on many fronts,' with strongly inclusive strategies (Soini et al., 2016, p. 464). Fullan (2016) recommends focusing on capacity building, results and action with a means of using information about what happens during implementation to refine the strategies.

How to address barriers to change, including the need for training and development?

Barriers to change may include lack of capacity, lack of resources and resistance from staff, parents, students or other stakeholders. Resistance and resources have already been considered in the preceding sections which focused on challenges and on how teachers respond to change. This section, then, focuses on the issue of capacity building through professional development in relation to change. Chapter 6 provides further discussion of professional development more generally in schools.

It is obvious that if teachers do not have the knowledge or skills to address or initiate change, then it will not take place. Professional development is, thus, vital for school change. At the same time, some teachers do not accept change, despite participating in professional development (Dudar et al., 2017). Johnson (2004, p. 282) describes how teachers in the five Australian case study schools in his research failed to engage with development opportunities linked to change:

> For example, some teachers at Mansfield Park quietly declined to participate in certain staff workshop activities they deemed to be 'too personal' or 'too threatening', even though they related to building better relationships with the students. An assistant principal at Eastern Fleurieu said that she noticed several teachers 'creeping off' from after-school workshops before they were finished. Others failed to return to sessions after short breaks. Others dutifully fulfilled their attendance requirements but contributed little to discussions or activities; some dozed or knitted to avoid full participation. These staff members passively 'went along with' whatever was presented or proposed but invariably returned to their classrooms unaffected by the experience …

Johnson's (2004) example demonstrates a form of passive resistance which had to be addressed by the leaders of the case study schools. There are times, however, when teachers do not engage with professional development because they view it as inappropriate. In order to prevent this, enabling teachers to contribute to decisions about professional development when a school is undergoing change helps to ensure its relevance and prevents it from being seen as part of a 'deficit model of training' (Priestley et al., 2011, p. 279).

Sanders (2011) suggests that, to support change, the system of staff learning in schools needs to:

- be systematic, assisted by a culture of professional enquiry
- enable the development of leadership skills
- allow individuals and groups of staff to share ideas and initiate their own projects
- recognise and value staff knowledge and use it to inform decisions about educational change.

The best form of professional development in relation to change is collaborative learning. Soini et al.'s (2016) research found that collective professional learning enabled staff to feel that they could participate in the problem-solving process and that their contributions were valued. Fullan (2016) suggests that group learning in schools is more powerful than individuals attending training alone. However, collaborative professional development does not suit everyone. In Finland, where Soini et al.'s (2016) research took place, teacher autonomy and professional freedom appeared to be valued more highly than collaborative learning, which suggests that some might prefer to identify their own skills development rather than learn with others. Fullan (2016), too, acknowledges the importance of individualistic, maverick teachers who are reluctant to collaborate with others but may be brilliant in the classroom.

Again, this leaves school leaders with mixed messages: to set up collaborative training opportunities (which might mean compelling teachers to attend even if they are not interested); to ask teachers what training they need and only deliver that; or to offer training but make participation optional (which might mean that the staff who need it most opt out).

How to monitor results and celebrate success, bearing in mind accountability?

The process of monitoring and evaluating change is sometimes presented as the last stage of a cyclical process, in which monitoring and evaluation leads to further change (for example, Lyng and Mortimer, 2011). There is a difference between monitoring and evaluation, however. Monitoring is the process of assessing the implementation of change at regular intervals, whereas evaluation is undertaken at the end of a project to check whether the original aims have been met. Monitoring the progress of change enables school leaders to gather timely feedback from staff in order to gauge the impact of the initiative/s and assess whether any adjustments are needed. In the example of formative assessment in Box 4.3, regular monitoring would have enabled the school to identify problems with the implementation of formative assessment before a whole year had passed.

There are a number of potential issues for evaluation in schools. It is sometimes difficult to assess the results of one particular change in the complex environment of a school (Fink and Stoll, 2005). How far can improvements in pupil progress be attributed to one change rather than another, for example? At what point should a particular change be evaluated? Many changes in schools have no clear endpoint; curriculum change, for instance, is likely to continue over several years. In addition, aims may be difficult to evaluate. White and Barber (1997, p. 51) state: 'Most of the educational aims which parents, teachers and ordinary citizens think important, happiness, personal autonomy, moral goodness, imaginativeness, civic-mindedness … do not appear to be measurable.' Schools need to identify how to measure what they value: otherwise there is a tendency to value what can be measured (Stoll and Fink, 1996).

In terms of who should be accountable for change, schools have to address both internal and external accountability. Internal accountability is when school staff take personal, professional and collective responsibility for school improvement (Hargreaves and Shirley, 2009). External accountability is when schools demonstrate their effectiveness through outside measures, such as inspection and attainment levels (Fullan, 2016). Clearly internal and external accountability are linked, and in recent years a school's ability to evaluate its own progress has become an important part of inspection (Macbeath, 2008). Accountability issues are particularly important for high-need schools. Coates et al. (2015, p. 199) argued that 'the need for accountability is especially pressing for schools in deprived communities where cycles of failure and low expectation can easily become entrenched'.

This is the backdrop against which school leaders need to identify accountability for change. For large-scale, national policy changes, the school leader is generally held accountable for the success of the change. The accountability for internal change is likely to vary, depending on the type of change and the structure of power within the school. For example, schools where there is distributed leadership are arguably more likely to distribute accountability for change. What seems important, however, is that the line of accountability for ensuring that change is implemented is clear to all participants.

Alongside accountability, it is important to celebrate success with participants (Dudar, 2013; Fullan, 2016). Praising staff for successful outcomes is a key part of the change process (Lyng and Mortimer, 2011). This can reinforce teachers' engagement with the change and applies a subtle positive pressure to keep going (Fullan, 2016).

How to maintain progress and create sustainability through cultural change?

Ensuring the sustainability of change is important but appears to be often overlooked by school leaders when planning change (Dudar, 2013). It is, perhaps, more difficult to sustain each individual initiative when many other external changes are constantly impacting on schools. The problems in sustaining change are illustrated by the struggle for schools in maintaining improvement: only about 10% of schools nationally in the UK improved consistently over a three-year period (Gray et al., 1999), while a study of 3,200 Californian schools found that only 16 maintained above-average achievement for three years running (Joyce et al., 1999). Consolidating change may be constrained by the type of school and its location: 'the daily challenge of maintaining a vibrant school in a deprived community is so great that we will never reach a stage where all we need to do is consolidate' (Coates et al., 2015, p. 227).

Change needs to be built into school structures in order to ensure sustainability (Sanders, 2011) – as indicated in Box 4.9.

> **BOX 4.9 BUILDING CHANGE INTO SCHOOL STRUCTURES**
>
> How are decisions about change made? If someone has an idea, how would it be communicated, discussed and approved? Is this routine or is it exceptional? (If the answer is 'my door is always open', then it is clearly not built into the structures of the school).
>
> (Sanders, 2011, p. 9)

The school leaders in Dudar's (2013) research study identified a number of factors which they felt contributed to sustainability: ongoing professional development, clear communication channels, consistent leadership, appropriate staffing, long-term plans and the trust of those who continued to support the change. Trust was developed through collaboration between the leaders and stakeholders. Change was more likely to be sustained if it proved to be effective and was properly resourced. Parents who committed to fundraising for the change helped to ensure its sustainability.

How long does a change need to continue in order to be judged sustainable? Box 4.10 provides an example of a school that was failing in 2003, transformed by the leadership team and where the most recent Ofsted inspection in 2016 indicates that the changes have been sustained in the intervening years.

> **BOX 4.10 LEADING CHANGE: MANNING SCHOOL**
>
> The Manning girls' school described at the start of the change process in 2003:
>
> > The walls are drab with the occasional example of graffiti. A couple of students run from under the stairwell at the sound of footsteps. Over the radio is the voice of a teacher calling for help with an unruly class. The site manager grumbles as he takes down another damaged display. A few students lounge around the edge of the Physical Education lesson, completely disengaged. The buildings from the outside look worn and tired with broken window frames and cracked windows. On looking up, a number of students are leaning out of upstairs windows, shouting to their mates on the tennis courts. As the bell rattles for break, students pour noisily onto the corridors, pushing and shoving to get to the queue, shouting and occasionally swearing. The staffroom fills with a cheerful yet tired-looking staff, dispirited yet again by this year's exam results and wondering if they will make it to the end of term.
>
> (Lyon, 2011, p. 72)

Leading change **109**

> At Manning School, the leader embarked on a major transformational process, which started by consulting with the students about teaching and learning. The school worked with external 'creative partners' to establish a range of creative projects. These were then extended through partnerships with local schools. Creative practice became embedded throughout the school, and it made a successful application to become a School of Creativity.
>
> Manning School has become Nottingham Girls Academy. In its 2016 Ofsted inspection, 13 years after Lesley Lyon became the headteacher, the school had maintained the changes which were put in place. It was deemed to be 'Good' and the inspection report commented on the 'harmonious relationships among the very diverse range of pupils'. Other comments included:
>
> - 'The school's values run through its work like the proverbial letters through a stick of seaside rock.'
> - 'Some of the pupils need a lot of support, emotionally, with their behaviour, and with their learning. They receive the support and told us themselves that … staff "go the extra mile" on their behalf.'
>
> (Ofsted, 2016)
>
> **More recently, the 2021 Ofsted inspection noted that:**
>
> - 'This is an inclusive popular and thriving school.'
> - 'A culture of high expectation connects all aspects of school life.'
> - 'Pupils feel well cared for.… Leaders ensure that they look after pupils with protected characteristics well. A group for lesbian, gay, bisexual and transgender pupils (LGBT+), for example, is further raising awareness of diversity.'

Clearly the culture of Manning School has fundamentally changed, with its values permeating the school and enabling continued progress. Changing a school's culture is considered to be crucial in turning it around, and cultural change is often achieved through appointing a new leader (Liu, 2020). Further discussion of organisational cultures is provided in Chapter 3.

The difficulties in sustaining innovation are described in Fink's (1999) account of the 'attrition of change' at Lord Byron High School in Canada. Lord Byron High School was a newly built school which began as a beacon of creativity, with a charismatic headteacher and dedicated, radical staff. Over time, however, and after two changes of headteacher, the school became much more traditional, losing many of the innovative practices that had distinguished it at the start. Fink (1999) suggests a number of factors which caused this reversal, including parents' preference for traditional schools, antagonism from other schools (which had, perhaps, envied the attention given to Lord Byron High School in its heyday), staff who were loyal to the headteacher rather than the values and concepts of the school and staff burnout after the initial exhilaration faded but lengthy working hours continued. A practical difficulty was that the school expanded, and this created problems for some of the original, cross-disciplinary structures, with a corresponding impact on the school's culture. It also proved difficult to maintain innovation while consolidating existing practices.

Fink (1999) concludes that, although Lord Byron High School became less innovative over the years, the staff who departed and continued their careers at other schools spread some of its pioneering practices throughout the education system. So perhaps sustainability of change needs to be viewed in the long term and across many school sites rather than simply the school where innovation began.

Conclusion

School leaders undoubtedly have a key role in leading change. They 'name and frame what it is possible to think and do in the school' (Sanders, 2011, p. 8). In order to lead change effectively, headteachers need a range of skills and traits. However, if they do not possess the appropriate abilities themselves, they need to identify staff who can supplement their own skillset. See Appendix 4.4, Characteristics of effective change leaders, for a list of the skills needed to lead change.

As indicated earlier, strategies for change need to be adapted to meet the needs of the school context: the students, staff, parents, governors and local community. What works in one school is not guaranteed to work in another. However, the research studies outlined in this chapter suggest that, in order for teachers to engage with change, collaborative, facilitative approaches are generally effective as they support their sense of agency. Building strong relationships between staff and leader also aids this process, as does relevant professional development. Establishing a coherent programme of change combining national and school-based strategies is an important task for school leaders. Promoting an appropriate culture with a clear vision and explicit moral values is also vital. Appropriate communication, planning, monitoring and evaluation are all considered key to leading change effectively.

It is not possible to conclude with a foolproof recipe prescribing how to implement change successfully in schools. As indicated at the beginning of this chapter, advice for those leading change is sometimes contradictory and much depends on the school's context. There are a number of criticisms of some of the theories which need to be borne in mind. For example, the idea of combining top-down and bottom-up change (Fullan, 2016) suggests that these may dovetail together. However, top-down change can interfere with and undermine bottom-up change and vice versa. The recommended approaches in much of the literature appear to be for large-scale change rather than the small-scale, incremental change undertaken by teachers on a daily basis.

Some of the theories seem to assume a certain kind of school in which there exists a team (or potential team) of hard-working, engaged staff, willing to add to their workloads in order to participate in and develop change, even if they do not agree with it. Many small primary schools have insufficient staff to create such a team of change agents. Schools in areas of economic deprivation tend to have high staff turnover, making the sustainability of change much harder, even if participatory processes are used. There is an assumption in the theories that people behave rationally when confronted with change, but emotions, past experiences and social interactions may result in unexpected responses from the teachers who are not amenable to rational solutions.

There seems to be insufficient acknowledgement of the difficulties facing school leaders whose staff are not functioning well, who have very limited resources and who are facing multiple problems (for example, poor pupil behaviour and attainment, staff vacancies or sickness, inadequate buildings, new national policies to implement). In these circumstances, a rapid correction may be needed, which makes the time-consuming process of consulting and engaging with staff more difficult.

There is also an assumption that there are adequate resources for change – but in England long years of austerity have left schools teetering on the brink of financial collapse. There is barely sufficient funding to maintain current activities, let alone embark on any large-scale reforms.

This leaves leaders in a dilemma: how can they encourage participation and collaboration without relinquishing their own responsibility to ensure progress? Ultimately it is the leader's head on the block if the school flounders. It is, perhaps, easiest to identify what not to do when leading change, as suggested in Box 4.11.

BOX 4.11 HOW TO MAKE CHANGE FAIL/WHAT NOT TO DO IF INITIATING CHANGE

- Regard any guiding principles such as an overall aim, vision or stated values as superfluous to requirements (because they are obvious).
- Trust no one.
- Adopt a change that has worked well in another school and stick rigorously to the same formula even if your own school context is very different.
- Avoid planning at all costs. As John Harvey-Jones said: 'Planning is an unnatural process. It is much more fun to do something. The nicest thing about not planning is that failure comes as a complete surprise, rather than being preceded by a period of worry and depression.'
- When preparing for the change, *either* spring it on your staff without any warning, discussion or explanation; *or* hold lengthy consultation meetings with your staff and

> then ignore all their suggestions. Whichever route you take, never forget you are the boss and the teachers are your minions.
>
> ■ When communicating with staff, *either* tell them nothing until the last minute (because it will make them anxious and because it's a useful way to avoid conflict), thus ensuring it's far too late for them to be able to prepare for the change; *or* send out multiple messages, often contradicting each other and/or so vague as to be meaningless. Regard any attempts at clarification by teachers as essentially hostile. Announce any major change on a Friday as it gives staff a whole weekend to reflect on (or stew about) what it might mean for them without being able to contact you.
>
> ■ Assume everyone will be as enthusiastic as you are about the change, even if it means more work for them. Ridicule anyone who makes any criticisms of it.
>
> ■ View the meaning of collaboration as consorting with the enemy instead of sharing with colleagues.

The preceding suggestions are somewhat tongue-in-cheek, but it is possible that, by avoiding these mistakes, school leaders could adopt change processes that are more likely to be effective and are best suited to their school's circumstances.

> **BOX 4.12 QUESTIONS FOR REFLECTION AND ACTION**
>
> ■ What do you regard as the main challenges of change at your school in relation to policy, stakeholders, resources and context?
>
> ■ What is the best approach to engage teachers positively with change in your own school context?
>
> ■ How will you plan and implement change, bearing in mind the need to establish aims, identify change agents, communicate with stakeholders, resolve obstacles, evaluate and celebrate success?
>
> ■ How will you ensure the sustainability of changes that you implement?

Appendix 4.1: Values and aims of schools in different Ofsted categories

Following are four examples of school values and aims (none of these schools included a vision on their website). The schools are all located in the same city, but each is in a different Ofsted category (outstanding, good, requires improvement, inadequate). See if you can identify which school is in which category based on their statements (answers in the footnote at the bottom of the next page).

School A (Primary)

Safe, Secure and Successful

In order to achieve this we must ensure that we:

- *Meet the needs of the whole child*
- *Provide all children with a relevant, personalised curriculum*
- *Develop pupil independence*
- *Raise pupil self-esteem*
- *Remove barriers to children's learning*
- *Value every child and take into account their views*
- *Work alongside parents, enabling them to support their child's education*
- *Support children to be aware of their rights which are set out in the UN Convention on the Rights of the Child.*

School B (Primary)

Push the Limits, Be Big Hearted, Discover What's Possible, Be Unusually Brave

We aspire to instil in all our pupils a desire to succeed in whatever they do, across all areas of school life and beyond. Our school is dedicated to providing the best possible education for every pupil in a stimulating and safe environment.

School C (Secondary)

Acceptance, Achievement, Aspiration, Resilience, Respect, Reward

Aims:

- *To ensure the process of education is a partnership between the learner, the school and the parents, together with the governors, employers and the community.*
- *To keep the child at the centre of this process.*
- *To strive to equalise the opportunities for each child to develop their talents to the fullest extent.*
- *To make the curriculum equally accessible to all pupils, raising their own expectations and society's expectations of them.*

- *To provide each pupil with the experience of challenging learning styles that value not only individual thinking, but also the collaborative skills of investigating, discussing and communicating.*

- *To engender in each pupil a thirst for knowledge that will be enjoyed throughout her or his life.*

School D (Secondary)

Think Big, Do the Right Thing, Show Team Spirit

These [core values] underpin everything we do. We strive to work extremely hard to support all our students to ensure they achieve their very best, not just academically but as well-rounded citizens equipped with the skills needed to be successful and to contribute positively to modern society.

See the footnote to check the Ofsted categories of the four schools[1].

There is a striking similarity in the values and aims featured on school websites – as evident in the preceding examples. This inevitably brings into question the significance of individual schools' visions, since it would be highly unlikely for any school not to want to ensure the maximum learning and development for every child. Nevertheless, while it is a question of nuance rather than a strong difference, the schools that are 'Good' and 'Outstanding' have a much stronger focus on the child in their aims.

Appendix 4.2: Surfacing your educational values

These questions (in Hallinger and Heck, 2003) can form a useful self-reflection exercise, or can be discussed by pairs or small groups of staff:

1. What brought you into education in the first place?

2. What are the elements of the school that you would want your own children to attend?

3. What would the school environment in which you would most like to work look like, feel like and sound like?

4. If your school were threatened, what would be the last things that you would be willing to give up?

5. On what issues would you make your last stand?

Appendix 4.3: Preparedness for change and improvement

Invite staff to complete the following questionnaire assessing the 'norms' evident at the school, based on Stoll and Fink (1996, pp. 92–98).

Cultural norms in improving schools	Extent to which this norm is evident at this school			
	Not at all	To a limited extent	Fairly wide-spread	School-wide
1. **Shared goals – 'we know where we're going'** Staff and leaders share a sense of direction which values teaching, learning and pupils' interests. This shared vision is regularly discussed and evaluated.				
2. **Responsibility for success – 'we must succeed'** Staff and leaders share a belief that all children can learn and that everyone contributes. Expectations are high, pupil success is paramount, and this is conveyed to pupils by their teachers.				
3. **Collegiality – 'we're working on this together'** There is a recognition of the importance of shared commitment and collaboration, for example, team teaching, mentoring, action research, peer coaching, planning and mutual observation and feedback.				
4. **Continuous improvement – 'we can get better'** However effective the school is already, the staff believe that there is still room for more improvement and they are encouraged to experiment with new approaches.				

(Continued)

Cultural norms in improving schools	Extent to which this norm is evident at this school			
	Not at all	To a limited extent	Fairly wide-spread	School-wide
5. Lifelong learning – 'learning is for everyone' Staff at the school are committed to developing their own skills and knowledge alongside those of their pupils. Teachers are encouraged to share their expertise with colleagues.				
6. Risk-taking – 'we learn by trying something new' Staff feel safe to try out new practices, even if the results may be uncertain. They are willing to admit to problems and find solutions with colleagues.				
7. Support – 'there's always someone there to help' There is a sense that the school is a nurturing environment, where kindness and supporting each other is prioritised even when people are busy.				
8. Mutual respect – 'everyone has something to offer' Trust and respect for each other, including for pupils, is important and diversity is perceived to be a strength.				
9. Openness – 'we can discuss our differences' People are willing to disagree openly and criticism is constructive. Conflicts are addressed appropriately.				
10. Celebration and humour – 'we feel good about ourselves' Pupils and teachers feel that their efforts are recognised, valued and celebrated. Staff socialise together.				

This activity can be used as the basis for a discussion activity in a staff meeting. It helps to identify what aspects of culture need to be addressed in order to enable change and improvement at the school.

Appendix 4.4: Characteristics of effective change leaders

Headteachers could draw on this list of characteristics of effective change leaders when appointing their senior leadership team:

- a lack of hesitancy (Bastin, 2017), high confidence in leading (Steiner et al., 2008), an unshakeable belief in their knowledge of what is best for the pupils (Berry, 2011)
- a focus on student outcomes (Bastin, 2017)
- commitment (Berry, 2011) and motivation to achieve the end results (Steiner et al., 2008)
- strong interpersonal skills (Bastin, 2017); able to engage diverse groups and individuals and offer emotional and psychological support (Fullan, 2016); strong influence on others to achieve results jointly (Steiner et al., 2008); flexibility and openness to thought processes and other people's way of thinking (Berry, 2011)
- able to change leadership styles from directive to facilitative and back again (Liu, 2020)
- self-reflective behaviours (Steiner et al., 2008)
- strong capacity in problem-solving (Steiner et al., 2008)
- humility (Fullan, 2016)
- trust (Berry, 2011).

The most important characteristic identified by Bastin (2017) is that head teachers need an understanding of their own weaknesses and the ability to find others to address those gaps.

Note

1 Ofsted categories. School A: Good; School B: Inadequate; School C: Outstanding; School D is Requires Improvement (on an upward trajectory after an inspection in 2017 when the pupils threw food at the Ofsted inspectors and the school was put into special measures).

References

Akshir Ab Kadir, M. (2019). Singapore's educational policy through the prism of student voice: Recasting students as co-agents of educational change and 'disrupting' the status quo? *Journal of Education Policy*, vol. 34, no. 4, pp. 547–576. DOI: 10.1080/02680939.2018.1474387

Barber, M. (1997). *The Learning Game: Arguments for Education Revolution*. Arizona: Phoenix.

Bastin, T. (2017). Accelerating change in schools: Leading rapid, successful and complex change initiatives. *Leadership and Policy in Schools*, vol. 18, no. 3, pp. 503–506.

Bennis, W.G. and Nanus, B. (1985). *Leaders: The Strategies for Taking Charge*. London: Harper and Row.

Berry, J. (2011). It can only happen on a Thursday. In E. Sanders (ed). *Leading a Creative School: Initiating and Sustaining School Change*. Abingdon: Routledge, pp. 17–28.

Black, P. and Wiliam, D. (2003). In praise of educational research: Formative assessment. *British Educational Research Journal*, vol. 29, no. 5, pp. 623–638.

Bottery, M. (2007). New Labour policy and school leadership in England: Room for manoeuvre? *Cambridge Journal of Education*, vol. 37, no. 2, pp. 153–172.

Braun, A., Maguire, M. and Ball, S. (2010). Policy enactments in the UK secondary school: Examining policy, practice and school positioning. *Journal of Education Policy*, vol. 25, no. 4, pp. 547–560.

Bryk, A. and Schneider, B. (2002). *Trust in Schools*. New York, NY: Russell Sage.

Burke, W. (2008). *Organization Change: Theory and Practice*, 2nd edition. Thousand Oaks, CA: Sage.

Carnall, C. (2003). *Managing Change in Organizations*, 4th edition. Harlow: Pearson Education.

Coates, S., Adcock, S. and Ribton, M. (2015). *Headstrong. 11 Lessons of School Leadership*. Woodbridge: John Catt Educational.

Collinson, V. (2012). Leading by learning, learning by leading. *Professional Development in Education*, vol. 38, no. 2, pp. 247–266.

Coleman, M. and Glover, D. (2010). *Educational Leadership and Management: Developing Insights and Skills*. Maidenhead: Open University Press.

Cuban, L. (1988). A fundamental puzzle of school reform. *Phi Delta Kappan*, vol. 69, no. 5, pp. 340–344.

Cook-Sather, A. (2002). Authorizing students' perspectives: Toward trust, dialogue, and change in education. *Educational Researcher*, vol. 31, no. 4, pp. 3–14.

Dudar, L. (2013). *Timesensitive change: Leaders and stakeholders' perspectives*. (Unpublished doctoral thesis). University of Calgary, AB.

Dudar, L., Scott, S. and Scott, D. (2017). *Accelerating Change in Schools: Leading Rapid, Successful and Complex Change Initiatives*. Bingley, UK: Emerald.

Edwards-Groves, C., Grootenboer, P., Hardy, I. and Rönnerman, K. (2019). Driving change from 'the middle': Middle leading for site based educational development. *School Leadership and Management*, vol. 39, no. 3-4, pp. 315–333.

Everard, K.B., Morris, G. and Wilson, I. (2004). *Effective School Management*. London: Sage.

Fink, D. (1999). The attrition of change: A study of change and continuity. *School Effectiveness and School Improvement*, vol. 10, no. 3, pp. 269–295.

Fielding, M. (2013). Beyond the betrayal of democracy in schools: Lessons from the past, hopes for the future. *Research in Teacher Education*, vol. 3, no. 2, pp. 47–50.

Fielding, M. (2015). Student voice as deep democracy. In C. McLaughlin (ed). *The Connected School: A Design for Well-Being*. London: Pearson/National Children's Bureau, pp. 26–32.

Fink, D. and Stoll, L. (2005). Educational change: Easier said than done. In A. Hargreaves (ed). *Extending Educational Change*. Dordrecht: Springer, pp. 17–41.

Fullan, M. (2016). *The New Meaning of Educational Change*, 5th edition. Abingdon: Routledge.

Fullan, M. (2013). *Stratosphere: Integrating Technology, Pedagogy, and Change Knowledge*. Toronto, Canada: Pearson.

Fullan, M. (2010). *All systems Go; the Change Imperative for Whole School Reform*. Thousand Oaks, CA: Corwin.

Fullan, M. (2008). *The Six Secrets of Change: What the Best Leaders Do to Help Their Organizations Survive and Thrive*. San Francisco, CA: Jossey-Bass.

Fullan, M. (2001). *Leading in a Culture of Change*. San Francisco, CA: Jossey-Bass.

Fullan, M. (1991). *The New Meaning of Educational Change*. New York: Teachers' College Press.

Gibson, M. and Simon, S. (2020). Losing your head: Are principals attached to their school? *Educational Management Administration and Leadership*, vol. 48, no. 1, pp. 25–44.

Gillard, D. (2018). *Education in England: A History*. www.educationengland.org.uk/history. Accessed 16 April 2020.

Gunter, H. (2012). *Leadership and the Reform of Education*. Bristol: The Policy Press.

Gray, J., Hopkins, D., Reynolds, D., Wilcox, B., Farrell, S. and Jesson, D. (1999). *Improving Schools: Performance and Potential*. Buckingham: Open University Press.

Hallinger, P. and Heck, R. (2003). Understanding the contribution of leadership to school improvement. In M. Wallace and L. Poulson (eds). *Learning to Read Critically in Educational Leadership and Management*. London: Sage, pp. 216–235.

Hargreaves, A. (1997). Cultures of teaching and educational change. In B.J. Biddle, T.L. Good and I.F. Goodson (eds). *International Handbook of Teachers and Teaching*. Springer International Handbooks of Education, vol 3. Dordrecht: Springer, pp. 1297–1319.

Hargreaves, A. (2004). Inclusive and exclusive educational change: Emotional responses of teachers and implications for leadership, *School Leadership and Management*, vol. 24, no. 2, pp. 287–309.

Hargreaves, A. and Shirley, D. (2009). *The Fourth Way: The Inspiring Future for Educational Change*. London: Corwin.

Hatch, T. (2002). When improvement programs collide. *Phi Delta Kappan*, vol. 83, no. 8, pp. 626–639.

Henning, E. (2016). *Transforming challenging schools through the leadership of superheads*. https://e-space.mmu.ac.uk/618718/1/Elizabeth%20Henning%20EdD%20thesis%20June%202017.pdf (Unpublished doctoral thesis) Manchester Metropolitan University. Accessed 15 April 2020.

Hotho, S. (2013). Higher education change and its managers: Alternative constructions. *Educational Management Administration and Leadership*, vol. 41, no. 3, pp. 352–371.

Hyman, P. (2005). *1 Out of 10: From Downing Street Vision to Classroom Reality*. London: Vintage.

Igoe, M. (2011). Change as an evolutionary process. In E. Sanders (ed). *Leading a Creative School: Initiating and Sustaining School Change*. Abingdon: Routledge, pp. 42–55.

Johnson, B. (2004). Local school micropolitical agency: An antidote to new managerialism. *School Leadership and Management*, vol. 24, no. 3, pp. 267–286.

Joyce, B., Calhoun, E. and Hopkins, D. (1999). *The New Structure of School Improvement: Inquiring Schools and Achieving Students*. Buckingham: Open University Press.

Kavanagh, M.H. and Ashkanasy, N.M. (2004). Management approaches to merger evoked cultural change and acculturation outcomes. In C.L. Cooper and S. Finkelstein (eds). *Advances in Mergers and Acquisitions*, vol. 3. Oxford: Elsevier, pp. 1–33.

Kotter, J. (2012). Accelerate! *Harvard Business Review*, vol. 90, no. 11, pp. 44–58.

Kurland, H., Peretz, H. and Hertz, L. (2010). Leadership style and organization learning: The mediate effect of school vision. *Journal of Educational Administration*, vol. 48, no. 1, pp. 7–30.

Lewin, K. (1947). Frontiers in group dynamics: Concept, method and reality in social science; social equilibria and social change. *Human Relations*, vol 1, no. 1, pp. 5–41.

Li, S., Poon, A., Lai, T. and Tam, S. (2021). Does middle leadership matter? Evidence from a study of system-wide reform on English language curriculum. *International Journal of Leadership in Education Theory and Practice*, vol. 24, no. 2, pp 226–243.

Liu, P. (2020). Understanding turnaround leadership research: Continuity and change (2009–2016). *Educational Management Administration and Leadership*, vol. 48, no. 1, pp. 6–24.

Lukacs, K. and Galluzzo, G. (2014). Beyond empty vessels and bridges: Toward defining teachers as the agents of school change. *Teacher Development*, vol. 18, no. 1, pp. 100–106.

Lyng, T. and Mortimer, J. (2011). Dance as key to full and effective student engagement and driver of whole school change. In E. Sanders (ed). *Leading a Creative School: Initiating and Sustaining School Change*. Abingdon: Routledge, pp. 56–70.

Lyon, L. (2011). If you always do what you've always done, you will always get what you've always got. In E. Sanders (ed). *Leading a Creative School: Initiating and Sustaining School Change*. Abingdon: Routledge, pp. 71–86.

MacBeath, J. (2008). Leading learning in the self-evaluating school. *School Leadership and Management*, vol. 28, no. 4, pp. 385–399.

Mackey, J., O'Reilly, N., Jansen, C. and Fletcher, J. (2017). Leading change to co-teaching in primary schools: A 'Down Under' experience. *Educational Review*, vol. 70, no. 4, pp. 465–485.

Maguire, M., Braun, A. and Ball, S. (2015). 'Where you stand depends on where you sit': The social construction of policy enactments in the (English) secondary school. *Discourse: Studies in the Cultural Politics of Education*, vol. 36, no. 4, pp. 485–499. DOI: 10.1080/01596306.2014.977022

McInerney, L. (2016). Superheads: The true cost to schools. *Schools Week*, Friday 16 April https://schoolsweek.co.uk/superheads-the-true-cost-to-schools/. Accessed 16 April 2020.

Nadler, D.A. and Tushman, M.L. (1995). Types of organizational change: From incremental improvement to discontinuous transformation. In D. Nadler, R. Shaw and E. Welton (eds). *Discontinuous Change: Leading Organizational Transformation*. San Francisco, CA: Jossey-Bass.

Netolicky, D. (2019). Redefining leadership in schools: The Cheshire Cat as unconventional metaphor. *Journal of Educational Administration and History*, vol. 51, no. 2, pp. 149–164. DOI: 10.1080/00220620.2018.1522296

Ofsted (2016). Short inspection of Nottingham Girls Academy [formerly Manning School]. https://files.ofsted.gov.uk/v1/file/2622055. Accessed 21 April 2020.

Peacock, A. (2011). Circles of influence: A democratic whole school alternative to a school council. In E. Sanders (ed). *Leading a Creative School: Initiating and Sustaining School Change*. Abingdon: Routledge.

Peters, A. (2012). Leading through the challenge of change: African-American women principals on small school reform. *International Journal of Qualitative Studies in Education*, vol. 25, no. 1, pp. 23–38.

Priestley, M. (2005). Making the most of the curriculum review: Some reflections on supporting and sustaining change in schools. *Scottish Educational Review*, vol. 37, no. 1, pp. 29–38.

Priestley, M., Miller, K., Barrett, L. and Wallace, C. (2011). Teacher learning communities and educational change in Scotland: The Highland experience. *British Educational Research Journal*, vol. 37, no. 2, pp. 265–284.

Pritchard, R.M.O. and Williamson, A.P. (2008). Long-term human outcomes of a 'shotgun' marriage in higher education: Anatomy of a merger, two decades later. *Higher Education Management and Policy*, vol. 20, no. 1, pp. 47–69.

Rayner, S. (2014). Playing by the rules? The professional values of head teachers tested by the changing policy context. *Management in Education*, vol. 28, no. 2, pp. 38–43.

Reck, C. and Reitzung, U. (2014). School turnaround fever. *Urban Education*, vol. 49, no. 1, pp. 8–38.

Ries, E. (2012). *The Lean Startup: How Today's Entrepreneurs Use Continuous Innovation to Create Radically Successful Businesses.* New York, NY: Crown Publishing.

Rudduck, J. (2007). Student voice, student engagement, and school reform. In Thiessen, D. and Cook-Sather, A. (eds). *International Handbook of Student Experience in Elementary and Secondary School.* Dordrecht: Springer, pp. 587–610.

Sanders, E. (ed). (2011). *Leading a Creative School: Initiating and Sustaining School Change.* Abingdon: Routledge.

Saunders, R. (2013). The role of teacher emotions in change: Experiences, patterns and implications for professional development. *Journal of Educational Change*, vol. 14, pp. 303–333.

Sarason, S. (1990). *The Predictable Failure of Educational Reform.* San Francisco: Jossey-Bass.

Sebring, P. and Bryk, A. (2000). School leadership and the bottom line in Chicago. *Phi Delta Kappan*, vol. 81, no. 6, pp. 440–443.

Sitkin, S.B. and Pablo, A.L. (2004). Leadership and the M & A process. In A.L. Pablo and M. Javidan (eds). *Mergers and Acquisitions: Creating Integrative Knowledge.* Oxford: Blackwell Publishing, pp. 181–193.

Smith, E. and Gorard, S. (2005). 'They don't give us our marks': The role of formative feedback in student progress. *Assessment in Education: Principles, Policy and Practice*, vol. 12, no. 1, pp. 21–38.

Soini, T., Pietarinen, J. and Pyhältö, K. (2016). Leading a school through change – principals' hands-on leadership strategies in school reform. *School Leadership and Management*, vol. 36, no. 4, pp. 452–469.

Spencer, D. (2001). Torsten Friedag. *Times Education Supplement*, 11 May 2001 https://www.tes.com/news/torstenfriedag. Accessed 16 April 2020.

Spillane, J., Gomez, L. and Mesler, L. (2012). Reframing the role of organisations in policy implementation: Resources *for* practice, *in* practice. In M. Preedy, N. Bennett, and C. Wise (eds). *Educational Leadership. Context, Strategy and Collaboration.* Milton Keynes: The Open University, pp. 131–144.

Starr, K. (2011). Principals and the politics of resistance to change. *Educational Management Administration and Leadership*, vol. 39, no. 6, pp. 646–660.

Steiner, L., Hassel, E. and Hassel, B. (2008). *School Turnaround Leaders: Competencies for Success.* Chapel Hill, NC: Public Impact.

Stoll, L. and Fink, D. (1996). *Changing Our Schools.* Buckingham: Open University Press.

Terhart, E. (2013). Teacher resistance against school reform: Reflecting an inconvenient truth. *School Leadership and Management*, vol. 33, no. 5, pp. 486–500.

Vahasantanen, K. (2015). Professional agency in the stream of change: Understanding educational change and teachers' professional identities. *Teaching and Teacher Education*, vol. 47, pp. 1–12.

White, J. and Barber, M. (eds). (1997). *Perspectives on School Effectiveness and School Improvement.* London: Institute of Education.

Woodward, W. (2001). Head on the block. *The Guardian*, 31 May 2001, https://www.theguardian.com/education/2001/may/31/schools.uk. Accessed 16 April 2020.

5 The empowered and/or squeezed middle?

Introduction

Distributed and middle leadership are two of the 85 'adjectival' leadership styles identified by Morrison (2009), which included authentic, autocratic, contingent, instructional, participative, toxic and transformational leadership. Distributed and middle leadership arguably move beyond a headteacher's personal 'style', however, because they are underpinned by the structure and culture of the school. Both have been shown to have a positive impact on learning outcomes (Leithwood et al., 2020; Harris and Jones, 2017; Li et al., 2021). Distributed leadership was, until recently, enshrined in the National Standards of Excellence for Headteachers in England (DfE, 2015). It was also identified as one of the 'nine pillars' of a great school (Woods and Macfarlane, 2022). Middle leaders have potentially more impact than headteachers on teaching and learning in schools because of their direct influence on teachers' classroom practice and professional development (Harris et al., 2019). Hence the focus in this chapter is on middle and distributed leadership.

Over the past three decades, there has been a strong emphasis on leadership, rather than management, in schools (Mertkan, 2014). This has a bearing on distributed and middle leadership because arguably, those working below the senior leadership level may be managers rather than leaders. Differences between leadership and management focus on vision and direction (leadership) compared to task efficiency (management). Leadership is about deciding what are the right things to do, management is about doing things right (Bennis and Nanus, 1985). Leadership is focused on culture while management is concerned with structure (Schein 1985) to maintain day-to-day activity. Arguably, it appears leadership is 'know-what' and management is 'know-how'; in other words, leaders have the vision which provides the rationale for action, while managers have the skills to implement actions to realise the vision. So management could potentially be just as important as leadership in creating an effective school. This point is made in a heartfelt plea by Ian Craig (2021), a former teacher, head teacher, inspector and government official – see Box 5.1.

DOI: 10.4324/9780429260612-5

> **BOX 5.1 THE LEADERSHIP VS MANAGEMENT DEBATE**
>
> Why are we, particularly in the United Kingdom, emphasising 'leadership' to aspiring heads and others rather than, or as well as, 'management'. Although 'leadership' within the profession is important, are we losing sight of what most heads and senior staff in schools and colleges are expected to do every day, and for most of their time, administer and manage? Headship, even good headship, is perhaps 80% management and only 20% leadership ... Let's not totally abandon our current leadership focus but let us once more also focus on management of the service. It is essential that we promote good leadership as a desired goal, but this should not be at the expense of effective management ....
>
> The 2020 Covid-19 crisis has clearly illustrated that governments and public services throughout the world have needed to adapt quickly and that good ideas are worthless without clear management of them. Educational institutions have been required to adapt their teaching methods, the management of staff and resources to deal with the pandemic, and it is clear that this will change the way in which education will be delivered in the future ... As never before, high-quality managers are necessary in all our educational organisations to ensure that new processes are clearly evaluated, managed into and during practice, and then constantly re-evaluated to ensure this. The 2020 Covid-19 'crisis' has undoubtedly highlighted the need for both high-quality management and clear leadership across all public services. A clear mission and clear goals are of little use without the efficient management of the processes and resources to achieve them.
>
> (Craig, 2021, pp. 55–6)

A key part of middle leadership is to develop and focus the activity of teams (De Nobile, 2018) within departments, year groups or key stages. Yet there has been relatively little research on how teams operate in schools and how best to lead them. In addition to a review of research into distributed and middle leadership, particularly in relation to challenging schools, this chapter will outline some key propositions and reflections about teams, team leadership and the differences between effective and ineffective teams. This chapter, therefore, provides a detailed analysis of distributed and middle leadership, identifies the strengths and potential difficulties of both and reviews theories and research regarding teamwork.

What is the difference between distributed and middle leadership?

Essentially, distributed leadership is shared leadership throughout the school, including everyone. Middle leadership is the layer of leaders between senior leadership teams and other staff. However, both terms are somewhat opaque and challenging to clarify, which has constrained research into distributed and middle leadership.

Distributed leadership defined

Leadership that is distributed has been dispersed throughout the school (Harris, 2010). It is a shift from solo or hero leadership to an approach that is shared or collaborative (Crawford, 2012). Leadership can be distributed to anyone, including Teaching Assistants (Amels et al., 2021), and allows influence and decision-making to occur at all levels in the school, not just the top (Leithwood et al., 2006; OECD, 2018). In Miškolci's (2017) in-depth study of two primary schools, one in Australia and one in Slovakia, the teachers in both schools understood distributed leadership to mean teachers could influence the decision-making process at all levels of the school and would collaborate on specific activities and to solve problems.

In their extensive literature review, Tian et al. (2016) defined distributed leadership as having both organisational and individual aspects. In organisational terms, they argue leadership is a resource which is multiplied through distribution. In relation to individuals, distributed leadership gives people agency at all levels in the school (Tian et al., 2016).

In distinguishing between distributed leadership and delegation the Gates Foundation (2017, n.p.) draws the following helpful distinction:

> **Distributed leadership is not about dividing tasks and responsibilities among individuals**. Instead, distributed leadership is concerned with the interactions among individuals (leaders and those whom they lead) to drive instructional improvement and improved student outcomes through the development of high-quality teaching and a culture where all students can thrive.

Distributed leadership can be top-down or bottom-up, democratic and autocratic (Tian et al., 2016). Top-down approaches, where authority has been delegated by the head, have been termed atomistic (Gronn, 2010) or devolved (Bolden et al., 2009), while bottom-up models, when small groups focus on an area of improvement, are holistic (Gronn, 2010) or emergent (Bolden et al., 2009). Lumby (2019, p.10) calls the latter the unique selling point of distributed leadership: 'the possibilities and potentialities of emergent spontaneous leadership, alongside the deliberative leadership of those in formal and informal roles.'

Middle leadership defined

Prior to the turn of the century, middle leaders were considered to be primarily heads of department in secondary schools (Harris and Jones, 2017). Since then, conceptions of middle leadership have expanded to include primary schools, a variety of roles (including pastoral responsibilities) and broader expectations. The change in terminology from 'middle managers' to 'middle leaders' reflects a development of the role from mainly administration to strategic activities that could have a significant impact on students (de Nobile, 2018). Management is, however, still important (Fleming, 2014) and is perhaps needed just as much as leadership in the middle tiers.

Middle leadership has been defined as teachers who have additional responsibilities beyond those of a classroom practitioner (Bassett and Shaw, 2018). This is a broad definition which encompasses anyone leading a subject, year group, key stage, special needs, pastoral care or project team. Essentially, middle leaders occupy a space between senior leaders and teachers or other staff and they have to liaise with them all (de Nobile, 2018). This 'go-between' role can be challenging.

Middle leadership practices include 'facilitating, mentoring, coaching, modelling, advising, workshopping, researching, managing, consulting, negotiating, collaborating and teaching' (Grootenboer et al., 2019, p. 253). Middle leaders also shape the work of beginning and novice teachers (Grootenboer et al., 2019). The breadth and demands of middle leaders' work will be discussed later in the section on the 'squeezed middle'.

From these definitions, it appears that distributed leadership is a concept, operational mode and cultural approach whereas middle leadership is a practice embedded within the hierarchical structure of the school. Distributed and middle leadership can be entwined because middle leaders are often active participants in distributed leadership. Research has tended to focus on one or the other, however, rather than both. The next sections expand on the popularity of distributed leadership and the importance of middle leadership while also examining the problems of each.

Why has distributed leadership become such a popular concept?

Some leadership approaches have had periods in the limelight (particularly transformational and instructional leadership), but distributed leadership has become the zeitgeist for our times (Lumby, 2019). It appears to fit the current more egalitarian, inclusive, culturally responsive role of schools in society (Brown et al., 2019). It is also a potential panacea for the complexity, intensification and extension of the headteacher's role: one person cannot do it all (Gumus et al., 2018). While transformational leadership offers inspirational motivation (Shatzer et al., 2014) and instructional leadership provides a focus on teaching and learning (Bush, 2013), both tend to rely heavily on the headteacher. Distributed leadership appears instead to offer an opportunity to relieve overworked headteachers of some of their burdens, a 'leader plus' approach enabling multiple individuals to be involved (Du Plessis and Heystek, 2020). It may enable a more diverse range of leaders working together to address the complex issues facing schools (Hatcher, 2005). In addition, there is some evidence that distributed forms of leadership improve student learning outcomes (Leithwood et al., 2020), but there are difficulties in proving this causal relationship in a complex school environment (Tian et al., 2016).

Distributed leadership offers potential benefits for teachers too, by empowering staff and giving them a sense of ownership (Hartley, 2010). A 2021 research study that included a large-scale survey of 787 Dutch primary school teachers and interviews with 58 Dutch primary school principals found that, in the schools with a distributed leadership approach, teachers were more likely to engage in joint work, share common goals and provide collegial support, and they had a higher sense of self-efficacy (Amels et al., 2021).

Distributed leadership is particularly appropriate for high-need schools in areas of poverty. In an in-depth study of ten schools in challenging circumstances, Harris (2002) found the most effective headteachers had adopted a distributed leadership approach (although the heads also recognised at times they used a more autocratic style). The headteachers of these schools worked through teams, involved staff in decision-making, built strong relationships and emphasised professional development – see Box 5.2 for participants' comments about distributed leadership.

BOX 5.2 EXPERIENCES OF DISTRIBUTED LEADERSHIP

The head has given real leadership responsibilities to others. It's not a case of just delegating headship tasks.

(Teacher S3)

The middle managers now have greater responsibility and authority for leading. The days of being in charge of stock cupboards are over.

(SMT S10)

In many respects we have more power than before. We are involved in decision making, we are able to take ideas forward and to challenge new ideas and developments. I guess we are more involved, more part of the decision-making process than before. (Teacher S6)

(Harris, 2002, pp. 20, 22)

Leadership in these case study schools was more fluid than fixed, with blurred distinctions between followers and leaders. There was 'a redistribution of power and a re-alignment of authority within the school as an organisation' (Harris, 2002, p. 24). These aspects of distributed leadership may also help to explain its popularity. Box 5.3 describes distributed leadership in two inner-city primary schools, from the perspective of the headteachers.

BOX 5.3 TWO EXAMPLES OF DISTRIBUTED LEADERSHIP IN LARGE, INNER-CITY PRIMARY SCHOOLS

Leadership has changed over time to give a lot more responsibility to the middle leaders and this year it is about what teachers can do for themselves and taking responsibility for their own classrooms and really being their own leaders in their own classrooms. This year we are looking at TAs developing their own practices and again become their own leaders. So you move from a top-down approach into

> a bit of versatility to be able to allow some people to fail sometimes and learn from their mistakes and take risks.
>
> Headteacher participant, Leadership for Learning Project
> (Menter and McGregor, 2015)
>
> We ditched the pointless subject leadership roles. That was step one; they don't really serve a useful purpose. We organised all teachers into leadership teams that include NQTs. Everybody gets into leadership teams. Everybody's experiencing leadership. We allow the teams to prioritise their work, set their own challenges and their objectives and we do that in as hands off way as we can afford and we budget time and money for teachers to do that work.
>
> Headteacher participant, Leadership for Learning Project
> (Menter and McGregor, 2015)

Despite its apparent benefits for schools there are both practical and theoretical challenges with distributed leadership which are discussed next.

Problems with distributed leadership

Distributed leadership is a slippery term, used to mean different things. There is a question about whether it is 'little more than a palatable way of encouraging gullible teachers to do more work' (Harris, 2013, p. 548). Instead of supporting innovatory practices, it may reinforce standardisation and hide the top-down delivery of policies under a democratic cloak (Hargreaves and Fink, 2009). In this scenario, the usual responsibilities of teachers are 'rebadged' as distributed leadership while the headteacher still orchestrates activities at the school (Lumby, 2013).

The issue of power in relation to distributed leadership is a thorny one and exists both within and beyond the school. Since headteachers operate within a hierarchical school system, they need to be empowered themselves in order to empower others (Du Plessis and Heystek, 2020). The tension between the need to 'achieve a workable balance between central control and local discretion' (Gronn, 2008, p. 174) applies to school systems just as much as to the experience of distributed leadership within a school. School leaders currently face unprecedented pressures (see Chapter 1), and with the high stakes of accountability it may be hard for them to 'let go' and support others to make key decisions. Du Plessis and Heystek (2020, p. 855) suggest those in the higher echelons of the hierarchy need to develop new skills, attitudes and knowledge in order to encourage distributed leadership in schools.

In state schools formal authority tends to stay with the headteacher (Gronn, 2010; Hartley, 2010), which inevitably limits the distribution of leadership. An in-depth study by Murphy et al. (2009, p. 187) found 'the principal's fingerprints were distinctly visible' in the creation of grade- or subject-level teams as part of a new, distributed leadership approach. Murphy et al. (2009) described how the headteacher intervened to bolster distributed leadership, for example, when the teams set up as part of the new approach proved to be ineffective, the principal 'tapped' a teacher to act as the informal leader and provided protocols on how to structure meetings. Lumby (2019) later used this case study as an example of the way in which power remains largely unaltered when headteachers distribute leadership, with other staff unable to take decisions independently. This was not the conclusion of Murphy et al. (2009), however. They believed that, by taking action to support distributed leadership, the school principal played a key role in ensuring its success (Murphy et al., 2009).

In more recent research into teachers' perceptions of distributed leadership in Australia and Slovakia (Miškolci, 2017), there appeared to be an assumption that the head had greater authority and more power than the teachers in both the case study primary schools involved. Miškolci (2017) concludes the very act of distributing leadership confirms the autocratic power of the headteacher. Similarly, in all three of Torrance's (2013) case study schools in Scotland the headteacher determined the way in which distributed leadership was enacted and retained overall control in the school. Lárusdóttir and O'Connor (2017), too, comparing interview data from middle leaders in Iceland and Ireland, found that the middle leaders did not feel that they had any power in their roles, possibly because there had not been a genuine distribution of authority and agency.

Authority is a crucial issue, which is linked to power. Leaders lower down the school can only carry out their work if other teachers see their role as legitimate. Murphy et al. (2009) found legitimisation was an important element of distributed leadership, which was achieved by the headteacher demonstrating links between teacher leadership and improved grades, advocating shared leadership and making explicit the power given to teachers to do their work. In some schools, however, it appears there is more focus on the technical aspects of achieving goals without staff having the authority and legitimacy to do the work, or to choose not to do it (Gunter, 2005).

The issue of teachers being free to choose *not* to carry out distributed leadership activities or to undertake activities in their own, rather than the headteacher's way, lies at the heart of the distribution of power and authority. If leadership has been distributed, teachers should have sufficient agency to be able to make those decisions; however, the headteachers are accountable for the school operating effectively. Thus, the differing interpretations of the headteacher's actions in Murphy et al.'s (2009) research (seeing the headteacher as nurturing distributed leadership as opposed to Lumby's (2019) view that the principal retained control) demonstrate a central dilemma of distributed leadership. Without a distribution of power, distributed leadership is disguised delegation, but when power is fully distributed, headteachers may be in danger of losing control of their school. Thus a key question about distributed leadership is: how feasible is it for school leaders to distribute power and decision-making to others when the headteacher continues to be accountable for effective teaching and learning, knowing that their leadership could be in jeopardy if pupil outcomes decline?

Trust, too, is an important aspect of distributed leadership (MacBeath 2009). If headteachers do not trust their staff, they are unlikely to distribute leadership to them. In high-stakes environments, it may be harder for headteachers to risk trusting their staff to lead key activities. Where trust is misplaced, there is a danger of distributing incompetence rather than leadership (Timperley, 2009). In a study of two secondary schools in Australia, Grice (2019) found some principals diminished trust by distributing leadership to 'spies' who could monitor compliance with their wishes. In one of the schools, teachers started meeting in secret to develop their own professional learning because they were unhappy with the middle leadership arrangements (Grice, 2019). This could be described as 'emergent' distributed leadership, but the development of such subcultures could also be seen as subversive and damaging to the development of professional trusting relationships.

A number of incorrect assumptions about distributed leadership are highlighted in Torrance's (2013) research. This study focused on three primary schools in Scotland. Four in-depth semi-structured interviews were carried out with each headteacher, who also completed a reflective diary over four weeks. This was combined with staff questionnaires exploring how far leadership had been distributed. The study findings challenge five taken-for-granted assumptions:

1. *Every staff member is able to lead.* Although the headteachers made efforts to develop leadership capabilities, this did not mean all staff felt confident to lead colleagues. Personal and interpersonal abilities meant it was unrealistic for some to undertake leadership roles.

2. *Every staff member wishes to lead.* In all the schools some members of staff resisted taking on a leadership role; others felt leadership was an extra which required additional time to be made available. Those who undertook leadership roles resented those who had opted out, undermining a positive staff atmosphere.

3. *Leadership roles of staff are legitimised simply by the headteacher's endorsement.* Staff did not necessarily share the headteacher's view of their colleagues' leadership potential: 'calling someone a leader did not make that person a leader' (Torrance, 2013, p. 364). Leadership roles for support staff proved particularly problematic.

4. *A distributed perspective occurs naturally.* The headteachers had to make concerted efforts to establish distributed leadership and it was an iterative process in which they needed to learn from their staff and vice versa. It was not a question of turning on a tap and allowing the leadership to flow across the school.

5. *A distributed perspective is unproblematic.* The move to distributed leadership caused friction, anxiety and resistance, and there were problems in determining the level of autonomy for staff. There was a lack of consensus about what distributed leadership meant and what expectations were reasonable.

Torrance (2013) concluded 'distributed leadership' might be an oxymoron and there could be better adverbs to describe leadership processes and practices in schools. Gurr and Drysdale (2013, p. 62) had similar findings in their research into secondary school middle leaders in Australia: 'The current focus on distributed leadership seems unhelpful and may indeed be exacerbating the problems as people who do not want to be leaders, nor who have the skills, attitudes or aptitudes to be leaders, are being forced into roles that have leadership as an expectation.'

Headteachers need to ensure the shift from hierarchy to heterarchy (shared power) does not result in anarchy, as there is a danger multiple leadership voices may create confusion for staff. Tian et al. (2016) noted teachers' commitment drops if multiple leaders supervise them. In addition, the role of senior leaders inevitably changes as leadership is distributed: they need to focus more on monitoring (Gronn, 2008) as well as staff development and ensuring relationships work well (Harris, 2002).

Other assumptions about the benefits of distributed leadership have also been questioned. Amels et al. (2021) found distributed leadership did not increase teachers' job satisfaction nor professional growth (in the sense of keeping up to date, innovating and reflecting). Lumby (2013) argues that distributed leadership does not address discrimination in relation to gender, ethnicity and other minority characteristics.

Clearly distributed leadership is complex, context-dependent and, to some extent, contradictory. It cannot be seen as a panacea, a simplistic solution to the multiple pressures on school leaders. A problem shared is not necessarily a problem halved. If distributed leadership does not work well it may result in more work, a problem multiplied. It is perhaps for this reason it has been dropped from the latest version of the National Standards for Headteachers in England, which 'move away from the aspirational nature of the 2015 standards' (DfE, 2020a, p. 4). In the latest version, headteachers 'ensure staff are deployed and managed well with due attention paid to workload' (DfE, 2020b, p. 7). Distributed leadership is not mentioned.

Why are middle leaders so important?

Middle leaders are usually active teachers who are responsible for other teachers or an aspect of the school, such as pastoral care. They combine working in the classroom with a leadership role, which makes them ideally placed to exert a positive influence on teachers' practice (Grootenboer, 2018) and on teaching quality (de Nobile, 2018). They play a key role in promoting the use of data as evidence (LaPointe-McEwan et al., 2017) and are seen as critical to school improvement because of their insider knowledge and their role in staff development (Harris et al., 2019). Li et al.'s (2021) large-scale survey of teachers indicated that, compared to headteachers:

> middle leaders such as subject department heads or curriculum leaders play a pivotal role in facilitation of professional learning, teachers' receptivity

towards change initiatives, implementation of new practices and, most importantly, enhancement of student learning experiences.

(Li et al., 2021, p. 239)

Although Li et al.'s (2021) research focused on English language teachers in Hong Kong, there have been similar findings elsewhere in the world (Harris and Jones, 2017). In England, Stoll et al. (2018) have reported on a project involving 16 'catalyst' middle leaders who had engaged with other 'Challenge Partner' schools. They concluded middle leadership had the greatest impact on pupil progress through networking, modelling best practice, championing improvement, supporting and coaching colleagues and tracking progress. The work of middle leaders is considered in more detail in the next section.

What do middle leaders do?

The work of middle leaders varies from one school to another and their roles are often ambiguous and lack clarity (Lipscombe et al., 2020; de Nobile, 2018). Although there are a number of activities and priorities that appear fundamental to middle leadership, some of these activities appear more applicable to heads of department or subject leaders than to heads of year or key stage co-ordinators. This illustrates the ambiguities of the role of middle leaders, but essentially, teaching and learning, managing relationships, professional development and administration are important for all the middle leadership roles.

Teaching and learning

A key quality of effective middle leaders is knowledge of curriculum, pedagogy and assessment (de Nobile, 2018). Middle leaders are essentially 'agents of teaching and learning' (Grice, 2019, p. 167). Their 'moral purpose' is having a strategy to transform learning (de Nobile, 2018).

It is essential for middle leaders to be expert teachers in order to gain the respect of colleagues; hence classroom teaching is an important aspect of their identity (Bassett, 2016). Within their dual role of teaching and leading, teaching tends to be their main priority. Indeed, in Busher's (2005) research study of six middle leaders in secondary schools, he found middle leaders identified with teachers rather than managers. In Bassett and Shaw's (2018, p. 753) study of principals and middle leaders in New Zealand primary schools, the headteachers believed the core role of the middle leaders was 'to be a classroom teacher first and a leader second'. This chimes with Netolicky's (2019) contention that middle leaders are teachers who lead while senior leaders are leaders who teach.

Appendix 5.1 offers a list of questions to help clarify the key tasks in curriculum leadership.

Managing relationships and supporting collaborative professionalism

Middle leaders manage relationships with senior leaders, teachers and other middle leaders – hence they work up, down and across the school (Bassett, 2016). They also manage relationships with pupils and parents. Building collaborative cultures and providing constructive feedback have been found to help middle leaders improve pupil outcomes (Stoll et al., 2018). Hargreaves and Shirley (2018, p. 20) advocate 'collaborative professionalism': 'forms of collaboration among educators that are professional in the sense of being open, rigorous, challenging, and evidence-informed'. Developing trust, being honest and respectful and providing support are all important ways that middle leaders engage with other staff (de Nobile, 2018). Linked to managing relationships, team leadership is often a key part of a middle leader's role (considered further later in this chapter).

A starting point for managing relationships is appointing the right staff, the most important task in running a department according to Smith (2001), in his memoir about working as the head of an English department in a secondary school. Yet this aspect of middle leadership is barely mentioned in the research literature, perhaps because appointments are often made in collaboration with the headteacher and other senior leaders, or because some middle leaders (such as heads of year/key stage) may not be involved in appointing staff. Box 5.4 summarises Smith's (2001) views about staff appointments.

Professional development

Developing teachers is a vital part of middle leaders' work. It is not just a question of sending staff on external training courses. Middle leaders improve teachers'

BOX 5.4 APPOINTING STAFF

Appoint the right team and it works in a creative, lively spirit. Such a department, with the saving graces of fun and tolerance, can take any setback in its stride ... People matter more than resources, more than facilities, more than the size of the classroom or the numbers in the set. Much more. Good colleagues inspire and encourage each other. They pass on what is 'working' for them; bad colleagues keep it to themselves and hope to show up the others. Good colleagues compliment and complement each other, suggest books, articles, radio and TV programmes, films, plays, approaches, strategies and hunches. They swap perceptions of pupils. They keep themselves and they keep each other alive. Such a department is as fulfilled and happy as a hard-pressed group of professionals can ever expect to be. On special days it hums, you feel moments of perfect harmony between yourself and your world and you walk tall.

(Smith, 2001, p. 196)

performance by modelling best practice, encouraging professional sharing, working with colleagues to identify strengths and weaknesses, recommending appropriate professional development, praising members' expertise and providing opportunities for them to exercise leadership (Li et al., 2021). Coaching and mentoring are also important means of professional development for both teachers and middle leaders.

Middle leaders gather information about teachers' practice through observation as well as through checking marking and assessment results. In some cases, however, the middle leader's knowledge of their teachers' needs is overridden by the principal's priorities. Bassett and Shaw's (2018) research on first-time middle leaders (in their first three years of practice) in New Zealand primary schools found that, although the middle leaders were key to developing their staff, in all six of the schools studied the SLT determined the priorities for development. This could prevent middle leaders from providing appropriate and targeted training for their teachers.

Bassett and Shaw (2018) also found there was a lack of development opportunities for first-time middle leaders. They concluded most of the leadership development in their study 'focused on the needs of the school rather than the needs of the leader' (Bassett and Shaw, 2018, p. 758). In England, in addition to development opportunities within school, middle leaders used to be able to take an external training course directed at their needs: the National Professional Qualification for Middle Leaders. This was replaced in 2021 by a suite of other qualifications:

- National Professional Qualification (NPQ) for Leading Teaching
- NPQ for Leading Behaviour and Culture
- NPQ for Leading Teacher Development.

From September 2022, two further NPQs became available:

- NPQ for Leading Literacy
- NPQ for Early Years Leadership.

Arguably these new qualifications better reflect the varied roles of middle leaders in primary and secondary schools than a general course for all middle leaders. It remains to be seen whether they will fulfil the needs of middle leaders to have an 'individual, co-created, leadership development plan that focuses on the dual purpose of achieving organisational and personal goals' (Bassett and Shaw, 2018, p. 758). The NPQs have been criticised by the Universities Council for the Education of Teachers (UCET, 2022) for relying heavily on limited sources of evidence: a narrow range of research produced by the Education Endowment Fund, focusing on 'what works'. Participants are not encouraged to critique the research or to carry out research themselves (UCET, 2022). Box 5.5 describes the impact of

> **BOX 5.5 PROFESSIONAL DEVELOPMENT FOR MIDDLE LEADERS: ACTION LEARNING SETS**
>
> As part of the Oxford City Council's 'Leadership for Learning' project, the middle leaders from 13 primary schools in areas of deprivation joined action learning sets which focused on different topics. Each middle leader then chose a project which would help to address issues within their own school context. For example, one middle leader focused on the teaching of phonics, because the outcomes of their school's KS1 reading test were poor. Through observation she determined the teachers and TAs were not using the correct methods and structures in their teaching of phonics. After discussions within the action learning set, sharing experience and advice, this middle leader worked with teachers in the classrooms, modelling practice as well as observing and giving feedback. This gave her teachers clear direction as to how to improve their teaching of phonics. In addition, she ran in-service training for all staff on the teaching of phonics. The impact was that the number of children passing the KS1 phonics test rose from 27% to 79%.[1]

an action learning set on the professional development of a middle leader (carried out as part of the Leadership for Learning project described in the preface).

For more details about different approaches to professional development, see Chapter 6.

Administration

Many middle leaders have to plan strategically, run effective meetings, manage resources, allocate teachers to classes and rooms, undertake timetabling, arrange supply teachers, oversee assessments, discipline pupils and liaise with parents, but research studies on middle leadership have tended to focus less on their administrative work than on other aspects of their role. It is, perhaps, concerning that less effective middle leaders tend to focus on administrative and lower-level management tasks at the expense of more strategic priorities (White, 2000). Yet middle leaders' power, such as it is, can be exercised most clearly in their administrative duties. Developing an appropriate bank of resources within a limited budget helps to support teaching and learning while, for a secondary head of department, timetabling decisions about which teacher will teach which class in which room at what time are an important element of managing teaching and learning appropriately. Smith (2001, p. 199) suggests the departmental timetable is the second most important task for middle leaders, after making staff appointments:

> You are deciding not only the overall picture but the precise daily nature of the job that all your colleagues will be doing: who teaches whom, each workload, who takes on the problem areas, how many lessons, how big the sets,

who shares with whom, etc. The head of department cuts the cake and there is a clear judgement being made in the cutting ….

Thus while administration appears to be a minor element of the work and has been neglected by research, it is nevertheless an important aspect of middle leadership. Appendix 5.2 provides advice on chairing meetings, a key administrative element of middle leadership.

How are middle leaders squeezed?

Middle leaders in schools are 'squeezed' in a number of different ways, including pressure from above (the SLT) and below (their own team), mixed identities as leader and teacher, and balancing individual with whole-school needs. More details of these tensions are as follows:

Whole school versus department/key stage/management area (Bennett et al., 2007). Middle leaders are torn between demands made by senior leaders in the interests of the whole school and the needs of their own department or area of responsibility.

Pressure from above and below (Harris et al., 2019). Middle leaders feel pressures of accountability and responsibility from senior leaders, on the one hand (to meet targets and demonstrate their effectiveness) and the teachers in their team, on the other (to listen to their concerns and communicate them to the SLT). Middle leaders have reported problems in their go-between role: they have to act as 'bridge and broker' between senior management and the teaching staff (Grootenboer et al., 2019) and may be in the unfortunate position of conveying bad news to both.

Leader versus teacher. Lipscombe et al. (2020, 1064) give the example of a school-based initiative, when a middle leader will 'often be the instigator, driver and facilitator, but as a teacher they will also engage as a co-learner and participant.' As well as combining their leadership and teaching identities, middle leaders may be torn between the demands of each area of their work. As expert teachers they value working with the students in their classes. It follows that time away from the classroom to attend to their leadership responsibilities is seen as potentially adverse to their effectiveness as a teacher and 'inconsistent with valued ideals' (Murphy et al., 2009, p. 192). One head of year in a challenging secondary school described the problem of being called in to help when teaching her own class:

> I shut my door, and I'm in my teacher mode and that's where I switch off and that's where I eventually find some time to relax in school, because the rest of the time I would have to say I'm very highly stressed…. People have knocked on my door, "Oh you need to …". Kids have been sent over, my personal phone being rung to come and deal with an incident while I've been teaching.
> (Middle leader, inner-city secondary school, Teacher Retention Research Project)

This middle leader felt torn between the demands of her leadership role and the importance to her of being able to focus, without interruption, on her classroom teaching.

Line manager versus colleague (Bennett et al., 2007) or *control versus collaboration* (Netolicky, 2019). Harris and Jones (2017, p. 214) noted a tension for middle leaders between 'a growing culture of line management within a hierarchical framework versus a professional rhetoric of collegiality'. Middle leaders have to balance collaborating with colleagues while at the same time exercising control. This was a major challenge for the six middle leaders in Netolicky's (2019) study.

Individual versus collective (Netolicky, 2019). It can be stressful for middle leaders to find the right balance between meeting an individual teacher's needs and expectations while ensuring the team is kept on track and moving in the right direction. Individuals may want to attend a particular training course, for example, which would consume the whole budget for CPD. The middle leader has to find an appropriate balance between satisfying individuals and supporting the team.

Restricting information versus trust (Lárusdóttir & O'Connor, 2017). Middle leaders may face the problem that they are in receipt of confidential information which they cannot share with colleagues. At the same time, it is very important they develop trusting relationships with their team. A two-year ethnographic case study involving three secondary schools in Australia found 'middle leaders lead with trust' (Edwards-Groves and Grootenboer, 2021, p. 279). Trusting relationships combined interpersonal trust (through mutual respect), intersubjective trust (through shared norms), interactional trust (through open communication and mutual learning) and intellectual trust (through middle leaders having appropriate professional knowledge) (Edwards-Groves and Grootenboer, 2021). Trust is based on transparency and honesty, so concealing information, even confidential information, may undermine it.

Moving slowly versus moving fast (Netolicky, 2019). Middle leaders need to maintain forward momentum to improve student learning while ensuring that the speed of new developments allows all staff to come on board. This might mean a slower pace is more appropriate for some staff, but the middle leader's targets require a faster trajectory. This has parallels with the need for slower, incremental learning as a way of embedding new practice (Grice, 2019) when there is pressure for quick results. See Chapter 4, 'Leading Change', for more discussion about introducing innovations.

In balancing these competing requirements, middle leaders face a further pressure: time. In a number of research studies, middle leaders reported they did not have time to complete their work to a satisfactory standard (Bassett and Shaw, 2018; de Nobile, 2018; Lárusdóttir & O'Connor, 2017). Lack of time leads to 'pressure, frustration, stress and worse' (de Nobile, 2018, p. 407). In Bassett and Shaw's (2018) study of middle leadership in New Zealand primary schools, middle leaders were expected to undertake much of their leadership work outside school hours. Even if this is not a requirement, some middle leaders in primary schools choose to do this to prevent an adverse effect on their class (Bassett and Shaw, 2018).

This is the case in England too: 'teachers' first experience of leadership is through subject coordinator roles, but these roles come without time release from the classroom, they come without any budget' (Headteacher of a challenging primary school, Leadership for Learning project). Time is also an issue for secondary school middle leaders. For example, in the Teacher Retention research study, one participant said the pressure of her middle leadership role led to frequent late nights:

> I could never get any marking done at school, because my free time is taken up by head of year, so I take my marking home ... I go to bed at one o'clock, that's probably every night, catching up on work I can't do in school.
> (Middle leader, inner-city secondary school, Teacher Retention research project)

Loneliness is another problem for middle leaders caught between conflicting identities. In Struyve et al.'s (2014) study of 26 teacher leaders in Flemish primary and secondary schools, middle leaders expressed a sense of not belonging anywhere. In addition, pressures of time may mean middle leaders are not able to interact socially with colleagues:

> I feel sometimes lonely at work, because I don't come down to the staff room ... I sit the majority of the time in my office with my door shut because I don't want to burden anyone else with my job, otherwise I don't get it done.
> (Middle leader, inner-city secondary school, Teacher Retention research project)

Middle leaders may find it hard to deal with difficult staff, particularly teachers who generally have an expectation of autonomy. Their own power is limited so they tend to rely on influence rather than formal authority in changing teachers' behaviours (Lipscombe et al., 2020). Such influence comes through collaboration and staff empowerment, engaging teachers actively in projects to improve teaching. However, middle leaders would benefit from more power. Those in Lárusdóttir and O'Connor's (2017, p. 432) research would have welcomed 'greater autonomy, responsibility and decision-making powers in their day to day practice than currently exists in the schools in which they work'. For those new to the role, having to prove themselves to more experienced colleagues while still learning the ropes is a challenge (Bassett and Shaw, 2018). To accomplish this (and other tasks) middle leaders need the support of their headteacher (Gurr and Drysdale, 2013).

How do middle leaders create effective teams?

A shift from the hero headteacher to distributed and middle leadership inevitably means a focus on teams rather than individuals (Harris and Spillane, 2008). School teams are also an essential part of managing change (Benoliel and Berkovich, 2017). Much of the research into middle and distributed leadership emphasises the need

> **BOX 5.6 BENEFITS OF TEAMWORK**
>
> In one particular school, a sceptical head realised how 'teams' of middle leaders could make a notable difference (McGregor and Browne, 2016). He indicated that he was 'reluctant to let go of control' but he enabled projects focused on developing different areas of school activity to be successfully led, driven and managed by middle leaders. One particular project he outlined, designed to improve the quality of writing throughout the school, was led by a middle leader working with a team of staff. New curriculum materials, ways of teaching and methods of monitoring impact were devised. The headteacher recognised 'growing your own leaders' was fundamental to future improvements. He had seen how the various teams meant that voids from staff being promoted and on maternity leave, for example, were more easily overcome. He also acknowledged it was easier for staff to share in-house their leadership skills to develop others' potential.
>
> (Primary Headteacher, Leadership for Learning project)

for strong teams in schools and collegial working, which is, of course, part of teamwork. Yet there is a lack of recent literature on how teams operate in schools.

Teams are defined as 'a small number of people with complementary skills, committed to a common purpose, for which they all hold themselves mutually accountable' (Katzenbach and Smith, 1993, p. 45). In Woodland and Mazur's (2019) survey, an overwhelming majority of their 1106 respondents felt that membership of a team impacted positively on their teaching. Teams can encourage shared understanding and expertise, develop teachers' skills and offer support to those who are struggling. As a result, they play an important role in improving schools. Box 5.6 gives an example of a headteacher's experience of developing teams in order to benefit the school.

What are the key theories about teams?

Although developed outside the educational sphere, the team theories frequently cited in the education literature are Tuckman's (1965) stages of team development, Belbin's (1981) team roles and Adair's (1988) consideration of the relationship between task, team and individual. Unlike other theories, these have avoided the 'tissue rejection difficulties which have afflicted many other attempts to transplant approaches from mainstream management into the working processes of schools' (O'Neill, 1997, p. 76). These theories are discussed in more detail and critiqued in the following sections.

Stages of team development

Tuckman was a social psychologist for the US Navy when he developed a groundbreaking theory on how teams form. His review of 50 articles dealing with stages of group development over time proposed a model for team development which has become well established. Tuckman (1965) argued that teams go through four distinct stages:

- *forming*, when team members develop an understanding of their task and agree on ground rules
- *storming*, when group members resist the group structure, express hostility to each other and react emotionally to the demands of the task
- *norming*, when the group develops cohesion, harmony and an openness to other group members
- *performing*, when members adopt roles to support the task activities, solve problems and have constructive interpersonal processes which allow the achievement of the task.

Tuckman and Jensen (1977) subsequently added a fifth stage, adjourning, when the task has been completed.

While helpful in understanding team processes, there are some problems in applying Tuckman's theory to schools. Unlike Tuckman's (1965) groups which were set up to accomplish a specific task and then disbanded, teams in schools are generally long-term (such as departmental, year group or special needs teams). In schools there are multiple teams, with some staff being in different teams, possibly with competing tasks to accomplish. School team development is influenced by external accountability constraints, limited resources and relationships with other teams in the school (O'Neill, 1997), none of which applied to Tuckman's (1965) groups. The model does not take into account changes in team members, which happen regularly in schools, and it ignores historical, political and social contexts, as well as under-performing teams. Although some short-term teams in schools may be formed by headteachers for a specific purpose and may also emerge from teachers' shared passions, they do not necessarily go through the linear stages proposed by Tuckman (1965). As O'Neill (1997, p. 81) argues: 'with many teams consisting of a fluid mixture of full-time, part-time and temporary staff, experienced and inexperienced teachers and professional, para-professional and lay members, it is reasonable to assume that team development is a fragmented, non-linear process'. So, while Tuckman's (1965) theory may be helpful in explaining, for example, conflict in a recently formed team, it does not necessarily assist an understanding of how long-standing teams in schools operate.

Morgeson et al. (2010) compressed Tuckman's (1965) stages of development into just two phases: transition and action. Based on an extensive review of the literature, they argue that, in the transition phase, teams focus on planning or evaluation to achieve their goals, while in the action phase, they implement activities. Teams constantly move between these two phases. The leadership functions for each of these phases are summarised in Table 5.1.

Table 5.1 Leadership functions in the transition and action phases of teamwork

Transition phase leadership functions	Action phase leadership functions
• *Compose team*, ensuring the team has the knowledge and skills to achieve the task • *Define mission*, ensuring the team is clear about its purpose • *Establish expectations and goals*, setting performance expectations and team goals • *Structure and plan*, developing a shared understanding of how to coordinate action and work together • *Train and develop team*, for example, through coaching and mentoring • *Sense making*, helping the team to understand events and gain perspective on their work • *Provide feedback*, reviewing team performance against expectations	• *Monitor team*, examining its processes, performance and context • *Manage team boundaries*, particularly the team's relationships with the rest of the organisation • *Challenge team* by confronting its assumptions and approaches in order to find the best way for achieving its goals • *Perform team task* as a leader by taking an active role in its work in order to enhance its performance • *Solve problems* by finding ways to overcome barriers faced by the team • *Provide resources*, including information, financial support, material resources and staff • *Encourage team self-management*, for example, by distributing leadership • *Support social climate* by respecting team members' ideas and addressing interpersonal issues and emotions

Morgeson et al., 2010

While useful, Morgeson et al.'s (2010) literature review did not focus on schools and, like Tuckman (1965), their conception of a team appears to be a project team with a fixed goal, which is different from the long-term teams usually found in schools. Teams in schools often go through a cycle of planning, action and evaluation, which is not reflected in the two phases described by Morgeson et al. (2010). In addition, Morgeson et al. (2010) do not consider the culture, values or beliefs of team members.

Team roles

Belbin's (1981) team roles theory has, like Tuckman (1965) been widely cited, although it is perhaps an urban myth that enthusiastic headteachers have subjected candidates to Belbin's team roles questionnaire when recruiting new staff. Belbin developed his theory about team roles while working at the Henley Business School. He and colleagues observed groups of managers undertaking a business simulation game in order to study how management teams work in practice. After looking at whether IQ influenced team success (it did not), they noticed that in the most successful teams people played nine key roles which helped them to achieve their goal. The original roles described by Belbin (1981) have been revised over the years and the most recent version with the positive and negative elements of each role follows (Belbin, 2022):

1. *Resource investigator*: seeks out ideas and resources for the team, is outgoing and enthusiastic but may lose interest rapidly

2. *Teamworker*: helps the team to operate smoothly, is cooperative and diplomatic but may be indecisive especially if a decision might result in conflict

3. *Co-ordinator*: focuses on goals, identifies skills and delegates work but may be seen as manipulative

4. *Plant*: solves problems creatively, is imaginative and generates ideas but may fail to communicate effectively

5. *Monitor evaluator*: makes impartial judgements and takes strategic decisions but may be seen as too critical of others

6. *Specialist*: has expert knowledge and skills and is single minded, but may focus on the technicalities rather than the bigger picture

7. *Shaper*: keeps the team's momentum and focus, has a drive to overcome problems, but may offend people

8. *Implementer*: develops and carries out a strategy efficiently, is practical and efficient but may be inflexible

9. *Completer finisher*: scrutinises work to ensure a high standard, is painstaking and conscientious but may be seen as a perfectionist.

Belbin's (2022) theory of team roles may not be entirely applicable in schools. The original research involved mainly white male managers, so the theory may not be appropriate for more diverse settings with predominantly female staff, such as schools. In schools, teams are rarely chosen to cover all of Belbin's (2022) roles. However, Belbin (2022) argues that people can play more than one role in a team and not all the roles are necessary the whole of the time.

Another difficulty in relating Belbin's (1981) theory to schools is that staff are likely to play different roles in various teams so it may not be easy to categorise them. Some teams may have vertical membership, for example, secondary subject departments that involve senior leaders, teachers and the head of department. This might lead to a clash of roles and values. Asong's (2005) research into teamwork in two socio-economically and geographically dissimilar secondary schools found that, for the four middle-level teams studied, it was the 'aggregate team profile' that mattered rather than individual roles. Nevertheless an important message from Belbin (2022) is that teams need to be diverse to achieve their goals effectively and a discussion of roles may help staff to reflect on their contribution and enable them to work more cohesively together.

Task, team and individual

Adair's (2009) theory concerns leaders balancing three overlapping aspects: the different needs of individuals, the task that has to be accomplished and the development of the team itself.

In order to achieve the task, the leader has to identify and communicate the team's aim and vision and develop an appropriate plan with targets, standards, resources and roles, together with implementing a process for monitoring and evaluation. Building and maintaining the team requires the leader to decide on its composition, establish and agree ground rules, address conflict, develop team spirit, identify team training needs, communicate and give feedback. In order to develop the individual members of the team, not surprisingly, the leader has to know each person; identify their strengths; agree their roles and responsibilities; support them; recognise, praise and, if appropriate, reward good work and understand their training needs (Adair, 2009).

Again, Adair's (2009) theory was developed in a business rather than school setting, with the idea that teams are set up to achieve a project, rather than exist long-term. However, creating a vision offers the possibility of a team functioning for a longer period. While it is useful to consider these three different aspects of teamwork, the focus is on the leader, whereas in many school teams there is a more collegial approach. Adair (2009) does not offer any solutions to the challenges for middle leaders in schools of managing well-established and resistant members of their team (O'Neill, 1997).

While these theories about teams were not developed in schools, they can nevertheless be useful to school leaders as a means of analysing how teams are working. For example, it is possible to consider whether a team is at one of Tuckman's stages, review whether Belbin's roles are sufficiently covered or identify the extent to which the task, team and individual needs of the team are being met.

What is the difference between effective and ineffective teams?

MacDonald (2013) has developed a 'team function, impact matrix' which suggests there are four types of collaborative teams in schools, based on how well they function and the level of their impact (see Figure 5.1). In the top right quadrant, teams work well together and have a high impact on students. They have a shared purpose and clear goals, make action plans which are monitored, and they transform teaching and learning. In the top left quadrant, team members collaborate well, but their work does not achieve measurable gains for students. They appear to function efficiently, but their chosen goals do not impact on student learning, for example, they might concentrate on a system for collecting homework, but not how to improve students' learning from homework. The bottom right quadrant represents teams that do not work well together, but nevertheless have a positive impact on student learning. In some cases these teams have excellent individual

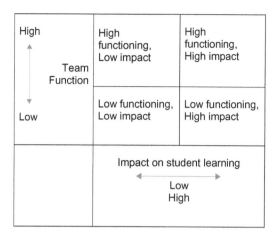

Figure 5.1 Team Function Impact Matrix (MacDonald, 2013, p. 31)

teachers who perform well. In other cases, a highly capable person can 'carry' the team. In the latter two instances, the team function is limited. The least desirable quadrant is the bottom left, in which teams neither function well, nor impact on student learning. These teams typically have limited goals, lack systems and procedures and tend to have disagreements and conflict.

MacDonald (2013, p. 5) argues that, to enable teams to move into the High functioning, High impact quadrant, team leaders need to value and act on the following:

- *Collaboration*, particularly shared learning of members focused on improving student learning
- *Shared leadership*, in terms of taking responsibility for each other's learning
- *Goal setting and attainment*, ensuring agreed goals will impact on student learning
- *Rigorous discourse*, encouraging evidence-based discourse and challenging cultural assumptions
- *Continuous improvement*, developing long-lasting change.

These values have some similarity with Goodall's (2013) description of high performing school leadership teams. Based on a study of nine schools, Goodall (2013) identified the following aspects of effective teams:

- *Creating and sustaining a team ethos*, which included the school's values and the attitude of team members
- *Clear roles*, including the role of the senior leadership team (SLT) and the roles of individual members of the SLT
- *Flexibility*, the need to be able to respond to change and new challenges
- *Valuing experience of other team members.*

Humour is also an often forgotten but important element of effective teamwork. As a deputy headteacher said in Wallace and Hall's (1997, p. 134) research, 'a team that can joke together can work together'.

While the focus of this chapter is on middle leadership, it is also important to consider the way in which senior leadership teams (SLT) operate in schools, partly because some middle leaders belong to the SLT. Senior leadership teams are different from other school teams in composition, activity and focus. They tend to include the headteacher, deputy heads and any middle leaders with school-wide responsibilities. Their focus is on the whole school, rather than a subsection of it. Based on in-depth research into senior leadership teams in larger primary schools (over 300 pupils), Wallace (2002) describes a number of characteristics that either promote or inhibit the effectiveness of SLTs, summarised in Table 5.2. SLTs may find it useful to review these in relation to their own team.

Table 5.2 Promotion and inhibition of effectiveness of SLTs, based on Wallace (2002, p. 176)

Aspect of SLT	Promoting effectiveness	Inhibiting effectiveness
Teamwork process and team tasks	• All members contribute to the debate • Shared sense of humour • Positive relationships • Good communication within the SLT • Head protected by SLT members • All SLT members collaborate	• Head dominates internal hierarchy • Personal disputes within SLT • Fail to communicate openly • Some SLT members do not accept head's ultimate responsibility for decisions • Bogged down with detailed administration
Links between SLT and others	• Good communication with others • SLT members united in public • SLT members approachable and accessible • SLT support and encourage involvement of other staff • SLT members protect other staff • SLT members foster consistent practice • Representation of all other staff on SLT	• Poor communication with other staff • SLT members disunited in public • Some SLT members unapproachable or inaccessible • SLT fail to consult other staff sufficiently and harness their expertise • Head out of touch with other staff • Head and deputy exclude other staff from decision-making • Head does not delegate enough to other staff • Individuals do not praise other staff • SLT fails to gain support of other staff • No time to socialise with other staff

Based on Wallace (2002, p. 176)

What are the obstacles to team effectiveness?

There are a number of obstacles to team effectiveness in schools. Teachers often work alone in their classrooms and value autonomy and control; characteristics that militate against teamwork (O'Neill, 1997). Intolerance by some team members and personality clashes may be problematic for teams (Middlewood, 2003). While constructive conflict is part of a healthy team, disagreements can make open interactions more difficult: effective communication is easier when people like each other (Nias et al., 1989). Where team processes and focus are not well-defined, time may be wasted in idle chatter, gossip and general discussions about students and teaching challenges rather than how to improve instructional practice (Woodland and Mazur, 2019). Agreeing on ground rules and occasional reflections on how the team is working may help to address this problem.

For senior leadership teams, Wallace (2001) observed that different expectations regarding hierarchy versus an equal contribution by team members could create problems. Where the head expected to operate hierarchically but the rest of the team wanted to have an equal contribution, there was likely to be conflict. Where the opposite was true, the team members contributed little to the SLT and expected the headteacher to make key decisions. Synergy could only be reached where the headteacher and the rest of the SLT had similar expectations about either a hierarchical or collaborative mode of operation.

Two major obstacles to team effectiveness relate to the context within which many schools are working. Firstly, the accountability framework that holds headteachers responsible for their school continues to render shared leadership 'as risky for heads as it is necessary' (Wallace, 2001, p. 156). Secondly, the high-pressure working environment of many schools reduces the time available for team meetings, shared professional development and social interactions.

Appendix 5.3 frames discussions to address problems in teamwork.

Conclusion

Distributed, middle and team leadership all appear to contribute to school effectiveness and improvement, but none of them provides a silver bullet for schools. For those looking for answers to the question, 'What works?' the response is, inevitably, 'It's complicated'.

For headteachers working in a system that emphasises checks (for example, Ofsted inspections, school league tables) rather than balances, distributed leadership will continue to be a chancy option. It appears to work best when heads trust their staff, engage them in decision-making and support their legitimacy as leaders, while recognising that some may not wish to get involved. Leadership roles defined by the headteacher need to be clear to all, including any boundaries to power and decision-making. Building strong relationships between staff throughout the school is important, through eliciting teacher voice and building teams that are mutually supportive throughout the school community. Appropriate professional development is needed to enable people to undertake new leadership roles effectively.

The term 'distributed' leadership seems misleading, suggesting something that is handed out or spread over a wide area. At the risk of adding yet more to the 85 adjectival leadership styles, perhaps this kind of developing leadership should be called 'empowering', 'enabling' or 'encouraging' (the three 'Es' of leadership) instead of distributed leadership.

For middle leaders to make a positive difference in schools, achieving balance is key, including between the needs of the school and of their team, between those above and those below them and between the needs of individuals and the collective. It means middle leaders valuing their leadership role as well as their teaching role in order to improve teaching and learning. Modelling expert teaching and encouraging professional development are important, as is understanding the needs of the students (for example, pastoral care, specific kinds of academic interventions, development of bespoke assessment systems). Middle leaders also need to maintain collegiality while addressing poor performance. Managing relationships is key to all these processes and, together with effective administration, empathy, professional development and performance management, provides the foundations for middle leaders to make improvements in teaching and learning. In addition, achieving a good work-life balance is important, given the pressures middle leaders face in schools.

In some ways, ensuring good teamwork requires similar skills to middle leadership. O'Neill (1997, p. 87) suggests: 'encouraging norms of openness, interdependence and a clarity of focus together with a clear, task-driven purpose and an explicitly collaborative process'. This is similar to the collaborative, shared leadership and goal-setting that MacDonald (2013) advocates.

Finally, it is useful to consider metaphors illustrating the role of headteachers which would be appropriate for empowering those in the middle strata. Portin (2013, p. 194) takes a musical stance, suggesting 'Principals can be one-man-bands, leaders of jazz combos or orchestra conductors'. This illustrates the difference between the lone hero at the top (a one-man band), those leading collaboratively (a jazz combo) and those directing teams of different players (orchestra conductor). Perhaps a more appropriate metaphor to encourage an 'empowered middle' would be a team captain in, for example, a football or netball team. The captain takes responsibility for the team's performance and upholds the strategy, but each member of the team has a clearly defined role and plays alongside the captain to achieve the goals. The captain maintains the team's morale, especially when going through difficult times. He or she ensures discipline in the team and mediates between players, as well as assigning positions based on levels of skill and experience. Of course, no metaphor is perfect, and this one, while encompassing some of the tasks of a middle leader, does not cover the importance of professional development and the way in which other 'players' take on leadership roles as well (Box 5.7).

BOX 5.7 QUESTIONS FOR REFLECTION AND ACTION

- To what extent is leadership distributed at your school? What, if any, of the problems identified in this chapter have you encountered in relation to distributing leadership? How have you addressed those issues?
- How are middle leaders at your school supported, particularly in relation to the inherent tensions in their role?
- What professional development is provided for your middle leaders and what professional development do they, in turn, offer to their staff?
- How effective is teamwork at your school? What steps could be taken to strengthen teamwork in your school?

Appendix 5.1: Key tasks in curriculum leadership[2]

The following questions are intended to help middle leaders to clarify their role and that of others in the school.

1. **Teacher supervision, development and performance management**

   - Who looks at teacher plans?
   - Who has an oversight of your work, ensuring it reflects agreed policies and practices?
   - Who is responsible for performance management, both for you and for teachers working in your curriculum area?
   - What opportunities exist to observe colleagues teaching?
   - What regular opportunities do you have to learn about teaching from your colleagues?
   - To what extent are there opportunities for self-evaluation?
   - Are there clear guidelines on effective teaching in the school?
   - Who is the CPD co-ordinator? How do they go about this task?

2. **Policies for teaching and curriculum**

   - Who plays the leading role(s) in formulating policies?
   - Who decides upon specific programmes of work or syllabuses?
   - Who considers the sequencing and continuity of programmes of work as taught by a group of teachers or across a number of departments?

3. **Resource management**

    - Who ensures resources are acquired and allocated in ways consistent with goals, needs and policies?
    - Who considers the use and allocations of time for both teachers and pupils?

4. **Quality control**

    - Who examines and evaluates programmes of study?
    - Who looks at the quality of the received curriculum (the actual experiences pupils have in the classroom and elsewhere)?
    - Who considers learning outcomes? (For example: Are we meeting our aims and objectives? How well are pupils learning? What criteria for success are there?)
    - Who regularly looks at pupil progress?

5. **Co-ordination**

    - Who looks at planning across programmes and teams of teachers?
    - Who examines the contributions of temporary and supply teachers in terms of pupils' learning?

Appendix 5.2: Running effective meetings

An important part of a middle leader's role is to chair meetings effectively. The following is a checklist of how to do this:

- Circulate an agenda in advance of the meeting – the agenda could include timed items and decision points
- Start on time
- Welcome people to the meeting. Ensure someone is taking the minutes.
- Remind the team of the purpose of meeting, perhaps identifying key items on the agenda.
- Pay attention to timing so that essential items have enough time allocated for discussion
- Encourage discussion through the Chair
- Clarify where necessary; ask for clarification if needed
- Ensure everyone is involved, prevent anyone from dominating, act impartially

- Following discussion of each item ensure appropriate actions (by whom, by when) are recorded in the minutes
- If necessary, summarise key relevant points during (and at the end of) the meeting
- End on time and thank participants.

Appendix 5.3: Addressing problems in teamwork

One way to overcome problems in teamwork is to go through the following processes with the team (based on MacDonald, 2013):

- identify the hurdle(s)
- explore possible causes/issues
- surface/elicit unspoken concerns
- acknowledge feelings about how things could be better/improved
- address the reasons for resistance/giving a voice to others to offer propositions and
- make a proactive response/develop action plan(s).

Action plans might include talking to individuals one-to-one, co-designing a lesson, modelling a new strategy, providing positive feedback, focusing on core principles in relation to curriculum, developing teaching materials or modes of assessment, establishing what is valued in learning and taking control.

Notes

1 For more information about this and other Leadership for Learning projects, see: https://mycouncil.oxford.gov.uk/documents/s17302/year%201%20Leadership%20evaluation%20for%20scrutiny%20groupo%20with%20whole%20page%20posters.pdf
2 Based on a questionnaire in O'Shea, A. and Southworth, G. (1992). *Management of Learning in Schools*. Milton Keynes: Open University.

References

Adair, J. (1988). *Effective Leadership*. London: Pan Books.
Adair, J. (2009). *Effective Teambuilding: How to Make a Winning Team*, 2nd edition. London: Pan Books.
Amels, J., Kruger, M., Suhre, C. and van Veen, K. (2021). The relationship between primary school leaders' utilization of distributed leadership and teachers' capacity to change. *Educational Management Administration and Leadership*, vol. 49, no. 5, pp. 732–749.

Asong, S. (2005). *Teamworking in Two Dissimilar Comprehensive Schools*. Nottingham: National College for School Leadership.
Bassett, M. (2016). The role of middle leaders in New Zealand secondary schools: Expectations and challenges. *Waikato Journal of Education*, vol. 21, no. 1, pp. 97–108.
Bassett, M. and Shaw, N. (2018). Building the confidence of first-time middle leaders in New Zealand primary schools. *International Journal of Educational Management*, vol. 32, no. 5, pp. 749–760.
Belbin, M. (1981). *Management Teams: Why They Succeed or Fail*. London: Butterworth-Heine.
Belbin, M. (2022). *Belbin Team Roles*. https://www.belbin.com/about/belbin-team-roles. Accessed 13 June 2022.
Bennett, N., Woods, P., Wise, C. and Newton, W. (2007). Understandings of middle leadership in secondary schools: A review of empirical research. *School Leadership and Management*, vol. 27, no. 5, pp. 453–470.
Bennis, W. and Nanus, B. (1985). *Leaders*. New York, NY: Harper and Row.
Benoliel, P. and Berkovich, I. (2017). There is no 'I' in school improvement: The missing team perspective. *International Journal of Educational Management*, vol. 31, no. 7, pp. 922–929.
Bolden, R., Petrov, G and Gosling, J. (2009). Distributed leadership in higher education: Rhetoric and reality. *Educational Management Administration and Leadership*, vol. 37, no. 2, pp. 257–277.
Brown, M., McNamara, G., O'Hara, J., Hood, S., Burns, D. and Kurum, G. (2019). Evaluating the impact of distributed culturally responsive leadership in a disadvantaged rural primary school in Ireland. *Educational Management Administration and Leadership*, vol. 47, no. 3, pp. 457–474.
Bush, T. (2013). Instructional leadership and leadership for learning: Global and South African perspectives. *Education as Change*, vol. 17, no. 1, pp. 5–20.
Busher, H. (2005). Being a middle leader: Exploring professional identities. *School Leadership & Management*, vol. 25, no. 2, pp. 137–153. DOI: 10.1080/13632430500036231
Craig, I. (2021). Whatever happened to educational management? The case for reinstatement. *Management in Education*, vol. 35, no. 1, pp. 52–57. DOI: 10.1177/0892020620962813
Crawford, M. (2012). Solo and distributed leadership: Definitions and dilemmas. *Educational Management Administration & Leadership*, vol. 40, no. 5, pp. 610–620.
De Nobile, J. (2018). Towards a theoretical model of middle leadership in schools, *School Leadership & Management*, vol. 38, no. 4, pp. 395–416. DOI: 10.1080/13632434.2017.1411902
Department for Education (2020a). *Headteachers' Standards: Report of the Review*. https://www.gov.uk/government/publications/national-standards-of-excellence-for-headteachers/headteachers-standards-report-of-the-review. Accessed 21 May 2022.
Department for Education (2020b). *National Standards of Excellence for Headteachers*. https://www.gov.uk/government/publications/national-standards-of-excellence-for-headteachers/headteachers-standards-2020. Accessed 21 May 2022.
Department for Education (2015). *National Standards of Excellence for Headteachers*. https://www.gov.uk/government/uploads/system/uploads/attachment_data/file/396247/National_Standards_of_Excellence_for_Headteachers.pdf. Accessed 23 November 2016.
Du Plessis, A. and Heystek, J. (2020). Possibilities for distributed leadership in South African schools: Policy ambiguities and blind spots. *Educational Management Administration and Leadership*, vol. 48, no. 5, pp. 840–860.
Edwards-Groves, C. and Grootenboer, P. (2021). Conceptualising five dimensions of relational trust: Implications for middle leadership. *School Leadership & Management*, vol. 41, no. 3, pp. 260–283. DOI: 10.1080/13632434.2021.1915761
Fleming, P. (2014). *Successful Middle Leadership in Secondary Schools*. London: Routledge.

Gates Foundation (2017). Four key things to know about distributed leadership. https://usprogram.gatesfoundation.org/news-and-insights/articles/4-key-things-to-know-about-distributed-leadership. Accessed 22 May 2022.

Grice, C. (2019). 007 Spies, surveillance and pedagogical middle leadership: For the good of the empire of education. *Journal of Educational Administration and History*, 51:2, 165–181. DOI: 10.1080/00220620.2019.1583173

Goodall, J. (2013). Recruit for attitude, train for skills: Creating high performing leadership teams. *Educational Management Administration and Leadership*, vol. 41, no. 2, pp. 199–213.

Gronn, P. (2008). The future of distributed leadership. *Journal of Educational Administration*, vol. 46, no. 2, pp. 141–158.

Gronn, P. (2010). Where to next for educational leadership? In T. Bush, L. Bell, and D. Middlewood (eds). *The Principles of Educational Leadership and Management*. London: Sage, pp. 70–85.

Grootenboer, P. (2018). *The Practices of School Middle Leadership*. Singapore: Springer.

Grootenboer, P., Edwards-Groves, C. and Rönnerman, K. (2019). Understanding middle leadership: Practices and policies, *School Leadership & Management*, vol. 39, nos. 3–4, 251–254. DOI: 10.1080/13632434.2019.1611712

Gumus, S., Bellibas, M.S., Esen, M. and Gumus, E. (2018). A systematic review of studies on leadership models in educational research from 1980 to 2014. *Educational Management Administration & Leadership*, vol. 46, no. 1, pp. 25–48. DOI: 10.1177/1741143216659296

Gunter, H. (2005). *Leading Teachers*. London: Continuum.

Gurr, D. and Drysdale, L. (2013). Middle-level secondary school leaders. *Journal of Educational Administration*, vol. 51, no. 1, pp. 55–71. DOI: 10.1108/09578231311291431

Hargreaves, A. and Fink, D. (2009). Distributed leadership: Democracy or delivery? In A. Harris (ed). *Distributed Leadership: Different Perspectives*. Dordrecht, the Netherlands: Springer Press, pp. 181–193.

Hargreaves, A. and Shirley, D. (2018). *Leading from the Middle: Spreading learning, wellbeing and identity across Ontario*. Council of Ontario Directors of Education Report. Ontario: Code Consortium.

Harris, A. (2002). Effective leadership in schools facing challenging contexts. *School Leadership & Management*, vol. 22, no. 1, pp. 15–26. DOI: 10.1080/13632430220143024a

Harris, A. (2013). Distributed leadership: Friend or foe? *Educational Management Administration and Leadership*, vol. 41, no. 5, pp. 545–554.

Harris, A. (2010). Distributed leadership: Current evidence and future directions. In T. Bush, L. Bell, and D. Middlewood (eds). *The Principles of Educational Leadership and Management*. London: Sage, pp. 55–69.

Harris, A., Jones, M., Ismail, N. and Nguyen, D. (2019). Middle leaders and middle leadership in schools: Exploring the knowledge base (2003–2017). *School Leadership and Management*, vol. 39, nos. 3–4, pp. 255–277 DOI: 10.1080/13632434.2019.1578738

Harris, A. and Jones, M. (2017). Middle leaders matter: Reflections, recognition, and renaissance. *School Leadership & Management*, vol. 37, no. 3, pp. 213–216. DOI: 10.1080/13632434.2017.1323398

Harris, A. and Spillane, J. (2008). Distributed leadership through the looking glass. *Management in Education*, vol. 22, no. 1, pp. 31–34.

Hartley, D. (2010). Paradigms: How far does research in distributed leadership stretch? *Educational Management, Administration and Leadership*, vol. 38, no. 3, pp. 271–285.

Hatcher, R. (2005). The distribution of leadership and power in schools. *British Journal of Sociology of Education*, vol. 26, no. 2, pp. 253–267.

Katzenbach, J. and Smith, D. (1993). *The Wisdom of Teams*. New York, NY: Harper Collins.

LaPointe-McEwan, D., DeLuca, C. and Klinger, D. (2017). Supporting evidence use in networked professional learning: The role of the middle leader. *Educational Research*, vol. 59, no. 2, pp. 136–153. DOI: 10.1080/00131881.2017.1304346

Lárusdóttir, S.H. and O'Connor, E. (2017). Distributed leadership and middle leadership practice in schools: A disconnect? *Irish Educational Studies*, vol. 36, no. 4, pp. 423–438. DOI: 10.1080/03323315.2017.1333444

Leithwood, K., Harris, A. and Hopkins, D. (2020). Seven strong claims about successful school leadership revisited. *School Leadership & Management*, vol. 40, no. 1, pp. 5–22. DOI: 10.1080/13632434.2019.1596077

Leithwood, K., Macsall, B., Strauss, T., Sacks, R., Memon, N. and Yaskina, G. (2006). *Distributed Leadership to Make Schools Smarter*. Ontario: Research Report Social Sciences and Humanities Research Council of Canada.

Li, S., Poon, A., Lai, T. and Tam, S. (2021). Does middle leadership matter? Evidence from a study of system-wide reform on English language curriculum. *International Journal of Leadership in Education Theory and Practice*, vol. 24, no. 2, pp 226–243.

Lipscombe, K., Tindall-Ford, S. and Gootenboer, P. (2020). Middle leading and influence in two Australian schools. *Educational Management Administration and Leadership*, vol. 48, no. 6, pp. 1063–1079.

Lumby, J. (2013). Distributed leadership: The uses and abuses of power. *Educational Management Administration & Leadership*, vol. 41, no. 5, pp. 581–597.

Lumby, J. (2019). Distributed leadership and bureaucracy. *Educational Management Administration and Leadership*, vol. 47, no. 1, pp. 5–19.

MacBeath, J. (2009). Distributed leadership: Paradigms, policy and paradox. In K. Leithwood, B. Mascall, T. Strauss (eds). *Distributed Leadership According to the Evidence*. London: Routledge, pp. 49–57.

MacDonald, E. (2013). *The Skillful Team Leader: A Resource for Overcoming Hurdles to Professional Learning for Student Achievement*. London: Sage.

McGregor, D. and Browne, L. (2016). Review of the Impact of Oxford City Council's Education Attainment Programme (2012–2014) Oxford City Council. Available at https://www.oxford.gov.uk. Accessed 1 May 2023.

Menter, I. and McGregor, D. (2015). *Leadership for Learning 2012 – 2014. Evaluation Report. Oxford City Council*. Available at https://www.oxford.gov.uk. Accessed 9 June 2023.

Mertkan, S. (2014). In search of leadership: What happened to management? *Educational Management Administration & Leadership*, vol. 42, no. 2, pp. 226–242. DOI: 10.1177/1741143213499252

Middlewood, D. (2003). Managing through teams. In J. Lumby, D. Middlewood and E. Kaabwe (eds). *Managing Human Resources in South African Schools*. London: Commonwealth Secretariat, pp. 171–186.

Miškolci, J. (2017). Contradictions in practising distributed leadership in public primary schools in New South Wales (Australia) and Slovakia. *School Leadership & Management*, 37:3, 234–253. DOI: 10.1080/13632434.2017.1293632

Morgeson, F.P., DeRue, D.S. and Karam, E.P. (2010). Leadership in teams: A functional approach to understanding leadership structures and processes. *Journal of Management*, vol. 36, no. 1, pp. 5–39.

Morrison, M. (2009). *Leadership and learning: Matters of social justice*. Charlotte, N.C.: Information Age Publishing.

Murphy, J., Smylie, M., Mayrowetz, D. and Seashore Louis, K. (2009). The role of the principal in fostering the development of distributed leadership. *School Leadership and Management*, vol. 29, no. 2, pp. 181–214. DOI: 10.1080/13632430902775699

Netolicky, D. (2019). Redefining leadership in schools: The Cheshire Cat as unconventional metaphor. *Journal of Educational Administration and History*, vol. 51, no. 2, pp. 149–164. DOI: 10.1080/00220620.2018.1522296

Nias, J., Southworth, G. and Yeomans, R. (1989). *Staff Relationships in the Primary School*. London: Cassell.

O'Neill, J. (1997). Managing through teams. In T. Bush and D. Middlewood (eds). *Managing People in Education*. London: Paul Chapman Publishing, pp. 76–90.

Organisation for Economic Co-operation and Development. (2018). *TALIS 2018 technical report*. https://www.oecd.org/education/talis/TALIS_2018_Technical_Report.pdf

Portin, B. (2013). What does it take to lead a school? In J. Harvey, N. Cambron-McCabe, L. Cunningham, R. Koff (eds). *The Superintendent's Fieldbook*, 2nd edition. London: Corwin, pp. 194–203.

Schein, E.H. (1985). *Organizational Culture and Leadership*. San Francisco, CA: Jossey-Bass.

Shatzer, R., Caldarella, P., Hallam, P. and Brown, B. (2014). Comparing the effects of instructional and transformational leadership on student achievement: Implications for practice. *Educational Management, Administration and Leadership*, vol. 42, no. 4, pp. 445–459.

Smith, J. (2001). *The Learning Game: A Teacher's Inspirational Story*. London: Abacus.

Stoll, L., Brown, C. and Spence-Thomas, K. (2018). Teacher leadership within and across professional learning communities. In A. Harris, M. Jones and J. Huffman (eds). *Teachers Leading Educational Reform*. Abingdon: Routledge, pp. 67–87.

Struyve, C., Meredith, C. and Gielen, S. (2014). Who am I and where do I belong? The perception and evaluation of teacher leaders concerning teacher leadership practices and micropolitics in schools. *Journal of Educational Change*, vol. 15, no. 2, pp. 203–230. DOI: 10.1007/s10833-013-9226-5

Tian, M., Risku, M. and Collin, K. (2016). A meta-analysis of distributed leadership from 2002 to 2013: Theory development, empirical evidence and future research focus. *Educational Management Administration and Leadership*, vol. 44, no. 1, pp. 146–164. DOI: 10.1177/1741143214558576

Timperley, H. (2009). Distributing leadership to improve outcomes for students. In K. Leithwood, B. Mascall, T. Strauss (eds). *Distributed Leadership According to the Evidence*. London: Routledge, pp. 197–223.

Torrance, D. (2013). Distributed leadership: Challenging five generally held assumptions. *School Leadership and Management*, vol. 33, no. 4, pp. 354–372. DOI: 10.1080/13632434.2013.813463

Tuckman, B. (1965). Developmental sequence in small groups. *Psychological Bulletin*, vol. 63, no. 6, pp. 384–399. DOI: 10.1037/h0022100

Tuckman, B. and Jensen, M. (1977). Stages of small-group development revisited. *Group & Rganization Studies*, vol. 2, no. 4, pp. 419–427. DOI: 10.1177/105960117700200404

UCET (Universities' Council for the Education of Teachers) (2022). Golden thread or gilded cage? An analysis of Department for Education support for the continuing professional development of teachers. Accessed 5 October 2023.

Wallace, M. (2001). Sharing leadership of schools through teamwork: A justifiable risk? *Educational Management and Administration*, vol. 29, no. 2, pp 153–167. DOI: 10.1177/0263211X010292002

Wallace, M. (2002). Modelling distributed leadership and management effectiveness: Primary school senior management teams in England and Wales. *School Effectiveness and School Improvement*, vol. 13, no. 2, pp. 163–186. DOI: 10.1076/sesi.13.2.163.3433

Wallace, M. and Hall, V. (1997). The dynamics of teams. In M. Crawford, L. Kydd and C. Riches (eds). *Leadership and Teams in Educational Management*. Buckingham: Open University Press, pp. 130–143.

White, P. (2000). *The Leadership of Curriculum Area Middle Managers in Selected Victorian Government Secondary Schools*, doctoral thesis, The University of Melbourne, Melbourne.

Woodland, R.H. and Mazur, R. (2019). Of teams and ties: Examining the relationship between formal and informal instructional support networks. *Educational Administration Quarterly*, vol. 55, no. 1, pp. 42–72. DOI: 10.1177/0013161X18785868

Woods, D. and Macfarlane, R. (2022). What makes a great school now? In T. Greany and P. Earley (eds). *School Leadership and Education System Reform*, 2nd edition. London: Bloomsbury, pp. 61–70.

6 Leading professional development

Introduction

When candidates for headteacher posts are asked how they will bring about the change they want to see in the school a common response is, 'By developing the staff'. A simplified equation derived from this assumption might look like this:

> Headteacher strategy + Teacher professional development = Improvement throughout the school

Somewhat similar to the idea of an equation, a logical chain has been proposed for teacher professional development, leading eventually to improvements in pupil achievements:

> Professional development → changes within teacher → enacted through teaching → changes within pupil → pupil performance (achievement).
> (Sims et al., 2021, p. 12)

These imply the school leader is 'the grand manipulator of inputs in a rational system, coordinating school improvement by applying 'CPD apps' to teacher deficits' (Mitchell, 2013, p. 395). The problem with equations or logical chains of action (Ofsted, 2006), however, is that schools are complex organisations where multiple unexpected events can derail the best-laid plans.

As well as embedding change, professional development (PD) enables teachers to develop new skills and insights (Sims et al., 2021) and should ultimately lead to improvements in pupils' academic achievement (Fletcher-Wood and Zuccollo, 2020). Despite these important effects, however, the average teacher in England spends only four days a year undertaking courses, observational visits, seminars or in-service training, compared to 10.5 days a year averaged across 36 OECD countries (Sellen, 2016).

The formal types of teachers' PD that are currently popular include professional qualifications, 'lesson study', filming oneself teaching, instructional coaching, peer observation, action research, collaborative enquiry and 'TeachMeets' (Sims et al., 2021; Holmes, 2019; Cravens and Hunter, 2021; Porritt et al., 2022). Also popular is the idea of the school as a 'learning organisation' (Senge, 2006) or 'professional learning community' in which teachers' learning and development are embedded in the structure and systems of the school (Mitchell, 2013). Of course, organised professional development is only one way in which teachers develop their practice. Collegiality, mutual support and one-to-one discussions are also important (Fullan, 2016). Collaborative professional communities, in which teachers share responsibility for student learning and work together to develop effective classroom practices, have also been shown to embed positive innovations (McLaughlin and Talbert, 2001).

School leaders are keen to know what types of professional development are effective and efficient. When looking for what can work, however, researchers have found it difficult to isolate professional development from other factors which make a difference to pupil progress and it is hard to prove causality, that is, that a particular PD intervention is directly responsible for improved outcomes (Sims et al., 2021). Furthermore, PD usually takes place outside the classroom, but is designed to encourage teachers to make changes within the classroom (Kennedy, 2016). This means that teachers may learn about and even say that they support a particular idea yet continue with their habitual teaching approaches, without necessarily even noticing they are doing so (Kennedy, 2016).

This chapter considers to what extent the equation and logical chain work in practice, what assumptions may stifle success and how school leaders can ensure their staff gain maximum benefits from professional development. It includes what constitutes effective PD, what leaders need to pay attention to when supporting PD and what PD is appropriate for aspiring leaders. The chapter summarises key theories about adult learning and professional development, considers the available evidence about which kinds of PD are effective and includes a critique of existing research.

What does professional development mean?

At its most basic, professional development is defined as the 'enhancement of individuals' professionalism' (Evans, 2011, p. 864). This begs the question, 'What does professionalism mean?' – particularly as teaching has not always been classified as a profession (Whitty, 2000).

Professionalism

Professionalism is generally deemed to involve:

- specialist expertise
- shared standards of practice
- a moral or ethical commitment to service

- autonomy
- self-regulation
- career-long learning.

(Eraut, 1994; Earley, 2004)

Teaching fits these categories, although in recent years teachers' autonomy and self-regulation have diminished, to some extent, due to a combination of national policies and Ofsted inspections which together govern and judge teachers' work.

While all professionals are expected to engage in learning (in some cases this is a mandated requirement), such development varies from that which is 'restricted' to 'extended' (Hoyle, 1974; Menter et al., 2010) as explained in Box 6.1.

Performativity and professionalism

Ball (2003) argues that, increasingly, rewards and sanctions determine teachers' performance rather than the ethics of professional collaboration, leading to 'performativity' replacing professionalism. In this scenario, professional development is a means for teachers 'to "add value' to themselves [and] improve their productivity' (Ball, 2003, p. 217). This is a shift away from the ethic of public service, self-development and collaborative learning which lie at the heart of professionalism.

Definitions of professional development

The ethical aspects of professionalism are included in Day's (1999, p. 4) definition of teachers' professional development, which is 'the process by which, alone and

---

BOX 6.1 MODELS OF TEACHER PROFESSIONALISM

Menter et al. (2010) describe four models of professionalism, categorising them as restricted or extended:

Restricted professionalism	Extended professionalism		
The *effective* teacher, judged to be competent by national standards	The *reflective* teacher, committed to personal professional development through practice	The *enquiring* teacher, engaging in systematic enquiry in their classrooms, improving their own practice and sharing insights with colleagues	The *transformative* teacher, combines reflection and enquiry, taking an activist approach and contributing to social change

with others, teachers review, renew and extend their commitment as change agents to the moral purposes of teaching'. In this definition, professional development promotes the ability to make a difference to students' lives – which is the key moral purpose of teaching (Fullan, 2002).

Day (1999) regards both 'natural' learning experiences and planned activities as intrinsic to professional development. Other definitions of PD are narrower, for example, 'activities that aim to develop an individual's skills, knowledge, expertise and other characteristics as a teacher' (OECD 2014, p. 86). The OECD definition, like others in the literature, focuses on 'activities' which can be evaluated rather than the many informal sources of learning for teachers, such as staffroom conversations or their personal observations and reflections. Other definitions see PD as a lifelong process for teachers (Burner and Svendsen, 2020) and as a shift in teachers' individual sense of self or identity (Edwards, 2021).

In defining professional development, one issue is whether PD can be considered to have taken place if it makes no impact on teachers' practice. This has led Porritt et al. (2022) to distinguish between professional learning and professional development. Professional learning includes all the ways in which teachers can 'learn something new, update skills, be informed of new developments, explore new techniques or resources and refresh subject-specific knowledge' (Porritt et al., 2022, p. 104). Professional development is the process whereby teachers put new understandings into practice in order to improve pupils' experience and outcomes (Porritt et al., 2022). Thus 'professional learning and development' implies teachers making practice changes as a result of learning something new. Of course, in some cases, PD confirms what teachers are already doing and justifies them continuing with their current practice.

For the purposes of this chapter, professional development is defined as all the formal and informal education that leads teachers and school leaders to improve their practice and make a greater difference to children and young people. This definition encompasses professional learning and development. While informal learning is important to teachers' and others' professional development, this chapter focuses primarily on PD in formal contexts, because research has tended to concentrate on specific activities designed to enhance practice.

The next section looks at theoretical perspectives and teachers' learning, illustrated by recent examples of professional development activities.

What are the key theories about learning and professional development?

It is useful to have an understanding of theories about adult learning and professional development because many types of teachers' PD appear to be built on these theories. The theories considered in this section include adult learning approaches, enquiry-based PD, communities of practice, learning organisations and professional learning communities, all of which continue to inform professional development in schools today.

Adult learning approaches

Experiential learning theory has dominated this field. Developed by Kolb (1984, 2015) and influenced by John Dewey, Kurt Lewin and Jean Piaget, experiential learning theory emphasises the importance of practical experience as the starting point for learning (Gunter et al. 2001). Four stages of learning are located within a circle or spiral, see Figure 6.1 (Kolb, 2015). The learner begins with a concrete experience, in which they are fully involved, without bias, in the here and now. The next stage is reflective observation, when the learner considers their experience from different perspectives. The third stage is abstract conceptualisation, in which the learner's observations are integrated into abstract concepts. Finally the learner undertakes active experimentation, testing out the implications of the abstract concepts developed (Kolb, 2015). This has been summarised as, 'something happens; we reflect on our observations; form an abstract concept around what happened; and experiment with our concept in the real world' (Ryder and Downs, 2022, p. 2).

Although experiential learning theory has been highly influential, there are a number of criticisms of it. For example, it is considered to ignore the context of learning (Fenwick, 2003); to oversimplify a complex process which does not necessarily occur in neat, linear stages (Seaman, 2008); and to assume a relatively static environment instead of the multiple changes that take place in most organisations (Ryder and Downs, 2022), which is particularly the case for schools.

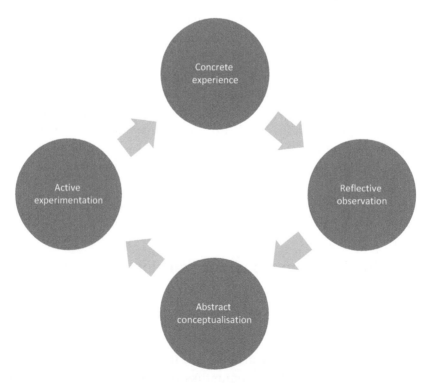

Figure 6.1 Kolb's (2015, p. 51) experiential learning cycle

Despite these criticisms, experiential learning has fostered developments in cyclical approaches to learning and reflective practice which have taken root in some schools. It also has similarities with action research, which continues to be important in teachers' PD.

Reflective practice

Reflection is included in the *Teachers' Standards* (DfE, 2022) as an important way in which teachers can improve their practice. Reflection is a systematic process in which teachers take a self-critical approach to consider their decisions and actions in order to make improvements (Tripp and Rich, 2012). It can include several dimensions: intellectual, emotional, motivational, personal and embodied (Šarić and Šteh, 2017).

Dewey (1933) was the first exponent and advocate of reflective teaching. Schön (1991) developed Dewey's (1933) ideas to identify different types of reflection, arguing it was possible to reflect 'in-action', for example, while teaching is taking place, and to reflect 'on-action', for example, after teaching has happened. Reflection 'for-action' enables teachers to identify changes they wish to make. McGregor and Cartwright (2011) suggest, when reflecting to develop practice, the process of replaying or rewinding in one's mind events that are of concern may be useful. Thinking back on what happened, and reflectively considering how and why an event unfolded as it did, can render more explicit what has previously remained tacit or implicit.

The reflective process is cyclical (see Figure 6.2) and is a little similar to Kolb's learning cycle. Teachers reflect on issues they face or a practical classroom problem,

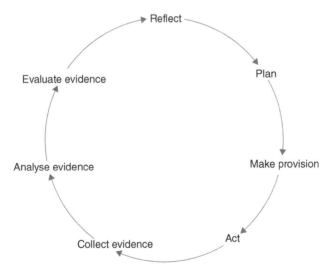

Figure 6.2 The process of reflective teaching
(Pollard et al., 2019, p. 87)

using evidence such as pupils' progress data, classroom observations and recent research. The teachers then plan how to address the issues and take action. Next, they collect, analyse and evaluate evidence of the impact of their action and this informs their subsequent reflections.

Typically reflective practice involves setting aside time to reflect on one's work, asking oneself questions about an event. Rolfe et al. (2001) scaffold the process by suggesting a number of key questions (see Table 6.1).

Driscoll (2007) related the 'what', 'so what' and 'now what' questions to the stages of the experiential learning cycle: 'what' (description) comes after the concrete experience; 'so what' (analysis) comes after the reflective observation; 'now what' (plan of action) comes after the abstract conceptualisation and leads to active experimentation.

While some advocates of reflective practice assume teachers undertake reflection as a matter of course, critics have expressed doubt about whether this happens in practice and whether such reflection is of sufficient quality for teachers to change what they do. Some teachers may not be interested in reflection and learning (Van Eekelen et al., 2006), while others may find self-criticism emotionally challenging. Knowledge is a complex phenomenon, with multiple layers linked to the body, intellect, past experiences and social interactions. Reflective practice can be based on a relatively simplistic version of knowledge: the assumption that teachers are able to represent accurately what happened in their reflections and that their perceptions are a sufficient basis to learn and improve (Summerscales, 2010). It assumes teachers are able to know something by taking a look at it individually.

Table 6.1 Questions that assist the process of developing reflective practice

What? (descriptive)	So what? (knowledge and meaning)	Now what? (plan of action)
... happened?	... does this tell me about my relationship with my teaching and my students?	... do I need to do to improve the situation/prevent recurrence?
... was my role in the situation?		
... was I trying to achieve?	... did I base my actions on?	... are the broader issues that need to be considered if new action is to be successful?
... action did I take?	... should I have done?	
... were the consequences for me and for my students?	... other knowledge can I bring?	
... was the response of others?	... is my new understanding of what has occurred?	... might the consequences be?
... feelings did it evoke?	... other broader issues have arisen?	... can I do to transfer this learning to other contexts?
... was good/bad about the experience?		

Based on Rolfe et al., 2001

Even if a teacher has an accurate perception of an event that has occurred, there is no guarantee that they will know how to deal with such an event better in the future. There is a danger that reflective practice has become a competence to be monitored and checked, rather than being a positive contribution to a teacher's professional development (Summerscales, 2010).

Bearing in mind these criticisms, it is important for school leaders to ensure that reflective practice operates at a complex, nuanced level in relation to knowledge and that teachers are supported to deal with any emotional challenges or issues that may arise from their reflections. There is some evidence that undertaking shared critical reflection through collaborative enquiry can strengthen teachers' willingness to reflect critically on their practice and make improvements to their work (Pareja Roblin and Margalef, 2013). This could help to enhance the powerful contribution that evidence-informed reflection can make throughout a teacher's professional life (Pollard et al., 2019).

Box 6.2 describes three practical examples of reflective PD: reflective circles, critical reflection and reflection using video-recordings.

BOX 6.2 EXAMPLES OF REFLECTIVE PD ACTIVITIES IN SCHOOLS

Reflective circles

Reflection in the form of 'reflective circles' has been used in Australia as a type of peer supervision and was found to 'foster mutually supportive and enabling and empowering practice' (Gardner et al., 2022, p. 380). Reflective circles are where small groups (of four to six members) reflect, initially individually, on a school-based experience, including their assumptions, the meaning of the experience, how their response might have been influenced by their own background and how it might have been perceived externally. The members of the group then present a summary of their reflection on personal and professional dimensions of their experience and other members respond with questions or comments to encourage and/or enable further understanding (Gardner et al., 2022).

Critical reflection

A study in Norway investigated the impact of a PD programme to encourage enquiry-based science teaching. Teacher reflection was defined as 'the teachers' capacity to look back on their teaching and make it the object of purposeful critical thinking' (Svendsen, 2016, p. 319). In this project, the teacher participants reflected together on their implementation of the enquiry-based teaching approach. This enabled them to think about their teaching differently, understand the dynamics of their classrooms better and try out new methods. Svendsen (2016) saw critical reflection as key to the teachers' growing confidence, trust and motivation. It should be noted, however, her research was confined to just three schools so may not be generalisable.

> **Reflection using video recordings**
>
> A reflective approach that has become increasingly popular in England is the use of video technology to record a teacher simultaneously with the pupils who are learning. Teachers can reflect on their recording alone, with colleagues or with a mentor and the outcomes can range from providing individual material for reflection on a specific activity to collating exemplar episodes of good/effective practice. Several schools in the Leadership for Learning project in Oxford used this approach and reported that teachers found the recording of their lessons a powerful means of learning (Menter and McGregor, 2015). One school, which raised their Ofsted inspection rating from 'Requires Improvement' to 'Good', adopted the use of video recordings to create a bank of video materials demonstrating the many different ways that Assessment for Learning had been carried out in the school (Menter and McGregor, 2015).
>
> However, the issue identified earlier with reflective practice, that individual teachers may not have the expertise to make improvements to what they observe, is relevant to the use of video recordings. A review of research into the use of video coaching found conflicting evidence about the extent to which video coaching changed teachers' classroom practice (van der Linden et al., 2022). While teachers' knowledge improved, van der Linden et al. (2022) noted that they did not always benefit from reflections on their practice when they simply described events or made quick judgements. However, coaching or expert feedback focused on a particular aspect of practice or learning can help to deepen their reflections.

Enquiry-based professional development

From Stenhouse (1975) onwards, teachers have been encouraged to undertake research in the classroom as part of their professional development. In the United States there has been a 'teachers as researchers' movement for several decades (Holmqvist et al., 2018). Timperley (2011, p. 104) argued that promoting 'inquiry habits of mind throughout the school' is the best way to achieve coherent PD.

Teachers have long been the subject of university research studies in which they are scrutinised and questioned by researchers external to the school, but there is now an acknowledgement that they should be co-designers of research in order to develop their agency in learning. Kyza and Agesilaou's (2022) research found, however, that in university/school partnerships, existing power imbalances tend to favour the university researchers, so teacher-researcher collaborations need to examine roles, expectations and interactions explicitly in order to ensure professional learning for the teachers. Where collaboration is successful, teacher-researchers are more likely to have their ideas accepted by the school than outsiders (Holmqvist et al., 2018).

Action research (AR) is frequently promoted as PD for teachers as it can help to develop teachers' autonomy, motivation, self-efficacy and collaboration as well as research skills (Edwards, 2021). It is a 'common-sense approach to personal and professional development that enables practitioners everywhere to investigate and evaluate their work, and to create their own theories of practice' (McNiff and Whitehead, 2012, p. 1). The kinds of questions that can help to scaffold an action research project (McGregor, 2021, p. 6) include:

1. What am I concerned about?

2. Why is this issue a worry or concern?

3. What evidence do I have that illustrates the issue or concern?

4. What *could* I do to improve the situation?

5. What *will* I do about it?

6. What kind of evidence would show the situation has improved?

Action research is often represented as a circle or spiral (see Figure 6.3). It starts with identifying a problem, carrying out an audit and planning an intervention ('Plan 1'). Next is 'Enactment 1' when the plan is implemented and data collected about its impact. The third stage, 'Evaluate 1' is an evaluation of the action, based on an analysis of the data. Then, during the 'Reflective review 1' the researcher starts to develop a theory which will underpin the next cycle. The results from the first cycle of action research feed into the next cycle, starting with 'Revised Plan 2' which leads eventually to new principles for teaching and learning.

Sometimes overlooked (because of the focus on improvements to teaching and learning), an important aspect of action research is the generation of 'living educational theory' (Whitehead and Huxtable, 2022, p. 1). Living educational theory can be developed using a wide range of different methods and provides explanatory principles for researchers about their findings. At its heart lies the possibility of

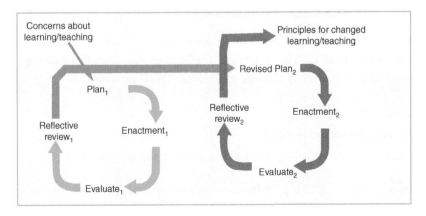

Figure 6.3 Action research spiral
(McGregor, 2021, p. 10)

bringing about positive social change through the sharing of theory (Whitehead and Huxtable, 2022).

There are a number of criticisms of action research, however. One is that the evidence it produces is, by its nature, small-scale and subjective, so it may not be generalisable to other teachers and schools. Another is that, like reflective practice, it assumes teachers have appropriate knowledge to generate solutions and theories from analysing their experiences, which may not always be the case. In addition, on a practical level, action research can be burdensome in terms of time and resources (Edwards, 2021). However, as McGregor (2021) emphasises, teachers can work collaboratively as a department, or even as a whole school to implement an AR project. AR can also offer the versatility to examine the impact of an innovation or to pilot an approach before implementing it more widely, possibly beyond individual schools (McGregor et al., 2020; McGregor et al., 2022). Collaborative action research is generally less taxing for individuals and addresses the problem of subjectivity.

Box 6.3 provides an example of teacher-led collaborative inquiry, where 'teachers work in teams and engage in continuous efforts to identify specific student-learning goals and instructional improvement strategies' (Cravens and Hunter, 2021, p. 565).

Communities of practice

Teacher participation in communities of practice has been found to support improvements in classroom teaching (Cravens et al., 2017). Communities of practice occur when people are engaged together in a joint enterprise with a shared approach, including the way they do things and the way they talk about work (Wenger, 1998). The members of a community of practice have a collective

---

BOX 6.3 EXAMPLE OF COLLABORATIVE ENQUIRY: TEACHER PEER EXCELLENCE GROUPS

Cravens and Hunter (2021) describe an approach to collaborative enquiry which they call Teacher Peer Excellence Groups. The Teacher Peer Excellence Groups in 14 Tennessee schools studied by Cravens and Hunter (2021) involved:

- lesson co-planning
- peer observation and feedback
- collaborative lesson plan revision by groups of participating teachers.

Cravens and Hunter (2021, p. 594) found that improvements in instructional quality were more likely when 'teachers share common instructional objectives, follow inquiry-focused protocols, and deprivatize their practice' (Cravens and Hunter, 2021, p. 594).

understanding and knowledge which underpins their work (Wenger, 1998). When newcomers join an existing community of practice, they are initially on the periphery ('legitimate peripheral participation') before becoming more involved as they learn the community's ways of working (Lave and Wenger, 1991). As the novices are gradually assimilated, they learn how to behave like the rest of the community and their identity becomes increasingly aligned with it. In a similar way, when new teachers join a school, they engage with the community there and gradually develop their identity and repertoires of practice as educators.

In schools, teachers may be in more than one community of practice; for example, they could be in a community of English teachers and also in an overarching community focused on improving learning (Wenner and Campbell, 2018). Wenner and Campbell's (2018) study of the influence of communities of practice on teacher leaders' PD found they supported improved instruction as well as curriculum and assessment. Their research was small scale, however, focusing on just two teacher leaders, so may not be generalisable. Other studies have found that communities of practice that enhance teacher learning involve collaborative participation linked to school curricula and policies, with enquiry-based learning approaches (Cravens and Hunter, 2021).

There are some problems with applying the theory of communities of practice to schools. Lave and Wenger (1991) developed their theory from research into the way in which apprentices learned in relatively slow-moving organisations (for example, tailors in Liberia). These apprentices had low levels of existing knowledge and gradually acquired a more complex understanding through practice. Teachers, on the other hand, arrive at a school with a relatively high level of pre-existing knowledge as well as abstract, theoretical understandings about their practice. The communities of practice described by Lave and Wenger (1991) were consensual, but there is not necessarily a consensus in schools about teachers' practice (Huang and Shimizu, 2016). Furthermore, when experienced teachers join a school, for example, as a head of department, they have a more complex process of assimilation than that described by Lave and Wenger (1991), acting as full members in some ways, while being peripheral in others (Fuller et al., 2005). They also may have a recognised identity prior to joining a school which impacts on their entry and development (Fuller et al., 2005).

Box 6.4 describes TeachMeet as an example of a teacher community of practice.

BOX 6.4 EXAMPLE OF TEACHER COMMUNITY OF PRACTICE: TEACHMEET

Teacher-led PD has been linked to the theory of communities of practice because it is a joint enterprise, with shared approaches to teaching (Holme et al., 2020). Sometimes called 'unconferences', 'Guerilla PD', 'Bottom-up PD', 'Grassroots PD', 'DIY PD' or 'Rogue PD' (Basnett, 2021; Holme et al., 2020), teacher-led PD involves teachers taking the initiative to organise PD for themselves. One example, TeachMeet, originated in Scotland in 2006 as a means for teachers to share ideas with other teachers and has since become a global movement (Basnett, 2021; Holme et al., 2020). TeachMeet events consist of short presentations followed by discussions in which participants can share and develop ideas. Most TeachMeets focus on a specific topic or theme. The benefits have been identified as:

- learning about different pedagogical approaches
- leaving with ideas and resources that can be used straightaway
- collaborating with like-minded teachers
- allowing isolated teachers to talk about their subject with others
- motivating teachers
- encouraging community and personal learning networks with teachers from other schools.

(Basnett, 2021)

While there is little research into TeachMeets, studies of a similar phenomenon in the United States called EdCamp have found that teachers valued learning from and collaborating with others (Holme et al., 2020).

Although teacher-led PD is similar to a community of practice, there are some problems with this comparison. In communities of practice there is generally a consensus about expertise and the community is relatively cohesive. Teacher-led PD is often organised by volunteers who may not share the same views about teaching and the events do not attempt to show a 'one right way' to teach. Also, participants come from different schools so are not working within the same community of practice.

Learning organisations and professional learning communities

Whereas the theory about social learning in communities of practice provides an explanation of how newcomers learn from 'old-timers', the theory of learning organisations suggests a way in which existing staff in an organisation can learn together. Senge (2006) proposed five elements (or 'disciplines') of learning organisations. Table 6.2 indicates how these might apply to schools.

While all of Senge's (2006) five disciplines appear to be positive, there is a danger they ignore potential divisions of class, culture, religion, education and politics among teachers. Unless efforts are made to include all staff, some of the disciplines could lead to 'in-groups' who enjoy learning and sharing together, and 'out-groups' who, for whatever reason (it could be as simple as having to leave promptly in order to look after children), are unable to participate.

In spite of this criticism, the theories about learning organisations and communities of practice underpin the popular notion of professional learning communities

Table 6.2 Senge's (2006) five disciplines and how they apply to schools

Senge's (2006) five disciplines	Application to schools
Personal mastery: commitment to lifelong learning	Everyone in the school is involved in a learning community and committed to their own learning and the learning of pupils.
Mental models: identifying and understanding deeply held (and often hidden even from ourselves) 'internal pictures' of the world, and working to make them consonant with positive goals and attitudes	Staff are encouraged to make explicit their values and cultural understandings, linked to the idea of social justice.
Building a shared vision: a common identity and sense of destiny	All the staff are engaged in and contribute to the development of the School Improvement Plan and vision and mission statements. Improving pupil learning is the main focus of everyone in the school.
Team learning: suspension of personal attitudes and assumptions, and the pursuit of open and true dialogue	Collaborative learning among staff is developed through open communication and acceptance of differences.
Systems thinking (the 'fifth discipline'): integrates the other four and helps the organisation relate more positively and effectively with the wider world	Connections are created with the local community and beyond.

in schools as a key source of teachers' PD. Professional learning communities (PLCs) are teams of teachers who use regular meetings to plan lessons, review students' work and progress, identify ways to improve teaching and attend to their professional learning needs (Blitz and Shulman, 2016).

Based on a national survey and 16 case study schools at different stages of development as a PLC, Bolam et al. (2005, p. i) identified the following characteristics of PLCs:

- shared values and vision
- collective responsibility for pupils' learning
- collaboration focused on learning
- individual and collective professional learning
- reflective professional enquiry
- openness, networks and partnerships

- inclusive membership

- mutual trust, respect and support.

(Bolam et al., 2005, p. i)

In addition to the benefits of learning with colleagues, by collaborating in a PLC, teachers are able to engage in discussing challenging subjects, for example, about racism, leading to more equitable classroom practices (Leonard and Woodland, 2022). Stoll et al. (2006, p. 247) conclude a wide-ranging literature review by noting that PLCs are 'worth the considerable effort put into creating and developing them'.

Bolam et al. (2005) created a useful checklist which school leaders can use to assess how far their school meets the criteria of being a PLC (see Appendix 6.1).

Despite their benefits, PLCs have not yet become widespread, and there are a number of reasons for this. Policymakers do not appear to be interested in them. Some teachers prefer to work 'privately' or autonomously and changing a long-standing culture is hard (Fullan, 2016). In addition, group dynamics may adversely affect some PLCs (Stoll et al., 2006). PLCs need time and external support to work effectively (Stoll et al., 2006), which is not always possible for hard-pressed leaders to provide. Box 6.5 provides two examples of PLCs: teacher learning communities, in which 'teachers come together over time for the purpose of reconsidering their existing beliefs and practice, gaining new professional knowledge and skills and constructing a reform agenda that enhances student learning and professional practice' (Chow, 2016, p. 288).

BOX 6.5 EXAMPLE OF PLCS: TEACHER LEARNING COMMUNITIES

Van Es (2012) notes that teacher learning communities (TLCs) do not necessarily develop simply by bringing teachers together. Van Es's research took place at one school, with nine teachers from the fourth and fifth grades meeting ten times over the course of one year to view videos of colleagues teaching. Van Es (2012) noted it took time for the community to develop and the participants needed to learn how to interact before they felt comfortable analysing the clips in relation to teaching and learning. It was important for a facilitator to assist this process. Focusing on student thinking helped the group to engage in a more substantive analysis of teaching in a supportive and collegial way.

Chow (2016) studied three teacher learning communities in secondary schools in Hong Kong, interviewing the participant teachers to assess the impact of different leadership styles. She found the need for leaders to take control and hold teachers accountable was, to some extent, in conflict with the need for teachers to be able to explore collaboratively in order to enhance their PD.

While professional learning communities may have positive outcomes, criticisms of PLCs include:

- if professional learning communities share the same values and vision, this may lead to a conformity which suppresses possibilities for change
- forced collaboration may stifle individual innovation
- harmony and cohesion may prevent helpful conflict which leads to questioning and challenge.

(Watson, 2014)

The effectiveness of learning communities depends on the participants and their interactions. Kennedy (2016) notes that one PD programme that used video-based lesson analysis within learning communities impacted negatively on student learning, partly because the teachers were mainly working individually to respond to pre-set questions. She suggests 'we need to move past the concept of learning communities *per se* and begin examining the content such groups discuss and the nature of intellectual work they are engaged in' (Kennedy, 2016, p. 972).

Collaborative approaches

In a much-cited review of the literature, Cordingley et al. (2003, p. 2) defined collaborative PD as: 'teachers working together on a sustained basis and/or teachers working with LEA [Local Education Authority] or HEI [Higher Education Institution] or other professional colleagues'. Thus, sending two or more teachers on a training course would not count as collaborative PD. Instead, collaborative PD would involve, for example, a group of teachers undertaking collaborative enquiry or collaborative lesson study (Demir, 2021). The positive outcomes of collaborative PD include improved job satisfaction, teacher retention and student achievement, but Woodland and Mazur (2019, p. 43) warn 'the pitfalls may be as thorny as the promises are rosy'. They point out some teachers prefer to work individually and see collaboration as an intrusion, while school leaders may find practical difficulties in creating the right conditions for collaboration, particularly in relation to time and space.

Despite these concerns, the widespread support for collaborative PD in the literature has been influential, and Box 6.6 describes two different types which are currently popular: lesson study and collegial visits/peer observation.

Coaching and mentoring

Although coaching and mentoring both involve one-to-one conversations, they are defined differently in education. Generally, mentoring refers to a skilled and experienced staff member who guides trainees or new teachers, while coaching

BOX 6.6 EXAMPLES OF COLLABORATIVE PD: LESSON STUDY AND COLLEGIAL VISITS

Lesson study

Lesson study involves a group of teachers working together to make improvements to their lessons and follows an established process, with a group of teachers undertaking a number of steps:

- analyse school/class data and set goals
- explore current research relating to the goals and linked to the curriculum
- action planning: jointly plan a lesson
- teach the designated lesson while being observed by colleagues
- debrief and reflect with each other in an open and collaborative setting with final comments by an invited expert.

(Midgette et al., 2018; Porritt et al., 2022; Seino and Foster, 2021)

While lesson study has merits, for example, encouraging student-centred teaching practices, enabling teachers to grow as professionals and enhancing the professional community's knowledge (Midgette et al., 2018), there are some practical problems with its implementation. It requires a fairly heavy investment of time by the participants, which is a challenge when teachers are time-poor (Holmqvist et al., 2018). It may be difficult to arrange to observe a colleague teaching the designated lesson when other staff are teaching at the same time. It is, of course, possible to film a lesson, but this does not have the same depth as observing the whole class and teacher simultaneously. Also, lessons can vary in their impact depending on where and when they take place and which class is involved. The final stage of debriefing and reflection may not always be effective, as it requires detailed notes from the observers, frank discussion and useful input from the invited expert (Seino and Foster, 2021).

Collegial visits/peer observation

Collegial visits offer opportunities for teachers to observe their colleagues teach, either in their own school or in other schools. Such peer observation is common practice in effective schools (Visone, 2018) and encourages collaborative learning among staff. Different types of collegial visits include

- small teams making short visits to different classrooms to observe a particular aspect of instruction
- teams viewing recorded lessons filmed at their own school or a different school
- teams of teachers observing others teaching followed by a debrief which includes visiting and host teachers.

(Visone, 2022)

> Visone (2022) investigated the impact of collegial visits on professional learning at a case study high-need elementary school in the United States. There, the collegial visits involved a number of teachers viewing a short lesson (25 to 30 minutes) on guided reading, followed by a debriefing session using predetermined questions. The visits had positive impacts, for example, the school's guided reading pedagogy improved and 'peer support, alignment of thinking and group learning' developed among the staff (Visone, 2022, p. 214). It should be noted, however, the participants felt they did not necessarily see authentic teaching (because of the presence of observers) and one of the hosts expressed anxiety about being observed and felt distracted by the observers. Similar to lesson study, there were also some practical difficulties arranging for teachers to leave their own classrooms for an hour in order to observe others, particularly because in this school several visits took place on the same day.
>
> A study in New Zealand (Parr and Hawes, 2017) looked at peer observation of classroom practice in writing at a state middle school (ages 11 to 13). Eleven pairs of teachers undertook peer observation, discussion and feedback seven times during the course of the year. They used an observation guide which focused on four areas: learning goals, how far these linked to teaching, classroom interactions, and feedback to pupils about their writing.
>
> The participants found giving and receiving feedback from colleagues was not straightforward. It required expertise in how to teach writing as well as interpersonal skills. However, there was a marked improvement in the students' writing during the course of the year. Participants valued the opportunity to observe their colleagues and, like Visone's (2022) teachers, found their collegial visits to be useful professional development.

is a means of helping established teachers to develop specific areas of expertise. Mentoring is seen as more about the person ('who and where I am') while coaching is about professional goals ('where I'm going and how to get there') (Bubb and Earley, 2007).

Coaching is sometimes used as part of PD programmes to try to assist teachers to implement what they have learned. Joyce and Showers (2002) identified coaching as making an important difference to the implementation of learning in the classroom (see Table 6.3).

Structured reflections through coaching have been shown to help to embed skills development (Wilkinson et al., 2020). Instructional coaching (which involves observation, feedback and practice, with guidance from an expert mentor) has been shown to change teachers' behaviours and has a positive impact on pupil outcomes (Sims and Fletcher-Wood, 2021). In a recent US experiment, teachers who were encouraged to implement new techniques with cycles of observation, feedback, further trials and reassessment, perhaps not surprisingly, were able to implement new approaches more effectively than those who were simply introduced to

Table 6.3 Impact of coaching

Components of training	Estimated percentage of learners who will …		
	… know how to do it %	… be able to do it %	… do it consistently in daily practice %
Presentation/lecture	10	5	0
+ Presenter modelling	30	20	0
+ Participant practice and feedback	60	60	5
+ Ongoing coaching and administration support	95	95	95

Joyce and Showers (2002)

them (Kraft and Blazar, 2017). Sims and Fletcher-Wood (2021) note coaching helps to encourage teachers to change their habits and put into practice what they have learned during professional development activities.

There are, however, different approaches to coaching which elicit variable results. In some cases, coaches use standardised templates to judge teachers' practices and whether they are complying with the PD approaches they have been taught. In other cases coaches take a collaborative, problem-solving approach. The latter appears to be more effective, as it allows teachers to have some agency over their decisions (Kennedy, 2016). Kennedy (2016) gives an example of two different versions of the same PD programme, one with a coaching component and the other without. In this case, the programme without coaching was, counterintuitively, more effective, and she suggests this might have been because the programme was prescriptive, so adding coaching to it exacerbated the lack of agency teachers experienced.

Mentoring in schools is primarily associated with trainees and new teachers, particularly as part of induction programmes. Mentoring involves helping new teachers to develop professional knowledge, skills, values and their identity (Kemmis et al., 2014). Mentors have been shown to be crucial in supporting early career teachers (Smith and Ingersoll, 2004), but other informal, collegial relationships are also important for new teachers' decisions to stay in the profession (Struyve et al., 2016). Interestingly, when in need of help and advice, lower-performing teachers were found to prefer approaching those with greater mentoring skills, rather than teachers with more expertise (Baker-Doyle and Yoon, 2011).

Different types of mentoring have been categorised as supervision, support and/or collaborative self-development, with different approaches adopted depending on the category (Kemmis et al., 2014). Kemmis et al. (2014) recommend mentoring as collaborative self-development, because it inducts new teachers into a democratic profession. Box 6.7 provides an example of mentoring as collaborative self-development as well as the GROW approach to coaching.

BOX 6.7 EXAMPLES OF COACHING AND MENTORING: THE GROW APPROACH AND THE CLASSROOM ASSESSMENT SCORING SYSTEM

The GROW approach

The GROW model of coaching (Whitmore, 2017) follows a standard format for each coaching session, in which the coach focuses on the following steps:

Goal: what do you want?
Reality: where are you now?
Options: what could you do?
Will (for action): what will you do?

It proved an effective approach to coaching in the Leadership for Learning project in Oxford. More detailed questions in relation to each step of the model can be found in Appendix 6.2.

The Classroom Assessment Scoring System

An example of a successful mentoring approach, which could perhaps reflect the idea of mentoring as collaborative self-development, is the Classroom Assessment Scoring System (Allen et al., 2011a). In this programme, an online 'teaching partner' (or mentor) was sent a fortnightly videotape of sample lessons by participating teachers, which were scored in relation to the following aspects of teacher-student interactions:

- positive climate (e.g. warmth and sense of connectedness in the classroom)
- teacher sensitivity (e.g. responsiveness to students' academic and emotional needs)
- teacher regard for adolescent perspectives (e.g. recognising and utilising student needs for autonomy, active roles and peer interaction)
- instructional learning formats (e.g. teacher use of varied and interesting materials and teaching techniques)
- analysis and problem solving (e.g. emphasis upon engaging students in higher-order thinking skills).

(Allen et al., 2011b, p. 6)

The trained teaching partners used brief segments from the recordings which demonstrated either positive teacher interactions or areas for growth in relation to the aforementioned dimensions. The teachers were asked to observe their behaviour and student reactions and to respond to their partner's prompts about the connection between them. In subsequent phone conversations, the teacher and partner discussed how to enhance the teacher-student interactions. Teachers participating in this programme made substantial improvements after completing it.

What is the role of induction in professional development?

Induction is an important process for teachers, middle and senior leaders and headteachers. It includes guidance, support and professional development for all those beginning a new role.

In England, the Department for Education (DfE, 2019) created an Early Career Framework comprising a compulsory two-year induction process for NQTs. This was intended to address the problem that 'too often, new teachers have not enjoyed the support they need to thrive, nor have they had adequate time to devote to their professional development' (DfE, 2019, p. 4). Early career teachers have a 10% timetable reduction for their first year of induction, followed by 5% reduction in their second year. School leaders need to ensure the school has an induction tutor and every Early Career teacher is assigned a trained mentor. Beginning teachers are assessed against the relevant standards. Table 6.4 indicates the skills they are expected to learn during the two years of induction (DfE, 2019, pp. 8–25).

An interim evaluation of the Early Career Framework (Institute for Employment Studies and BMG Research, 2022) included a baseline survey of Early Career teachers, mentors and induction tutors participating in the training (18,677 respondents) and discussions with the training providers. The participants were generally positive about the training they had experienced, particularly those in primary settings. A similar survey about induction in New Zealand (Langdon et al., 2014) found a comprehensive approach to induction made a positive difference to most, but not all novice teachers. Interestingly, Langdon et al. (2014) noted school leaders had a more positive perception of the induction and mentoring process than the beginning teachers who experienced it.

In relation to the Early Career Framework in England, there were 'high levels of enthusiasm for the provider-led programme' from early career teachers and mentors (Institute for Employment Studies and BMG Research, 2022, p. 10). Two issues that arose, however, were:

- the heavy workload for time-pressured early career teachers. Mentors, too, found it difficult to combine their induction responsibilities with their other commitments

- a lack of flexibility, which for some participants meant the training was not tailored to the school content.

These findings are similar to a small research study which found, in two schools, that it was difficult to arrange cover teachers to allow participants to undertake the early career training and for induction tutors and mentors to oversee the progress of new teachers (Hilton, 2022). Hilton (2022, p. 106) noted 'the interviewees were concerned with the rigidity of the programme and its lack of an approach that really worked for individuals and their specific needs, which all differ. It was, they thought, a "one size fits all approach" which is not helpful'.

Table 6.4 Standards and skills in the DfE Early Career Framework

Standard	Skills
Set high expectations	<ul><li>communicate a belief in the academic potential of all pupils</li><li>demonstrate consistently high behavioural expectations</li></ul>
Promote good progress	<ul><li>avoid overloading working memory</li><li>build on pupils' prior knowledge</li><li>increase likelihood of material being retained</li></ul>
Demonstrate good subject and curriculum knowledge	<ul><li>deliver a carefully sequenced and coherent curriculum</li><li>support pupils to build increasingly complex mental models</li><li>develop fluency</li><li>help pupils apply knowledge and skills to other contexts</li><li>develop pupils' literacy</li></ul>
Plan and teach well-structured lessons	<ul><li>plan effective lessons</li><li>make good use of expositions</li><li>model effectively</li><li>stimulate pupil thinking and check for understanding</li></ul>
Adapt teaching	<ul><li>develop an understanding of different pupil needs</li><li>provide opportunity for pupils to experience success</li><li>meet individual needs without creating unnecessary workload</li><li>group pupils effectively</li></ul>
Make accurate and productive use of assessment	<ul><li>avoid common assessment pitfalls</li><li>check prior knowledge and understanding during lessons</li><li>provide high-quality feedback</li><li>make marking manageable and effective</li></ul>
Manage behaviour effectively	<ul><li>develop a positive, predictable and safe environment for pupils</li><li>establish effective routines and expectations</li><li>build trusting relationships</li><li>motivate pupils</li></ul>
Fulfil wider professional responsibilities	<ul><li>develop as a professional</li><li>build effective working relationships</li><li>manage workload and well-being</li></ul>

Induction is not only needed for newly qualified teachers. It is also essential when teachers change roles or move schools and for new headteachers. In relation to headteachers, Bush (2018, p. 70) states that, 'Planned induction can minimize the sense of isolation and uncertainty reported by many new principals'. He argues that headteacher induction should move beyond administrative procedures to include mentoring (preferably by an experienced and successful headteacher), a personalised induction, guided by the new principal's needs and a focus on professional learning and school improvement. In England, headteachers are eligible for structured coaching in their first five years of headship (DfE, 2023). Box 6.8 describes a Local Education Authority's induction programme for new headteachers.

What are the key influences on teachers' professional development?

One of the problems with the 'logical chain' (Sims et al., 2021) at the start of this chapter is that individual teachers respond differently to PD depending on their

---

BOX 6.8 EXAMPLE OF A LOCAL EDUCATION AUTHORITY INDUCTION PROGRAMME FOR NEW HEADTEACHERS

The induction started with a 1.5 day event, 'New into Headship,' which focused on newly appointed headteachers getting to know each other, sharing their professional learning needs and identifying the needs of their school. During the event, the headteachers were divided into learning groups, one for the north and one for the south of the county. In each group there were a small number of experienced headteachers who had recently moved to schools in the county. The groups set their own ground rules, which included confidentiality.

Thereafter, the north and south learning groups met at regular intervals for a year, facilitated by an outside expert, with discussion topics chosen by the group. The meetings began with individuals describing their experiences and any issues that had arisen since the previous meeting. In many cases this led to expressions of empathy and support, recommendations of possible action and shared documents. Topics included: school improvement planning and sustainability, improving staff morale, performance management, teacher workload and support staff, health and safety, pupil tracking, preparing for Ofsted inspections, personal development and work-life balance. The groups met at each other's schools, and the meetings included a tour of the school.

The induction process was highly rated by participants. They all attended regularly because they found the support so helpful. They learned a lot from each other and also from seeing different schools. By the end of the year, they felt well-equipped to continue with their headships.

expectations, motivation, sense of efficacy and identity (Poekert et al., 2020). Thus any assumption about the impact of professional development depends partly on the teachers, who are driven by their own values and concerns (Demir, 2021). Teachers are also influenced by the unconscious habits they develop while teaching, which is why repeated practice of new behaviours is needed to overcome former routines (Sims and Fletcher-Wood, 2021).

Research studies show that, in addition, the school context, system of education and local community influence the outcomes of teachers' PD (Poekert et al., 2020). Undoubtedly financial pressures and school priorities also affect the way leaders make PD opportunities available to teachers. There are practical difficulties, too. When PD takes place during the day, teachers need to be released from lessons, which has implications relating to the cost of providing cover and the possible deficit experience for the pupils whose teacher is away. Conversely, when PD takes place after the school day, the participants are likely to be tired and may resent spending time on PD instead of marking and preparation.

School leaders play an important part in maximising the impact of professional development and facilitating teachers' engagement in it (Hustler et al., 2003). Sims et al. (2021) found that leadership was identified in 16 studies as a crucial barrier or support to successful PD. Bubb and Earley (2007, p. 40) suggest school leaders need to encourage 'a commitment on the part of the individual and school to professional and personal growth'. This means developing appropriate structures and policies to promote PD as well as creating a learning-focused culture in the school, for example encouraging collaborative practices such as lesson study and mentoring (Demir, 2021). However, it can be challenging for school leaders to do this if they are constrained by lack of funds and if the school has limited capacity for staff to be released to engage with PD in work time.

What can work in professional development for teachers?

Professional development for teachers needs to address four persistent challenges in schools (Kennedy, 2016):

- enabling pupils to make sense of curriculum content
- managing pupil behaviour
- persuading pupils to participate: 'school attendance is compulsory but learning is not' (p. 954)
- knowing and acting on what pupils understand.

It is important to know how to plan PD that addresses these needs appropriately. Systematic reviews of research have tried to elicit what makes professional development work. The characteristics for successful PD, identified by multiple research studies (though in some cases, still questionable), have been summarised by Sims and Fletcher-Wood (2021) as:

- sustained over time, rather than one-off
- collaborative rather than individual
- voluntary rather than mandatory – although obligatory PD may be effective if its purpose is justified to participants
- subject specific rather than general
- using external rather than internal expertise, on the basis that outside experts bring challenge and fresh ideas
- practice-based rather than purely theoretical, with opportunities to use, practise or apply what is learned.

Critique of what works

This consensus has influenced government policy in England, but there are a number of problems with these guiding principles and they may not be reliable predictors of effective PD (Sims and Fletcher-Wood, 2021). In some cases, professional development that included all these characteristics has not had a positive impact (Sims and Fletcher-Wood (2021). Conversely, Kennedy (2016) has identified at least one example of PD (Anderson et al., 1979) that had none of the characteristics but which resulted in long-term improvements in student learning.

Subject-specific PD is not necessarily more effective than general topics, as some programmes focusing only on content knowledge have had little effect on student learning (Kennedy, 2016). The need for external expertise is also questionable, as a number of studies indicate internal, teacher-led PD also leads to improvements in student progress (Cravens and Hunter, 2021). Furthermore, insiders appear to influence policy and practice more than outsiders (Holmqvist et al., 2018). In addition, Sims and Fletcher-Wood (2021) argue that much of the research evidence is based on systematic reviews of literature, so if the original articles were flawed, those failings have continued in subsequent analyses. In particular, there appears to be insufficient evidence that PD needs to be collaborative and long term in order to be effective (Sims and Fletcher-Wood, 2021). Sims and Fletcher-Wood (2021) also suggest that repeated practice may be what makes the difference, rather than sustained, long-term PD.

As mentioned earlier, research studies have struggled to demonstrate causality when linking teachers' PD with pupil progress (Cravens and Hunter, 2021). This is partly because of the many other influences on pupil progress, but also because it takes time for teachers to re-develop their practice (it is an incremental process), and changes may not be immediately visible after a PD intervention (Kennedy, 2016). Lindvall and Ryve (2019) conclude that existing research does not demonstrate definitively how best to invest in PD.

Guidelines for PD

Bearing in mind these concerns about the general principles of professional development, Box 6.9 offers guidelines for PD activities based on the following sources:

- The Effective Practices in CPD project, in which over 670 schools were involved (Earley and Porritt, 2014). A selection of 20 schools became case studies of good practice for PD, although even these schools found it hard to substantiate their claims of the success of PD through effective evaluation.
- Stoll et al.'s (2012) review of the literature.
- Sims et al.'s (2021) review of the literature and subsequent guidance by Collin and Smith (2021).

BOX 6.9 GUIDELINES FOR PD ACTIVITIES

Before undertaking PD
1. Assess individual and school needs
2. Establish clarity of purpose at the outset
3. Specify a focus and goal for PD activity aligned to clear timescales
4. Plan how to manage 'cognitive load' during PD (by focusing on the most relevant content, using a variety of examples and combining verbal and visual instructions)
5. Include a focus on pupil outcomes

During PD
1. Revisit prior learning
2. Motivate participants by agreeing goals, using credible sources and providing affirmation and reinforcement
3. Challenge thinking
4. Ensure ownership by participants
5. Develop teaching techniques by giving instructions on what to do, followed by modelling and practising the technique, providing feedback and support
6. Engage with a variety of activities

After PD
1. Allow time for reflection and feedback
2. Encourage teachers to practise new techniques in the classroom (at least twice in order to overcome existing habits)
3. Embed changed practices through email reminders, action planning, self-monitoring
4. Provide ongoing support through coaching
5. Understand how to evaluate the impact of PD

> **Long-term**
> 1. Use action research and enquiry
> 2. Create professional learning communities within and between schools
> 3. Develop strategic leadership of PD

Overall, in considering what works for teachers, their practice and their learners, it seems important that teachers have agency when undertaking PD. They need to be able to make sense of new ideas themselves rather than simply being provided with knowledge and prescriptive guidance. Kennedy (2016, p. 974) concludes, 'We need to replace our current conception of "good" PD as comprising a collection of particular design features with a conception that is based on more nuanced understandings of what teachers do, what motivates them, and how they learn and grow'. The same is true for the development of school leaders.

What can work in school leadership development?

Crow et al. (2008, pp. 2–3) suggest that, 'If school leaders and leadership are important, then perhaps we should be deeply concerned with how leaders learn to do their jobs'. But while there has been extensive research into effective professional development for teachers, the evidence of what works in school leadership development is relatively sparse. Research indicates, however, that effective preparation makes a difference to the competence of beginning headteachers (Bush, 2018).

How do aspiring leaders develop their skills? Like many other countries, in England most school leaders start their careers as teachers and gradually progress through middle and senior leadership roles to headship (Bush, 2018). At the early stages, effectiveness as a teacher is important for promotion, but thereafter leadership skills become increasingly significant.

In the past, school leadership development in England was offered by local education authorities and universities, in the form of higher degrees (Brundrett, 2001). From 2000, a national programme of leadership development was put in place, led by the National College for School Leadership (NCSL). The NCSL also took over the training for a compulsory qualification for headteachers, the National Professional Qualification for Headship (NPQH), introduced in 1997.

The system for preparing school leaders in England has become more ad hoc and fragmented since then (Bush, 2018). The National College for School Leadership has effectively disappeared (becoming part of the Teaching Agency in 2013), local authorities have little influence and the NPQH was made optional, rather than mandatory, in 2012 (Outhwaite et al., 2018). A national system of 'school to school support' (DfE, 2022) involving national, local, and specialist leaders of education who could provide training and expertise has been largely devolved to teaching schools. A recent survey (Cliffe et al., 2018) noted leadership and development opportunities for aspiring leaders included accredited courses, higher degrees and workplace experiences, but these opportunities varied from one school to another. Gibson (2018, p. 92) suggests the system has moved from being 'nationalised' in the first decade of the 21st century to being 'privatised' in the decade that followed.

Nevertheless, a whole suite of National Professional Qualifications has been developed by the Department for Education (DfE, 2023) for schools in England, including four relating to leadership: Senior Leadership; Headship; Executive Leadership; Early Years Leadership. These NPQs are now mainly delivered by charities and not-for-profit organisations instead of higher education institutions. They offer a more coherent programme which adds to professional development opportunities for Early Career Teachers (ECTs). An early evaluation of the reformed NPQs was largely positive, although the uptake of nearly 30,000 across all the qualifications in the first year was fewer than the DfE's aim of 50,000 participants a year (CFE/DfE, 2023). However, there have been criticisms of the NPQs from the Universities Council for the Education of Teachers (UCET). The prescribed content is narrowly and uncritically based on evidence from the Education Endowment Fund (EEF) and there is no encouragement for teachers and leaders to engage in enquiry and research (UCET, 2022).

National versus local systems of school leadership development

There are mixed views about whether it is preferable to have a national system of school leadership development or a local system which is more relevant to specific contexts. The benefit of a national system is that it provides a consistent, comprehensive programme with established career paths, which enable aspiring leaders to gain the knowledge and skills to lead in any school. The disadvantages are that it creates a uniformity of understanding about school leadership and the one-size-fits-all approach does not necessarily address the needs of leaders facing particular challenges in their own school (Brauckmann et al., 2023). On the other hand, a system that is dependent on individual schools may be contextually relevant but is neither coherent nor consistent nationally. Gibson (2018) argues that quality assurance systems are needed in England if leadership preparation and development remain largely the responsibility of multi-academy trusts and training schools.

School leaders' learning needs

New headteachers need to know what happens when for the first time they are 'balancing at the top of the greasy pole' (Walker and Qian, 2006, p. 297). Weindling and Dimmock (2006) undertook a longitudinal study over a period of 20 years, focusing on the challenges facing new headteachers. Forty-eight secondary heads were followed up after two years, five years, ten years and 20 years, by which time only five individuals remained in post. Weindling and Dimmock's (2006) initial findings were that new headteachers were surprised by the shadow left by the former leader, including existing routines and structures which staff were reluctant to change. Other challenges included the school buildings, communicating with staff, improving the school's public image, addressing low morale and dealing with weak members of the leadership team and incompetent teachers. These findings were similar to a 2003 study commissioned by the NCSL (Hobson et al., 2003) on the issues of early headship, with the addition of professional isolation and loneliness, managing time and resources, and implementing government initiatives.

Effective school leadership preparation

Aspiring school leaders have different professional development needs than teachers, but there is one similarity, which is that they need to be able to translate theoretical knowledge to practices which are relevant to their local context (Brauckmann et al., 2023). High-quality leadership preparation programmes appear to be:

1. related philosophically and theoretically to individual needs in leadership and professional learning, as well as the needs of the educational context
2. oriented to the goals of improvement in student learning and achievement
3. research-informed
4. sustained over time, to allow for learning to be 'interspersed with collegial support, in-school applications and reflective encounters'
5. practical, to enable leaders to use their knowledge in their school
6. designed for different levels of leadership
7. supported by peers and others within or beyond the school
8. sensitive to school contexts, enabling school leaders' knowledge of their circumstances to inform their learning
9. involved in partnership with associations, universities and the wider professional world
10. effectively evaluated, particularly the impact on leaders, as well as on their schools.

(Fluckiger et al., 2014, p. 564)

National Professional Qualification for Headship

The National Professional Qualification for Headship (DfE 2023) is designed for aspiring head teachers in England. It covers some, but not all of school leaders' learning needs and the preceding guidelines for effective leadership preparation. It currently includes the following topics:

- school culture
- effective teaching
- supporting curriculum and assessment development
- establishing and sustaining a positive, predictable and safe environment for pupils
- additional and special educational needs
- professional development
- organisational management
- implementation strategies
- working in partnership with parents and carers
- governance and accountability.

(DfE, 2023)

The main focus of the NPQH is on what Crow (2006) calls 'professional' and 'organisational' socialisation. Professional socialisation is 'the need to know culturally relevant learning strategies, to use data for assessment and to monitor and enhance teacher instruction and student learning' (Crow, 2006, p. 317), while organisational socialisation is the need to understand and manage the school culture and organisation. The NPQH does not include another important type of socialisation which could address the other problems facing new headteachers: personal socialisation. This concerns a change in self-identity and an understanding of the role of headteacher as an advocate for social justice in the context of an unequal society (Crow, 2006). It includes the headteachers' feelings as they grapple with the challenges of their new role and manage their relationships with other staff.

Professional development for aspiring headteachers, then, needs to focus on all aspects of the role, relevant to their school context, together with the personal and emotional needs linked to the changing identity of a headteacher. Once in post, headteachers need to continue their own professional development and this will be different depending on whether they are new to leadership or experienced headteachers. Collaborating with other heads may help to prevent a sense of isolation, and mentoring from experienced colleagues offers support to those new to headship. For headteachers interested in research, an education doctorate provides a framework for carrying out research and leads to a doctoral qualification.

How should professional development of teachers and leaders be evaluated?

Nearly 20 years ago, the Teacher Training Agency (TTA) in England noted that most schools lacked effective processes for evaluating the impact of teachers' PD on pupils, teachers and schools (TTA, 2005, p. 6). In a study of 40 high-performing schools, Ofsted found the evaluation of PD in terms of impact and value for money was 'the weakest aspect of continuing professional development' (Ofsted, 2010, p. 5). These findings were confirmed in the 'State of the Nation' study: 'School systems and processes for evaluating the effectiveness of CPD provision tend to be developed without reference to planned outcomes, specific criteria or value for money judgements' (Pedder and Opfer, 2010, p. 433). More recently, McChesney and Aldridge (2019) came to a similar conclusion, that evaluation was not properly conducted and schools had largely ignored recommendations about the best techniques.

Evaluation typically identifies the value of an activity in order to improve practice. It is often based on the original goals of the activity, to analyse how far they have been achieved (Arthur and Cox, 2013). The goals of teachers' PD are mainly linked to pupil progress but there are also impacts on teachers, the school as an organisation and potentially beyond the institution (Frost and Durrant, 2003). Thus a core task of evaluating PD is 'translating the complex, interactive, formal, and informal nature of teacher learning opportunities into manageable, measurable phenomena' (Desimone 2009, p. 183). The usual sources of evidence are evaluation questionnaires, teacher interviews, classroom observations, teacher surveys, written assessments of teacher knowledge, student achievement data, teacher reflections and portfolios (McChesney and Aldridge, 2019). The easiest form of evaluation is the participant satisfaction questionnaire at the end of an event (sometimes called the 'happy sheet') so perhaps it is not surprising that participant reactions are more likely to be evaluated than wider impacts (McChesney and Aldridge, 2019).

A range of different models are available for evaluating PD. Guskey's (2002) much-quoted work suggested that evaluation should focus on the following levels of impact:

- participants' reactions
- participants' learning
- organisation support and change
- participants' use of new knowledge and skills
- student learning outcomes.

Most importantly, evaluation needs to be incorporated into the planning of PD and used formatively (to make improvements) not just summatively (to identify what worked and what didn't). All too often, evaluation of PD appears to be an afterthought, focused on justifying expenditure rather than 'critical impacts such as teacher learning, changes in classroom practice and student outcomes' (McChesney and Aldridge, 2019, p. 312).

In order to establish whether PD has made a difference, it is important to gather baseline data to assess current practice and performance before teachers undertake it (Earley and Porritt, 2014). This data can then be used to identify what PD is most appropriate for teachers and, importantly, how to measure the difference it is likely to make. Afterwards, two key questions concerning impact are:

- What has been achieved (as a result of engaging in PD activity) that is making a difference for the practice of the staff, the school and to the learning of the children/students?
- What evidence is telling the school that it is making this difference?

(Earley and Porritt, 2014, p. 121)

In relation to students, the following aspects of their learning and experience could be included in evaluations:

- motivation and enjoyment
- more positive attitudes
- improved behaviour
- greater confidence and self-awareness
- subject knowledge and/or skills
- performance and progress in assessments
- engagement in a wider range of learning activities.

(Frost and Durrant, 2003)

Box 6.10 describes the approach of a PD coordinator at a large secondary school aiming to evaluate PD in relation to cost and impact.

BOX 6.10 EXAMPLE OF MEASURING THE IMPACT OF PROFESSIONAL DEVELOPMENT (PERSONAL COMMUNICATION)

The professional development coordinator (PDC) of a large secondary school measured the cost of professional development for different departments at the school against the 'subject residuals' showing how much progress students had made in one subject compared to another. The aim was to consider the potential cost-benefits of PD. However, analysing the results demonstrated the flaws in this approach. The Geography Department, which had spent a relatively low amount on PD, had outstanding pupil progress. This was because the charismatic head of department had persuaded all the geography teachers to attend regular, after-school meetings of a local subject specialist group at which teachers discussed the latest developments in geography and shared good practice in how to teach it. The cost was minimal, and it appeared to have had a

> positive impact. Conversely, the PE department had spent a large amount on PD, but the students did not appear to have performed any better as a result. This may have been because the training undertaken was related to health and safety, which was essential for PE, but did not help the teachers develop their practice. So, while useful for stimulating conversations with the heads of department about the impact of PD, the table produced from these figures did not demonstrate where and how the school should invest in PD in the future.
>
> The PDC adopted a more qualitative approach in relation to teachers who were under-performing. Less competent teachers were asked to choose six students, who were then interviewed by the PDC and asked how the teacher could improve their teaching. Appropriate professional development was provided to address these weaknesses, after which the six students were interviewed again and asked whether they had noticed any improvements. While anecdotal, this appeared to have had a positive impact.

There are a number of barriers to schools undertaking detailed impact evaluation, perhaps most importantly time, effort and cost (Desimone, 2009). Nevertheless, unless PD makes a difference to teachers' behaviours and pupil outcomes it is arguably not worth doing. McChesney and Aldridge (2019) contend that teachers' self-reporting is valid evidence in evaluations and can include what teachers have learned, what changes they have made in classroom practices and any pupil changes they have observed. Two evaluation forms are available in Appendix 6.3, one identifying goals for the future as a result of the PD and the other reviewing a course or PD activity several months later. Ideally, school leaders will follow up with teachers who have engaged in PD some months afterwards, or possibly as part of a performance appraisal, to explore how far the teachers have been able to achieve their goals.

Conclusion

This chapter began with an equation and logical chain, suggesting that there is a relatively simple pathway from teachers' professional development to improvements in student outcomes. The chapter has, however, identified a number of ways in which this assumption is over-optimistic due to, for example, the different ways in which individuals respond to professional development, the extent to which PD relates to the school context, the way in which teachers work together, the amount of time available and teachers' own level of interest in developing their careers.

It is evident that PD in schools is much more than a range of training courses. Teachers and leaders learn from many sources and in multiple ways (Hallinger and Kulophas, 2020). While a simple list of 'what works' is problematic, it is important that schoolteachers and leaders have a sense of agency in determining the PD that will suit their needs. This means that school leaders have an important role to play in balancing individual needs and wishes with the school's priorities.

School leaders have most impact on PD when they promote and participate in teacher learning and development (Robinson et al., 2009). By engaging staff with an inspiring vision of learning, they can motivate them to develop their skills and knowledge (Hallinger and Kulophas). School leaders can maximise the effect of professional development by:

- understanding how PD makes a difference and developing strategic leadership and evaluation of PD
- approaching PD strategically by clarifying purpose, specifying timescales and including a focus on pupil outcomes
- improving the quality of PD by ensuring that school staff have a sense of ownership, are able to engage with a variety of PD opportunities, have time for reflection and feedback and the opportunity to collaborate with colleagues.

(Earley and Porritt, 2014)

A key and ongoing difficulty for school leaders is ensuring that teachers and other staff have the time and resources to make the most of professional development opportunities. This is a stumbling block noted in many research studies about the impact of professional development. There are always pressures on school staff and budgets, so this is undoubtedly a challenging task for headteachers, but the potential benefits of professional development seem worth it. Setting up robust systems of evaluation can provide evidence to help ensure that investment in professional development pays dividends in school improvement (Box 6.11).

BOX 6.11 QUESTIONS FOR REFLECTION AND ACTION

- How do leaders at your school support, encourage and evaluate professional development?
- To what extent does your school's Professional Development Strategy follow the Guidelines for PD activities in Box 6.9?
- How far are the key theories of professional development analysed in this chapter reflected in your Professional Development Strategy?
- Is there an appropriate induction programme for newly qualified teachers, experienced teachers, middle leaders and senior leaders at your school?
- Does your school's Professional Development Strategy address the learning needs of the head teacher and senior leadership team?

Appendix 6.1 Professional learning community development profile

The following development profile, created by Bolam et al. (2005) offers schools (or teams) the opportunity to self-audit the extent to which it has a professional learning community. Staff are invited to complete the table indicating the extent to which the following dimensions are evident at the school.

Dimensions of a professional learning community	Not evident	Slightly evident	Reasonably evident	Strongly evident
Shared values and vision				
Collective responsibility for pupils' learning				
Collaboration focused on learning				
Professional learning: individual and collective				
Reflective professional enquiry				
Openness, networks and partnerships				
Inclusive membership				
Mutual trust, respect and support				
Optimising resources and structures to promote the professional learning community				
Promoting professional learning, individual and collective				
Evaluating and sustaining the PLC				
Leading and managing the PLC				

Appendix 6.2 The GROW model. Possible questions (Whitmore, 2002, pp. 174–176)

Following are possible questions for coaches to ask, linked to each of the four steps of the GROW model.

Goal

- What is the subject matter or the issue on which you would like to work?
- What form of outcome are you seeking by the end of this coaching session?

- How far and how detailed do you expect to get in this session?
- In the long term, what is your goal related to this issue? What is the timeframe?
- What intermediate steps can you identify, with their timeframes?

Reality

- What is the present situation in more detail?
- What and how great is your concern about it?
- Who is affected by this issue other than you?
- Who knows about your desire to do something about it?
- How much control do you personally have over the outcome?
- What action steps have you taken on it so far?
- What stops you from doing more?
- What obstacles will need to be overcome on the way?
- What, if any, internal obstacles or personal resistances do you have to taking action?
- What resources do you already have? Skill, time, enthusiasm, money, support, etc.?
- What other resources will you need? Where will you get them from?
- What is really the issue here, the nub of the issue or the bottom line?

Options

- What are all the different ways in which you could approach this issue?
- Make a list of all the alternatives, large or small, complete and partial solutions.
- What else could you do?
- What would you do if you had more time, a larger budget or if you were the boss?
- What would you do if you could start again with a clean sheet, with a new team?
- Would you like to add a suggestion from me?
- What are the advantages and disadvantages of each of these in turn?
- Which would give the best result?
- Which of these solutions appeals to you most or feels best to you?
- Which would give you the most satisfaction?

Will

- Which option or options do you choose?
- To what extent does this meet all your objectives?
- What are your criteria and measurements for success?
- When precisely are you going to start and finish each action step?
- What could arise to hinder you in taking the steps or meeting the goal?
- What personal resistance do you have, if any, to taking these steps?
- What will you do to eliminate these external and internal factors?
- Who needs to know what your plans are?
- What support do you need and from whom?
- What will you do to obtain that support and when?
- What could I do to support you?
- What commitment, on a 1 to 10 scale, do you have to taking these agreed actions?
- What prevents this from being a 10?
- What could you do or alter to raise your commitment closer to 10?
- Is there anything else you want to talk about now or are we finished?

Appendix 6.3 Evaluation questionnaires

Making an impact (to be completed at the end of the course)
Please complete this form, which aims to help you to identify what you would like to achieve following this course/professional development.

Name:

Aims: within the next 6 months, I would like to …

Activities: in order to achieve my aims, I will do …

Support: in order to achieve my aims, I will need...

Possible obstacles: I anticipate that the following issues may cause difficulties in achieving my aims ...

Possible solutions: in order to overcome these potential problems, I will ...

Impact Evaluation Questionnaire (to be completed 1–3 months after the course)

1. Name:

2. Course/Professional development undertaken:

3. How much impact has your experience of this course/professional development had on the following? *Please rate each on a scale from 1 (no significant impact) to 5 (very significant impact).*

	1	2	3	4	5	Comment
Your professional development						
Your promotion prospects						
Your teaching skills						
Your self-confidence/self-esteem						
Your desire to learn more						
Your pupils' learning outcomes						
Your leadership skills						
Other (please specify)						

4. What impact has the course/professional development had on your professional practice:

    a) in relation to your work with children and young people? Are your pupils:

    - more positive and motivated?
    - behaving better?
    - more confident?
    - improving their subject knowledge and/or skills?
    - performing better in assessments?
    - engaging in a wider range of learning activities?

    b) in relation to colleagues?

    c) in relation to the school?

    d) in relation to communities beyond the school/organisation?

5. Have you faced any obstacles in completing the course/professional development or implementing activities, and if so, what are they?

6. Have you had any support in implementing activities, for example, resources, coaching?

7. How has the course/professional development influenced:

    a) your plans for your future career and professional development?

    b) taking up any new responsibilities/changing your professional role?

    c) the way you feel about yourself and your work?

    d) any changes to your school organisation?

8. Has anything unexpected happened as a result of the course/professional development?

9. What changes would you make to enhance the impact of the course/professional development for future practitioners?

10. Would you recommend the course/professional development to other people, and if so, what would you outline the benefits and weaknesses to be?

References

Allen, J.P., Pianta, R.C., Gregory, A., Mikami, A.Y. and Lun, J. (2011a). An interaction-based approach to enhancing secondary school instruction and student achievement. *Science*, vol. 333, no. 6045, pp. 1034–1037. DOI: 10.1126/science.1207998

Allen, J.P., Pianta, R.C., Gregory, A., Mikami, A.Y. and Lun, J. (2011b). Supporting online material for an interaction-based approach to enhancing secondary school instruction and student achievement. https://www.science.org/doi/10.1126/science.1207998. Accessed 26 August 2023.

Anderson, L.M., Evertson, C.M. and Brophy, J.E. (1979). An experimental study of effective teaching in first-grade reading groups. *Elementary School Journal*, vol. 79, no. 4, pp. 193–223. DOI: 10.1086/461151

Arthur, L. and Cox, E. (2013). From evaluation to research. *International Journal of Research and Method in Education*, vol. 37, no. 2, pp. 137–150.

Baker-Doyle, K.J. and Yoon, S.A. (2011). In search of practitioner-based social capital: A social network analysis tool for understanding and facilitating teacher collaboration in a US-based STEM professional development program. *Professional Development in Education*, vol. 37, no. 1, pp. 75–93.

Ball, S. (2003). The teacher's soul and the terrors of performativity. *Journal of Education Policy*, vol. 18, no. 2, pp. 215–228.

Basnett, J. (2021). TeachMeets: Continuing professional development for teachers by teachers. In T. Beaven and F. Rosell-Aguilar (eds). *Innovative Language Pedagogy Report*. pp. 139–144. Research-publishing.net. DOI: 10.14705/rpnet.2021.50.1249

Blitz, C.L. and Shulman, R. (2016). *Measurement instruments for assessing the performance of professional learning communities*. U.S. Department of Education, Institute of Education Sciences, National Center for Education Evaluation and Regional Assistance, Regional Educational Laboratory Mid-Atlantic. https://ies.ed.gov/ncee/edlabs

Bolam, R., McMahon, A., Stoll, L., Thomas, S., Wallace, M. with Greenwood, A., Hawkey, K., Ingram, M., Atkinson, A. and Smith, M. (2005). *Creating and Sustaining Effective Professional Learning Communities*. Bristol: University of Bristol. https://dera.ioe.ac.uk/5622/1/RR637.pdf. Accessed 21 January 23.

Brauckmann, S., Pashiardis, P. and Ärlestig, H. (2023). Bringing context and educational leadership together: Fostering the professional development of school principals. *Professional Development in Education*, vol. 49, no. 1, pp. 4–15. DOI: 10.1080/19415257.2020.1747105

Brundrett, M. (2001). The development of school leadership preparation programmes in England and the USA: A comparative analysis. *Educational Management and Administration*, vol. 29, no. 2, pp. 229–245. DOI: 10.1177/0263211X010292007

Bubb, S. and Earley, P. (2007). *Leading and Managing Continuing Professional Development*, 2nd edition. London: Paul Chapman Publishing.

Burner, T. and Svendsen, B. (2020). A Vygotskian perspective on teacher professional development. *Education*, vol. 141, no. 1, pp. 11–20.

Bush, T. (2018). Preparation and induction for school principals: Global perspectives. *Management in Education*, vol. 32, no. 2, pp. 66–71.

CFE Research/ Department for Education (2023). *Emerging findings from the NPQ evaluation: Interim report 1*. https://assets.publishing.service.gov.uk/government/uploads/system/uploads/attachment_data/file/1131108/Emerging_findings_from_the_evaluation_of_National_Professional_Qualifications_Interim_report_1.pdf. Accessed 3 March 2023.

Chow, A.W. (2016). Teacher learning communities: The landscape of subject leadership. *International Journal of Educational Management*, vol. 30, no. 2, pp. 287–307.

Cliffe, J., Fuller, K. and Moorosi, P. (2018). Secondary school leadership preparation and development: Experiences and aspirations of members of senior leadership teams. *Management in Education*, vol. 32, no. 2, pp. 85–91.

Collin, J. and Smith, E. (2021). *Effective Professional Development Guidance Report*. Education Endowment Foundation (EEF). https://files.eric.ed.gov/fulltext/ED615913.pdf. Accessed 29 August 2023.

Cordingley, P., Bell, M., Rundell, B. and Evans, D. (2003). The impact of collaborative CPD on classroom teaching and learning. In *Research Evidence in Education Library*. London: EPPI-Centre, Social Science Research Unit, Institute of Education.

Cravens, X. and Hunter, S. (2021). Assessing the impact of collaborative inquiry on teacher performance and effectiveness. *School Effectiveness and School Improvement*, vol. 32, no. 4, pp. 564–606. DOI: 10.1080/09243453.2021.1923532

Cravens, X., Drake, T., Goldring, E. and Shuermann, P. (2017). Teacher peer excellence groups (tpegs): Building communities of practice for instructional improvement. *Journal of Lesson and Learning Studies*, vol. 55, no. 5, pp. 283–292.

Crow, G. (2006). Complexity and the beginning principal in the United States: Perspectives on socialization. *Journal of Educational Administration*, vol. 44, no. 4, pp. 310–325.

Crow, G., Lumby, J. and Pashiardis, P. (2008). Introduction: Why an international handbook on the preparation and development of school leaders? In J. Lumby, G. Crow and P. Pashiardis (eds). *International Handbook on the Preparation and Development of School Leaders*. New York: Routledge, pp. 1–17.

Day, C. (1999). *Developing Teachers: The Challenges of Lifelong Learning*. London: Falmer Press.

Demir, E. (2021). The role of social capital for teacher professional learning and student achievement: A systematic literature review. *Educational Research Review*, vol. 33, pp. 1–33. DOI: 10.1016/j.edurev.2021.100391

Department for Education (DfE) (2019). *Early Career Framework*. London: DfE, Crown Copyright.

Department for Education (DfE) (2022). *Get school to school support from system leaders*. https://www.gov.uk/guidance/get-school-to-school-support-from-system-leaders. Accessed 28 February 2023.

Department for Education (DfE) (2023). *National Professional Qualifications*. https://www.gov.uk/government/publications/national-professional-qualifications-npqs-reforms/national-professional-qualifications-npqs-reforms. Accessed 3 March 2023.

Desimone, L.M., 2009. Improving impact studies of teachers' professional development: Toward better conceptualizations and measures. *Educational Researcher*, vol. 38, no. 3, pp. 181–199.

Dewey, J. (1933). *How We Think: A Restatement of the Relation of Reflective Thinking to the Educative Process*. Chicago: Henry Regnery.

Driscoll, J. (2007). *Practising Clinical Supervision: A Reflective Approach for Healthcare Professionals*, 2nd edition. Edinburgh: Baillière Tindall Elsevier.

Earley, P. (2004). 'Continuing professional development'. In P. Earley and S. Bubb (eds). *Leadership and Management of Education*. Oxford: Oxford University Press.

Earley, P. and Porritt, V. (2014). Evaluating the impact of professional development: The need for a student-focused approach. *Professional Development in Education*, vol. 40, no. 1, pp. 112–129.

Edwards, E. (2021). The ecological impact of action research on language teacher development: A review of the literature. *Educational Action Research*, vol. 29, no. 3, pp. 396–413. DOI: 10.1080/09650792.2020.1718513

Eraut, M. (1994). *Developing Professional Knowledge and Competence*. London: Routledge.

Evans, L. (2011). The 'shape' of teacher professionalism in England: Professional standards, performance management, professional development and the changes proposed in the 2010 White Paper. *British Educational Research Journal*, vol. 37, no. 5, pp. 851–870.

Fenwick, T. (2003). Reclaiming and re-embodying experiential learning through complexity science. *Studies in the Education of Adults*, vol. 35, no. 2, pp. 123–141.

Fletcher-Wood, H. and Zuccollo, J. (2020). The effects of high-quality professional development on teachers and students: A rapid review and meta-analysis. Wellcome Trust, https://epi.org.uk/wp-content/uploads/2020/02/EPI-Wellcome_CPD-Review__2020.pdf. Accessed 10 December 2022.

Fluckiger, B., Lovett, S. and Dempster, N. (2014). Judging the quality of school leadership learning programmes: An international search. *Professional Development in Education*, vol. 40, no. 4, pp. 561–575.

Frost, D. and Durrant, J. (2003). *Teacher-led Development Work*. London: David Fulton.

Fullan, M. (2016). *The New Meaning of Educational Change*, 5th edition. Abingdon: Routledge.

Fullan, M. (2002). *Moral Purpose Writ Large*. https://www.michaelfullan.ca/wp-content/uploads/2016/06/13396048660.pdf. Accessed 6 January 2023.

Fuller, A., Hodkinson, H., Hodkinson, P. and Unwin, L. (2005). Learning as peripheral participation in communities of practice: A reassessment of key concepts in workplace learning. *British Educational Research Journal*, vol. 31, no. 1, pp. 49–68.

Gardner, F., Southall, A. and Baxter, L. (2022). Effectively supporting teachers: A peer supervision model using reflective circles. *Teachers and Teaching*, vol. 28, no. 3, pp. 369–383. DOI: 10.1080/13540602.2022.2062727

Gibson, M. (2018). Leadership preparation and development within a multi-academy trust: Self-improving or self-serving? *Management in Education*, vol. 32, no. 2, pp. 92–97.

Gunter, H., McGregor, D. and Gunter, B. (2001). Teachers as leaders: A case study. *Management in Education*, vol. 15, no. 1, pp. 26–28. DOI: 10.1177/089202060101500106

Guskey, T. (2002). Does it make a difference? Evaluating professional development. *Educational Leadership*, vol. 59, no. 6, pp. 45–51.

Hallinger, P. and Kulophas, D. (2020). The evolving knowledge base on leadership and teacher professional learning: A bibliometric analysis of the literature, 1960-2018. *Professional Development in Education*, vol. 46, no. 4, pp. 521–540. DOI: 10.1080/19415257.2019.1623287

Hilton, G. (2022). NQT to ECT - The new induction programme for teachers in England: An overview. In BCES Conference Books (2022). *Towards the New Epoch of Education*. Sofia: Bulgarian Comparative Education Society, pp. 101–108.

Hobson, A., Brown, E., Ashby, P., Keys, W., Sharp, C. and Benefield, P. (2003). *Issues of Early Headship – Problems and Support Strategies*. Nottingham: National College of School Leadership.

Holme, R., Schofield, S., Lakin, E. (2020). Conceptualising and exploring examples of grassroots teacher professional development. *Teacher Education Advancement Network Journal*, vol. 12, no. 1, pp. 25–37.

Holmes, R. (2019). *Teacher reflection: Why filming yourself is essential*. https://blog.irisconnect.com/uk/blog/teacher-reflection-why-filming-yourself-is-essential. Accessed 12 January 2023.

Holmqvist, M., Bergentoft, H. and Selin, P. (2018). Teacher researchers creating communities of research practice by the use of a professional development approach. *Teacher Development*, vol. 22, no. 2, pp. 191–209. DOI: 10.1080/13664530.2017.1385517

Hoyle, E. (1974). Professionality, Professionalism and Control in Teaching. *London Educational Review*, vol. 3, no. 2, pp. 13–19.

Huang, R. and Shimizu, Y. (2016). Improving teaching, developing teachers and teacher educators, and linking theory and practice through lesson study in mathematics: An international perspective. *ZDM Mathematics Education*, vol. 48, no. 4, pp 393–409. DOI: 10.1007/s11858-016-0795-7

Hustler, D., McNamara, O., Jarvis, J., Londra, M., Campbell, A. and Howson, J. (2003). *Teachers' Perceptions of Continuing Professional Development*. Nottingham: DfES.

Institute for Employment Studies and BMG Research (2022). Evaluation of the national roll-out of the early career framework induction programmes. https://assets.publishing.service.gov.uk/government/uploads/system/uploads/attachment_data/file/1078234/ECF_evaluation_interim_research_brief_2022.pdf. Accessed 6 March 2023.

Joyce, B. and Showers, B. (2002). *Student Achievement through Staff Development*, 3rd edition. Alexandria, VA: ASCD.

Kemmis, S., Heikkinen, H., Fransson, G., Aspfors, J. and Edwards-Groves, C. (2014). Mentoring of new teachers as a contested practice: Supervision, support and collaborative self-development. *Teaching and Teacher Education*, vol. 43, pp. 154–164.

Kennedy, M.M. (2016). How does professional development improve teaching? *Review of Educational Research*, vol. 86, no. 4, pp. 945–980. DOI: 10.3102/0034654315626800

Kolb, D.A. (1984). *Experiential Learning: Experience as the Source of Learning and Development* (Vol. 1). Englewood Cliffs, NJ: Prentice-Hall.

Kolb, D. (2015). *Experiential Learning: Experience as the Source of Learning and Development*, 2nd edition. Upper Saddle River, NJ: Pearson Education Inc.

Kraft, M.A. and Blazar, D. (2017). Individualized coaching to improve teacher practice across grades and subjects: New experimental evidence. *Educational Policy*, vol. 31, no. 7, pp. 1033–1068. DOI: 10.1177/0895904816631099

Kyza, E. and Agesilaou, A. (2022). Investigating the processes of teacher and researcher empowerment and learning in co-design settings, *Cognition and Instruction*, vol. 40, no. 1, pp. 100–125. DOI: 10.1080/07370008.2021.2010213

Langdon, F.J., Alexander, P.A., Ryde, A. and Baggetta, P. (2014). A national survey of induction and mentoring: How it is perceived within communities of practice. *Teaching and Teacher Education*, vol. 44, pp. 92–105.

Lave, J. and Wenger, E. (1991). *Situated Learning: Legitimate Peripheral Participation*. Cambridge, UK: Cambridge University Press.

Leonard, A. and Woodland, R. (2022). Anti-racism is not an initiative: How professional learning communities may advance equity and social-emotional learning in schools. *Theory into Practice*, vol. 61, no. 2, pp. 212–223.

Lindvall, J. and Ryve, A. (2019). Coherence and the positioning of teachers in professional development programs. A systematic review. *Educational Research Review*, vol. 27, pp. 140–154.

McChesney, K. and Aldridge, J. (2019). A review of practitioner-led evaluation of teacher professional development. *Professional Development in Education*, vol. 45, no. 2, pp. 307–324. DOI: 10.1080/19415257.2018.1452782

McGregor, D. (2021). Action research: Applying the principles to frame a professional development project. *Journal of Emergent Science*, vol. 21, pp. 5–13.

McGregor, D. and Cartwright, L. (2011). *Developing Reflective Practice: A Guide for Beginning Teachers*. Berkshire, England: Open University Press.

McGregor, D., Frodsham, S. and Wilson, H. (2020). The nature of epistemological opportunities for doing, thinking and talking about science: Reflections on an effective intervention that promotes creativity. *Research in Science and Technological Education*, vol. 40, no. 3, pp. 363–388. DOI: 10.1080/02635143.2020.1799778

McGregor, D., Wilson, H., Frodsham, S. and Alexander, P. (2022). Practical theorising in the professional development of primary teachers: Outcomes of the 'Thinking, doing, talking science' project. In K. Katharine Burn, T. Trevor Mutton and I. Ian Thompson (eds). *Practical Theorising in Teacher Education: Holding Theory and Practice Together*. London: Routledge.

McLaughlin, M. and Talbert, J. (2001). *Professional Communities and the Work of High School Teaching*. Chicago: University of Chicago Press.

McNiff, J. and Whitehead, J. (2012). *Action Research for Teachers: A Practical Guide*. Abingdon: David Fulton.

Menter, I., Hulme, M., Elliot, D., Lewin, J. et al. (2010). *Literature Review on Teacher Education in the 21st century*. Edinburgh: The Scottish Government. www.gov.scot/binaries/content/documents/govscot/publications/research-and-analysis/2010/10/literature-review-teacher-education-21st-century/documents/0105011-pdf/0105011-pdf/govscot%3Adocument/0105011.pdf. Accessed 24 August 2023.

Menter, I. and McGregor, D. (2015). Leadership for learning 2012-1014. Evaluation Report. Oxford City Council. Available at https://www.oxford.gov.uk. Accessed 26 August 2023.

Midgette, A., Ilten-Gee, R. and Powers, D. (2018). Using lesson study in teacher professional development for domain-based moral education. *Journal of Moral Education*, vol. 47, no. 4, pp. 498–518.

Mitchell, R. (2013). What is professional development, how does it occur in individuals, and how may it be used by educational leaders and managers for the purpose of school improvement? *Professional Development in Education*, vol. 39, no. 3, pp. 387–400.

OECD (Organisation for Economic Co-operation and Development) (2014). *TALIS 2013 Results: An International Perspective on Teaching and Learning*. Paris: OECD.

Ofsted (2006). *The Logical Chain: CPD in Effective Schools*. London: Ofsted.

Ofsted (2010). Good professional development in schools: How does leadership contribute? Available from: https://dera.ioe.ac.uk/1109/1/Good%20professional%20development%20in%20schools.pdf. Accessed 20 February 2023.

Outhwaite, D., Close, P. and Kendrick, A. (2018). Special issue on leadership, preparation and development. *Management in Education*, vol. 32, no. 2, pp. 63–65.

Pareja Roblin, N. and Margalef, L. (2013). Learning from dilemmas: Teacher professional development through collaborative action and reflection. *Teachers and Teaching*, vol. 19, no. 1, pp. 18–32.

Parr, J. and Hawes, E. (2017). Facilitating real-time observation of, and peer discussion and feedback about, practice in writing classrooms. *Professional Development in Education*, vol. 43, no. 5, pp. 709–728. DOI: 10.1080/19415257.2016.1241818

Pedder, D. and Opfer, V. (2010). Planning and organisation of teachers' continuous professional development in schools in England. *The Curriculum Journal*, vol. 21, no. 4, pp. 433–452.

Poekert, P., Swaffield, S., Demir, E. and Wright, S. (2020). Leadership for professional learning towards educational equity: A systematic literature review. *Professional Development in Education*, vol. 46, no. 4, pp. 541–562. DOI: 10.1080/19415257.2020.1787209

Pollard, A. with Black-Hawkins, K., Cliff Hodges, G., Dudley, P., Higgins, S., James, M., Linklater, H., Swaffield, S., Swann, M., Winterbottom, M. and Wolpert, M.A. (2019). *Reflective Teaching in Schools*, 5th edition. London: Bloomsbury Academic.

Porritt, V., Spence-Thomas, K. and Tahylor, C. (2022). Leading professional learning and development. In T. Greany and P. Earley (eds). *School Leadership and Education System Reform*. London: Bloomsbury Publishing, pp. 103–113.

Robinson, V., Hohepa, M. and Lloyd, D. (2009). *School Leadership and Student Outcomes: Identifying What Works and Why: Best Evidence Synthesis*. Wellington, NZ: New Zealand Ministry of Education. https://www.educationcounts.govt.nz/__data/assets/pdf_file/0015/60180/BES-Leadership-Web-updated-foreword-2015.pdf. Accessed 20 February 2023.

Rolfe, G., Freshwater, D. and Jasper, M. (2001). *Critical Reflection for Nursing and the Helping Professions: A user's guide*. London: Palgrave Macmillan.

Ryder, M. and Downs, C. (2022). Rethinking reflective practice: John Boyd's OODA loop as an alternative to Kolb. *The International Journal of Management Education*, vol. 20, no. 3, pp. 1–12.

Šarić, M. and Šteh, B. (2017). Critical reflection in the professional development of teachers: Challenges and possibilities. *Center for Educational Policy Studies Journal*, vol. 7, no. 3, pp. 67–85.

Schön, D. (1991). *The Reflective Practitioner: How Professionals Think in Action*. London: Temple.

Seaman, J. (2008). Experience, reflect, critique: The end of the 'learning cycles' era. *Journal of Experiential Education*, vol. 31, no. 1, pp. 3–18.

Seino, T. and Foster, C. (2021). Analysis of the final comments provided by a knowledgeable other in lesson study. *Journal of Mathematics Teacher Education*, vol. 24, pp. 507–528. DOI: 10.1007/s10857-020-09468-y

Sellen, P. (2016). *Teacher workload and professional development in England's secondary schools: Insights from TALIS*. Education Policy Institute, https://epi.org.uk/wp-content/uploads/2018/01/TeacherWorkload_EPI.pdf. Accessed 10 December 2022.

Senge, P.M. (2006). *The Fifth Discipline: The Art and Practice of the Learning Organization*, 2nd edition. London: Random House Business.

Sims, S. and Fletcher-Wood, H. (2021). Identifying the characteristics of effective teacher professional development: A critical review. *School Effectiveness and School Improvement*, vol. 32, no. 1, pp. 47–63. DOI: 10.1080/09243453.2020.1772841

Sims, S., Fletcher-Wood, H., O'Mara-Eves, A., Cottingham, S., Stansfield, C., Van Herwegen, J. and Anders, J. (2021). *What are the Characteristics of Teacher Professional Development that Increase Pupil Achievement? A Systematic Review and Meta-Analysis*. London: Education Endowment Foundation. https://educationendowmentfoundation.org.uk/education-evidence/evidence-reviews/teacherprofessional-development-characteristics. Accessed 26 January 2023.

Smith, T.M. and Ingersoll, R.M. (2004). Reducing teacher turnover: What are the components of effective induction? *American Educational Research Journal*, vol. 41, no. 3, pp. 681–714.

Stenhouse, L. (1975). *An Introduction to Curriculum Research and Development*. London: Heinemann Educational Books.

Stoll, L., Bolam, R., McMahon, A., Wallace, M. and Thomas, S. (2006). Professional learning communities: A Review of the Literature. *Journal of Educational Change*, vol. 7, no. 4, pp. 221–258.

Stoll, L., Harris, A. and Handscomb, G. (2012). *Great Professional Development Which Leads to Consistently Great Pedagogy: Nine Claims from Research*. Nottingham: NCTL.

Struyve, C., Daly, A., Vandecandelaere, M., Meredith, C., Hannes, K. and De Fraine, B. (2016). More than a mentor. *Journal of Professional Capital and Community*, vol. 1, no. 3, pp. 198–218.

Summerscales, I. (2010). *Attentive educational practice: A philosophical analysis*. EdD thesis. Sheffield University. Unpublished.

Svendsen, B. (2016). Teachers' experience from a school-based collaborative teacher professional development programme: Reported impact on professional development. *Teacher Development*, vol. 20, no. 3, pp. 313–328. DOI: 10.1080/13664530.2016.1149512

Timperley, H. (2011). *Realizing the Power of Professional Learning*. London: McGraw-Hill Education.

Tripp, T. and Rich, P. (2012). Using video to analyse one's own teaching. *British Journal of Educational Technology*, vol. 43, no. 4, pp. 678–704.

TTA (Teacher Training Agency) (2005). *The Teacher Training Agency's Role in the Future of Continuing Professional Development: Response to the Secretary of State.* London: TTA.

UCET (Universities' Council for the Education of Teachers) (2022). Golden thread or gilded cage? An analysis of Department for Education support for the continuing professional development of teachers. https://www.ucet.ac.uk/downloads/14605-Gilded-Cage-UCET-CPD-position-paper-%28full-version%29.pdf. Accessed 5 October 2023.

van der Linden, S., van der Meij, J. and McKenny, S. (2022). Teacher video coaching, from design features to student impacts: A systematic literature review. *Review of Educational Research*, vol. 92, no. 1, pp. 114–165.

Van Eekelen, I., Vermunt, J. and Boshuizen, H. (2006). Exploring teachers' will to learn. *Teachers and Teaching Education*, vol. 22, no. 4, pp. 408–423.

Van Es, E. (2012). Examining the development of a teacher learning community: The case of a video club. *Teaching and Teacher Education*, vol. 28, no. 2, pp. 182–192.

Visone, J. (2018). Developing social and decisional capital in US national blue ribbon schools. *Improving Schools*, vol. 21, no. 2, pp. 158–172. DOI: 10.1177/1365480218755171

Visone, J. (2022). What teachers never have time to do: Peer observation as professional learning. *Professional Development in Education*, vol. 48, no. 2, pp. 203–217.

Walker, A. and Qian, H. (2006). Beginning principals: Balancing at the top of the greasy pole. *Journal of Educational Administration*, vol. 44, no. 4, pp. 297–309.

Watson, C. (2014). Effective professional learning communities? The possibilities for teachers as agents of change in schools. *British Educational Research Journal*, vol. 40, no. 1, pp. 18–29.

Weindling, D. and Dimmock, C. (2006). Sitting in the 'hot seat': New Head Teachers in the UK. *Journal of Educational Administration*, vol. 44, no. 4, pp. 326–340.

Wenger, E. (1998). *Communities of Practice: Learning, Meaning, and Identity.* Cambridge University Press. DOI: 10.1017/CBO9780511803932

Wenner, J. and Campbell, T. (2018). Thick and thin: Variations in teacher leader identity. *International Journal of Teacher Leadership*, vol. 9, no. 2, pp. 5–21.

Whitehead, J. and Huxtable, M. (2022). Developing a living educational theory research approach to community-based educational research. *Educational Research for Social Change*, vol. 11, no. 2, pp. 1–23.

Whitmore, J. (2017). *Coaching for Performance: The Principles and Practice of Coaching and Leadership*, 5th edition. London: Nicholas Brearley publishing.

Whitmore, J. (2002). *Coaching for Performance: The Principles and Practice of Coaching and Leadership*, 3rd edition. London: Nicholas Brearley publishing.

Whitty, G. (2000). Teacher professionalism in new times. *Journal of In-Service Education*, vol. 26, no. 2, pp. 281–295.

Wilkinson, S., Freeman, J., Simonsen, B., Sears, S., Byun, S.G., Xin, X. and Luh, H.-J. (2020). Professional development for classroom management: A review of the literature. *Educational Research and Evaluation*, vol. 26, nos. 3–4, pp. 182–212. DOI: 10.1080/13803611.2021.1934034

Woodland, R. and Mazur, R. (2019). Of teams and ties: Examining the relationship between formal and informal instructional support networks. *Educational Administration Quarterly*, vol. 55, no. 1, pp. 42–72. DOI: 10.1177/0013161X18785868

7 Recruitment and retention of staff: Leadership implications

Introduction

It may seem obvious that a key aim for school leaders should be to recruit and retain the best teachers in order to ensure high-quality teaching and learning in the classroom. However, it is not quite so obvious how to do this. School leaders will be painfully aware of fluctuating teacher numbers, meaning that sometimes they may be swamped with prospective candidates, while at other times they may have to advertise several times before receiving a single suitable application. One headteacher of a high-need school recently offered her staff a reward of £500 if they recommended a suitable candidate for vacancies at the school (Secondary headteacher, Teacher Retention research project). Recruiting good staff and persuading them to remain, particularly in deprived areas, is crucial and challenging for school leaders.

In the UK, the DfE has acknowledged the increasing difficulties of enlisting and keeping staff in its *Recruitment and Retention Strategy* (DfE, 2019b). The DfE (2019b, p. 10) summarises the problems as follows: 'We need even more teachers at a time when we have the most competitive labour market on record. At the same time, we are losing more teachers from the profession than we can afford'. As will become clear later in this chapter, the DfE's past policies, including a reduction of resources and punitive accountability structures may be partially responsible for teacher attrition: a point that its *Recruitment and Retention Strategy* does not altogether address, although the *Strategy* does recognise that 'there are unintended consequences in the current system that make it harder for school leaders to create the right environment for their staff' (DfE, 2019b, p. 8).

Recruitment problems are likely to worsen in England's secondary schools because of a 'demographic bulge'. It has been calculated that there will be 14.7% more pupils in secondary schools in 2025 than there were in 2018 (DfE, 2019a). In the most recent statistics, the exit rate for teachers was relatively high; 40,000 teachers resigned from state schools in 2022 (almost 9% of the workforce) while a further 4000 retired (DfE, 2023). The number of teacher vacancies increased from

2021 to 2022, as did the number of temporarily filled posts (McLean et al., 2023; DfE, 2023).

These are indications of potential teacher shortages (Worth and Van den Brande, 2019), particularly when combined with an under-recruitment of student teachers. The number of ITT entrants was 20% lower in 2022/3 than before the COVID-19 pandemic (McCLean et al., 2023). In some cases teachers leave a school but remain within the teaching profession (for example, moving for a promotion in a different school), but there is some evidence that the number moving out of teaching has been rising, partly driven by lower pay rates than equivalent graduate posts outside teaching (McClean et al., 2023).

The DfE (2019b, p. 10) is particularly concerned about the retention of early career teachers: 'Over 20% of new teachers leave the profession within their first two years of teaching, and 33% leave within their first five years'. The latest statistics show that just over 10% of newly qualified teachers left teaching by the end of their first year in 2022 (DfE, 2023), and one in three teachers departed within the first five years after qualifying (Long and Danechi, 2022). McClean et al. (2023, p. 13) surmise that: 'Along with substantially lower recruitment into teaching, higher leaving rates will exacerbate existing teacher shortages, and likely mean that many schools will continue to struggle with recruitment challenges this year'.

This chapter will cover the key aspects of recruitment and retention of teachers, including national supply and demand, recruitment strategies, succession planning, turnover and attrition. Of interest to school leaders may be the factors that lead teachers to leave either a school or the profession as well as potential solutions to recruitment and retention problems. The chapter includes evidence and illustrations from the Teacher Retention research project (2020) described in the Preface.

How do teacher supply and demand differ?

In considering how school leaders can address the challenges of recruitment and retention, it is useful to review the national picture. When there is an abundance of qualified teachers, it may be challenging for individuals to find an appropriate post, with large numbers of applicants for each opening. Conversely, times of teacher shortage present difficulties for schools in recruiting suitable staff.

Supply

In order to ensure there are sufficient teachers in schools, availability and demand for them needs to be balanced. Newly qualified teachers are the most numerous annual additions to the general population of teachers, but there are also some who return after a period away (for example, due to maternity leave, travel or other employment). The DfE's Teacher Workforce Model (TWM) shows how the number of teachers at the start of the year is increased by new and returning entrants and decreased by those leaving. Estimates are carried out for future years and if it appears that more teachers will be leaving than entering (i.e., demand will exceed estimated 'stock' size), the number of places for teacher training is increased. This does not necessarily mean, however, that it will be possible to recruit sufficient teacher trainees to meet the demand.

Teacher numbers are also affected by the proportion of part-time staff, and there is an increasing desire by teachers for part-time work: 'About a quarter of full-time teachers (23%) would like to reduce their working hours even if it means less pay, compared to 17% of similar professionals' (Worth and Van den Brande, 2019, p. 6). If two teachers job-share a single post, inevitably that means more teachers are needed overall in the workforce.

A 2022 report on Teacher Recruitment and Retention indicated that if the supply of teachers is not meeting demand, class sizes will inevitably increase, with an impact on teacher workload.

> In general, over the past decade or so the overall number of qualified teachers in state-funded schools has not kept pace with increasing pupil numbers. This means the pupil to teacher ratio (number of pupils divided by number of qualified teachers) has increased from 17.6 in November 2010 to 18.5 in 2021. In addition, the teacher vacancy rate has risen over this period.
> (Long and Danechi, 2022, p. 5)

The postgraduate teacher training recruitment target has only been achieved once since 2015/16 – in 2020/21, immediately after the COVID-19 pandemic (Long and Danechi, 2022). The recruitment of secondary teacher trainees in 2022/23 was 41% below target and the number of primary teacher trainees was 7% below target. As a result, there continues to be a squeeze on the supply of teachers available to schools, particularly in shortage subjects such as maths and science.

Demand

In schools, the number of staff required is influenced by the overall number of pupils, and that in turn depends on the birth rate, how many children attend private schools and, potentially, immigration. The DfE (2019a) reported, however, that the direct immigration of children born outside the UK had had minimal effect on the school-age population.

Government policies also impact on the demand for teachers. For example, in 2002 the then Labour government introduced a maximum class size of 30 for Key Stage 1 (ages 5–7 in primary schools), so schools had to recruit more staff in order to cover the additional classes required. More recently, in 2017, the government's teacher supply model took into account the following policies which were likely to affect the number of teachers needed:

- an increase in hours spent teaching mathematics at key stages 4 and 5
- an assumption that the new GCSE for English would lead to an increase in hours spent teaching English at key stage 4 (ages 14–16)
- the removal of the option to take Core Science GCSE from September 2016 meant an increase in teaching time for pupils who had previously taken one GCSE and would need to take two.

(DFE, 2017a, p. 7)

Government policies may also influence class contact and non-contact time. For example, in 2005, planning, preparation and assessment (PPA) time was introduced. This allowed all teachers 10% of their regular teaching hours to plan and prepare lessons and carry out assessment. Schools needed to cover this time, either with more teachers or, as has been happening recently, by closing the school for half a day each week. Government policies also determine the amount of funding given to schools. If funding is reduced, as happened during the years of austerity, teaching posts are cut. A survey of headteachers in 2022 found that, because of budget cuts, 58% were considering or likely to reduce teaching staff and increase class sizes (ASCL, 2022).

What should be considered in teacher and headteacher recruitment?

Research into recruitment in effective schools indicates they have rigorous systems for finding the right staff (Podolsky et al., 2019), see Box 7.1.

BOX 7.1 RECOMMENDED RECRUITMENT PRACTICES (PODOLSKY ET AL., 2019)

- Where possible, undertake recruitment before the beginning of the school year. Teachers recruited later in the year are often less effective and more likely to leave (Papay & Kraft, 2016).
- Provide extensive information to ensure there is a good fit between the teacher candidate and the needs of the school. This should include a clear job description and person specification, information about the context and culture, links to the school's website and Ofsted report, current improvement strategies.
- Undertake a careful screening of applications before selecting candidates for interview. The staff who will work with the candidate should contribute to the screening process as well as senior leaders.
- Organise a teaching demonstration and debrief.

> - Arrange for candidates to visit the school and meet other teachers and members of the school community.
> - Undertake interviews with the school principal and, depending on the role, middle leaders.

Appendix 7.1 provides a selection of interview questions that could be used when recruiting teachers.

Internationally, a popular approach to boost recruitment in hard-to-staff areas is to offer financial incentives in the form of, for example, higher salaries or remission of student loans (See et al., 2019). Apart from the issue of whether financial incentives are affordable, research has indicated that retention rates only last as long as the financial incentive and that in the long term they are ineffective in retaining teachers (Klassen et al., 2021).

Recruitment and retention of headteachers

Similar to concerns about teacher shortages, the rates of recruitment and retention of headteachers in England are worryingly low. There has been a 36% rise in headteacher vacancies from 2021 (1924 vacancies) to 2022 (2619 vacancies) (Howson, 2023). It is possible this is due to an increase in headteachers retiring after the pressures of the COVID-19 pandemic (Howson, 2023). More than half (53%) of deputy and assistant heads do not aspire to become headteachers (NAHT, 2022). In addition, the attrition rates of headteachers are high. Over a quarter of primary leaders and more than a third of secondary heads left their posts within five years of appointment (NAHT, 2022).

While school governors have primary responsibility for appointing headteachers in England, school leaders play an important role in assisting with succession planning as well as developing future heads (see Chapter 6 on professional development). However, there are potential problems with succession planning. As Ritchie (2020, p. 33) points out, 'No successful leader wants to plan their exit', and school governors may feel awkward about discussing successors with the person in post.

Nevertheless, similar to disaster relief plans, having a succession plan in place helps to ensure a smooth transition, whatever the circumstances of a headteacher's departure. Ritchie (2020) recommends that the succession plan should identify:

- the steps to take when a leader decides to leave, including leadership responsibilities during any interim phase
- the process for recruiting a new head
- the installation and induction of the new head.

The process for recruiting a new head includes, for example, deciding on the budget, who will be involved, the role of pupils and staff in the process, preparing a job description, person specification, background information about the school and a link to the school's website, advertising, application form or letter and CV, shortlisting, references, interviews, tasks to be undertaken by candidates in addition to the interviews, making a decision and salary level. Information about the process in England is provided by the DfE's (2017b) *Recruiting a headteacher, Staffing and employment advice for schools* (DfE, 2017c) and the *Governance handbook and competency framework* (DfE, 2020).

A research study on the recruitment of primary headteachers, including surveys and interviews (James et al., 2019) found that some aspects of the process were problematic. Although the recruitment procedure appears to be linear, it is complex, resource intensive and time-consuming. Governing bodies may not have appropriate expertise for the appointment process (but can and do seek external advice). There may be a shortage of candidates and it is not always possible to make an appointment. It can also be particularly challenging when there are internal candidates (James et al., 2019). While James et al.'s (2019) study focused on primary schools, these problems are likely to occur in secondary schools too. This makes succession planning and a clear recruitment strategy all the more important. Box 7.2 provides a vignette of a primary school in which the succession of a long-established and successful headteacher was well-planned, leading to a continuation of the school's outstanding status.

BOX 7.2 SCHOOL CASE STUDY: SUCCESSION PLANNING

The Willows is a large (over 800 pupils), high-need primary school in the Midlands. The school carefully planned for the retirement of the experienced headteacher who successfully led the school to 'outstanding' status (as judged by Ofsted).

Fortuitously, the deputy headteacher went on maternity leave. Instead of recruiting a temporary deputy head, the governors appointed an associate headteacher to work alongside the outgoing head over the course of a year, while his hours were gradually reduced.

The school has always had a very strong vision and philosophy. Teaching and learning remained the highest priority both before the associate headteacher arrived at the school and while she worked with the outgoing head. She ensured the same philosophy and vision continued once he left although some changes were dictated by curriculum directives and a new Ofsted framework. The subject-led curriculum required changes in approach and leadership, with every subject requiring a subject lead. Despite these changes, many underlying processes from the previous head teacher are still evident at the school and, if anything, have been strengthened. A rigorous monitoring schedule continues to be essential to ensure delivery across the school around agreed frameworks.

> Performance management is still a strength of the school as are systems of distributive leadership.
>
> The school retains an underlying intention to be the best it can be and this has ensured that its 'outstanding' status has continued.

What does teacher turnover mean?

Teacher turnover is the rate at which teachers are leaving schools. Location appears to play a role in the turnover of teachers, with London and the south-east of England placing the highest number of advertisements for secondary classroom teachers (Howson, 2018). Teacher turnover in these regions could be due to higher local wages, as retention is affected by the relative pay of teachers compared to other workers in the area (Allen et al., 2016). The cost of living inevitably influences teacher turnover as, apart from London, in England teachers' pay is the same, however expensive the area in which they work. Box 7.3 gives two headteachers' views about the impact of the cost of living on teacher retention.

Teacher turnover in high-need schools

The level of deprivation appears to make a difference to teacher retention, with the highest turnover occurring in schools serving the poorest areas: 'More than one in

> **BOX 7.3 HEADTEACHERS TALKING ABOUT THE IMPACT OF THE COST OF LIVING**
>
> London is sucking people out of this school, because we are still within a critical distance of London, and one of the issues we have here is actually house prices in [County X] are high, the cost of living in [County X] is not unlike London, and actually why would you then live here as a young person, when you can live in London and get London weighting? (Headteacher, high-need secondary school in Shire County)
>
> We have London-type problems in schools like this, but we don't have the money to back up what needs to be done. And [County Y] in particular is a nightmare for recruitment and retention, especially with young teachers, because no-one can afford to live here. You can't. So they end up going elsewhere.... So it's very very difficult to find, a) people who want to work in a tough school, and b) people who can afford at all to be a teacher in [County Y]. (Headteacher, high-need primary school in Shire County)
>
> (Headteacher interviewees from the Teacher Retention research project)

ten teachers from the most disadvantaged secondary schools leave to teach in other schools: about twice the proportion who make the same move from the least disadvantaged schools' (DFE, 2019b, p. 10). If disadvantaged schools are located where house prices and the cost of living are high, this exacerbates recruitment difficulties (Worth et al., 2015). High turnover in challenging schools may be linked to the working conditions in these schools – in their extensive longitudinal study of 300 teachers over three years, based on twice-yearly interviews, Gu and Day (2013, p. 29) found teachers in socio-economically disadvantaged schools were 'more likely to report unstable, fluctuated, personal, situational and professional scenarios'.

Nevertheless, some teachers commit to staying in schools with a high proportion of children living in social and economic deprivation. Lynch et al. (2016) found no evidence that the proportion of pupils eligible for free school meals in a school influenced teachers' intentions to leave the profession. Ronfeldt et al. (2012, p. 6) noted: 'A growing body of evidence indicates that more effective teachers are at least as likely, and sometimes more likely, to stay in schools than their less effective peers and that this is true even in schools with historically underserved student populations'. Gu and Day (2013) found that, despite the potential difficulties in high-need schools, resilience was high in the most deprived contexts, due to a sense of vocation and team spirit. One explanation for the higher turnover in challenging schools is that such schools tend to employ younger teachers, who are more likely to leave in order to develop their careers (Allen et al., 2012).

Costs and benefits of teacher turnover

There are a number of reasons why high teacher turnover is viewed negatively. Research in the United States found that turnover is related to and reduces student achievement, especially in lower-ranking schools. This adversely affects the pupils of teachers who stay as well as those who leave (Ronfeldt et al., 2012). The possible explanations for this are that teacher turnover has a negative impact on collegiality among staff or perhaps causes a loss of institutional memory. High levels of turnover make workforce planning difficult and disrupt pupils' schooling (Worth et al., 2015). It may not be easy for leaders to replace staff, especially when the economy is buoyant (Worth et al., 2015). Where turnover is persistent, such as in high-need schools, leaders may have to keep 'starting over' rather than making strategic progress (Ronfeldt et al., 2012). Recruitment may drain financial resources (Darling-Hammond and Sykes, 2003) and place additional burdens on leaders who are responsible for hiring and training new staff (Barnes, Crowe and Schaefer, 2007).

Conversely, there can be benefits when teachers leave schools. Carlsson et al. (2019, p. 244) suggest that attrition could be viewed as 'active career decisions among teachers with a strong sense of agency'. Adnot et al. (2017) found that when low-performing teachers leave, student achievement improves, but their research was carried out in the District of Columbia, where there appeared to be a pool of effective teachers available to replace leavers. Certainly, few headteachers would regret the departure of poorly performing staff, and the movement of teachers provides an opportunity for leaders to reassess the school structure and staffing needs.

Teacher turnover also occurs when teachers are promoted to managerial posts in different schools, which could be regarded as a positive reason for leaving (Carlsson et al., 2019). In some professions, job mobility is viewed as an indication of motivation, with those who remain in post seen as 'lacking professional dynamic' (Kelchtermans, 2017, p. 964). In some cases, teachers who leave are demonstrating a sense of ambition and will take to their next school their positive attitude towards career development and a wider professional experience.

Training and teacher turnover

Interestingly, the type of training that a teacher has undertaken may influence how long they stay in the profession. Allen et al. (2016) found that school-led routes such as the graduate training programme (GTP) have higher retention rates after five years than postgraduate courses in universities and other higher education institutions (HEIs). However, the worst retention rates are for the school-based training course Teach First (37–44%). This is perhaps because the graduates who opt for Teach First sign a contract for three years' service, so may not be considering a long-term career in teaching.

What makes teachers leave?

Decisions to leave teaching are driven by a number of different factors, of which workload is the most important. For some, there is a particular 'trigger' point which pushes them to resign, such as a negative review of their work or a specific behavioural issue (DfE, 2018). In addition to workload, the reasons for attrition include stress, pupil behaviour, school leadership and professional support, reduced autonomy and resilience. These are discussed in more detail next.

Workload

In the 2018 TALIS international survey, full-time lower secondary school teachers in the UK worked an average of 49.3 hours a week, compared to the OECD average of 41 hours a week (Jerrim and Sims, 2019). Full-time primary school teachers worked 52.1 hours a week, longer than any other country apart from Japan. Over 50% of teachers reported that their workload was unmanageable. In the NAHT (2018) survey, 75% of respondents identified work-life balance and workload pressures as the reasons for teachers leaving the profession.

In Ofsted's (2019, p. 6) survey of 2293 staff from 290 schools, the main causes of heavy workload were:

> the volume of administrative tasks, the volume of marking, staff shortages, lack of support from external specialist agencies (such as for special educational needs and disabilities [SEND], or behaviour), challenging behaviour of pupils, changes to external examinations, frequently changing government policies and regulations, and in some cases, lack of skills or training.

The DfE's (2019b) *Recruitment and Retention Strategy* acknowledged that workload is the primary reason for teachers resigning. Conversely, however, research investigating the workload of teachers in 12 secondary schools found some highly motivated teachers worked long hours by choice and that 'job satisfaction is dependent on a more complex set of factors than hours worked' (Butt and Lance, 2005, p. 420). Arthur and Bradley's (2023) research into teacher retention in challenging schools found that workload was not necessarily a reason for veteran teachers to leave. Some teachers recognised that their own perfectionism and commitment were partially responsible for their workload. Box 7.4 provides illustrative teachers' comments about workload.

Stress

Teaching is undoubtedly a challenging job. Richardson and Watt's (2014, p. 8) survey of over 1000 Australian teacher trainees found that they believed teaching to be a 'highly demanding, emotionally testing, expert career'. Whereas most

---

BOX 7.4 TEACHERS TALKING ABOUT WORKLOAD

One of the big things I've grappled with my whole career, is it's never done, you can't finish it. Like you can't finish planning a lesson, because you could still fiddle around with it. You can't really finish marking a set of books…. (Secondary school teacher, high-need coastal school)

It follows you. You know, it's on the sofa at home…. You don't ever put it away in the same way as a job. (Secondary school teacher, high-need coastal school)

I don't feel like I ever do a good job of anything. And I know that that's partly because I'm a bit of a perfectionist anyway, but I want to do a good job and I want to do a good job for those kids. But it's enormous, and there are so many pressures. And it's, and it's partly my own pressure of wanting to be good at my role, it's partly because I look at the children, I'm going "I need to be better for you", it's partly because of the accountability…. That I think is what for me the workload is. (Secondary school teacher, high-need coastal school).

(Teacher interviewees in Teacher Retention research project)

professionals have moments of crisis, teachers face 'regular and cumulative difficulties' (Clarà, 2017, p. 83). Worth and Van den Brande's (2019) annual report of the teacher labour market compared teachers' working conditions with other professionals. They found that job-related stress was higher among teachers and that they were more likely to feel tense or worried about their work.

Stress for teachers is partly caused by the intensity of their work during term time: 'While their working hours averaged over the whole year are similar to those in other professions, working intensively over fewer weeks of the year leads to a poorer work-life balance and higher stress levels among teachers' (Worth and Van Den Brande, 2019, p. 6). The stressful and intensive nature of teachers' work perhaps explains why workload is consistently the major factor in teachers deciding to leave the profession. Teachers' feelings about stress are provided in Box 7.5.

Pupil behaviour

Pupil behaviour is another key reason teachers leave the profession. Smithers and Robinson (2003) undertook a large-scale survey of 1066 teachers who had left. While workload was the most important reason for leaving, poor pupil behaviour was identified as a particular concern for secondary school teachers. More recently, research carried out by the Policy Exchange (Williams, 2018) produced similar results. Williams' (2018) survey on pupil behaviour was completed by 743 teachers in state secondary schools. In this research, one of the main reasons for teachers leaving the profession was 'the damaging impact of dealing with low-level persistent disruption on a regular basis' (Williams, 2018, p. 32). Of the teacher respondents, 63% had considered leaving the teaching profession because of poor pupil behaviour and 72% knew teachers who left for this reason.

BOX 7.5 TEACHERS TALKING ABOUT STRESS

You're constantly being scrutinised and being picked up on it. That can be incredibly stressful. (Secondary school teacher, high-need, inner-city school)

My family are still, like, why on earth are you working your fingers to the bone? Why don't you go and work somewhere nice? Like why are you coming home in floods of tears about this kid, or why, why? Stop. (Secondary school teacher, high-need coastal school)

It is exhausting, and like I think I certainly live my life in sort of six to eight week chunks, where I'm like, work every hour God made, and then I sort of fall off the end into a holiday. And then I have this holiday and I'm like oh, that's absolutely amazing, and then, and then I go again.... It's a bizarre flow. (Secondary school teacher, high-need coastal school).

(Teacher interviewees in Teacher Retention research project)

Conversely, many teachers find their relationships with young people in the classroom to be positive and rewarding (Kelchtermans, 2017) and a key reason for remaining in the profession. Paradoxically, in high-need schools, pupils' behaviour can be a reason for teachers to remain because it tends to be most challenging when staff are new to a school (Arthur and Bradley, 2023). Box 7.6 provides some insights into teachers' relationships with the pupils in high-need schools, which made them want to remain at the school.

School leadership and professional support

Professional support in schools comes mainly from school leaders and colleagues. Leadership support may be related to a teacher's instructional, environmental or emotional needs and it can also include recognition of a teacher's work (Hughes et al., 2015). Lack of leadership support has been identified as a reason for teacher turnover in Australia and England (Gallant and Riley, 2017; Towers and Maguire, 2017), while a number of research surveys in the United States have identified the quality of leadership as a top reason for teachers to leave or stay in the profession (Podolsky et al., 2019). Communication and trust, together with a facilitative rather than top-down leadership style, are likely to influence teachers to stay in post (Podolsky et al., 2019).

Ofsted (2019) reported that teachers felt they did not have sufficient support from senior leaders to control pupils. Pupil behaviour is a key reason for leaving

---

BOX 7.6 HEADTEACHER AND TEACHERS TALKING ABOUT THE DEMANDS AND REWARDS RELATING TO PUPILS

[Teachers] stay for the children, because obviously you can see where we are, it's a very, very deprived area, we have an awful lot of involvement with social services, we've got housing issues around. The children are fantastic, they love being at school, because they see it as a little safety haven. They have the routines and they have the structures here. So I think any member of staff that you'll speak to here will say, "we do it for the children", and I can hand on heart say they put the children first in every decision that's made. It's what's best for the children. (Primary school head teacher, high-need, inner-city school)

They're demanding, challenging, they're hard work, but you see a light bulb moment, it is brilliant. (Secondary school teacher, high-need inner-city school)

The difference you can make and see an impact, almost immediately some days, when suddenly a child can do something they couldn't three weeks ago. It actually gives you such a buzz and such a good feeling. (Primary school teacher, high-need coastal school).

(Teacher interviewees, Teacher Retention research project, 2020)

(Williams, 2018). It is, of course, possible that weak teachers cite a lack of leadership support because their performance is inadequate. Consequently, their work is more likely to be scrutinised and criticised, causing them to leave.

Support from colleagues is also important in teacher retention. In Newberry and Allsop's (2017) research in Utah (the US state with the highest attrition rates), 'collegial relationships' were identified as the key influence on teachers' decisions about whether to leave or stay in teaching. The level of social-professional support trumped all other factors in teachers' decisions to leave. However, Newberry and Allsop's (2017) research was based on just six interviews with teachers who had left the profession, so may not be generalisable. Collegial support is, however, linked to teacher resilience, which is important for teacher retention (see next section). Box 7.7 provides illustrative comments from teachers about the importance of support.

In addition to internal collegial and leadership support, professional assistance from outside the school is needed for some pupils. For example, schools are reliant on external support for children and young people with mental health and behavioural difficulties. There has been an increase in the number of children and young people experiencing a mental health problem, one in six in 2022 compared to one in nine in 2017 (Rainer et al., 2022). The number of children and young people with special needs has also increased (DfE, 2022). But the support systems for schools in England, such as NHS Children and Young People's Mental Health Services, specialist services and social care have suffered from government spending cuts and can be challenging to access, with long waiting times (Rainer et al., 2022). As a result, schools are dealing with complex cases while waiting for assessments and diagnoses which would enable the children and young people to access

---

BOX 7.7 TEACHERS TALKING ABOUT SUPPORT

If you feel supported on a day-to-day, you know, you feel you can put up with anything, you can do those days where you wonder why you're bothering! (Secondary school teacher, high-need coastal school)

Nobody's left floundering. It's like some schools, someone starts floundering, it's a bit like blood in the water and the sharks attack to get them out. Here it's a case of, members of staff are having difficulty, how can we help? (Primary school teacher, high-need inner-city school)

I work with a lot of colleagues who I really respect as teachers, and there's nobody sort of slacking; everyone pulls their weight, everybody is trying to give 100% all the time. It makes you raise your game and feels like if you don't give that 100% as well you're letting the team down. (Secondary school teacher, high-need inner-city school).

(Teacher interviewees, Teacher Retention research project, 2020)

> **BOX 7.8 HEADTEACHERS TALKING ABOUT SUPPORT SERVICES**
>
> Parents increasingly turn to us for things they would have never dreamed of going to school for. That puts a demand on us that we're not trained or prepared for, and that's what causes the challenge.... Just even on a very fundamental level, over Christmas we supplied probably 50 of our families with food parcels. Parents didn't have enough money to provide a Christmas meal for their child. (Secondary head teacher, high-need coastal school)
>
> You could make a referral to the mental health services for children, and they may or may not be seen in six months for their triage appointment, they might not get to see somebody properly for 12 months. That's too late, so we end up picking that up a lot here. (Primary head teacher, high-need, inner-city school)
>
> We've been doing some work with our staff on understanding some of our young people a bit better, and understanding childhood trauma. Because there are children that are in this academy that five, ten years ago, they would have been in a specialist provision, getting significant help and support from people that are professionally trained to deal with those kinds of children. (Secondary head teacher, high-need coastal school)
>
> The numbers of children that can go to a short-term placement at the PRU has been cut significantly. So we have built our own in-school provision for some children who are just not either safe or appropriate to be in five lessons a day with teachers. They would just make everybody else's life difficult and disrupt learning to the extent that it's not fair on the other children. (Secondary headteacher, high-need coastal school).
>
> (Headteacher interviewees, Teacher retention research project, 2020)

specialist support (Rainer et al., 2022). In Box 7.8, headteachers comment on the pressure that results from inadequate support services.

Resilience

Teacher resilience contributes to retention (Clarà, 2017; Gu and Day, 2013; Mansfield et al., 2012). Some might argue, however, that the focus of school leaders should be on creating a better work environment for teachers, rather than depending on their resilience to remain motivated in adverse conditions.

Resilience has a number of different definitions but is often regarded as the ability to adapt positively to adversity (Clarà, 2017). The capacity to 'bounce back' was the most frequent response from 125 early career and 75 graduating teachers answering the question 'How would you describe a resilient teacher?' (Mansfield et al., 2012, p. 361). Conversely, Gu and Day (2013, p. 26) argue that, rather than the ability to recover from traumatic challenges, resilience is 'the capacity to maintain equilibrium and a sense of commitment and agency in the everyday world in which teachers teach'. This 'everyday resilience' helps teachers to maintain their well-being in the face of regular difficulties (Clarà, 2017).

Resilience is considered to depend on inner strengths, including strong beliefs about core purposes and values (Gu and Day, 2013). There is a recognition that resilience is complex and may include a range of different factors: cognitive, emotional, physical, spiritual/motivational, relational, behavioural/social and organisational (Gu and Day, 2013; Mansfield et al., 2012).

Support from colleagues is fundamental to teacher resilience. In Gu and Day's (2013) research, 75% of respondents rated 'supportive relations with colleagues' of key importance to their resilience. This appears to be particularly the case in schools in areas of deprivation (Gu and Day, 2013). Yet it is not only a question of colleagues offering support; resilient teachers also seek help (Mansfield et al., 2012). This also links to aspects of the 'achievement goal' approach to motivation (see next chapter).

The ability to find support where it is needed partly depends on teachers' goals. Teachers with 'mastery goals' (that is, goals that develop expertise) are more likely to pursue help when they need it, whereas those with 'ability goals' (that is, goals that demonstrate competence) may see help-seeking as an admission of failure or poor ability (Butler, 2014).

In summary, teacher resilience is a 'complex, dynamic and multi-dimensional phenomenon which may draw on a range of likely overlapping profession-related, emotional, motivational and social aspects, at varying levels of intensity' (Mansfield et al., 2012, p. 364). Clearly this complexity makes it difficult for school leaders and teacher educators to help build resilience. Individuals' inner strengths may have developed from childhood or may be linked to spiritual beliefs, neither of which is possible to replicate in teachers who are less resilient. Teachers' emotional engagement, too, may be affected by circumstances in their personal lives, which school leaders are not able to address. The social environment of the school, however, is an arena in which school leaders can make a difference, and providing timely support to teachers may be crucial in strengthening their resilience. In Box 7.9, a headteacher and two teachers comment on the need for resilience in challenging schools.

BOX 7.9 HEADTEACHER AND TEACHERS TALKING ABOUT RESILIENCE

We think teachers need to be really resilient to work here, and so if we feel they're not we don't take them on. (Primary headteacher, high-need coastal school)

You just need that inner, like, grit. (Secondary school teacher, high-need shire county school)

> You have to be very resilient with our parents, as I'm sure everyone else will agree. You know, you can't expect to walk in and ... they're going to be smiley, happy all the time.... (Primary teacher, high-need coastal school)
>
> (Headteacher and teacher interviewees, Teacher Retention research project, 2020)

Autonomy, agency and performativity

Teachers' autonomy is a key aspect of their professional status (Hargreaves, 2006; Brock, 2013) and an important reason for teachers to stay in teaching (Hunter-Quartz et al., 2010). A recent research study found that teacher autonomy is 'strongly correlated with job satisfaction, perceptions of workload manageability and intention to stay in the profession' (Worth and Van den Brande, 2020, p. 3). Yet autonomy has been significantly diminished by successive governments in England (Gu and Day, 2013).

Worth and Van den Brande (2020) found that teachers appear to have less autonomy than similar professionals over what they do, the order in which they carry out tasks, their pace of work and their working hours and that they have little or no influence over their professional development. An imposed curriculum and assessment practices also limit teachers' autonomy. Glazer (2018, p. 66) interviewed 25 effective and experienced teachers who had decided to leave the profession ('invested leavers') and found that a key reason for their decision was the imposition of a curriculum that 'did not feel right' and a requirement to 'teach to the test'. Deciding to leave was a form of resistance: 'They were asserting their professionalism, their judgment within accepted teaching practices, and they felt this judgment was ignored in the moves to impose curriculum' (Glazer, 2018, p. 66).

Meanwhile, accountability has increased (Towers and Maguire, 2017) through the advent of Ofsted inspections, league tables and the collection of large quantities of data in schools to measure pupil progress and teacher performance. In 'The teacher's soul and the terrors of performativity', Ball (2003) argues that teachers are seen less as professionals than as units of production, controlled through rewards and sanctions. Accountability systems have a particularly negative effect on teacher retention in low-performing schools. Ironically, the policies designed to ensure a good education for low-achieving students may instead worsen their education by making it harder for schools to keep teachers in post (Podolsky et al., 2019). Box 7.10 provides comments from a teacher and headteacher about the impact of accountability on retention.

> **BOX 7.10 TEACHER AND HEADTEACHER TALKING ABOUT ACCOUNTABILITY**
>
> I think the thing that makes me want to leave is the accountability … I'm accountable for the history, RE and geography results, and sometimes that pressure keeps me awake at night. (Secondary school teacher, high-need inner-city school)
>
> I hate the fact we're judged by SATs results, and the pressure all comes from the high accountability. I know if we don't get good SATs results, that will affect our Ofsted judgment, ultimately that will make me lose my job. (Secondary headteacher, high-need coastal school)
>
> (Teacher and headteacher interviewees,
Teacher Retention research project, 2020)

What are the solutions to recruitment and retention?

See and Gorard (2019) proposed several ways to address teacher shortfalls at a national level, including

- more coherent policies accounting for teacher demand and supply
- revisions to the ITT application and selection process
- robust evaluations of the cost and benefits of recruitment incentives.

As indicated earlier, financial incentives are expensive and do not appear to be effective in the long term after the enticement has been removed. This is true even in cases in the USA when financial incentives are tied into a teacher's commitment to stay at the school for a longer period, with penalties for leaving earlier (See et al., 2019). Nevertheless, it is important for the government to narrow the gap between teachers' pay and the wider labour market to ensure salaries are more competitive (McCLean et al., 2023).

Other national strategies include reducing teacher workload (McClean et al., 2023), identifying a foundation of key attributes needed in the teaching profession, evaluating teacher recruitment strategies, learning from relevant research into recruitment in other fields and exploring innovative methods of recruitment (Klassen et al., 2021). Values-based recruitment strategies, in which organisations try to find candidates whose values fit their own, have been successful in the public sector (Klassen et al., 2021). Providing detailed information about the school's context and culture can encourage a good fit between the institution and teacher/headteacher applicants. It is important to be realistic: attrition is higher when teachers feel disillusioned and deceived by a false picture of the school (Klassen et al., 2021).

A review of the literature about retention found that the factors that most influence teachers' job satisfaction and career decisions are the quality of leadership, positive collegial relationships and the school culture (Podolsky et al., 2019). Collaborative, communicative, empowering leadership supporting teachers' professional autonomy and influence is associated with higher retention levels (Podolsky et al., 2019). Teachers in the Teacher Retention research project valued school leaders who listened to and supported them.

There is little that headteachers can do about the cost of living and the level of teachers' pay, but school leaders can demonstrate how much they value teachers with relatively inexpensive rewards. Participants in the Teacher Retention research project (2020) valued small gifts or simply a thank-you card to recognise extra effort; an occasional 'duvet day' or time off to go to a child's nativity play; end-of-term celebrations; regular lunchtime buffets while senior staff undertook playground duties; a half-termly staff member award (nominated by anyone); subsidised child care (one secondary school had a nursery attached for teachers to use).

Flexible working arrangements also encourage teachers to stay in post (McClean et al., 2023). It is particularly helpful for teachers with young families and/or elderly parents. Supporting part-time staff is important, for example, through scheduling meetings at times when they can attend and encouraging them to apply for promotion where appropriate.

School leaders can also make efforts to reduce teachers' workload. Schools in the Teacher Retention research project had introduced a number of ways to decrease the time spent on marking, for example, 'live' marking in lessons; whole-class feedback rather than individual book marking (identifying the key problems through a 15-minute appraisal of a set of books); marking one assessment per half-term; quality marking only ten books a day. Some schools allowed staff to work at home occasionally in order to complete an important project, which relieved the pressure on them. Other schools closed for half a day a week to allow staff sufficient planning and preparation time without having to cover lessons. However, this strategy has been criticised by parents and politicians.

Addressing pupil behaviour is a way to reduce teachers' stress and enable more positive relationships. Effective and consistent behaviour policies help to support teachers in the classroom. Some schools survey their teachers regularly to ascertain their experiences and explore ways to ensure their well-being and development.

'Growing your own' by developing teaching assistants or even former pupils is recommended by some headteachers, but there is not yet empirical evidence which establishes causation, that is, teachers recruited and trained within the local community are more likely to stay long term at a school (See et al., 2019). Nevertheless, growing your own teachers is recommended as a strategy by Podolsky et al. (2019) and also by the headteachers in the Teacher Retention research project, see Box 7.11.

> **BOX 7.11 HEADTEACHERS TALKING ABOUT 'GROWING YOUR OWN'**
>
> People maybe come in as TAs or as unqualified teachers, but they've got degrees, and then we start them off and we then grow them, grow them into teachers, and that's been successful. And people like that, they feel invested in. (Secondary headteacher, high-need shire county school)
>
> It's our best strategy for getting teachers in and then retaining them. (Primary headteacher, high-need shire county school)
>
> For some of our sixth formers, if they're going off to university, we contact them in their third year at university and we say do you want to train to be a teacher with us? (Secondary headteacher, high-need shire county school)
>
> From a teacher perspective: 'Every time I've thought about leaving, I got promoted!' (Secondary school teacher, high-need coastal school)
>
> (Headteachers and teacher interviewees, Teacher Retention research project, 2020)

Conclusion

Recruitment and retention are part of a national educational framework. Currently the supply of teachers and headteachers is outstripped by the demand. This means that the approach of individual school leaders to recruitment and retention is vital to ensure that their school is not understaffed. Succession planning and systematic recruitment strategies are important, since hiring staff at all levels in a school is potentially problematic.

The message for school leaders seems to be to develop a collaborative school culture (see Chapter 3) with shared values and vision, to provide teachers with opportunities for growth (see Chapter 6) and to support teamwork and collegial relationships (see Chapter 5). It is also important to create a nurturing school, where teachers feel valued and supported. Recruiting staff who like children and young people and who are motivated by making a difference in their lives will also enhance retention (Box 7.12).

> **BOX 7.12 QUESTIONS FOR REFLECTION AND ACTION**
>
> - Which of the recruitment practices recommended in the literature (see Box 7.1) has your school adopted?
> - Does your school have a succession plan for senior leaders, particularly the headteacher?

- How does your school demonstrate that you value all staff?
- What are your school's strategies for retaining staff, including
  - reducing stress and workload
  - managing pupil behaviour
  - providing support
  - strengthening resilience
  - encouraging autonomy

Appendix 7.1: Thinking about interviews

Recruiting good staff committed to inclusive teaching is key to leading a successful school. The following suggestions offer a list of questions headteachers (or senior leaders) might ask of potential new recruits to the school.

Prior to interview, asking potential applicants to teach a class is likely to be very revealing (Podolsky et al., 2019). Questions can elicit from the candidate their reflections about the positive aspects and the aspects of the lesson that could be improved. This strategy will demonstrate the extent to which the candidate is self-aware, not only of their teaching competency but also recognising how they can improve.

Ten key questions

1. Why are you attracted to teaching in this school? What can you offer?

   [This can elicit whether or not the candidate has researched information about the school and has some knowledge of it already. This is indicative of their personal commitment and enthusiasm for teaching in the school. Resonance between the capabilities they describe and the needs of the school also suggests prior preparatory work has been done.]

2. What is it about [subject/s to be taught] that you think is important for pupils to learn?

   [This elicits whether the candidate is well informed about the nature of subject matter/specialism they are applying for. Levels of knowledge about the discipline will be demonstrable here.]

3. What are the skills and capabilities you have that this role requires?

   [This elicits whether the candidate is well informed about the role they want to undertake. Levels of knowledge and experience will become apparent here.]

4. How did you feel the lesson you taught went? How typical was it of your teaching generally? What was successful and what could be improved?

   [This elicits the extent to which a candidate is reflective and knows their own capability, limits and areas for development.]

5 Please describe the most challenging situation you have faced in your classroom and explain how you dealt with it.

[This response provides insight into the candidates' likely behavioural/pedagogical limits and conveys the extent to which they were resourceful in remediating teaching situations that are not successful.]

6 If you overheard colleagues talking about your teaching in the staff room, what do you think they would say?

[This can elicit the candidate's views about their teaching and persona generally. If they share positives and negatives this suggests whether they have a more rounded self-awareness. It could also elicit their contributions beyond the classroom to the school.]

7 If you asked the pupils what they think about your lessons, what would they say?

[This can elicit the candidate's views about their teaching from pupils' perspectives. It will demonstrate the extent to which they are empathetic about what they do in classrooms.]

8 If it was decided that we would not appoint you, what would the school miss out on?

[This response could reveal aspects of the longer-term aspirations the candidate holds, beyond just classroom teaching.]

9 Please describe the most effective lesson you have taught using technology.

[This elicits the extent to which they are able to utilise IT.]

10 Where would you like to be in five years' time?

[This elicits the candidate's longer-term view of their career, both at the school and even beyond. Energetic and aspirational teachers who will be determined to progress and are therefore 'doers', may indicate head of department/middle leadership roles etc.]

References

ASCL (Association of School and College Leaders) (2022). ASCL Funding Survey October 2022. https://www.ascl.org.uk/ASCL/media/ASCL/News/Press%20releases/ASCL-funding-survey-October-2022.pdf. Accessed 23 June 2023.

Adnot, M., Dee, T., Katz, V. and Wyckoff, J. (2017). Teacher turnover, teacher quality and student achievement in DCPS. *Educational Evaluation and Policy Analysis*, vol. 39, no. 1, pp. 54–76.

Allen, R., Burgess, S. and Mayo, J. (2012). *The Teacher Labour Market, Teacher Turnover and Disadvantaged Schools: New Evidence for England*. Bristol: The Centre for Market and Public Organisation.

Allen, R., Belfield, C., Greaves, E., Sharp, C. and Walker, M. (2016). *The Longer-Term Costs and Benefits of Different Initial Teacher Training Routes.* Institute for Fiscal Studies Report 118 https://www.ifs.org.uk/publications/8368. Accessed 10 February 2020.

Arthur, L. and Bradley, S. (2023). Teacher retention in challenging schools: Please don't say goodbye! *Teachers and Teaching*, vol. 29, no. 7–8, pp. 1–19. DOI: 10.1080/13540602.2023.2201423

Ball, S. (2003). The teacher's soul and the terrors of performativity. *Journal of Education Policy*, vol. 18, no. 2, pp. 215–228.

Barnes, G., Crowe, E. and Schaefer, B. (2007). *The Costs of Turnover in Five Districts: A Pilot Study.* Washington, DC: National Commission on Teaching and America's Future.

Brock, A. (2013). Building a model of early years professionalism from practitioners' perspectives. *Journal of Early Childhood Research*, vol. 11, no. 1, pp. 27–44.

Butler, R. (2014). What teachers want to achieve and why it matters: An achievement goal approach to teacher motivation. In P. Richardson, S. Karabenick and H. Watt (eds). *Teacher Motivation, Theory and Practice.* Abingdon: Routledge, pp. 20–35.

Butt, G. and Lance, A. (2005). Secondary teacher workload and job satisfaction. *Educational Management Administration and Leadership*, vol. 33, no. 4, pp. 401–422.

Carlsson, R., Lindqvist, P. and Nordanger, U. (2019). Is teacher attrition a poor estimate of the value of teacher education? A Swedish case. *European Journal of Teacher Education*, vol. 42, no. 2, pp. 243–257.

Clarà, M. (2017). Teacher resilience and meaning transformation: How teachers reappraise situations of adversity. *Teaching and Teacher Education*, vol. 63, pp. 82–91.

Darling-Hammond, L. and Sykes, G. (2003). Wanted: A national teacher supply policy for education: The right way to meet the "Highly Qualified Teacher" challenge. Education Policy Analysis Archives https://epaa.asu.edu/ojs/article/viewFile/261/387. Accessed 17 March 2020.

Department for Education (DfE) (2023). *School workforce in England.* https://explore-education-statistics.service.gov.uk/find-statistics.school-workforce-in-england. Accessed 23 June 2023.

Department for Education (DfE) (2022). *Special educational needs in England.* https://explore-education-statistics.service.gov.uk/find-statistics.special-educational-needs-inengland/2021-22. Accessed 24 June 2022.

Department for Education (DfE) (2020). *Governance Handbook and Competency Framework.* London: DfE and National College for Teaching and Leadership. https://www.gov.uk/government/publications/governance-handbook. Accessed 8 August 2023.

Department for Education (DfE) (2019a). National pupil projections – future trends in pupil numbers: July 2018 (2019 update) https://assets.publishing.service.gov.uk/government/uploads/system/uploads/attachment_data/file/815634/National_pupil_projections__future_trends_in_pupil_numbers_July_2019_update.pdf. Accessed 8 February 2020.

Department for Education (DfE) (2019b). *Recruitment and Retention Strategy.* https://assets.publishing.service.gov.uk/government/uploads/system/uploads/attachment_data/file/786856/DFE_Teacher_Retention_Strategy_Report.pdf. Accessed 8 February 2020.

Department for Education (DfE) (2018). Factors affecting teacher retention: Qualitative investigation. https://assets.publishing.service.gov.uk/government/uploads/system/uploads/attachment_data/file/686947/Factors_affecting_teacher_retention_-_qualitative_investigation.pdf. Accessed 24 June 2023.

Department for Education (DfE) (2017a). Postgraduate Initial Teacher Training (ITT) places and the Teacher Supply Model (TSM), England 2017/18. https://assets.publishing.service.gov.uk/government/uploads/system/uploads/attachment_data/file/655038/SFR42_2017_TSM_Main_Text.pdf. Accessed 8 February 2020.

Department for Education (DfE) (2017b). *Recruiting a Headteacher: A Guide to the Recruitment and Selection of Headteachers and Other Leadership Roles.* London: DfE/

National Governance Association. https://assets.publishing.service.gov.uk/government/uploads/system/uploads/attachment_data/file/1156153/Recruiting-a-headteacher-v2.pdf. Accessed 8 August 2023.

Department for Education (DfE) (2017c). Staffing and employment advice for schools. https://www.gov.uk/government/publications/staffing-and-employment-advice-for-schools. Accessed 8 August 2023.

Gallant, A. and Riley, P. (2017). Early career teacher attrition in Australia: Inconvenient truths about new public management. *Teachers and Teaching*, vol. 23, no. 8, pp. 1–18.

Glazer, J. (2018). Learning from those who no longer teach: Viewing teacher attrition through a resistance lens. *Teaching and Teacher Education*, vol. 74, pp. 62–71. DOI: 10.1016/j.tate.2018.04.011

Gu, Q. and Day, C. (2013). Challenges to teacher resilience: Conditions count. *British Educational Research Journal*, vol. 39, no. 1, pp. 22–44.

Hargreaves, A. (2006). Four ages of professionalism and professional learning. In H. Lauder, P. Brown, J. Dillabough and A.H. Halsey (eds). *Education, Globalisation and Social Change*. Oxford: Oxford University Press.

Howson, J. (2018). Recruitment, retention and region: The three 'R's challenging school performance in England. *Berabites*, vol. 2, pp. 16–19.

Howson, J. (2023). *School leadership trends in 2022*. https://johnohowson.wordpress.com/tag/head-teacher-recruiment/. Accessed 8 August 2023.

Hughes, A., Matt, J. and O'Reilly, F. (2015). Principal support is imperative to the retention of teachers in hard-to-staff schools. *Journal of Education and Training Studies*, vol. 3, no. 1, pp. 129–134.

Hunter-Quartz, K., Olsen, B., Anderson, L. and Barraza-Lyons, K. (2010). *Making a Difference: Developing Meaningful Careers in Education*. New York: Paradigm.

James, C., Fitzgerald, S., Fellows, T., Goodall, J., Costas Batlle, I. and Jones, J. (2019). Primary school headteacher recruitment and selection in England: The processes and the problematic aspects. *School Leadership & Management*, vol. 39, no. 5, pp. 478–495. DOI: 10.1080/13632434.2018.1525699

Jerrim, J. and Sims, S. (2019). *The Teaching and Learning International Survey (TALIS) 2018. Research Report*. London: UCL Institute of Education.

Kelchtermans, G. (2017). 'Should I stay or should I go?': Unpacking teacher attrition/retention as an educational issue, *Teachers and Teaching*, vol. 23, no. 8, pp. 961–977.

Klassen, R., Rushby, J., Durksen, T. and Bardach, L. (2021). Examining teacher recruitment strategies in England. *Journal of Education for Teaching*, vol. 47, no. 2, pp. 163–185.

Long, R. and Danechi, S. (2022). *Teacher Recruitment and retention in England*. London: House of Commons Library. https://researchbriefings.files.parliament.uk/documents/CBP-7222/CBP-7222.pdf. Accessed 23 June 2023.

Lynch, S., Worth, J., Bamford, S. and Wespieser, K. (2016). *Engaging Teachers: NFER Analysis of Teacher Retention*. Slough: NFER.

Mansfield, C., Beltman, S., Price, A. and McConney, A. (2012). 'Don't sweat the small stuff': Understanding teacher resilience at the chalk face. *Teaching and Teacher Education*, vol. 28, pp. 357–367.

McClean, D., Worth, J. and Faulkner-Ellis, H. (2023). *Teacher Labour Market in England. Annual Report 2023*. Slough: NFER. https://www.nfer.ac.uk/media/5286/teacher_labour_market_in_england_annual_report_2023.pdf. Accessed 23 June 2023.

National Association of Head Teachers (NAHT) (2018). *The NAHT School Recruitment Survey 2016*. 8 February 2020.

National Association of Head Teachers (NAHT) (2022). Gone for good: Leaders who are lost to the teaching profession. https://www.naht.org.uk/Portals/0/PDF's/Campaigns/NAHT-Retention-rate-report-FINAL.pdf. Accessed 8 August 2023.

Newberry, M. and Allsop, Y. (2017). Teacher attrition in the USA: The relational elements in a Utah case study. *Teachers and Teaching: Theory and Practice*, vol. 23, no. 8, pp. 863–880.

Papay, J.P. and Kraft, M.A. (2016). The productivity costs of inefficient hiring practices: Evidence from late teacher hiring. *Journal of Policy Analysis and Management*, vol. 35, no. 4, pp. 791–817.

Ofsted (2019). Teacher wellbeing at work in schools and further education providers [online]. https://assets.publishing.service.gov.uk/government/uploads/system/uploads/attachment_data/file/819314/Teacher_well-being_report_110719F.pdf. Accessed 10 February 2020.

Podolsky, A., Kini, T., Darling-Hammond, L. and Bishop, J. 2019. Strategies for attracting and retaining educators: What does the evidence say? *Education Policy Analysis Archives*, vol. 27, pp. 1–43. DOI: 10.14507/epaa.27.3722

Rainer, C., Le, H. and Abdinasir, K. (2022). *Behaviour and Mental Health in Schools*. https://cypmhc.org.uk/wp-content/uploads/2023/06/Behaviour-and-Mental-Health-in-Schools-Full-Report.pdf. Accessed 24 June 2023.

Richardson, P. and Watt, H. (2014). Why people choose teaching as a career: An expectancy-value approach to understanding teacher motivation. In P. Richardson, S. Karabenick and H. Watt (eds). *Teacher Motivation, Theory and Practice*. Abingdon: Routledge, pp. 3–19.

Ritchie, M. (2020). Succession planning for successful leadership: Why we need to talk about succession planning! *Management in Education*, vol. 34, no. 1, pp. 33–37.

Ronfeldt, M., Loeb, S. and Wyckoff, J. (2012). How teacher turnover harms student achievement. *American Educational Research Journal*, vol. 50, no. 1, pp. 4–36.

See, B. and S. Gorard. (2019). Why don't we have enough teachers? A reconsideration of the available evidence. *Research Papers in Education*, vol. 35, no. 4, pp. 416–442. DOI: 10.1080/02671522.2019.1568535

See, B., Gorard, S., Morris, R. and El Soufi, N. (2019). Attracting and retaining teachers in hard to staff areas: What does the evidence say? *Durham University Evidence Centre for Education*. https://www.durham.ac.uk/media/durham-university/research-/research-centres/durham-university-evidence-centre-for-education/resources/TeacherSupplyFullPaper-1.pdf. Accessed 9 August 2023.

Smithers, A. and Robinson, P. (2003). Factors affecting teachers decisions to leave the profession. https://webarchive.nationalarchives.gov.uk/20130404090352/https://www.education.gov.uk/publications/eOrderingDownload/RR430.pdf. Accessed 12 February 2020.

Towers, E. and Maguire, M.. (2017). Leaving or staying in teaching: A 'vignette' of an experienced urban teacher 'leaver' of a London primary school. *Teachers and Teaching: Theory and Practice*, vol. 23, no. 8, pp. 946–960.

Williams, J. (2018). It just grinds you down: Persistent disruptive behaviour in schools and what can be done about it. https://policyexchange.org.uk/wp-content/uploads/2019/01/It-Just-Grinds-You-Down-Joanna-Williams-Policy-Exchange-December-2018.pdf. Accessed 12 February 2020.

Worth, J. and Van den Brande, J. (2019). *Teacher Labour Market in England: Annual Report 2019*. Slough: NFER.

Worth, J. and Van den Brande, J. (2020). *Teacher Autonomy: How Does It Relate to Job Satisfaction and Retention?* Slough: NFER. https://www.nfer.ac.uk/publications/teacher-autonomy-how-does-it-relate-to-job-satisfaction-and-retention/. Accessed 24 February 2020.

Worth, J., Bamford, S. and Durbin, B. (2015). *Should I Stay or Should I Go? NFER Analysis of Teachers Joining and Leaving the Profession*. Slough: NFER.

8 Motivating teachers

Introduction

Motivating teachers is crucial for ensuring a positive learning environment in schools. Roth (2014) illustrates how motivated teachers can motivate students through practices that offer more engaging learning opportunities. Motivation is also important because 'teachers who are more satisfied and motivated are more likely to stay' (Worth and Van den Brande, 2019, p. 10). Therefore, if school leaders identify and enact ways to motivate their staff, there are likely to be positive outcomes for both pupil progress and teacher retention.

Motivation has been defined simply as 'to be moved to do something' (Ryan and Deci, 2000, p. 54). However, in thinking about how to motivate others, it is more useful to conceive of motivation as 'a process that activates, orients, reinforces and maintains the behaviour of individuals towards the achievement of intended objectives' (Roussel, 2000, p. 5). School leaders are likely to focus on motivating their staff towards achieving whole-school goals that they have identified as important. Motivation is different to job satisfaction, which concerns teachers' perceptions about their job meeting their needs and expectations at work (Evans, 1999). Motivation extends beyond individual job satisfaction, encouraging staff to achieve more in the workplace.

There are numerous theories of motivation, most of which have been developed in and for commercial organisations, so are not directly related to education. As a result, it may be difficult to understand what motivates teachers by using established motivation theories (Urdan, 2014). This chapter, therefore, will focus on the theories that researchers have applied to schools. These theories comprise: intrinsic and extrinsic motivation, self-determination theory, self-efficacy theory, teacher agency, Herzberg's 'two-factor' theory and achievement goal theory. The chapter also includes a critique of these theories.

What is intrinsic and extrinsic motivation?

Intrinsic motivation describes engagement in activities for inherent enjoyment or interest, while extrinsic motivation involves external stimuli influencing achievement of a particular outcome (Ryan and Deci, 2000). So a teacher who delights in working with young people or providing opportunities to learn is intrinsically motivated, whereas a teacher who is mainly interested in their salary and the school holidays is extrinsically motivated (Box 8.1 highlights COVID-19 as an external factor impacting negatively on teachers' motivation). Extrinsic motivation is sometimes seen as an 'impoverished' incentive, where activity tends to be instrumental ('I am only doing this in order to meet my targets'). However, if teachers recognise the value of the goal they wish to achieve (such as students achieving better learning outcomes), extrinsic motivation can be positive and give a sense of control and agency (Ryan and Deci, 2000). Thus some aspects of extrinsic motivation can be internalised even if they began initially as externally driven aspirations.

Alongside intrinsic and extrinsic influences, Klassen et al. (2011) suggest teachers have 'altruistic' motivation, which is about helping others, for example, making a difference in children's lives. A study of the motivations of 'veteran teachers' (who had been in the profession for ten years or longer) found that they had higher rates of intrinsic and altruistic motivations than those less experienced, whereas novice teachers were more influenced by extrinsic motivation (Chiong et al., 2017). The OECD's (2005) survey in seven developed countries found the main motivations to become a teacher were: wanting to work with young people and children, intellectual fulfilment and making a social contribution, all of which are intrinsic or altruistic. In developing countries, however, extrinsic motivations such as salary, job security and career status have been ranked more highly (Richardson and Watt, 2014). There are, however, problems with drawing valid comparisons internationally because different survey instruments have been used in different countries and there is a lack of shared understanding of the meaning of intrinsic, extrinsic and altruistic motivation (Richardson and Watt, 2014).

BOX 8.1 EXTRINSIC FACTOR: COVID-19

A survey of more than 2000 teachers carried out in January 2021 indicated that 52% of classroom teachers were less motivated to teach because of the pandemic (Fullard, 2021a). This is likely to have an impact on pupil progress, since teachers' motivation affects pupils' learning and well-being (Fullard, 2021a). The survey also found that the impact of COVID-19 negatively influenced teachers and school leaders, leaving them more likely to leave the profession, due to the government's handling of the pandemic (Fullard, 2021a).

> **BOX 8.2 EXTRINSIC FACTOR: TEACHERS' PAY**
>
> 'Teachers' pay affects teachers' effort and motivation, which then has an impact on their pupils' cognitive attainment, measured by test scores. Specifically, over an academic year, a ten per cent increase in teachers' wages has roughly the same effect that existing evidence has found for a one pupil reduction in class size ... While there are a range of other factors that are likely to affect teacher motivation (such as senior leadership and work–life balance) ... money does matter. In a wider context this means that salaries are not only important for the recruitment and retention of excellent teachers, they also help ensure that teachers feel valued and are motivated' (Fullard, 2021b, n.p.).

Intrinsic motivation depends on competence, so offering professional development to help teachers improve their practice can increase their motivation (Firestone, 2014). Firestone (2014) points out that emphasising extrinsic incentives, such as additional salary or threats, may undermine intrinsic motivation because it encourages teachers to focus on external targets rather than developing their inherent interest in their work or sense of professionalism. Yet extrinsic factors appear to remain an important influence in teachers' motivation (see Box 8.2 for research on the impact of teachers' pay on their motivation).

What is self-determination theory?

Self-determination theory (SDT) is, as the name implies, linked to a sense of personal empowerment and relates to intrinsic motivation. Conceptualised by Deci and Ryan (1985), SDT focuses on 'autonomous' motivation, which combines intrinsic and internalised extrinsic motivation. Individuals who are autonomously motivated have a sense of agency over what they do; they can make their own choices about how they work. Conversely, 'controlled' motivation is based on rewards and punishments so people who experience controlled motivation look for approval and feel pressurised to work or behave in a particular way (Deci and Ryan, 2008).

Self-determination theory identifies three psychological needs:

- competence (the ability to perform well in one's job)
- relatedness (having a connection with and support from one's colleagues)
- autonomy (freedom to make one's own decisions).

There is a balance between these psychological needs, so, for example, too much autonomy for inexperienced teachers may be inappropriate for their level of competence (Worth and Van den Brande, 2020); instead they may need more support until they have reached an appropriate standard. Work pressure, such as high workload and accountability, reduces teachers' ability to satisfy their psychological needs, which in turn adversely affects autonomous motivation (Taylor et al., 2008). A recent large-scale survey of teachers in England found that there is a 'positive relationship between autonomy, job satisfaction and retention' (Worth and Van den Brande, 2020, p. 6). Box 8.3 describes a case study school in which teachers' competence and relatedness needs were met, but not their need for autonomy and involvement in decision-making, which resulted in demotivation.

There is some evidence that teachers with controlled motivation (based on rewards and punishments) have a tendency to teach in a style that does not encourage autonomy in their students (Roth, 2014). Research in Spain, based on 584 questionnaires from secondary teachers, found that those who felt more pressurised tended to adopt 'ego-oriented' approaches to teaching, for example, they were more likely to encourage students to compare their results, which adversely affected the students' own autonomous motivation (Abos et al., 2018). Abos et al. (2018) conclude that teachers' psychological needs (competence, relatedness, autonomy) should be better supported at work. However, there were some limitations of the study. There was a lack of longitudinal data (it was a snapshot at a particular time) and a lack of analysis of different teacher tasks (for example, lesson preparation, marking). However, Abos et al. (2018) provided an evidence base indicating that supporting teachers' psychological needs seems likely to result in positive outcomes.

It may seem problematic for school leaders to encourage autonomy and agency, because it means trusting teachers to carry out their work effectively without measures of accountability. There is some evidence that transformational leadership

---

BOX 8.3 LACK OF SELF-DETERMINATION IN A US SCHOOL

The incoming principal of an elementary, high-need school in the United States adopted a number of strategies to improve student outcomes, which included mentoring teachers, professional development, performance data meetings and developing a sense of community. In addition, to reduce teacher workload and job stress, she took responsibility for key decisions and duties at the school. She was surprised when teacher turnover at the school continued to increase over the next three years, while student academic outcomes declined. After undertaking a staff survey and analysing the exit interviews of those who had resigned, the principal was taken aback to find that, despite her efforts, the teachers felt stressed, overworked and unsupported, particularly in relation to student behaviour. Seventy-seven per cent reported that they were rarely or never involved in instructional decisions. The lack of teacher involvement in decision-making proved to be a key contributing factor to the loss of morale and motivation in the school. The teachers had not felt able to contribute their views about, for example, how to improve student behaviour.

(Baker et al., 2022)

styles support teacher autonomy, based on research carried out in Israel (Eyal and Roth, 2011). This study comprised a questionnaire survey completed by 122 Israeli teachers. Eyal and Roth (2011) found that the leadership styles of school principals have a significant effect on teachers' motivation and well-being. A transformational leadership style, in which there was a clear vision and teachers felt empowered, led to autonomous motivation. Conversely, transactional leadership styles, in which principals closely monitored staff and ensured that they complied with the regulations, resulted in controlled motivation and higher burnout. The limitations of this study are that the teachers involved were from elementary schools and the great majority (107) were women. The study did not identify which aspects of transformational leadership had the most impact on motivation, and leadership style is only one of the factors that influences motivation and burnout. Nevertheless, Eyal and Roth's (2011) findings were confirmed by a more recent study by Polatcan et al. (2023). This research, which involved 349 teachers from primary, middle and secondary schools in 15 city regions of Anatolia, Turkey, also found that transformational leadership increased teacher agency. Polatcan et al.'s (2023) findings suggest both direct and indirect effects of transformational practice on teachers' behaviours. Clearly, more research is needed to be able to develop generalisable conclusions from both Eyal and Roth's (2011) and Polatcan et al.'s (2023) studies.

In research evidence to date, there is a lack of causal inferences about self-determination theory in schools. In other words, while different factors may be identified, there is no evidence that one variable causes or affects another. Thus although self-determination theory suggests school leaders could motivate staff more by addressing the three psychological needs of competence (by providing appropriate professional development as needed), relatedness (by encouraging teamwork and collegiality) and autonomy (by empowering staff and enabling them to engage in decision-making), there is no direct evidence that this results in better learning outcomes for students.

What is self-efficacy theory?

Self-efficacy is the belief that one is capable of achieving one's goals (Bandura, 1997); in the case of teachers, this is about the ability to help students learn (Klassen et al., 2011b). Self-efficacy determines which tasks individuals choose to focus on (which are generally the ones that they are more likely to achieve), how much effort they expend on an activity, how long they persevere and their level of resilience (Schunk and DiBenedetto, 2016). Teachers are more likely to persist in the face of difficulties if they are confident that they have the ability to succeed (Tschannen-Moran and Woolfolk Hoy, 2001). Calkins et al. (2023, p. 4) argue that 'a teacher's motivation and self-efficacy are related and a teacher's desire to teach is, in part, related to their beliefs about their teaching ability'.

Self-efficacy can increase with experience. As might be expected, veteran teachers have higher levels of self-efficacy than novices (Bullock et al., 2015). A snapshot survey of 1430 practising teachers in Canada confirmed that teachers' self-efficacy appeared to increase until it peaked at 23 years of experience (Klassen et al., 2014). Day and Gu (2007) suggest self-efficacy declines towards the end of a teacher's career.

Teachers' self-efficacy has an impact on the learning environment and on the achievement of their students (Gilbert et al., 2014). Teachers with high self-efficacy have more positive classroom environments and quality of instruction (Holzberger et al., 2013), as well as greater levels of job satisfaction (Klassen and Chiu, 2010). They also increase student learning outcomes and motivation (Calkins et al., 2023). Teachers with lower self-efficacy tend to struggle at work, with reduced job satisfaction and higher stress levels (Klassen et al., 2014).

There are a number of self-efficacy questionnaires which aim to assess teachers' self-efficacy beliefs. Two of them are provided in Appendix 8.1, Tschannen-Moran and Woolfolk Hoy's (2001) Teachers' Sense of Efficacy Scale and Appendix 8.2, Bandura's (1990) Self-Efficacy Scale. While the full scales are given in the appendices, some sample questions are:

- How well can you implement alternative strategies in your classroom?
- How well can you keep a few problem students from ruining an entire lesson?
- How much can you influence the decisions that are made in the school?
- How much can you do to make students enjoy coming to school?

School leaders could encourage staff to complete the questionnaires in Appendix 8.1 or 8.2 and offer professional development to help with areas where they lack confidence.

There are problems in assessing self-efficacy, however, because a teacher may have a belief in their ability to teach one topic or subject but not another (Ball and Bass, 2000). Teaching combines elements that are externally determined (the curriculum, for example) and interaction with students, who do not behave in predictable ways. Much of the research on teacher self-efficacy has relied on validated questionnaires through which teachers report on their own beliefs about their effectiveness. There is a lack of corroborating evidence about whether their self-efficacy is justified by their performance. Box 8.4 gives an example of unjustified self-efficacy.

Collective self-efficacy involves teachers collaborating to improve student learning and to help each other cope with difficulties. It can include teachers' shared beliefs about the capabilities of the whole staff, is characteristic of successful schools and influences teachers' engagement and well-being (Klassen et al., 2014).

How can school leaders help to strengthen self-efficacy in their staff? Bandura (1997) suggested that self-efficacy develops from a range of factors including one's own performance ('I can do it'), observing how others perform ('if s/he can do it,

> **BOX 8.4 UNJUSTIFIED SELF-EFFICACY**
>
> An example of a mismatch between teachers' self-efficacy and performance is a challenging secondary school known to the authors, which employed a number of teachers who were confident about their abilities and were found by the leadership team to have excellent behaviour management skills. This was not, however, matched by their teaching approaches. The pupils made little progress in their learning, despite being well behaved. This indicates a misplaced sense of self-efficacy for the teachers, which needed to be addressed by appropriate professional development.

so can I'), positive persuasion ('you can do it') and physiological states ('I feel like this when I do it'). A key aspect of self-efficacy is that it represents a teacher's confidence in having the capability to achieve professional effectiveness, even if they are currently not able to do some aspect of their work.

Good communication and regular feedback may help to support self-efficacy (Leithwood and Beatty, 2008). Professional feedback should give teachers confidence as well as help identify areas where they can improve. Encouraging perceptions of collective self-efficacy across the school can help to reduce problem behaviours and improve student achievement (Sorlie and Torsheim, 2011). In addition, social and professional capital, developed through teacher interactions, access to resources and research-informed projects, have been found to improve teacher self-efficacy (Neugebauer et al., 2019; Qvortrup, 2016).

How to build motivation through community and agency?

Ideas about the social nature of learning have been extended through the theory of communities of practice (Lave and Wenger, 1991; Wenger, 1998). Wenger (1998) proposes that a community of practitioners (such as teachers in a school) may share challenges, passions and interests and through their interactions learn from and with each other. He argues that a community can work effectively with novice and experienced practitioners collaborating to enable novices to learn. In working together as a community he suggests that they can improve their ability to do what they care about. More information about communities of practice can be found in Chapter 6.

Karlberg-Granlund (2019) supports this in her discussion about the nature of teachers' work. She elaborates on context – that is, all the factors that affect how schools operate. These factors include the particular place or environment within which a school is situated and the social, cultural, political, institutional and historical factors that impact on the school community. Karlberg-Granlund (2019) argues that the context of the community can affect how teachers carry out their work, that is, the extent to which they can be agentive. McGregor and Frodsham

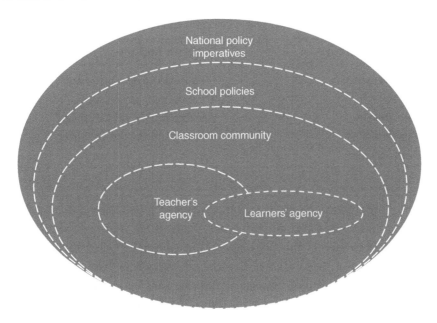

Figure 8.1 Relationally locating teacher and learner agency to indicate structural and others' influences

(2022, p. 3) theorised about how these influences affect teacher and learner agency and provide the illustration in Figure 8.1 to suggest how they are connected.

Manninen et al. (2022) extend the factors affecting the context of a school to include diversity and migration. In their Finnish study, involving 15 interviews with staff, they found that, faced with the challenging situation of a more diverse student population, teachers could be empowered in developing new strategies to deal with their learners' needs. They also recognised that the headteacher promoting shared (or distributed leadership) enabled staff to contribute to decision-making and facilitate the demands of reshaping their work to generate new practices to deal with the challenges of diverse student education.

Working with their school communities, headteachers can shape the culture of the school to enable teachers to have agency, that is, given sufficient space and support to engage in meaningful and useful activities, to contribute to school life. This in turn strengthens teachers' motivation.

What is Herzberg's motivation-hygiene theory/two factor theory?

Herzberg et al.'s (1993) theory has shaped much of the research into teacher job satisfaction (Buyukgoze et al., 2022). Herzberg et al. (1993) found that the aspects of work that lead to motivation are not the same as those that lead to dissatisfaction. He and his team differentiated between 'motivation' and 'hygiene' factors as follows (see Table 8.1):

Table 8.1 Herzberg et al.'s (1993) motivation and hygiene factors

Motivation factors	Hygiene factors
• Achievement	• Policies and administration systems
• Recognition	• Competent supervision
• Job interest	• Interpersonal relationships
• Responsibility	• Salary and related benefits
• Advancement	

Herzberg et al. (1993) argued that if the 'hygiene' factors are deficient, this leads to staff being dissatisfied at work, but when the hygiene factors are met, it does not necessarily lead to greater motivation. So, for example, if the classrooms are not cleaned regularly, teachers will feel dissatisfied, but, while extra cleaning may help them to feel better, it will not necessarily increase their motivation.

It might appear that Herzberg et al.'s (1959) research cannot easily be generalised to education, since the original interviewees in the study were all male accountants and engineers while the majority of teachers, particularly in primary schools, are women. Teachers work in the public sector and are often motivated by altruistic values, such as making a difference. Altruism was not identified as a motivator by Herzberg et al.'s (1959) original research. Nevertheless, a number of research projects have applied motivation-hygiene theory to education (for example, Nias, 1981; Klassen and Anderson, 2009).

Back in 1981, teacher motivation was a relatively unexplored topic, so Nias' (1981) study broke new ground by interviewing 99 graduates who had been teaching for between two and nine years in primary schools and asking them what they liked or disliked about their job and what their plans were for the future. Some of her findings were consistent with Herzberg's theory that personal achievement, recognition and growth were important for motivation. Most of the teachers, however, said that the children were what they liked most in the job. The reasons teachers gave for not liking their work were more complex than Herzberg's 'hygiene' factors. Although the factors of administration, poor communication and inadequate leadership were all mentioned, the interviewees' main concern was the way in which these elements prevented them from fulfilling their expectations of teaching, rather than causing them to be dissatisfied with their work. Nias (1981) suggested that factors such as inefficient administration, poor communication and uncongenial colleagues should be seen as 'negative satisfiers' which, if improved, could help raise the level of job satisfaction and motivation.

Another research study looking at teacher motivation (Klassen and Anderson, 2009, p. 756), which involved a survey of 210 secondary teachers in south-west England, concluded that it was difficult to categorise teachers' inspirations into motivation and hygiene factors or negative satisfiers, because 'teachers' job

> **BOX 8.5 TEACHERS TALKING ABOUT MOTIVATION FACTORS**
>
> **Recognition**
>
> 'It's a really hard job, but when you just come in and find a little thank you card in your pigeonhole or a bottle of wine on your desk or just an e-mail that just says that was really good, and you just think you don't have to keep thanking me, but actually it really does help' (Secondary school teacher, high-need inner city school)
>
> **Achievement**
>
> 'I've got a great sense of pride in what's achieved in my department' (Secondary school teacher, high-need shire county school)
>
> **Pupils**
>
> 'I look back and think there's been tougher years, and easier years, and I think you just.... It's that moment, isn't it. It's the moment when a kid says something, or asks a question, and that's what we're here for. It's all about them. The rest's not relevant' (Secondary school teacher, high-need shire county school)
>
> **Rewards**
>
> 'It's just tiny things ... like... we get free tea and coffee here.... They do an end of term buffet every half term' (Secondary school teacher, high-need inner city school)
>
> (Teacher Retention research project)

satisfaction relies heavily on a series of interactive and reciprocal relationships'. As a result neither Herzberg et al.'s (1993) theory, nor Nias' (1981) study could fully explain their findings. It appears that the complex interactions in schools are difficult to classify into motivation and hygiene factors. Nevertheless, Box 8.5 provides some examples of factors that motivated teachers in high-need schools.

What is achievement goal theory?

Achievement goal theory has been developed from the work of Locke (1968, p. 157), whose systematic review of the literature noted that 'hard goals produce a higher level of performance than easy goals; specific hard goals produce a higher level of performance than a goal of 'do your best'; and behavioural intentions regulate choice behaviour'. In other words, clear, specific, reasonably challenging goals help to motivate individuals to work harder. Hard goals are more motivating because there is a greater sense of accomplishment in achieving them. Individuals are motivated to achieve goals that satisfy their emotions and desires, so the amount of effort made depends on the difficulty of the goal and the level of commitment to it.

This theory was investigated in Portugal by Jesus and Lens (2005). Their questionnaire survey measured 272 elementary and secondary teachers' expectancies of control, success and efficacy, intrinsic motivation and perceived goal value levels, and how these interacted to influence professional engagement. Jesus and Lens (2005) found that although professional goals are very important for teacher performance, if they fail to attain goals that they value highly, it reduces their professional engagement. In addition, they found that if teachers perceive work problems to be caused *internally* because of personal inadequacies, and success to be due to *external* factors, such as luck, they feel helpless and demotivated, believing that nothing they do will make a difference. In short, high goals and low expectancy of achieving them can lead to low motivation (Jesus and Lens, 2005).

Butler (2014, p. 21) distinguishes between 'mastery' goals (to develop competence) and 'ability' goals (to demonstrate performance). Teachers with mastery goals are more likely to attribute success to their effort, prefer challenging tasks and see difficulties as opportunities to learn. Teachers with ability goals are more likely to judge their competence in relation to others, attribute success to their ability rather than effort and avoid seeking help when they experience problems because it might expose their inadequacies (Butler, 2014).

There are a number of different measures of teachers' achievement goals, including Butler's (2012) own questionnaire which includes mastery, ability-approach (demonstrating superior teaching ability), ability-avoidance (avoiding failure) and work-avoidance (minimising effort) goals. It appears, perhaps rather obviously, that mastery goals for teaching result in more constructive responses to difficulty than ability-avoidance and work-avoidance goals. Mastery goals are also linked to greater job satisfaction and reduced burnout, whereas the opposite is true for work avoidance and ability-avoidance. Butler (2014) suggests that 'relational' goals need to be included for teachers, since teachers' relationships with students (and other staff members) are an important element of the profession. She also points out that teachers may have a variety of goals of different kinds which they aspire to achieve. Examples of Butler's (2007, p. 244; 2012, p. 729) questions which demonstrate the differences between these goals are in Table 8.2.

School leaders who are interested in encouraging mastery goals should perhaps bear in mind that performance pressure from the school principal tends to result in teachers focusing on ability goals, while directive leadership styles, causing additional work for the teacher, appear to encourage work-avoidance. It is possible that the most appropriate leadership approach to boost mastery goals is transformational leadership, when school leaders inspire teachers to embrace their vision and values while empowering them to develop their own skills.

Table 8.2 Extracts from Butler's (2007, 2012) Goal Orientations for Teaching

Teachers differ in what makes them feel they had a successful day in school; when would you feel that you had a successful day?	1 2 3 4 5

Mastery goals
- I saw that I was developing professionally and teaching more effectively than in the past.

Ability-approach goals
- My classes did better than those of other teachers on an exam.

Ability-avoidance goals
- No one asked a question that I could not answer.

Work-avoidance goals
- Some of my classes were cancelled because pupils were on a school trip.

Identify how far you agree with the following statements:

Personal relationships with students
- I would feel most successful as a teacher if I saw that I was developing closer and better relationships with students in my classes.

What are the shortcomings of motivation theories?

One criticism of motivation theories is that they sometimes use the terms 'motivation', 'job satisfaction' and 'satisfying' interchangeably when these words have different meanings for research participants (Evans, 1999). For example, if researchers ask teachers about times when they felt satisfied at work, this could elicit a different response than asking when they felt motivated. Herzberg (1959), in particular, discusses job satisfaction and motivation as well as dissatisfaction, without ever defining these terms.

Another problem for the psychological theories of motivation is that the challenges facing teachers may lead them to adopt 'ego-protective' behaviours which influence their responses to questionnaires about motivation (Urdan, 2014). Since many questionnaires involve self-reporting of, for example, self-efficacy or self-determination, there is a danger that the results may be biased. Butler (2014, p. 25) makes the point that teachers' reports of their behaviour 'tend to be only weakly correlated, if at all, with both student and observer reports, and thus may be rather poor indicators of [ways] teachers actually behave in the classroom'. In addition, teachers may only focus on a few students when they answer questionnaires rather than providing a balanced view, drawing on their work with a range of different pupils.

Several of the theories draw links between individual motivation preferences and greater engagement, improved pupil outcomes and reduced burnout. Thus it seems possible that the different theories may be measuring the same underlying characteristics, for example, 'internally motivated individuals experience both autonomy and self-efficacy' (Firestone, 2014, p.101). Opfer (2014), too, notes the inter-connectedness of the concepts relating to motivation.

Conclusion

A critical issue for school leaders is whether teachers' motivations can be significantly influenced and this depends on whether their motivations are dependent on the school context and their relationships within it or on the individual's personal history. Individuals have different motivations and may not necessarily share these openly. This makes it challenging for leaders to build motivation across a whole school (Bingham and Bubb, 2022).

Nevertheless, the theories of motivation give some useful indications about what appears to inspire teachers. Professional development, coaching and recognising achievement are likely to build self-efficacy. Empowering teachers to take ownership of their work and involving them in decision-making help to develop a sense of agency, self-determination and autonomy. Offering opportunities to collaborate with colleagues across the school strengthens relationships and helps to develop collective efficacy and agency. Providing career progression supports the 'motivators' of job interest, responsibility and advancement. School leaders can also support teachers' psychological needs and well-being as a means of improving job satisfaction. In addition, it is important to ensure effective management in the school, so that communication, administration and resource provision are a source of satisfaction to staff.

> **BOX 8.6 QUESTIONS FOR REFLECTION AND ACTION**
>
> - How far are the psychological needs of competence, relatedness and autonomy supported at your school?
> - Have you identified staff levels of self-efficacy at your school in order to provide appropriate professional development (see Appendix 8.1 and 8.2)? Is there a system for providing professional feedback to build teachers' confidence?
> - Are teachers and other staff given sufficient agency to increase motivation?
> - Is the senior leadership team aware of 'hygiene' factors (such as administration, salary, resources and communication) which might cause dissatisfaction? How are these factors regularly reviewed and addressed?
> - To what extent are teachers encouraged to work towards 'mastery' goals (to develop competence) rather than 'ability' goals (to demonstrate performance)? In other words, is the school's main focus on test results or on developing teaching and learning?
> - How could your leadership be adapted to a more transformational approach which motivates teachers?

APPENDIX 8.1: TSCHANNEN-MORAN AND WOOLFOLK HOY'S (2001) TEACHERS' SENSE OF EFFICACY SCALE (ALSO CALLED THE OHIO STATE TEACHER EFFICACY SCALE BECAUSE IT WAS DEVELOPED AT OHIO STATE UNIVERSITY)

Teachers could use this questionnaire to assess their own sense of self-efficacy. The outcomes could be reviewed with a colleague or manager. Professional development could also be provided to address aspects of work where they feel less confident.

Efficacy for instructional strategies									
1. To what extent can you use a variety of assessment strategies?	Nothing	2	Very Little	4	Some Influence	6	Quite a Bit	8	A Great Deal
2. To what extent can you provide an alternative explanation or example when students are confused?	Nothing	2	Very Little	4	Some Influence	6	Quite a Bit	8	A Great Deal
3. To what extent can you craft good questions for your students?	Nothing	2	Very Little	4	Some Influence	6	Quite a Bit	8	A Great Deal
4. How well can you implement alternative strategies in your classroom?	Nothing	2	Very Little	4	Some Influence	6	Quite a Bit	8	A Great Deal
5. How well can you respond to difficult questions from your students?	Nothing	2	Very Little	4	Some Influence	6	Quite a Bit	8	A Great Deal
6. How much can you do to adjust your lessons to the proper level for individual students?	Nothing	2	Very Little	4	Some Influence	6	Quite a Bit	8	A Great Deal

(Continued)

7. To what extent can you gauge student comprehension of what you have taught?	1 Nothing	2	3 Very Little	4	5 Some Influence	6	7 Quite a Bit	8	9 A Great Deal
8. How well can you provide appropriate challenges for very capable students?	1 Nothing	2	3 Very Little	4	5 Some Influence	6	7 Quite a Bit	8	9 A Great Deal

Efficacy for classroom management

9. How much can you do to control disruptive behaviour in the classroom?	1 Nothing	2	3 Very Little	4	5 Some Influence	6	7 Quite a Bit	8	9 A Great Deal
10. How much can you do to get children to follow classroom rules?	1 Nothing	2	3 Very Little	4	5 Some Influence	6	7 Quite a Bit	8	9 A Great Deal
11. How much can you do to calm a student who is disruptive or noisy?	1 Nothing	2	3 Very Little	4	5 Some Influence	6	7 Quite a Bit	8	9 A Great Deal
12. How well can you establish your classroom management system with each group of students?	1 Nothing	2	3 Very Little	4	5 Some Influence	6	7 Quite a Bit	8	9 A Great Deal
13. How well can you keep a few problem students from ruining an entire lesson?	1 Nothing	2	3 Very Little	4	5 Some Influence	6	7 Quite a Bit	8	9 A Great Deal
14. How well can you respond to defiant students?	1 Nothing	2	3 Very Little	4	5 Some Influence	6	7 Quite a Bit	8	9 A Great Deal
15. To what extent can you make your expectation clear about student behaviour?	1 Nothing	2	3 Very Little	4	5 Some Influence	6	7 Quite a Bit	8	9 A Great Deal

16. How well can you establish routines to keep activities running smoothly?	1 Nothing	2	3 Very Little	4	5 Some Influence	6	7 Quite a Bit	8	9 A Great Deal

Efficacy for student engagement

17. How much can you do to get students to believe they can do well in schoolwork?	1 Nothing	2	3 Very Little	4	5 Some Influence	6	7 Quite a Bit	8	9 A Great Deal
18. How much can you do to help your students value learning?	1 Nothing	2	3 Very Little	4	5 Some Influence	6	7 Quite a Bit	8	9 A Great Deal
19. How much can you do to motivate students who show low interest in schoolwork?	1 Nothing	2	3 Very Little	4	5 Some Influence	6	7 Quite a Bit	8	9 A Great Deal
20. How much can you assist families in helping their children do well in school?	1 Nothing	2	3 Very Little	4	5 Some Influence	6	7 Quite a Bit	8	9 A Great Deal
21. How much can you do to improve the understanding of a student who is failing?	1 Nothing	2	3 Very Little	4	5 Some Influence	6	7 Quite a Bit	8	9 A Great Deal
22. How much can you do to help your students think critically?	1 Nothing	2	3 Very Little	4	5 Some Influence	6	7 Quite a Bit	8	9 A Great Deal
23. How much can you do to foster student creativity?	1 Nothing	2	3 Very Little	4	5 Some Influence	6	7 Quite a Bit	8	9 A Great Deal
24. How much can you do to get through to the most difficult students?	1 Nothing	2	3 Very Little	4	5 Some Influence	6	7 Quite a Bit	8	9 A Great Deal

Appendix 8.2: Bandura's (1990) Self-Efficacy Scale

Teachers could use this questionnaire to assess their own sense of self-efficacy. They could review the outcomes with a colleague or manager. Professional development could also be provided to address aspects of work where they feel less confident.

Efficacy to influence decision-making

1. How much can you influence the decisions that are made in the school?

1	2	3	4	5	6	7	8	9
Nothing		Very Little		Some Influence		Quite a Bit		A Great Deal

2. How much can you express your views freely on important school matters?

1	2	3	4	5	6	7	8	9
Nothing		Very Little		Some Influence		Quite a Bit		A Great Deal

Efficacy to influence school resources

3. How much can you do to get the instructional materials and equipment you need?

1	2	3	4	5	6	7	8	9
Nothing		Very Little		Some Influence		Quite a Bit		A Great Deal

Instructional self-efficacy

4. How much can you do to influence the class sizes in your school?

1	2	3	4	5	6	7	8	9
Nothing		Very Little		Some Influence		Quite a Bit		A Great Deal

5. How much can you do to get through to the most difficult students?

1	2	3	4	5	6	7	8	9
Nothing		Very Little		Some Influence		Quite a Bit		A Great Deal

6. How much can you do to promote learning when there is a lack of support from the home?

1	2	3	4	5	6	7	8	9
Nothing		Very Little		Some Influence		Quite a Bit		A Great Deal

7. How much can you do to keep students on task on difficult assignments?	1 Nothing	2	3 Very Little	4	5 Some Influence	6	7 Quite a Bit	8	9 A Great Deal
8. How much can you do to increase students' memory of what they have been taught in previous lessons?	1 Nothing	2	3 Very Little	4	5 Some Influence	6	7 Quite a Bit	8	9 A Great Deal
9. How much can you do to motivate students who show low interest in schoolwork?	1 Nothing	2	3 Very Little	4	5 Some Influence	6	7 Quite a Bit	8	9 A Great Deal
10. How much can you do to get students to work together?	1 Nothing	2	3 Very Little	4	5 Some Influence	6	7 Quite a Bit	8	9 A Great Deal
11. How much can you do to overcome the influence of adverse community conditions on students learning?	1 Nothing	2	3 Very Little	4	5 Some Influence	6	7 Quite a Bit	8	9 A Great Deal
12. How much can you do to get children to do their homework?	1 Nothing	2	3 Very Little	4	5 Some Influence	6	7 Quite a Bit	8	9 A Great Deal
Disciplinary self-efficacy									
13. How much can you do to get children to follow classroom rules?	1 Nothing	2	3 Very Little	4	5 Some Influence	6	7 Quite a Bit	8	9 A Great Deal
14. How much can you do to control disruptive behaviour in the classroom?	1 Nothing	2	3 Very Little	4	5 Some Influence	6	7 Quite a Bit	8	9 A Great Deal

(*Continued*)

15. How much can you do to prevent problem behaviour on the school grounds?

1	2	3	4	5	6	7	8	9
Nothing		Very Little		Some Influence		Quite a Bit		A Great Deal

Efficacy to enlist parental involvement

16. How much can you do to get parents to become involved in school activities?

1	2	3	4	5	6	7	8	9
Nothing		Very Little		Some Influence		Quite a Bit		A Great Deal

17. How much can you assist parents in helping their children to do well in school?

1	2	3	4	5	6	7	8	9
Nothing		Very Little		Some Influence		Quite a Bit		A Great Deal

18. How much can you do to make parents feel comfortable coming to school?

1	2	3	4	5	6	7	8	9
Nothing		Very Little		Some Influence		Quite a Bit		A Great Deal

Efficacy to enlist community involvement

19. How much can you do to get community groups involved in working with the school?

1	2	3	4	5	6	7	8	9
Nothing		Very Little		Some Influence		Quite a Bit		A Great Deal

20. How much can you do to get churches involved in working with the school?

1	2	3	4	5	6	7	8	9
Nothing		Very Little		Some Influence		Quite a Bit		A Great Deal

21. How much can you do to get businesses involved in working with the school?

1	2	3	4	5	6	7	8	9
Nothing		Very Little		Some Influence		Quite a Bit		A Great Deal

22. How much can you do to get local colleges and universities involved in working with the school?

1	2	3	4	5	6	7	8	9
Nothing		Very Little		Some Influence		Quite a Bit		A Great Deal

Efficacy to create a positive school climate

23. How much can you do to make the school a safe place?	1 Nothing	2	3 Very Little	4	5 Some Influence	6	7 Quite a Bit	8	9 A Great Deal
24. How much can you do to make students enjoy coming to school?	1 Nothing	2	3 Very Little	4	5 Some Influence	6	7 Quite a Bit	8	9 A Great Deal
25. How much can you do to get students to trust teachers?	1 Nothing	2	3 Very Little	4	5 Some Influence	6	7 Quite a Bit	8	9 A Great Deal
26. How much can you help other teachers with their teaching skills?	1 Nothing	2	3 Very Little	4	5 Some Influence	6	7 Quite a Bit	8	9 A Great Deal
27. How much can you do to enhance collaboration between teachers and the administration to make the school run effectively?	1 Nothing	2	3 Very Little	4	5 Some Influence	6	7 Quite a Bit	8	9 A Great Deal
28. How much can you do to reduce school dropout?	1 Nothing	2	3 Very Little	4	5 Some Influence	6	7 Quite a Bit	8	9 A Great Deal
29. How much can you do to reduce school absenteeism?	1 Nothing	2	3 Very Little	4	5 Some Influence	6	7 Quite a Bit	8	9 A Great Deal
30. How much can you do to get students to believe they can do well in schoolwork?	1 Nothing	2	3 Very Little	4	5 Some Influence	6	7 Quite a Bit	8	9 A Great Deal

Appendix 8.3: Janke et al.'s (2019) goal orientation questionnaire

Teachers could use this questionnaire to assess their own goal orientation, with the option to review the outcomes with a colleague or manager.

In my work, I aspire ...	1 Total	2	3 Total	4	5 Disagreement	6	7 Agreement
Learning goal orientation							
... to improve my pedagogical knowledge and competence							
... to improve my content knowledge and competence							
... to improve my pedagogical-content knowledge and competence							
Performance approach goal orientation							
... to demonstrate that I know more than other teachers							
... to show that I deal better with critical lessons than other teachers							
... for others to realise that I teach better than other teachers							
Performance avoidance goal orientation							
... to conceal when I do something less well than other teachers							

In my work, I aspire ...	1 Total	2	3 Total	4	5 Disagreement	6	7 Agreement
... not to show when I find it harder to meet the demands of the job than other teachers							
... that no one thinks that I do my job worse than other teachers							
Work avoidance goal orientation							
... not to have to work too hard							
... that the work is easy							
... to get through the day with little effort							

References

Abos, A., Haerens, L., Sevil, J., Aelterman, N. and Garcia-Gonzalez, L. (2018). Teachers' motivation in relation to their psychological functioning and interpersonal style: A variable- and person-centred approach. *Teaching and Teacher Education*, vol. 74, pp. 21–34.

Baker, R., Hill, J., Portwood, B., Smith-Harrah, E. and Sutherland, D.H. (2022). One size does not fit all: How leadership strategies affect teacher satisfaction and retention. *Journal of Cases in Educational Leadership*, vol. 25, no. 4, pp. 378–393.

Ball, D. and Bass, H. (2000). Interweaving content and pedagogy in teaching and learning to teach: Knowing and using mathematics. In J. Boaler (ed). *Multiple Perspectives on the Teaching and Learning of Mathematics*. Westport, CT: Ablex, pp. 83–104.

Bandura, A. (1997). *Self-efficacy: The Exercise of Control*. New York: Freeman.

Bandura, A. (1990). *Multidimensional Scales of Perceived Academic Efficacy*. Stanford, CA: Stanford University Press.

Bingham, D. and Bubb, S. (2022). Leadership for well-being. In Greany, T and Earley, P. (eds). *School Leadership and Education System Reform*, 2nd edition. London: Bloomsbury Academic, pp. 143–152.

Bullock, A., Coplan, R.J. and Bosacki, S. (2015). Exploring links between early childhood educators' psychological characteristics and classroom management self-efficacy beliefs. *Canadian Journal of Behavioral Science*, vol. 47, no. 2, pp. 175–183. DOI: 10.1037/a0038547

Butler, R. (2007). Teachers' achievement goal orientations and associations with teachers' help seeking: Examination of a novel approach to teacher motivation. *Journal of Educational Psychology*, vol. 99, no. 2, pp. 241–252.

Butler, R. (2012). Striving to connect: Extending an achievement goal approach to teacher motivation to include relational goals for teaching. *Journal of Educational Psychology*, vol. 104, no. 3, pp. 726–742.

Butler, R. (2014). What teachers want to achieve and why it matters: An achievement goal approach to teacher motivation. In P. Richardson, S. Karabenick and H. Watt (eds). *Teacher Motivation, Theory and Practice*. Abingdon: Routledge, pp. 20–35.

Buyukgoze, H., Caliskan, O. and Gümüş, S. (2022). Linking distributed leadership with collective teacher innovativeness: The mediating roles of job satisfaction and professional collaboration. *Educational Management Administration & Leadership*. DOI: 10.1177/17411432221130879

Calkins, L., Wiens, P., Parker, J. and Tschinkel, R. (2023). Teacher motivation and self-efficacy: How do specific motivations for entering teaching relate to teacher self-efficacy? *Journal of Education*, vol. 204, no. 2, pp. 427–438. DOI: 10.1177/00220574221142300

Chiong, C., Menzies, L. and Parameshwaran, M. (2017). Why do long-serving teachers stay in the teaching profession? Analysing the motivations of teachers with 10 or more years' experience in England. *British Educational Research Journal*, vol. 43, no. 6, pp. 1083–1110. DOI: 10.1002/berj.3302

Day, C. and Gu, Q. (2007). Variations in the conditions for teachers' professional learning and development: Sustaining commitment and effectiveness over a career. *Oxford Review of Education*, vol. 33, no. 4, pp. 423–443. DOI: 10.1080/03054980701450746

Deci, E. and Ryan, R. (2008). Self-determination theory: A macrotheory of human motivation, development, and health. *Canadian Psychology*, vol. 49, no. 3, pp. 182–185.

Deci, E. and Ryan, R. (1985). *Intrinsic Motivation and Self-determination in Human Behavior*. New York: Plenum Press.

Evans, L. (1999). *Managing to Motivate: A Guide for School Leaders*. London: Cassell.

Eyal, O. and Roth, G. (2011). Principals' leadership and teachers' motivation: Self-determination theory analysis. *Journal of Educational Administration*, vol. 49, no. 3, pp. 256–275.

Firestone, W. (2014). Teacher evaluation policy and conflicting theories of motivation. *Educational Researcher*, vol. 43, no. 2, pp. 100–107.

Fullard, J. (2021a). The pandemic and teacher attrition: An exodus waiting to happen? Education Policy Institute. https://epi.org.uk/publications-and-research/the-pandemic-and-teacher-attrition-an-exodus-waiting-to-happen/. Accessed 17 August 2023

Fullard, J. (2021b). *Does money motivate teachers?* https://www.bera.ac.uk/blog/does-money-motivate-teachers. Accessed 17 August 2023.

Gilbert, R., Adesope, O. and Schroeder, N. (2014). Efficacy beliefs, job satisfaction, stress and their influence on the occupational commitment of English-medium content teachers in the Dominican Republic. *Educational Psychology*, vol. 34, no. 7, pp. 876–899.

Herzberg, F., Mausner, B. and Snyderman, B. (1993). *The Motivation to Work*, 2nd rev. ed.,. New Brunswick, NJ: Transaction Publishers.

Herzberg, F., Mausner, B. and Snyderman, B. (1959). *The Motivation to Work*. New York: John Wiley & Sons.

Holzberger, D., Philipp, A. and Kunter, M. (2013). How teachers' self-efficacy is related to instructional quality: A longitudinal analysis. *Journal of Educational Psychology*, vol. 103, pp. 649–663.

Janke, S., Bardach, L., Oczlon, S. and Lüftenegger, M. (2019). Enhancing feasibility when measuring teachers' motivation: A brief scale for teachers' achievement goal orientations. *Teaching and Teacher Education*, vol. 83, pp. 1–11. DOI: 10.1016/j.tate.2019.04.003

Jesus, S. and Lens, W. (2005). An integrated model for the study of teacher motivation. *Applied Psychology: An International Review*, vol. 54, no. 1, pp. 119–134.

Karlberg-Granlund, G. (2019). Exploring the challenge of working in a small school and community: Uncovering hidden tensions. *Journal of Rural Studies*, vol. 72, pp. 293–305.

Klassen, R., Al-Dhafri, S., Hannok, W. and Betts, S. (2011) Investigating pre-service teacher motivation across cultures using the teachers' ten statements test. *Teaching and Teacher Education*, vol. 27, no. 3, pp. 579–588.

Klassen, R.M. and Anderson, C.J.K. (2009). How times change: Secondary teachers' job satisfaction and dissatisfaction in 1962 and 2007. *British Educational Research Journal*, vol. 35, no. 5, pp. 745–759.

Klassen, R. and Chiu, M. (2010). Effects on teachers' self-efficacy and job satisfaction: Teacher gender, years of experience and job stress. *Journal of Educational Psychology*, vol. 102, pp. 741–756.

Klassen, R., Durksen, T. and Tze, V. (2014). Teachers' self-efficacy beliefs: Ready to move from theory to practice? In P. Richardson, S. Karabenick and H. Watt (eds). *Teacher Motivation, Theory and Practice*. Abingdon: Routledge, pp. 100–115.

Klassen, R., Tze, V., Betts, S. and Gordon, K. (2011b). Teacher efficacy research 1998-2009: Signs of progress or unfulfilled promise? *Educational Psychology Review*, vol. 23, pp. 21–43.

Lave, J. and Wenger, E. (1991). *Situated Learning: Legitimate Peripheral Participation*. Cambridge: Cambridge University Press.

Leithwood, K. and Beatty, B. (2008). *Leading with Teacher Emotions in Mind*. Thousand Oaks, CA: Corwin Press.

Locke, E.A. (1968). Towards a theory of task motivation and incentives. *Organisational Behavior and Human Performance*, vol. 3, no. 2, pp. 157–189.

Manninen, E., Hökkä, P., Tarnanen, M. and Vähäsantanen, K. (2022). Staff members' professional agency within the staff community and the education policies: Supporting integration in multicultural and multilingual school communities. *Education Sciences*, vol. 12, no. 12, p. 900. DOI: 10.3390/educsci12120900

McGregor, D. and Frodsham, S. (2022). Capturing the nature of teacher and learner agency demonstrating creativity: Ethical issues and resolutions. *Education Sciences*, vol. 12, no. 12, p. 394. DOI: 10.3390/educsci12060394

Neugebauer, S.R., Hopkins, M. and Spillane, J.P. (2019). Social sources of teacher self-efficacy: The potency of teacher interactions and proximity to instruction. *Teachers College Record*, vol. 121, no. 4, pp. 1–32.

Nias, J. (1981). Teacher satisfaction and dissatisfaction: Herzberg's 'two-factor' hypothesis revisited. *British Journal of Sociology of Education*, vol. 2, no. 3, pp. 235–246.

Organisation for Economic Cooperation and Development (OECD) (2005). *Teachers Matter: Attracting, Developing and Retaining Effective Teachers*. Paris: OECD Publishing.

Opfer, D. (2014). Section commentary: Teacher career trajectories. In P. Richardson, S. Karabenick and H. Watt (eds). *Teacher Motivation, Theory and Practice*. Abingdon: Routledge, pp. 214–226.

Polatcan, M., Arslan, P. and Balci, A. (2023). The mediating effect of teacher self-efficacy regarding the relationship between transformational school leadership and teacher agency. *Educational Studies*, vol. 49, no. 5, pp. 823–841. DOI: 10.1080/03055698.2021.1894549

Qvortrup, L. (2016). Capacity building: Data- and research-informed development of schools and teaching practices in Denmark and Norway. *European Journal of Teacher Education*, vol. 39, no. 5, pp. 564–576. DOI: 10.1080/02619768.2016.1253675

Richardson, P. and Watt, H. (2014). Why people choose teaching as a career: An expectancy-value approach to understanding teacher motivation. In P. Richardson, S. Karabenick and H. Watt (eds). *Teacher Motivation, Theory and Practice*. Abingdon: Routledge, pp. 3–19.

Roth, G. (2014). Antecedents and outcomes of teachers' autonomous motivation: A self-determination theory analysis. In P. Richardson, S. Karabenick and H. Watt (eds). *Teacher Motivation, Theory and Practice*. Abingdon: Routledge, pp. 36–51.

Roussel, P. (2000). La Motivation au Travail – Concept et Theories. Notes du Laboratoire Interdisciplinaire de Recherche sur les Ressources Humaines et l'Emploi (LIRHE). Note No. 326. Toulouse: LIRHE

Ryan, R. and Deci, E. (2000). Intrinsic and extrinsic motivation: Classic definitions and new directions. *Contemporary Educational Psychology*, vol. 25, no. 1, pp. 54–67.

Schunk, D. and DiBenedetto, M. (2016). Self-efficacy theory in education. In K. Wentzel and D. Miele (eds). *Handbook of Motivation at School*, 2nd edition. London: Routledge, pp. 34–54.

Sorlie, M. and Torsheim, T. (2011). Multilevel analysis of the relationship between teacher collective efficacy and problem behaviour in school. *School Effectiveness and School Improvement*, vol. 22, no. 2, pp 175–191.

Taylor, I., Ntoumanis, N. and Standage, M. (2008). A self-determination theory approach to understanding antecedents of teachers' motivational strategies in PE. *Journal of Sport and Exercise Psychology*, vol. 30, pp. 75–94.

Tschannen-Moran, M. and Woolfolk Hoy, A. (2001). Teacher efficacy: Capturing an elusive construct. *Teaching and Teacher Education*, vol. 17, no. 7, pp. 783–805.

Urdan, T. (2014). Concluding commentary: Understanding teacher motivation: What is known and more there is to learn. In P. Richardson, S. Karabenick and H. Watt (eds). *Teacher Motivation, Theory and Practice*. Abingdon: Routledge, pp. 227–246.

Wenger, E. (1998). *Communities of Practice: Learning, Meaning and Identity*. Cambridge: Cambridge University Press.

Worth, J. and Van den Brande, J. (2019). *Teacher Labour Market in England: Annual Report 2019*. Slough: NFER.

Worth, J. and Van den Brande, J. (2020). *Teacher Autonomy: How Does It Relate to Job Satisfaction and Retention?* Slough: NFER. https://www.nfer.ac.uk/media/3874/teacher_autonomy_how_does_it_relate_to_job_satisfaction_and_retention.pdf. Accessed 24 February 2020.

Leading more inclusively: Addressing diversity and equity

Introduction

Diversity in schools is important for a number of reasons. Different staff views and perspectives help to strengthen dealing with change, ensuring that new policies and strategies take into account the needs of all stakeholders (Fullan, 2016). A diverse teaching staff models the wider society, helping all pupils to feel included and welcomed. It may also impact on students' results, for example, Black and Minority Ethnic (BME) school leaders have been shown to have a positive influence on BME students' confidence and achievement (Francis, 2019).

People's identities are influenced by multiple facets: upbringing, family, race and ethnicity, gender, religion, sexual orientation, class, abilities and many more (Theoharis and Scanlan, 2015). Some of these aspects create advantages. In England it has traditionally benefited people to be White, English-speaking, middle-class, Christian, heterosexual, male and without disability. Conversely, being of colour, working class, non-Christian, female, lesbian, gay or transgender, speaking English as an additional language or having a disability has been associated with prejudice and marginalisation (Theoharis and Scanlan, 2015).

Although the Equality Act (2010) made discrimination on a range of factors illegal in England, some groups of learners and staff continue to experience disadvantage in schools and there is evidence of unequal outcomes for minority groups in terms of achievement (for pupils) and career development (for teachers).

Historically, school leadership has reflected those who are advantaged in our society, which means that those who 'diverge in any way from this ideal are seen as "outsiders" if they aspire to become leaders' (Coleman, 2012, p. 597). This restricted view of school leaders has been compounded by a tendency for people to appoint staff who are similar to themselves, thus entrenching the status quo (Coleman, 2012). While a larger percentage of head teachers are now women, it is still the case that women, Black and Minority Ethnic, disabled and LGBTQ teachers are less likely to be promoted to headship than White, heterosexual, able-bodied men (DfE, 2020).

DOI: 10.4324/9780429260612-9

251

Leadership for diversity is complex, sensitive and challenging (Coleman, 2012). It addresses issues of equal opportunities, equity and social justice. The *Headteacher Standards* state that headteachers will, within and outside the school, 'show tolerance of and respect for the rights of others, recognising differences and respecting cultural diversity within contemporary Britain' (DfE, 2020, n.p.). But tolerance, respect and recognition, while laudable as a first step, will not necessarily address the deep-seated divisions within our society. The difficult and demanding responsibility of the headteacher is to ensure inclusivity, valuing every person equally and enabling everyone to achieve their full potential (Brown et al., 2019).

Research on diversity has focused more on gender (Coleman, 2012), race and ethnicity (Poekert et al., 2020), than on sexual orientation or disability. This chapter includes all these different aspects of diversity, but it should be borne in mind that gender, race and sexuality are interrelated, they are 'connective tissue, each exerting force on the other' (Odell, 2023, p. 104). Intersectionality is increasingly recognised as important. This is where being in more than one category (for example, a leader who is Black, female and disabled) adds to the complexity of the individual's experience.

This chapter begins by defining the key terms linked to diversity and equity, followed by discussion of the role of school leaders in managing inclusion, the issue of social justice, different aspects of diversity (disability, race, gender, LGBTQ), what can work in leading for equity and how to embrace diversity. The chapter focuses primarily on teachers and other staff rather than pupils, although the two are inevitably related. In this chapter, the words Black and White are capitalised. Black, when referring to people, is not a colour (Black people are not actually black), but signifies a history and racial identity, so should be capitalised, like English or Asian. If Black is capitalised, White should be too (and White people are not white either).

What are the key terms linked to diversity and equity?

Diversity is, essentially, about differences between people. Some aspects of diversity are visible, for example, gender, ethnicity, certain physical disabilities, while others may not be evident, for example, sexual orientation, mental health, class (Coleman, 2012). Managing inclusivity means developing appropriate policies, systems and structures in a school to enable everyone to reach their full potential irrespective of their differences whilst ensuring no one is excluded (Grobler et al., 2006).

Equity and equality are two terms which are sometimes used interchangeably, but they hold different meanings. Equality means treating people similarly, but if their needs are different, treating people equally may be unfair, because some start from a more advantageous position. Equity aims to redress this balance and ensure a level playing field for all (Ibrahim, 2015). Poekert et al. (2020, pp. 541–2) define educational equity as a state in which dimensions of privilege and oppression (e.g. race, ethnicity, socioeconomic status, gender, sexual orientation, religion) are not predictive of or correlated with educational outcomes, broadly defined, in any significant way, and where all learners are able to participate fully in quality learning experiences.

In the UK, the Equality Act 2010 outlawed discrimination (direct and indirect), harassment and victimisation. Each of these terms is clarified as follows:

- Discrimination means treating a person differently because of their sex, race, disability, religion or belief, sexual orientation or gender reassignment (DfE, 2014). These are called 'protected characteristics'. *Direct* discrimination occurs when one person treats another less favourably than others because of one of these characteristics, for example, if a school had stricter disciplinary penalties for African Caribbean pupils. *Indirect* discrimination occurs when a general rule puts a particular group at a disadvantage, for example, holding an after-school club in a room which is inaccessible to wheelchair users.

- Harassment is unwanted behaviour relating to disability, race, sex or pregnancy and maternity which undermines a person's dignity or creates a hostile environment for that person (DfE, 2014). This includes bullying and actions which, whether intentionally or unintentionally, cause offence. For example, if a teacher used a derogatory term about a pupil's race or disability in class, this could be considered harassment.

- Victimisation occurs when a person is treated less favourably because of something they have done, for example, whistleblowing or making an allegation of discrimination (DfE, 2014).

Diversity is strongly linked with social justice. Many educational leaders are determined to address inequities in education and to prevent the marginalisation of any groups of pupils (Ishimaru and Galloway, 2014). Theoharis and Scanlan (2015, p. 3) state that socially just schooling is evident when:

> educational opportunities abound for all students, when ambitious academic goals are held and met by all students, when all students and families are made to feel welcome in the school community, when students are proportionally distributed across all groupings in the school, and when one dimension of identity (such as one's race or home language or gender or sexual orientation) does not directly correlate with undesirable aspects of schooling (such as being bullied, struggling academically, or dropping out of school).

Care and love also underpin the concept of social justice (Francis, 2019).

Culturally responsive school leadership is also important in relation to diversity. This is the ability of school leaders to respond effectively to the diverse needs of their students. In order to be culturally responsive, leaders need to be critically self-aware of their own values and beliefs, personal biases and assumptions (Khalifa et al., 2016).

Cognitive dissonance in relation to diversity occurs when a person's behaviour does not align with their values or beliefs. This results in a sense of discomfort, for example, if a person holds a negative unconscious bias against a particular group but believes themselves to be a good and moral person (Radd et al., 2021). Radd et al. (2021, p. 44) argue that 'when faced with these conflicting thoughts, most people will employ their defensive routines to dismiss the thought that puts them in a negative light. These routines serve as real barriers to equity'.

These definitions help to explain social justice in relation to pupils, but not in relation to adults, which reflects a trend in education. Issues of social justice in schools have tended to be linked to diversity among learners rather than staff (Morrison et al., 2007). Social justice should, however, encompass equitable treatment for everyone at a school, including adults and children. Inevitably, because much of the research has been focused on pupils, this chapter recognises both students and staff when considering diversity issues.

What is the role of school leaders in managing inclusion?

School leaders play a vital role in creating equitable schools, where all staff and pupils have equal opportunities (Theoharis and Scanlan, 2015; Galloway and Ishimaru, 2020). They need to recognise that some communities experience discrimination and maintain a focus on issues of equity and justice, facilitating engagement and positive relationships with marginalised communities (Theoharis and Scanlan, 2015; Rayner, 2008). Equity leaders need to 'promote a concern for the entire school community […] faculty and staff' (Radd et al., 2021, p. 29). By embracing diversity, leaders can enrich their school community and enhance the future of all young people, whatever their differences (see Box 9.1).

BOX 9.1 DEVELOPING MORE INCLUSIVE POLICY AND PRACTICE

After a district superintendent of a US suburban school district halted suspensions because they were used disproportionally for students of colour, schools became more unruly and learning outcomes declined. One school, however, continued to improve. Its principal, Susan, had been the head for six years of the district's most racially diverse middle school and had been leading with a clear focus on equity since her arrival. Her experience is described as follows:

> [Susan] had strong relationships with her staff and the school community, founded on gathering input and collective decision-making. To respond to the policy change in ways that improved the community and the learning environment, Susan convened a series of conversations with students, staff and families to discuss their concerns, values, needs, goals and approaches to social, emotional and behavioural learning at the school. Stakeholders identified what they needed to learn and do differently to reduce and eliminate suspensions. Topping their list were the following items:
>
> - help teachers create stronger, more inclusive classroom communities;
> - teach all school staff how to de-escalate tense situations in ways that maintain everyone's sense of dignity and belonging;
> - agree on a set of grounding principles/values to guide all community members in their interactions with one another;
> - create safe spaces and processes for supporting students when their emotions feel particularly intense;
> - create accessible pathways to strengthen the relationships and communications between families and school staff; and
> - adopt a restorative approach for responding to situations where someone has been harmed.
>
> The involvement of so many stakeholders in the process resulted in broad and deep engagement in implementing the plans they created. The process took a significant amount of time and the outcome was not perfect, but the school community continued to improve its approach to supporting students' development and sense of belonging, while also improving their learning.
>
> (Radd et al., 2021, p. 36)

However, the ideals of equitable leadership contrast with the negative way in which some leaders perceive diversity. A study in Spain (Gómez-Hertado et al., 2018), based in four socio-economically disadvantaged secondary schools in Andalusia, found the school principals viewed diversity (in relation to ethnicity) as a source of problems unless the number of immigrant pupils was small enough to allow for easy assimilation. Crucially the headteachers wanted to avoid labelling and segregating immigrant pupils, which meant they did not focus on their needs as a subgroup in the school.

Use of data to address inequalities

These attitudes to diversity could also be present at schools in England and elsewhere. In some cases, the desire to avoid segregating BME and other pupils leads to inaction which allows underachievement to continue. This applies to the use of disaggregated data to identify disparities in achievement for different student subgroups, information that should be used to develop leadership strategies to address differences. In a study in the United States, instead of looking at subgroups (for example, based on race/ethnicity, gender, disability) to observe differences in academic outcomes, the 18 principals in Roegman et al.'s (2018) research used disaggregated data to focus on the performance of teachers and students in relation to state assessments. Indeed, some of the headteachers viewed the disaggregation of data by demographic characteristics as discriminatory and contrary to the need to have high expectations of all students, rather than as a means of addressing systemic inequities.

While it is important to monitor the achievement of students who have been traditionally disadvantaged, one potentially negative aspect of disaggregating data is that it can confirm teachers' stereotypes and lower their expectations. Park (2018) notes that educators' understanding of data is influenced by their own assumptions and background so there is a danger the use of disaggregated data may augment, rather than challenge inequalities. Discussions of achievement disparities in Brown et al.'s (2011) research led to some teachers' beliefs about student deficits being reinforced (that students from that subgroup would never do well) rather than helping to identify and address the school's deficits in provision for those pupils. Box 9.2 highlights the dangers of stereotyping and low expectations in relation to African-Caribbean children.

BOX 9.2 THE DANGERS OF STEREOTYPING

A recent study by Wallace (2023) examined the reasons why Caribbean pupils do well in US schools but not in UK schools. As a Caribbean child educated in New York, who had experienced high expectations and exceptional achievement at school, Wallace (2023) was surprised to discover, when he moved to the UK, that the educational outcomes of children of Caribbean immigrants in London were low and their progress was worse than those of children from African immigrants. In the US, African Caribbean children outperform African Americans. In both countries, the lower level of achievement of some ethnic groups has been attributed to cultural differences in the family, particularly in relation to attitudes to education, rather than to institutional racism or lower expectations of some children by teachers (after all, if some Black children do well, this might suggest that schools are not institutionally racist). Wallace's (2023) research drew on observations, interviews and archives in London and New York City schools. He found that culture was sometimes used as an alibi for racism, and that institutional processes and colonially-based stereotypes influenced the school experience and achievement of those from ethnic minorities. These factors were what made a difference to educational outcomes, rather than particular cultural groups' commitment to education.

In order to address the problem of data confirming negative stereotypes, Park (2018, p. 617) recommends that school leaders should use 'conversation moves' to support teachers' capacity to analyse data. Conversation moves are ways to shift discussions towards learning and equity. Park (2018) identified the following positive conversation moves enacted by leaders as helpful in using data to address inequality:

- triangulating – because the data are never perfect, other sources of data can be used to confirm teachers' understanding. Data should be seen as a springboard for further information

- reframing deficit narratives – shifting attention to student strengths and focusing on specific skills

- pedagogical linking and student-centred positioning – using formative assessments to discuss students' thinking processes in relation to a specific skill

- 'extending moves' – asking for more concrete evidence or specific examples to justify conclusions or perceptions.

Organisational and community approaches

Organisational, as opposed to individual, leadership for equity, provides a strategy for engaging teachers, pupils, families and community members collectively to ensure every learner has access to high-quality education. Galloway and Ishimaru's (2020) research focused on leadership across two American case study schools with diverse pupil intakes. Both principals (one Black, one White) distributed leadership across teams, empowering teachers and encouraging multiple perspectives. Both developed a culture of enquiry, based on data, and both encouraged team members to reflect on their own biases and racialised assumptions, as well as collective understandings of power, privilege and oppression. Interestingly, although the two school leadership teams identified the analysis of data as being important to equity, they did not use that analysis to enquire about the reasons for any disparities in pupil achievement, which could have been used to inform more equitable decision-making. This is similar to Roegman et al.'s (2018) finding that principals tended not to use data about subgroups to address inequities.

Galloway and Ishimaru (2020) argue that equity-centred practice and development requires the development of organisational learning about power and inequality: 'Such leadership creates a culture where teachers and staff regularly examine their own and others' practice and collaborate around equitable teaching and learning' (Galloway and Ishimaru, 2020, p. 111). When school leaders initiate conversations about race, it helps to facilitate greater understanding about how racism plays out in the classroom, whereas when racism is not addressed, inequities are reinforced. Appendix 9.1 provides some questions to prompt discussion about diversity.

The way in which headteachers position themselves in relation to marginalised students also seems to be important. In a wide-ranging, systematic literature review, Poekert et al. (2020) noted the importance of taking an 'ally' rather than an 'altruistic' approach, in other words, working alongside marginalised students rather than 'othering' them. In addition, enabling young people to be involved in decision-making about their own education and to help shape policy can transform schools: 'the most valuable resources of all are the students themselves, their families and communities' (Poekert et al., 2020, p. 556).

How does social justice relate to diversity?

Social justice involves equitable access for all to a country's educational, cultural, economic and legal resources. Arguably, bringing about social justice is the key moral purpose of educational leadership (Fuller, 2012). While school leaders' main focus relates to schooling, social justice leaders move beyond this to address inequities in the wider society (Dudley-Marling and Dudley-Marling, 2015). When addressing problems of inclusivity, leaders for social justice focus on structures and services which will help to meet students' needs (Reed and Swaminathan, 2016).

Socially just school leaders recognise that marginalised students are treated inequitably in the wider society (Kelsey et al., 2015). As a result, they strive to create a culturally relevant, rich and engaging curriculum and adopt inclusive practices which have been informed by research (Kelsey et al., 2015). Conversely, a narrow curriculum with a focus on testing (as in England) appears to undermine social justice (Poekert et al., 2020) and exacerbate race-discrimination and other inequities (Gillborn et al., 2022).

The need for power-sharing is highlighted in the social-justice leadership literature, so it is important to consider inclusive practice across a school, rather than just the role of the headteacher (Ishimaru and Galloway, 2014). Distributed leadership, as a form of power sharing, has been advocated to support social justice (Brown et al., 2019). Conversely, instructional leadership may prioritise academic outcomes over some aspects of social justice leadership, such as preparing students to be active citizens who can challenge inequities (Shaked, 2020). Consequently, Shaked (2020) concludes that the present focus on instructional leadership as the best means of improving achievement in schools may undermine social justice. Box 9.3 describes a school which illustrates leadership for social justice.

> **BOX 9.3 SOCIAL JUSTICE AND DISTRIBUTED LEADERSHIP IN IRELAND**
>
> Distributed leadership does not automatically result in addressing social justice, but it helps leaders to become culturally responsive to the changing population of their school. Brown et al.'s (2019) research focused on four subcategories of school leadership:

> relationships with families and the wider community; connecting the school to the wider educational environment; a distributed culture of leadership, encouraging a shared sense of purpose; and establishing incentives for learning as well as team and group structures for problem solving. This ethnographic case study used interviews and observations to investigate the leadership of an effective primary school in Ireland. The school had 423 pupils, of which 145 had English as an Additional Language (EAL).
>
> The headteacher discussed her priorities with staff to ensure their participation. She personified the school's values of inclusion and courtesy. She set up a 'twilight club' where staff took turns in leading workshops for other teachers and ancillary staff twice a month. Textbooks were scrutinised to ensure that they reflected cultural diversity and did not stereotype culture or gender, as well as reflecting a variety of family compositions. First names were used by all teachers.
>
> The school had a buddying and peer tuition system to ensure the inclusion of children from different cultures and those who spoke different languages. Emojis (selected by the pupils) were used for communication with parents and guardians. The school had a well-developed garden, maintained by parents and grandparents of pupils and the produce was sold at the school fête.
>
> The researchers concluded that two interrelated approaches to management ensured the school's effectiveness: distributed leadership and 'culturally responsive leadership' (Brown et al., 2019, p. 470). Distributed leadership allowed the school to respond rapidly to change and enabled policies and practices to spread throughout the school. Culturally responsive leadership was a 'philosophy of care about social justice that guides every aspect of the response of a school to meeting the huge challenge of an increasingly diverse pupil population' (Brown et al., 2019, p. 470).

Challenges of addressing social justice

While social justice may seem to be self-evidently a moral duty for schools, it is not always easy to implement. Some individuals may be opposed to aspects of social justice. If it is seen to be primarily a means of redistributing wealth, those who are politically conservative may not support it (Reed and Swaminathan, 2016). If advocates of social justice challenge the structures which 'reproduce the dominant culture and values in society' (Bogotch, 2002, p. 140), those who are part of that dominant culture may feel uncomfortable and criticised. Obstacles that have been identified as obstructing a move towards social justice policies and practice include toxic teachers, national policies creating a test-driven culture, and school-based culturally unresponsive and socially unjust policies and practices (Ezzani, 2020). Box 9.4 describes two schools where the principals focused on social justice as a means to improve student achievement.

BOX 9.4 SOCIAL JUSTICE AND IMPROVING STUDENT ACHIEVEMENT IN THE USA

Two schools in the USA adopted social justice approaches to improve the progress of disadvantaged and EAL students. Both schools adopted distributed leadership and professional learning communities underpinned by a framework of social justice to bring about positive change.

At one elementary school in California, with poor outcomes for Hispanic and economically disadvantaged students, the teachers tended to work in silos, leading to instructional inconsistencies. There were 'toxic conversations about students in the faculty lounge' (Ezzani, 2020, p. 579) with deficit views of students being projected. The school adopted a combination of data-informed decision-making, the development of social learning communities and distributed leadership for social justice. The school leaders needed to ensure that data were used to support poorly performing students rather than to stigmatise them. Teachers were made partners in school-wide professional learning communities (despite initial resistance by a few). Ezzani (2020, p. 576) concluded that the problems identified at the school were resolved when the teachers engaged in a 'continuous culture of learning through authentic dialogue focused on student data with an eye on equity'.

At the second, urban school, the principal implemented a social justice framework by acquiring need-based resources from the district, working with teachers to ensure 'equitable learning opportunities' and addressing conflicts between students from different cultures (Reed and Swaminathan, 2016, p. 1115). The conflicts included clashes between Mexican American and Puerto Rican students, which were resolved through intensive conflict-resolution support from a local community-based organisation. There was a lack of support for 120 students from Burma, so the principal used central services as well as local colleges and universities to help the Burmese students. Student achievement for Black males was very low, so the principal asked teachers to develop specific strategies to address the achievement disparity for African American males, set achievement goals for this group on a bulletin board in the main office and worked with the maths department chair to bolster test preparation.

The school also received extra financial and human resources for a mandated school improvement model. The principal's adoption of distributed leadership and professional learning communities underpinned by a social justice framework exemplified 'culturally responsive leadership' (Reed and Swaminathan, 2016, p. 1118). This was demonstrated when the school leaders took into consideration the context of their school, used creative ingenuity to address the local needs and took a balanced approach between transformational and transactional leadership.

Action for social justice

In summary, school leadership for social justice involves developing school communities that reflect 'multiple dimensions of diversity' (Kelsey et al., 2015, p. 86) and includes

- raising student achievement
- improving school structures
- developing staff knowledge and skills
- strengthening school culture and community.

(Theoharis and Scanlan, 2015, p. 3)

How can school leaders address different aspects of diversity?

The following sections consider disability, race, LGBTQ and gender, which are all aspects of diversity covered by the Equality Act 2010 in England. However, most research has focused on gender and race, so these sections are lengthier than the others.

Disability and inclusion

Disability is a neglected aspect of diversity in relation to school leaders and teachers. Unfortunately, disability has traditionally been viewed as a deficit, negative trait (Theoharis et al., 2015). Perhaps this is the reason there is insufficient information about the number of teachers and school leaders with disabilities: individuals may be reluctant to admit that they have a disability. Despite questions in the school census in England, institutions have consistently failed to provide information about disabilities, for example, data about disabilities were missing for 56% of teachers in the November 2022 census (DfE, 2023). As a result, the 2023 national staff census (DfE, 2023) did not report on disability in relation to teacher characteristics: only gender, age and ethnicity were considered. Similarly, a summary of characteristics and trends in school leadership from 2010 to 2020 only focused on gender and ethnicity and neglected to mention disabilities in relation to school leaders (DfE, 2022). From the data available, there appear to be considerably fewer teachers (2%) and headteachers (1%) with disabilities than the population at large (17.8%, according to the Office for National Statistics (2021)). A 2004 survey of school leaders with 1100 respondents found that only 1% had a disability. Of this very small percentage, one was a wheelchair user, one had diabetes and the others stated their disability as deafness (Coleman, 2005b).

The government is currently encouraging people with disabilities to apply for teacher training, with a page on the DfE's website explaining what support is available (https://getintoteaching.education.gov.uk/funding-and-support/if-youre-disabled). The DfE has also commissioned research into why schools are not providing adequate data about teachers with disabilities, with a view to improving the staff census (Butler and Fisher, 2023). Despite these efforts, it seems unlikely that the proportion of, and disclosure about, school leaders and staff with disabilities is going to increase rapidly in the near future.

Leaders wishing to move towards fully inclusive schools for those with disabilities could undertake the following (originally developed in relation to pupils):

- set a bold, clear vision of full inclusion
- set goals based on the vision, focusing on school structures, school climate and meeting the needs of all staff and students
- conduct an equity audit (see Appendix 9.2), gather data to identify operational realities and areas that need to be addressed
- map current service delivery in relation to disabilities, identify how services are provided, how human resources are used and where staff and students receive such services
- realign school and staffing structures as appropriate
- monitor the implementation, adjust if necessary and celebrate successes.

(Theoharis et al., 2015, p. 21)

In addition, an important step to address a deficit orientation about disability is to presume competence from the outset (Radd et al., 2021).

Race

There has been no progress in the last decade in terms of BME teachers becoming senior leaders in England. In 2011, ethnic minorities were clearly underrepresented in senior leadership teams relative to student demographics and also to the ethnic mix of teachers (Allen and Rawal, 2013). At that time, a higher rate of headteachers were of a White ethnic background (95%) compared to teachers as a whole (90%) and compared to students (80%) (Allen and Rawal, 2013). Ethnic minority teachers and senior leaders tended to cluster in schools with larger proportions of ethnic minority students (Allen and Rawal, 2013). More recent data indicate that this deficit continues to exist. In England in 2021, the proportion of headteachers from ethnic minorities was: 1.4% Black or Black British, 2.1% Asian or Asian British and 96% White. The proportion of BME students was 27% (DfE, 2022). From 2015 to 2019, BME teachers were 18% less likely to be promoted to middle leadership than White British teachers, 16% less likely to be promoted from middle to senior leadership, and 21% less likely to be promoted from senior leadership to headship (DfE, 2022).

BME teachers' perceptions of their status were recorded in a large-scale survey on the status of teachers, the Teacher Status Project (TSP). Reporting on this data and an additional follow up study with Pakistani, Bangladeshi and Indian teachers, Hargreaves (2011) argued that, while Pakistani, Bangladeshi and Indian teachers were not deterred from entering the profession by the status or prestige of teaching, 'their treatment within the profession, and in particular the barriers they have faced in relation to promotion to senior leadership roles suggests a high degree of institutional racism within the teaching profession in England' (Hargreaves, 2011, p. 39).

The movement from schools to academies does not appear to have helped: few MATs have prioritised race and gender in relation to school leadership (Johnson, 2021). Johnson's (2021) longitudinal life history research involving eight Black and South Asian headteachers found that there had been little institutional support for them, so their personal resilience and networks were crucial in navigating their careers. Johnson (2021, p. 681) concluded that more effort and resources were needed from schools, MATs and government to support the recruitment, retention and promotion of Black and South Asian headteachers.

A large-scale survey of 1027 BME teachers in England in 2016 (51% secondary, 35% primary, 14% nursery, FE, PRU) found the following:

- BME teachers regularly experienced structural barriers such as racism and ethnic stereotypes about their capabilities. There appeared to be an 'invisible glass-ceiling' and a perception among senior leadership teams that BME teachers 'have a certain level and don't go beyond it' (Haque and Elliott, 2016, p. 6).

- Respondents had different views about the reasons for BME staff being excluded from senior leadership teams and promotion opportunities; some BME teachers felt that it was deliberate while others felt it was due to unconscious bias.

- The long-term outcome of many of the barriers to career progression was to damage the 'confidence and self-esteem of BME teachers'.

(Haque and Elliott, 2016, p. 6)

Box 9.5 describes a school in the United States where Black teachers were assigned to teaching only the lower classes, which had a negative effect on their careers, their status in the school, their access to teaching resources and their ability to act as role models for their students. While this is an American school, similar barriers to career progression for Black teachers also exist in England.

In England, Miller (2016) describes the importance of 'White sanction' for the participants in his research study of career progression for BME teachers. White sanction occurs when White people recognise and promote the skills of BME individuals. Miller (2016) suggests that White sanction serves to legitimate BME teachers and opens doors for them, enabling them to take up new opportunities. While

> **BOX 9.5 CASE STUDY: BME TEACHER SEGREGATION IN THE USA**
>
> Leon Middle School in the United States had shifted towards larger numbers of African American students (60% in a previously predominantly White school) due to district rezoning. Most of the teachers were experienced White women who had been at the school since before the increase in African American students. Three of the five Black teachers taught in the less well-resourced general education, remedial and special education classes, while the White teachers mainly taught in the well-resourced International Baccalaureate (IB) programme. The principal decided to prioritise placing the Black students with Black teachers as much as possible. She felt this would be 'more desirable for both parties' and that it would improve discipline (Stanley and Venzant Chambers, 2018, p. 77). She also referred to research indicating that Black students benefit from being taught by Black teachers.
>
> Placing Black students with Black teachers was seen as more important than ensuring that they could access higher level classes. It also meant that the Black teachers were effectively excluded from teaching any of the honours and IB courses because there were not many Black students in those classes. Since resources such as smart boards and other curricular supports had been funnelled to the IB, the Black teachers did not have access to them. In addition, the assignment of Black teachers to the lower-level classes may have given their students, fellow teachers, and parents the impression that they were less competent than their White colleagues.
>
> When the Black teachers complained to the principal that they had been allocated to the least well-resourced classes, she justified her actions and refused to move them. By the end of the year, four of the five Black teachers had found employment at other schools in the area which would treat them better. The authors concluded that:
>
>> This case study exemplifies the segregated and dichotomous nature of many of today's public school systems.... The gross underrepresentation of Black and Latinx teachers alike in advanced courses seems to be a combination of leadership bias, institutional racism and/or discrimination, internal school politics, and a lack of appreciation for teachers of color among other various factors.
>>
>> (Stanley and Venzant Chambers, 2018, pp. 81–82)

this may appear to be positive, it is clearly unjust if BME teachers have to depend on White teachers to support their career progression.

Black women leaders experience 'double jeopardy' because of the combination of Black and female subordinate identities (Bailey-Morrissey and Race, 2019). They face the challenges of racism, stereotyping, unspoken rules and invisible barriers, such as people who fit a certain profile being promoted (Bailey-Morrissey and Race, 2019). For three of Bailey-Morrissey and Race's (2019) participants, the challenges outweighed the benefits and they concluded that school leadership was not for them. On the other hand, where guidance and support were available, Black senior women leaders were able to take risks, develop their careers and become successful and dedicated leaders (Bailey-Morrissey and Race, 2019).

The absence of BME leaders in schools is problematic because they challenge racial stereotypes, provide positive role models for BME students and, through a process of 'co-identification', encourage BME students to become teachers (Miller, 2016). Black male leadership, based on justice and care, has a positive influence on Black male students' confidence and achievement (Francis, 2019).

School leaders can take action to address racism through undertaking the following:

- Building race consciousness, which may involve watching videos, using book circles with relevant books about race, running seminars on multicultural curriculum transformation and undertaking parent outreach in order to encourage involvement (Horsford and Clark, 2015).

- Undertaking race-based dialogue which allows BME staff to share their concerns about race and racism with White colleagues. Crucially this should not be diluted by engaging in discussions about multiple identities but should focus on the analysis of injustices experienced by BME staff (Horsford and Clark, 2015).

- Developing a better understanding of the different cultures of pupils, parents and communities (Mistry and Sood, 2011).

- Providing professional development – but this needs to include sustained exchanges which 'disrupt patterns of inequity' and reframe racial narratives. The focus should be on changing teacher attitudes, for example, through encouraging teachers to undertake self-reflection that challenges unconscious bias (Poekert et al., 2020) or through using members of staff from different cultures to describe their values and experience (Mistry and Sood, 2011). See Appendix 9.1 for questions to prompt discussion. Professional development that includes data-informed decision-making helps a shift towards greater equity for marginalized students (Ezzani, 2020), especially when accompanied by 'conversation moves' to prevent negative stereotyping (Park, 2018). Teacher education needs to develop 'teachers' racial literacy' and create 'racial affinity spaces' for teachers from marginalized groups (Poekert et al., 2020, p. 551).

Gender

Despite many years of anti-discrimination legislation and a general belief that equity issues for women have been resolved (Coleman, 2012), women continue to experience disadvantage in pursuing school leadership careers. Although there has been an improving trend over the last ten years, there are still fewer female headteachers compared to the proportion of female teachers in schools in England. According to the DfE (2022, p. 16), in 2019, female teachers were '14% less likely to be promoted to senior leadership and 20% less likely to be promoted to headship than male teachers'. Men also make faster progress to leadership roles than women, especially in primary schools (DfE, 2022).

Women may feel that they need to sacrifice marriage/relationships and children in order to achieve senior leadership positions. Coleman (2005a) found that a greater percentage of male secondary headteachers (96%) compared to female (79%) were married and more male heads (90%) were parents, compared to females (63%). It is undoubtedly the case that maternity leave interrupts women teachers' careers, which may make it more difficult for them to rise to senior positions.

There appear to be different assumptions about the ways in which men and women lead schools, based on gender stereotypes. The educational leadership literature suggests that women's strengths are being caring and good at relationships, which puts women into 'a bin defined by the way that they are socialised' (Odell, 2023, p. 101). Long-standing stereotypes link men with higher levels of discipline and good financial management and women with more domestic or supportive roles (Coleman, 2012). Aspiring female school leaders appear to be pressurised into developing stereotypical masculine leadership approaches (being aggressive, unemotional and decisive) (Weiner and Burton, 2016). The research study on Special Educational Needs Coordinators (SENCos) described in Box 9.6 confirms these assumptions about the different ways in which men and women lead and identifies how men are constrained by gender stereotypes just as much as women.

BOX 9.6 GENDER ISSUES FOR SPECIAL EDUCATIONAL NEEDS COORDINATORS (SENCOS)

Pulsford (2020) suggests that there is a tension between the feminised vision of teaching (human and emotional) compared to a masculinised view of a professional teacher focused on standards. His research focused on the experiences of four men working as SENCos, all White and all in primary schools serving relatively disadvantaged communities. The role of SENCo has typically been taken by women. Narrative interviews were recorded with each participant. Pulsford (2020) observes that, within primary schools, traditional images of gender are still well established. This was reflected in his participants' concerns that being 'nice' could compromise their (masculine) leadership credentials. Several participants expressed concerns about being seen as weak, to the extent that leading in an empathetic way seemed problematic. Pulsford (2020, p. 828) describes as 'emotional labour' the challenge for these men of relating to their female colleagues while leading special educational needs. Their focus as 'agents of change' was on addressing poor performance, which limited the possibility of developing relational trust and collegiality.

Pulsford's research confirms Gunter's (2001) concern that conflating being male with masculinity may put men off from applying for or feeling comfortable in the roles that they perform in schools.

How far do gender stereotypes exist in reality? Hallinger et al.'s (2016) systematic literature review found that female principals showed more active instructional and transformational leadership than males. Female principals tended to be more participatory, democratic and task focused as well as surpassing men on supportive and encouraging treatment of subordinates, individualised consideration and interpersonal interaction (Hallinger et al., 2016). These findings were confirmed in Shaked et al.'s (2018) study in Israel, involving in-depth, semi-structured interviews with 36 female principals (nine from the Arab sector) and 23 male principals (five from the Arab sector) in Israel. A substantial proportion of the female principals in this study 'linked instructional leadership to the maintenance of positive relationships with the school staff, which involves partnership, empowering others, and various forms of cooperation', whereas few male principals considered interpersonal relationships to be important in their instructional leadership role (Shaked et al., 2018, p. 429). It should be borne in mind, however, that the male interviewees in this study were mostly high school principals (61%), while the women interviewees were mostly elementary school principals (92%).

There are a number of actions that school leaders can take to support women moving into leadership roles:

- welcoming different approaches to leadership, ensuring that both men and women can use more empathetic, relational styles without being criticised for weakness

- providing female role models

- offering coaching and mentoring for women interested in leadership roles

- taking a sympathetic approach to childcare issues.

This last action should, of course, apply to both male and female teachers.

LGBTQ+

Sexuality has for many years been a thorny issue for schools, and the recent focus on transgender and transsexuals has highlighted conflicting views about sexual identity. In England the history of Clause 28 from 1988 to 2003, when it was forbidden to promote homosexuality in schools, has cast a long shadow. During that time teachers may have felt (with good reason) that coming out as gay or lesbian would jeopardise their career. Even though Clause 28 has long since been repealed, headteachers and school staff may still feel reluctant to discuss LGBTQ+ issues openly, which of course makes it impossible to support LGBTQ+ staff and students (Lee, 2020).

It is, perhaps, helpful to define what is meant by lesbian, gay, bi-sexual, transgender, transsexual, questioning (LGBTQ) and other terms, although these categories have become increasingly fluid over the years. A lesbian woman is attracted to other women and a gay man is attracted to other men. Someone who is bi-sexual is attracted to both men and women. Pan-sexual refers to a person whose sexual attraction is not based on gender and who may themselves have a fluid gender identity. An individual who is transgender believes that their biological sex does not match their gender identity, that is, their subjective experience of their gender (Hernandez and Fraynd, 2015). They may wish to present themselves as the opposite sex as this reflects their perception of their true identity. Transsexual refers to an individual who has had sex re-assignment surgery. Questioning is when a person has not yet decided on their sexual orientation. The terms binary and non-binary relate to divisions between male and female or between homosexual and heterosexual. Binary is when an individual has adopted one or other gender or sexuality; non-binary is when an individual's gender or sexual identity is not defined by these traditional binary oppositions. Cisgender is when an individual's sexual identity is the same as their biological sex.

Research evidence indicates that many LGBT teachers fear the prospect of coming out at school and, despite increasing support for young people with LGBT identities, 'it remains extremely challenging for LGBT teachers and in particular LGBT teacher leaders to reconcile their personal and professional identities in the workplace' (Lee, 2020, p. 6). In particular, faith-based schools have been seen as 'inhospitable places for minorities', especially in relation to LGBTQ+ (McNamara and Norman, 2010, p. 545). Some LGBT teachers are afraid of being labelled as paedophiles if they come out (Lee, 2020). Others feel pressured to come out, in order to provide role models for pupils, and feel guilty if they decide not to do so (Rasmussen, 2004). The concealment of personal identity and the vigilance this requires adds an extra layer of stress and anxiety for LGBT teachers on top of their teaching role (Lee, 2020).

Many LGBT teachers believe that their identity is an obstacle to promotion (Lee, 2020). Yet there are a number of strengths that LGBT teachers can bring to leadership roles: 'challenging the status quo of the organisational culture, risk-taking, being willing to listen and learn, fostering collaboration and inclusion, and empowering others, especially those on the margins of the workforce' (Lee, 2020, p. 7).

In order to create a safe and supportive environment for LGBTQ+ staff and pupils, school leaders need to 'create awareness, promote safety, and reduce stigma without resorting to reductionism or stereotyping' (Hernandez and Fraynd, 2015, p. 109). There is a need to avoid making heteronormative assumptions (for example, that a person's partner is the opposite sex, or a student's parents are heterosexual). Headteachers are recommended to undertake a school-wide equity audit regarding LGBTQ+ matters (see Appendix 9.2), to use policies to address bullying and inclusion and to develop communities in which staff and students can discuss LGBTQ+ issues (Hernandez and Fraynd, 2015). Staff may need training about being inclusive in their language and actions (Radd et al., 2021).

What can work in managing diversity and creating equitable schools?

Equitable leadership means shifting from top-down, 'hero' leaders with power and authority vested in the principal to more collaborative and inclusive forms of leadership which are shared and distributed (Ishimaru and Galloway, 2014). Leaders need to shift from a 'deficit' orientation, blaming the victim, to an 'equity' orientation, focusing on systemic barriers which prevent marginalised groups from succeeding (Ishimaru and Galloway, 2014). The process of enquiry and improvement, informed by data, is important to achieve equitable outcomes (Ishimaru and Galloway, 2014).

Numerous activities that support more inclusive approaches are recommended in the literature. In relation to the different aspects of diversity described earlier, key actions appear to be:

- set a bold, clear vision, promoting diversity
- adopt appropriate leadership approaches, particularly those that empower staff
- welcome different approaches to leadership
- organise school structures and school climate to meet the needs of all staff and students
- allocate resources to support diversity
- use data to audit gaps in achievement and career progression and to guide strategies for improvement
- encourage self-reflection and acknowledgement of unconscious bias and stereotyping
- provide appropriate professional development to change teachers' attitudes
- offer coaching and mentoring for marginalised groups
- create a positive and inclusive staff culture, with a strong sense of community
- create a positive learning environment which values all children
- develop a better understanding of diverse cultures at the school; know students well and affirm their home culture
- engage with parents and local communities
- campaign for social change.

The idea of campaigning for social change does not mean belonging to a particular political party. It is about identifying social change which will benefit all the staff and pupils at the school, based on the school's data and the evidence of systemic disadvantage which prevents staff and pupils from reaching their full potential. See Appendix 9.3 for a comparison of recommendations about leadership actions which support diversity.

In terms of how to address barriers to diversity, mentoring and networking have been highlighted as well as leadership training aimed at particular groups of 'outsiders' (Coleman, 2012). Expressing clear values that promote equality, fairness and respect is important (Walker et al., 2005), as is developing an inclusive culture (Gómez-Hurtado et al., 2018). Appendix 9.4 provides a questionnaire which could be used to assess a school's readiness to become inclusive.

How to embrace diversity?

Embracing diversity goes beyond management to encourage a positive attitude towards diversity. In England, there is sometimes a reluctance to tackle issues explicitly; culturally, there is a tendency to be polite and respectful rather than speak out about potentially delicate topics. Teachers can disrupt structural inequities, however, by raising the issues of class, culture, politics and oppression in their teaching. An example of a school leader encouraging a positive attitude to diversity in a predominantly White school is outlined in Box 9.7.

> **BOX 9.7 A CASE OF DEVELOPING INTERNATIONAL LINKS TO ADDRESS DIVERSITY**
>
> The head of a secondary school that had a pupil population that was almost exclusively White working class wanted to address the lack of cultural diversity. He explains:
>
> 'The students were not exposed to cultural diversity and therefore missed out on the rich experiences that mixing with others from a wide variety of cultural backgrounds could give them. Neither were they adequately prepared to live and work in an increasingly multicultural world. Also, the lack of aspiration was an issue because many students frequently showed little motivation to become high achievers and moved away from the local town once they left school'.
>
> The headteacher decided to set up a number of international links that would allow students exposure to a fairly wide range of cultures and even to visit other countries. The local authority had some connections with China, and these were used to establish a partnership with a similar school in the Guangzhou province. Each year students would either visit the partner school or host students in their own homes. Ongoing contacts using social media channels were also established for pupils to interact with their Chinese friends.
>
> Similar links were established with schools in France and in Romania, through a contact with one of the staff. There were also a few one-off visits to other countries.

> Even students in the school that were not directly involved in visits were able to interact with the visiting students when they appeared, spread across a number of classes during the school week. English students frequently expressed surprise at the level of knowledge that their new friends had of the English language and also of English culture, politics, history and geography. The overseas visitors took part in assemblies and joined local school visits as well as interacting at lunchtime and break.
>
> The project had the desired effect of exposing students to a variety of different cultures and opened their eyes to far more possibilities moving forward. As a motivating initiative it worked extremely well. As a bonus, racist incidents within the school declined from few to almost none.

More equitable approaches are also supported by raising awareness through personal and collaborative reflection, identifying the limitations and needs of the school and counteracting dominant narratives (Poekert et al., 2020). This means explicit discussions about potentially awkward issues.

A research study of two schools in the United States with diverse pupil intakes (Galloway and Ishimaru, 2020) found a number of routines that distinguished schools that were pro-diversity and equitable (although focused on students rather than staff):

- authentic conversations about race
- using trans-affirming language
- teacher co-planning to include students with special needs
- using restorative justice practices to repair harm and build and sustain community
- using disaggregated data to identify disparities in student achievement.

(Galloway and Ishimaru, 2020, p. 109)

One way to encourage greater diversity in school leadership is to offer leadership courses designed for those who are currently under-represented in school leadership positions. In Box 9.8, Elton-Chalcroft et al. (2018) report on the impact of three such courses: Future BME Middle Leaders, Aspirant Primary Headteachers and Women into Secondary Headship. The designers of these three courses noted the need to include opportunities for participants to reflect on their identities as well as to analyse critically important structural inequalities and the changes needed to enable the participants to gain leadership positions.

Appendix 9.5 provides an activity to design a school focused on equity, which can be carried out with a whole staff group.

> **BOX 9.8 THE IMPACT OF LEADERSHIP COURSES FOR UNDER-REPRESENTED GROUPS**
>
> Elton-Chalcroft et al. (2018) gathered data from participants on the three courses using a baseline questionnaire before the course started, mid-point focus groups and another questionnaire at the end. The participants identified structural inequalities, including sexism (particularly lack of equality of access and opportunities linked to maternity); faith-school leadership (requiring participants to be a practising Anglican or Catholic); and preconceptions linked to faith (such as judgements about wearing a veil). All the participants (male and female, BME and White) felt that having a family hindered their career aspirations because of the difficulty of retaining an appropriate work-life balance. Interestingly, as the BME participants' confidence grew, they became more interested in leadership roles, which they felt were less onerous than they had originally perceived; whereas the reverse was true for the White participants: their desire to become leaders decreased as the course progressed.

Conclusion

Leadership that is inclusive is rewarding, expansive and engaging but it is also challenging and sensitive. It requires a commitment to developing an inclusive culture, which may mean changes in staff attitudes that are never easy to achieve. It involves confronting one's own assumptions and biases, which can be uncomfortable and it may necessitate open conversations with staff about potentially sensitive topics, such as racism, sexism and homophobia.

There are difficult balances for school leaders to maintain, for example, between affirming a student's home culture while challenging aspects of that culture which do not support diversity (such as attitudes critical of LGBTQ+). In focusing on fairness, school leaders may find that treating one group fairly to promote equitable outcomes is seen as unfair by another, larger faction. There may be times when an individual's needs (for example, to attend to childcare responsibilities) are seen to be at the expense of the staff group (others may have to step in to cover an absent teacher).

School leaders also need to balance the need to highlight social justice and promote diversity with the pressure to increase achievement and ensure that the school has favourable judgements in Ofsted inspections.

Managing inclusivity is not easy, but it can help create vibrant communities within schools, help staff to develop openness, transparency and warmth and make an enormous difference to students from diverse backgrounds. Recognising diversity and focusing on inclusivity will ideally produce a win-win, with staff and pupils able to flourish and everyone in the school achieving their full potential.

BOX 9.9 QUESTIONS FOR REFLECTION AND ACTION

- Does your school have a clear vision promoting diversity?
- Do current leadership approaches empower staff and help to create an inclusive and positive staff culture?
- How does your school use data to ensure equitable outcomes for staff and students?
- Do you regularly carry out an equity audit to assess whether your school's structures and culture meet the needs of all staff and students?
- Are resources allocated to support equity and diversity?
- To what extent do staff and leaders at your school examine their own practice and assumptions in relation to equity?
- How do you address issues of social justice at your school?
- Are leaders and staff at your school engaging in race-based dialogue and ensuring a good understanding of diverse cultures?
- Does your school offer coaching and mentoring to encourage those from marginalised groups to apply for leadership roles?
- How far does professional development support equity, in particular changing teachers' attitudes?
- What action has your school taken to ensure a safe and supportive environment for LGBTQ+ staff and pupils?

Appendix 9.1: Critical reflection prompts

These questions are intended to frame reflections on equity issues:

- How am I reproducing or disrupting the experience for students in terms of their sense of community and social support around race, disability, gender and LGBTQ+?
- How am I reproducing or disrupting the culture and learning of the adults at the school (teachers, administrators, other staff) around race, disability, gender and LGBTQ+ to create a more inclusive staff?
- How am I reproducing or disrupting the structures, policies and practices around race, disability, gender and LGBTQ+?
- How am I reproducing or disrupting the curriculum in terms of race, disability, gender and LGBTQ+?

(Based on Radd et al., 2021)

These questions are intended to build self-awareness of privilege and power:

- If you are White, which aspects of this privilege are you aware of? In what ways, if any, do you feel defensive about your privilege?
- If you are a cisgender Male, which aspects of this privilege are you aware of? In what ways, if any, do you feel defensive about your privilege?
- As a school administrator [headteacher] or an educator in another role, what are the various ways in which you have positional decision-making authority that can powerfully affect others' lives? When are you aware of this positional authority? When, if at all, do you forget or ignore it? How often do you consciously think through how you will use your authority to redistribute power and privilege to create more equity?
- What other privileges are hard for you to acknowledge?

(Radd et al., 2021, p. 123)

Appendix 9.2: Equity audit

A school equity audit is the systematic analysis of data to understand whether, and how, particular groups are experiencing disadvantage. Data about staff recruitment and promotions as well as student performance are disaggregated according to race, nationality, religion, gender, disability, sexual orientation and poverty. Some of these categories, however, depend on students and staff disclosing information which they may not be willing to share. Each school should design a review relevant to its own context, but a typical audit might include the following:

	Gender		LGBTQ+	Race[1]					Nationality[2]			Religion				Disability	Pupil premium	EAL
	M	F	T		White	Asian	Black	Mixed				Christian	Muslim	Jewish	Other			
Staff																		
Head teacher																		
Deputy head																		
Middle leaders																		
Full-time teachers																		
Part-time teachers																		
Teaching assistants																		
Administrative staff																		
Pupils																		
Overall number																		

(Continued)

Leading more inclusively 275

	Gender		LGBTQ+	Race[1]				Nationality[2]		Religion				Disability	Pupil premium	EAL
Staff	M	F	T	White	Asian	Black	Mixed			Christian	Muslim	Jewish	Other			
Number in each year group																
Gifted and talented																
SEN																
Exclusions – temporary																
Exclusions – permanent																
Poor attendance																
Reaching expected level of achievement																
Not reaching expected level																
Participation in after-school clubs																

1   These are broad categories of race, because the numbers of different racial groups may be very small in some schools. It is possible to have more detailed subcategories, however.
2   Add nationalities present at the school, e.g. British, EU, Pakistani, Jamaican, Brazilian, Nigerian, South African, Australian

Appendix 9.3: Key activities of school leaders in managing diversity

The following table brings together the recommendations of three different research articles, one of which is a systematic literature review summarising existing research on diversity (Poekert et al., 2020), another offers a conceptual framework for ten key leadership practices which support diversity (Ishimaru and Galloway, 2014) and the third is based on case studies of head teachers who celebrate diversity (Fuller, 2012).

Key activities of school leaders	Fuller (2012)	Ishimaru and Galloway (2014)	Poekert et al. (2020)
Appropriate leadership approaches		• Developing organisational leadership for equity	• Building shared accountability for academic success, tapping into educators' motivations
Empathy	• Empathising with children, linked to experience of prejudice or injustice		
Positive learning environment	• Understanding the impact of difference: creating a positive learning environment for all children to feel safe and valued	• Supervising for equitable teaching and learning • Hiring and placing personnel, using assessments of cultural competence, exploring teachers' understanding of equity and placing the most effective teachers with the students who have the greatest need	• Supporting academic achievement with high expectations

(Continued)

Key activities of school leaders	Fuller (2012)	Ishimaru and Galloway (2014)	Poekert et al. (2020)
Allocation of resources	• Providing for difference: ensuring appropriate support and provision to meet children's needs	• Allocating resources (in an equitable, rather than equal way to address imbalances)	
Culture of enquiry	• Identifying individual and generic differences (by using data)	• Constructing and enacting an equity vision	• Developing a culture of enquiry
Critical reflection		• Engaging in self-reflection and growth for equity	• Examining own racial identity and explicitly identifying and challenging inequities in the school
Knowing students and affirming their home cultures	• Knowing children: able to use personal knowledge of a child's circumstances to help the whole family • Recognising uniqueness in relation to social identity, race, ethnicity and faith	• Fostering an equitable school culture	• Affirming students' home cultures and empowering students in the face of adversity
Community orientation	• Celebrating diversity by engaging with diverse communities	• Collaborating with families and communities	• Empowering parents and expressing confidence in their communities
Campaigning for social change	• Caring about difference: a moral imperative in relation to social justice and making a difference to children	• Influencing the sociopolitical context • Modelling: demonstrating behaviour that aligns with moral convictions about equity	• Advocating societal change

Appendix 9.4 Data collection for organisational readiness

- How is the organisational climate overall? The community climate? Where is there cohesiveness and where is there division?

- What is the attitude towards difference? Inclusivity?

- What are the varying definitions of equity? Whose job is it to work for equity? Who is equity for?

- Who is seen to be marginalised? Who is invisibly marginalised?

- Who are the formal and informal leaders? What are their priorities, commitments and styles in relation to equity? Who makes things happen? Who can prevent things from happening?

- Who cares enough about equity to go the extra mile? Whose support and engagement are available and needed?

- What are the pressing needs in the school buildings related to equity? What are the barriers that inhibit the ability to achieve equity?

- How capable do you feel to advance equity through your work here? What would help you feel more capable?

(Radd et al., 2021, p. 224)

Appendix 9.5 The school for equity (based on Scragg et al., 1993, p. 144)

This is an activity to be carried out by the whole staff, working in small groups. Each group should be given a poster-size sheet of paper.

The task for each group is to construct a school which is focused on equity and inclusion. What would it look like? For example:

- Imagine people, noticeboards, posters, social and cultural events.

- Think about the curriculum, the playground, the buildings, rules and regulations.

- Think about how and where to recruit staff, who to involve in interviewing and the criteria that staff who work at the school would need to fulfil.

- Consider the staff room: what would it look like? What kind of informal and formal events would take place? What would they consist of and who would be invited?

- Think about what would be rewarded and given attention.

Draw diagrams, noticeboards, words, cartoons and pictures on the sheet as ideas come to you. Everyone is allowed to draw on the sheet and no idea should be rejected. Spend about 20 minutes on this activity as a group and then report back to the whole staff.

References

Allen, R. and Rawal, S. (2013). The demography of school leadership. In P. Earley. *Exploring the School Leadership Landscape: Changing Demands, Changing Realities.* London: Bloomsbury, pp. 33–60.

Bailey-Morrissey, C. and Race, R. (2019). The lived experiences of black women leaders: Barriers to progression. In P. Miller and C. Callender (eds). *Race, Education and Educational Leadership in England: An integrated analysis.* London: Bloomsbury, pp. 121–141.

Bogotch, I. (2002). Educational leadership and social justice: Theory into practice. *Journal of School Leadership*, vol. 12, no. 2, pp. 138–156.

Brown, K., Benkovitz, J., Muttillo, A. and Urban, T. (2011). Leading schools of excellence and equity: Documenting effective strategies in closing achievement gaps. *Teachers College Record*, vol. 113, no. 1, pp. 57–96.

Brown, M., McNamara, G., O'Hara, J., Hood, S., Burns, D. and Kurum, G. (2019). Evaluating the impact of distributed culturally responsive leadership in a disadvantaged rural primary school in Ireland. *Educational Management Administration and Leadership*, vol. 47, no. 3, pp. 457–474.

Butler, A. and Fisher, L. (2023). *Disability Data Collection in Schools (Workforce).* London: Department for Education. assets.publishing.service.gov.uk/government/uploads/system/uploads/attachment_data/file/1137578/Disability_data_collection_in_schools__workforce.pdf. Accessed 26 June 2023.

Coleman, M. (2005a). Gender and secondary school leadership. *International Studies in Educational Administration*, vol. 33, no. 2, pp. 3–20.

Coleman, M. (2005b). *Gender and Headship in the 21st Century.* https://discovery.ucl.ac.uk/id/eprint/10004164/. Accessed 27 June 2023

Coleman, M. (2012). Leadership and Diversity. *Educational Management Administration and Leadership*, vol. 40, no. 5, pp. 592–609.

DfE (Department for Education) (2023). *School Workforce in England.* London: Department for Education. https://explore-education-statistics.service.gov.uk/find-statistics/school-workforce-in-england. Accessed 26 June 2023.

DfE (Department for Education) (2022). *School Leadership in England 2010 to 2020: Characteristics and Trends.* London: Department for Education. https://assets.publishing.service.gov.uk/government/uploads/system/uploads/attachment_data/file/1071794/School_leadership_in_England_2010_to_2020_characteristics_and_trends_-_report.pdf. Accessed 6 April 2023.

DfE (Department for Education) (2020). *Headteachers' Standards 2020.* https://www.gov.uk/government/publications/national-standards-of-excellence-for-headteachers/headteachers-standards-2020#section-1-ethics-and-professional-conduct. Accessed 13 April 2023.

DfE (Department for Education) (2014). The Equality Act 2010 and schools: Departmental advice for school leaders, school staff, governing bodies and local authorities. https://

assets.publishing.service.gov.uk/government/uploads/system/uploads/attachment_data/file/315587/Equality_Act_Advice_Final.pdf. Accessed 13 April 2023.

Dudley-Marling, C. and Dudley-Marling, A. (2015). Inclusive leadership and poverty. In G. Theoharis and M. Scanlan (eds). *Leadership for Increasingly Diverse Schools*. London: Routledge, pp. 39–57.

Elton-Chalcroft, S., Kendrick, A. and Chapman, A. (2018). Gender, race, faith and economics: Factors impacting on aspirin and school leaders. *Management in Education*, vol. 32, no. 4, pp. 176–184.

Ezzani, M. (2020). Principal and teacher instructional leadership: A cultural shift. *IJEM*, vol, 34, no. 3, pp. 576–585.

Francis, D. (2019). Male leaders of African Caribbean heritage: Leading with justice and care to enhance black male student achievement. In P. Miller and C. Callender (eds). *Race, Education and Educational Leadership in England: An Integrated Analysis*. London: Bloomsbury, pp. 37–58.

Fullan, M. (2016). *The New Meaning of Educational Change*, 5th edition. Abingdon: Routledge.

Fuller, K. (2012). Leading with emancipatory intent: Headteachers' approaches to pupil diversity. *Educational Management Administration and Leadership*, vol. 40, no 6, pp. 672–689.

Galloway, M. and Ishimaru, A. (2020). Leading equity teams: The role of formal leaders in building organizational capacity for equity. *Journal of Education for Students Placed at Risk*, vol. 25, no. 2, pp. 107–125.

Gillborn, D., McGimpsey, I. and Warmington, P. (2022). The fringes is the centre: Racism, pseudoscience and authoritarianism in the dominant English education policy network. *International Journal of Education*, vol. 115, pp. 1–16.

Gómez-Hurtado, I., González-Falcón, I. and Coronel, J. (2018). Perceptions of secondary school principals on management of cultural diversity in Spain: The challenge of educational leadership. *Educational Management Administration and Leadership*, vol. 46, no. 3, pp. 441–456.

Grobler, B., Moloi, K., Loock, C., Bisschoff, T. and Mestry, R. (2006). Creating a school environment for the effective management of cultural diversity. *Educational Management Administration and Leadership*, vol. 34, no. 4, pp. 449–472.

Gunter, H. (2001). *Leaders and Leadership in Education*. London: Paul Chapman.

Hallinger, P., Li, D. and Wang, W. (2016). Gender differences in instructional leadership: A meta-analytic review of studies using the principal instructional management rating scale. *Educational Administration Quarterly*, vol. 52, no. 4, pp. 567–601.

Haque, Z., & Elliott, S. (2016). *Visible and Invisible Barriers: The Impact of Racism on BME Teachers*. The Runnymede Trust and NUT. https://neu.org.uk/latest/library/barriers. Accessed 14 June 2024.

Hargreaves, L. (2011). The status of minority ethnic teachers in England: Institutional racism in the staffroom. *DEDiCA Revista de Educação e Humanidades (dreh)*, vol. 1, pp. 37–52. DOI: 10.30827/dreh.v0i1.7151

Hernandez, F. and Fraynd, D. (2015). Inclusive leadership and lesbian, gay, bisexual, transgendered and questioning students. In G. Theoharis and M. Scanlan (eds). *Leadership for Increasingly Diverse Schools*. London: Routledge, pp. 101–118.

Horsford, S.D. and Clark, C. (2015). Inclusive leadership and race. In G. Theoharis and M. Scanlan (eds). *Leadership for Increasingly Diverse Schools*. London: Routledge, pp. 58–81.

Ibrahim, A. (2015). Why should school leaders take equity seriously in their work? In D. Griffiths and J. Portelli (eds). *Key Questions for Educational Leaders*. Burlington, ON: Word and Deed Publishing, pp. 49–53.

Ishimaru, A. and Galloway, M. (2014). Beyond individual effectiveness: Conceptualising organisational leadership for equity. *Leadership and Policy in Schools*, vol. 13, pp. 93–146.

Johnson, L. (2021). Portraits of UK Black and South Asian head teachers five years on: Leadership retention in the age of academization. *Educational Management Administration and Leadership*, vol. 49, no. 4, pp. 662–684.

Kelsey, I., Campuzano, C. and Lopez, F. (2015). In G. Theoharis and M. Scanlan (eds). *Leadership for Increasingly Diverse Schools*. London: Routledge, pp. 82–100.

Khalifa, M., Gooden, M. and Davis, J. (2016). Culturally responsive school leadership: A synthesis of the literature. *Review of Educational Research*, vol. 20, no. 10, pp. 1–40.

Lee, C. (2020). Courageous leaders: Promoting and supporting diversity in school leadership development. *Management in Education*, vol. 34, no. 1, pp. 5–15.

McNamara, G. and Norman, J. (2010). Conflicts of ethos: Issues of equity and diversity in faith-based schools. *Educational Management Administration and Leadership*, vol. 38, no. 5, pp. 534–546.

Miller, P. (2016). 'White sanction', institutional, group and individual interaction in the promotion and progression of black and minority ethnic academics and teachers in England. *Power and Education*, vol. 8, no. 3, pp. 205–221.

Mistry, M. and Sood, K. (2011). Rethinking educational leadership to transform pedagogical practice to help improve the attainment of minority ethnic pupils: The need for leadership dialogue. *Management in Education*, vol. 25, no. 3, pp. 125–130.

Morrison, M., Lumby, J., Maringe, F., Bhopal, K. and Dyke, M. (2007). *Diversity, Identity, and Leadership*. Working Paper Series. Lancaster: Centre for Excellence in Leadership.

Odell, S. (2023). Listening as methodological resistance: Hearing voices at the margins of educational leadership. *Journal of School Leadership*, vol. 32, no. 2, pp. 98–117.

Office for National Statistics (2021). *Disability England and Wales: Census 2021*. https://www.ons.gov.uk/peoplepopulationandcommunity/healthandsocialcare/healthandwellbeing/bulletins/disabilityenglandandwales/census2021#:~:text=In%202021%2C%20across%20both%20England,19.5%25%20(10.0%20million). Accessed 26 June 2023.

Park, V. (2018). Leading data conversation moves: Toward data-informed leadership for equity and learning. *Educational Administration Quarterly*, vol. 54, no. 4, pp. 617–647. DOI: 10.1177/0013161X18769050

Poekert, P., Swaffield, S., Demir, E. and Wright, S. (2020). Leadership for professional learning towards educational equity: A systematic literature review. *Professional Development in Education*, vol. 46, no. 4, pp. 541–562. DOI: 10.1080/19415257.2020.1787209

Pulsford, M. (2020). 'I could have been the caretaker in a suit': Men as primary school SENCos in an era of change. *Education*, vol. 48, no. 7, pp. 820–832.

Radd, S., Generett, G., Gooden, M. and Theoharis, G. (2021). *Five Practices for Equity-Focused School Leadership*. Alexandria, VA: ASCD.

Rasmussen, M. (2004). The problem of coming out. *Theory into Practice*, vol. 43, no. 2, pp. 144–150.

Rayner, S. (2008). Complexity, diversity and management: Some reflections on folklore and learning leadership in education. *Management in Education*, vol. 22, no. 2, pp. 40–46.

Reed, L. and Swaminathan, R. (2016). An urban school leader's approach to school improvement: Toward contextually responsive leadership. *Urban Education*, vol. 51, no. 9, pp. 1096–1125.

Roegman, R., Samarapungavan, A., Maeda, Y. and Johns, G. (2018). Color-neutral disaggregation? Principals' practices around disaggregating data from three school districts. *Educational Administration Quarterly*, vol. 54, no. 4, pp. 559–588.

Scragg, T., Burton, J., Basset, T., Gaine, C. and Aiken, M. (1993). *Training for Equality*. Harlow: Longman.

Shaked, H. (2020). Social justice leadership, instructional leadership, and the goals of schooling. *International Journal of Educational Management*, vol. 34, no. 1, pp. 81–95.

Shaked, H., Glanz, J. and Gross, Z. (2018). Gender differences in instructional leadership: How male and female principals perform their instructional leadership role. *School Leadership & Management*, vol. 38, no. 4, pp. 417–434. DOI: 10.1080/13632434.2018.1427569

Stanley, D. and Venzant Chambers, T. (2018). The case of teacher tracking at Leon middle school. *Journal of Cases in Educational Leadership*, vol. 21, no. 3, pp. 75–87.

Theoharis, G. and Scanlan, M. (eds). (2015). *Leadership for Increasingly Diverse Schools*. London: Routledge.

Theoharis, G., Causton, J. and Woodfield, C. (2015). Inclusive leadership and disability. In G. Theoharis and M. Scanlan (eds). *Leadership for Increasingly Diverse Schools*. London: Routledge, pp. 13–38.

Walker, A., Dimmock, C., Stevenson, H., Bignold, B., Shah, S. and Middlewood, D. (2005). *Effective Leadership in Multi-Ethnic Schools*. Nottingham: NCSL.

Wallace, D. (2023). *The Culture Trap: Ethnic Expectations and Unequal Schooling for Black Youth*. Oxford: Oxford University Press.

Weiner, J. and Burton, L. (2016). The double bind for women: Exploring the gendered nature of turnaround leadership. *Harvard Educational Review*, vol. 86, no. 3, pp. 339–365.

Conclusion: Reflecting on school leadership

Introduction

At the start of this book we considered the turbulence in today's schools and the pressure this places on school leaders and teachers. The advertisement for an assistant headteacher in Chapter 1 illustrated that working as part of a school's leadership team can be exhausting, incredibly demanding in both a teaching and pastoral sense, require very long hours and the utmost commitment, and it may also intrude on one's personal life. Yet school leadership can also be immensely rewarding. A contrasting advertisement for a headteacher of a secondary school in the Wirral demonstrates the positive characteristics of school leadership which have been advocated in this book (Box 10.1).

> **BOX 10.1 EXCERPT FROM HEADTEACHER JOB DESCRIPTION**
>
> The Governors wish to appoint an outstanding professional to lead this successful school. The Headship presents an exceptional opportunity for a visionary, empathetic and determined leader to work with a talented, professional and caring staff to continue to provide an academically challenging, culturally rich and enjoyable education for future generations of pupils.
>
> **The Governors are seeking a Headteacher who:**
>
> - is inspirational and dynamic and will empower pupils and staff to excel
> - is a visionary leader with a strong sense of moral purpose, ethical principles and values
> - has excellent leadership skills demonstrating the ability to develop, articulate and realise the school's vision
> - is thoroughly committed to promoting exceptional opportunities for every pupil whatever their background

- is committed to and promotes diversity and equality
- values knowledge and a love of learning
- has a passion for developing outstanding Teaching and Learning
- has proven ability to implement effective change
- has exceptional interpersonal skills with the capacity to develop highly effective relationships with all parts of the school community
- has proven capacity for strategic leadership, demonstrating financial acumen and the capacity to maximise opportunities for the school.

This advert seems aimed at a headteacher with a transformational leadership approach described in Chapter 1: 'inspirational', 'visionary', with a strong 'moral purpose'. The requirement for a 'love of learning' and a 'passion for developing outstanding teaching and learning' resonates with the leadership for learning highlighted in Chapter 2 as does the need for an academically challenging, culturally rich and enjoyable education. Professional development, recruitment and retention (Chapters 6 and 7) are also directly linked to creating outstanding teaching and learning. The focus on implementing effective change resonates with Chapter 4. The school is looking for someone who also has 'exceptional interpersonal skills' – a characteristic that is needed in almost every aspect of school leadership, but particularly in relation to empowering and motivating staff (Chapters 5 and 8), and engaging with students, parents and the wider community. The commitment to promoting diversity and equality links to Chapter 9. Together these aspects of the school are likely to create a positive culture as outlined in Chapter 3.

School leadership: evidence of what can work in turbulent times

The current turbulence in schools is generated from many different sources: international comparisons, national policy, inspection criteria, learning strategies prioritised by Multi-Academy Trusts, headteachers and teachers, among others. As an indication of how some staff feel about constant change, one teacher told us that, in general elections, she voted to retain the existing government, irrespective of their manifesto, because she thought that this would minimise changes in education:

> At the times when we've had elections, I think very much about ... not again putting even more change on teachers as well. That's the thing we have to remember, is that change of government means... It could mean an entire different direction.
> (Primary school interviewee, Teacher Retention Research project)

Setting aside any concerns about what this means for the democratic process, unfortunately for this teacher, it is certain that change in education will continue, whichever government is in charge and whatever impact this has on teachers. In addition to national policies introduced by the government, new developments in research, changes in the pupil population, new technology, climate change and international pandemics are all likely to influence the nature of teaching and learning in schools. Leaders and teachers need to be able to navigate this turbulence and although there is no blueprint for action, there is, increasingly, research evidence that points to ways in which this can be done.

School leaders spearhead change and they do so to bring about improvements in learning. The most recent developments indicate the importance of leaders encouraging innovative practices within and beyond the national curriculum (Chapter 2). Data-driven decisions about learning also impact on pupil progress, by developing strategies to support groups of students or individuals who are under-performing, or areas of the curriculum that need more attention (Chapter 9). Developing a positive, supportive school culture in which challenge and debate are welcome is a vital prerequisite for change (Chapter 3). What is also important is that school leaders need to take into account the context of the school when developing change strategies and adopting leadership approaches. The downfall of some 'super heads' is testament to that (Chapter 4). One example of a headteacher leading positive change in her school is described in Box 10.2.

BOX 10.2 LEADING CHANGE IN A LARGE PRIMARY SCHOOL

One headteacher from a relatively large primary school (800+ pupils aged 5–11; 5% eligible for free school meals, 15% pupils related to service personnel; Ofsted-rated Good with outstanding features) described how she embedded change to improve her school.

'On moving to a new school very recently judged as satisfactory by Ofsted it was evident that standards and expectations were very low. Standards were poor, particularly in writing and there was little pace or rigour in teaching and learning.

In order to initiate improvements, I arranged for an external advisor to come to a staff meeting where we all did a book trawl. The outcome was that all staff realised changes were needed to improve the children's achievement in writing. The external review meant that someone else communicated to our teaching and support staff the difficult message that we needed to improve. This enabled me to empower us all to collaboratively work together and shape our future progress.

An INSET day was used to enable all staff to throw out or pass on any old and outdated resources we had in school. This was cathartic. We also used an INSET day for teachers and teaching assistants to visit other schools to witness outstanding practice. Each of the three schools visited had different approaches, but I knew that developing our own systems based on any of the individual approaches used, or on an amalgamation of all of them, would be an excellent way to develop teaching and learning at our own school. This meant that I was able to steer the direction of our improvement without adopting a "top-down" or authoritative approach. This enabled me to involve staff and develop new practices collegiately.

We used our staff meetings, led by the literacy co-ordinator, to develop writing assessment grids. We also developed a spreadsheet showing national expectations for writing at the end of each term. Subsequently this was used in pupil progress interviews with individual teachers to set challenging targets for each pupil and to discuss how to unlock the necessary progress. The beauty of the assessment grids was that they gave a very clear understanding of where a pupil was and clearly indicated what their next steps in learning should be. This meant that focused teaching and learning could take place. A half-termly piece of writing would go in each child's book. The teacher would assess the writing using the appropriate grid and then write a comment. The book would be sent home where the parent/carer could see it and write a comment before it was returned to school. This had several benefits:

- expectations of standards were very clear
- by using the book teachers were carrying out formative assessment
- teaching and learning became more focused
- pupils developed a pride in their book
- parents/carers felt included and knew about their child's progress and what was needed for next steps
- the book went with them from year to year and showed the progress they had made very clearly, which was particularly useful for external assessors such as Ofsted.

By introducing this system, it enabled staff to develop their own practice whilst at the same time raising standards. As a result of these changes we achieved a Good Ofsted outcome with outstanding features.

This however was only the first step. Once the system was embedded the approach changed from a whole school one to supporting individual members of staff with their own professional development.'

Within this headteacher's strategy to lead a significant development in the teaching of writing, she engages in practices (described in Chapter 2) that result in change (considered in Chapter 4) of both school policy and practice (resulting in a cultural shift, discussed in Chapter 3). Her concern about how to improve the level of writing across the school through bringing in an external expert to review the current situation provided gravitas and momentum to the whole school initiative. She supported the literacy co-ordinator in leading from the middle (examined in Chapter 5) and utilised the process of collaboratively developing a new assessment system to facilitate professional development (discussed in Chapter 6) to enhance staff teaching practices throughout the school, indicative of an inclusive approach (considered in Chapter 9). This systematic approach augmented teacher motivation (as outlined in Chapter 8) to develop their practices in new ways.

School leaders need to take into account the context of the school when developing change strategies and adopting leadership styles (Chapter 4). Throughout this book, it has become apparent that collaborative approaches to leadership, empowering staff and creating a nurturing environment are key to success. Whether this is through transformational leadership, leadership for learning or distributed leadership, collaborating with teachers motivates them and supports retention (Chapters 7 and 8). Although some staff have other commitments outside the school, most prefer a sense of ownership and agency over their work. Clear communication, planning, monitoring and evaluation are important for all aspects of school life, whether it is managing change, planning professional development or experimenting with innovative approaches to learning.

In order to maximise pupils' academic performance, school leaders need to foster a culture of continuous improvement. They need to ensure that decisions about teaching and learning are driven by data, to inform teaching practices, allocate resources and address inequities experienced by particular groups. Collecting and analysing performance and other informal forms of data can provide insights into different ways to tackle academic and achievement concerns (Chapter 2).

Creating a vibrant, inclusive school culture and ethos creates a warm and positive learning climate that engages all stakeholders and enables staff and pupils to achieve their full potential. The ethos also needs to promote positivity, respect and a supportive environment that is conducive to both staff and student collaboration (Chapter 3).

Distributed leadership has been advocated for many years as a means of improving schools. In an ideal context, leadership is dispersed throughout the school, with headteachers trusting their staff and engaging them in decision-making. Empowering, enabling and encouraging teachers underpins the concept of distributed leadership. Yet it should be recognised that in some schools, it is difficult for headteachers to distribute leadership, and other approaches may also be effective. Meanwhile, middle leaders (who are on the receiving end of distributed leadership) need to navigate between the needs of the school and their team, between those above and below them and between the needs of individuals and the group. As a result, managing relationships with both empathy and professionalism is crucial for this role in schools (Chapter 5).

Teachers benefit from interactions with their colleagues as well as with school leaders, in order to share good practice and offer mutual support. Encouraging teamwork and providing opportunities for collaboration between colleagues builds enduring relationships, which support teachers in the long term. At the same time, it should be recognised that some individuals may be excellent teachers despite not wanting to engage with others (Chapters 5 and 7).

Professional development offers a solution to many school leadership dilemmas. As well as motivating staff, it can prepare teachers for change, improve their skills and engage them in new approaches to teaching and learning. School leaders need to take a strategic approach to professional development, including how to evaluate interventions. At the same time, it is important to give school staff a sense of ownership over their own development – a balance that may be hard to achieve within limited budgets (Chapter 6).

Motivating teachers is an important part of school leadership, and while 'different strokes please different folks', there is research evidence that offering professional development and career progression as well as recognising teachers' achievements are likely to support motivation. In addition, building teachers' sense of self-efficacy and supporting their well-being improves job satisfaction (Chapter 8) and is likely to lead to retaining staff (Chapter 7).

In a world that is increasingly diverse, school leaders are faced with the challenge of developing an inclusive culture, confronting their own biases as well as tackling racism, sexism and homophobia in staff and parents. Ensuring equitable outcomes and social justice may be difficult, but can be life changing for both teachers and pupils (Chapter 9).

It is also important to extend community engagement beyond the school. Prioritising pupils and staff, but also involving everyone associated with the school (parents, guardians, governors and other stakeholders) to engage in partnerships focused on enhancing teaching and learning can underpin improved learner outcomes (discussed in Chapters 2 and 9).

In summary, headteachers should focus on understanding student needs with a view to maximising learning, implementing effective teaching strategies, using evidence for decision-making, fostering a positive school culture, allocating resources wisely, facilitating professional development, promoting equity and inclusion and engaging more widely with the community where appropriate.

As Mick Waters (2013, p. 309) suggests, the 'fabric of leadership' could be thought of as a tapestry. Each leader creates the school's own unique pattern, reflecting the bespoke nature of leadership practices required to maintain a successful and effective place of learning.

What is clear, when talking to headteachers who have navigated the turbulence of change and succeeded in leading their school successfully, is that there is a deep sense of satisfaction from the knowledge that they have actioned policies and practices in such a way that has benefited their school community and all who work and learn there, most particularly their pupils.

Reference

Waters, M. (2013). *Thinking Allowed on Schooling*. Carmarthen, Wales: Independent Thinking Press.

Glossary

Academy A type of state-funded school, directly funded by the national Department for Education, independent of local education authorities. Previously, schools were managed by local authorities in each county in England. Academies were originally opened to replace failing schools. These early academies were sponsored by businesses or individuals (sponsored academies). In 2010, the Academies Act allowed state-maintained schools to convert to academies (converter academies) without being sponsored and there were financial benefits to do so. Any school placed in special measures by Ofsted is forced to become a sponsored academy. In January 2023, 40% of primary schools and 80% of secondary schools were either academies or free schools (another type of school, set up by an organisation or group of individuals, funded by the government but not controlled by the local authority).

A-level Advanced-level subject-based assessments that lead to university, training or work, usually taken after 7 years of secondary education.

ASCL Association of School and College Leaders, a British trade union for school and college leaders.

BTEC Business and Technology Education Council qualifications, combining practical learning with theory, available at different levels.

CPD Continuing professional development, how education professionals learn and hone their skills.

DFE Department for Education, the government department responsible for education in England.

EAL English as an Additional Language, those pupils who have a mother tongue which is not English.

EEF Education Endowment Foundation, a charity aiming to improve teaching and learning through better use of evidence.

FSM Free school meals, available to children from low-income families and all children in reception, Year 1 and Year 2.

GCSE General Certificate of Secondary Education, national subject-based tests at age 16.

GTP Graduate Teacher Programme, a form of initial teacher training for graduates to gain Qualified Teacher Status while teaching in schools. It was subsequently replaced by School Direct, which is a similar, school-led route into teacher training for graduates, run by a lead school, other schools and an accredited teacher-training provider. Trainees are employed by a school as an unqualified teacher while completing their initial teacher training to gain Qualified Teacher Status.

HEI Higher education institution, a university or college providing degree-level (or higher) qualifications for students.

High-need schools Schools in areas of socio-economic deprivation.

ITT Initial Teacher Training, the training through which students gain Qualified Teacher Status.

KS Key stage. The key stages relate to different school years as follows:

Nursery and reception (3–5 years old)

Primary School

- Key Stage 1: years 1 to 2 (5–7 years old)
- Key Stage 2: years 3 to 6 (7–11 years old)

Secondary School

- Key Stage 3: years 7 to 9 (11–14 years old)
- Key Stage 4: years 10 to 11 (14–16 years old)
- Key Stage 5: years 12 to 13 (16–18 years old) – may be school, sixth form college or further education college

LEA Local Education Authority, also called Local Authority (LA); local council responsible for education in England, for schools that have not become academies or free schools.

MAT Multi-academy trust, an academy trust with more than one academy school. There are over 1000 MATs in England with more than two schools and the largest 29 MATs have 26 or more schools.

NCSL National College for School Leadership, which became the National College for Teaching and Leadership before being dissolved in 2018. NCTL aimed to improve school leadership through research, training and resources.

NHS National Health Service, a free health service for the UK population.

NPQH National Professional Qualification for Headship, a qualification for aspiring headteachers which was, at one time, compulsory for anyone appointed as a headteacher. Although optional now, it is widely expected by schools when appointing heads.

OECD Organization for Economic Cooperation and Development, an international organisation working towards prosperity, equality, opportunity and well-being. Members include mainly richer countries in Europe, North and South America and Asia.

Ofsted Office for Standards in Education, Children's Services and Skills, inspects schools and other organisations providing education and skills for learners, as well as services that care for children and young people.

PD Professional development, how education professionals learn and hone their skills.

PGITT Postgraduate Initial Teacher Training, to enable graduates to gain Qualified Teacher Status through a university-led, school-led or an apprenticeship teacher-training programme.

PISA Programme of International Student Assessment, part of the OECD which measures 15-year-olds' ability and knowledge in relation to reading, mathematics and science.

PPA Planning preparation assessment – time allocated to teachers for these activities during the working week. Some schools have started to close for half a day a week in order to enable teachers to undertake PPA without having to arrange for another teacher to cover their classes.

Progress 8 A means of assessing pupil progress, used to judge schools.

PRU Pupil Referral Unit – a special unit for children and young people who are experiencing problems at school, for example, those with social and behavioural difficulties, whose needs cannot be met in a mainstream school.

Pupil premium Additional funding for disadvantaged children, that is, those eligible for free school meals in the last 6 years and those who are or have been in the care of the local authority.

QTS Qualified Teacher Status, a legal requirement to teach in most English schools, awarded by the Teaching Regulation Agency.

RSC Regional schools commissioner, responsible for overseeing the academy system. There are eight across England.

SEND Pupils with special educational needs and disabilities, for example, difficulties in behaviour, socialising, ability to understand, concentration, physical ability and dyslexia. Children may be eligible for SEN support, such as speech therapy, or an Education, Health and Care plan with funding for a plan of care for those with more complex needs.

SLT Senior leadership team, sometimes called the senior management team (SMT) or senior strategic team (SST), the group of senior leaders at a school responsible for daily management, usually including the headteacher, deputy headteacher, assistant headteachers and others with schoolwide responsibilities (depending on the size of the school).

SWC School workforce census, carried out annually by the Department for Education to report on teaching and support staff working in schools.

TA Teaching assistant, also called classroom assistant or learning support assistant, supports teachers and pupils, for example, by helping teachers prepare lessons, working with individual students to help them understand the lesson, and looking after children who are upset or unwell.

TALIS Teaching and Learning International Survey, run by the Organisation for Economic Co-operation and Development (OECD) to compare the views and practices of teachers and headteachers in OECD countries.

TIMSS Trends in International Maths and Science Study, monitors trends in maths and science achievement every 4 years through tests in 64 countries

TWM Teacher workforce model, used by the Department for Education to illustrate the supply of teachers.

UCET Universities Council for the Education of Teachers, a national forum for discussion about the education of teachers, composed of HEIs involved in teacher education.

Index

Pages in *italics* refer to figures and pages in **bold** refer to tables

academies 3, 50, 83, 87, 109, 215; Act 30; cultural web 53; local 50, 77; multi-Trust 77, 263, 285; regional 90

accountability xx, 3–4, 6, 18, 20, 30, 35, **37**, 54, 78, 93, **99**, 106–107, 136, 140, 146, 185, 202, 211, 217–218, 229, **277**

action learning sets xix, 22–23, 36, **38**, 135; impact 22–23, 25; organisation 22, 40; setting up 38–40

action planning 23, 172, 181

action research 157, 161, 182; implementation in schools 31, 40, **115**; nature of 31, 164–166

agency 182, 188, 216, 226–229, 233; autonomy 209, 217; identity 238; opportunities 230

aims of schooling 32–33, 100–101, 106, 112–114, 149, 192–193, 252; goals 100, **115**, 124, 127, 129, 140–144, **141**, 147, 149, 166, 169, 172, 175, 181, 184, 188, 190, 192, 216, 226–227, 235–238, **237**, **246**; school mission **37–38**, 88, 100, 124, 141, 169; vision 4–7, 12–14, 16–18, **17**, 20, 26, 31–33, **37–38**, 41, 48, 50, 64, 67, 78, 87–88, **98–99**, 100–101, 103–104, 110–112, **115**

A level 77

approaches and practices xviii

assessment 2, 4, 8, 13–14, 18, 21, 23, **37**, 49, 53, 66, 77, 82–83, 85, 88, 93, 106, 132, 134, 147, 150, 164, 167, 175, **177**, 185–186, 205, 217, 219, **239**, 287

Association of School and College Leaders (ASCL) 205

audits 40, 165, 190, 262, 269, 273, **275**; aims and values 112, 114; diamond card sort, Hobby 60, 64–65, 68–69; effective meetings 149; evaluation questionnaires, PD 192–194; goal orientation, Janke et al **246**; GROW model 190; interview questions 221; key tasks in curriculum leadership 148; leadership practices 17, **277–278**; leaders of effective change **115–117**, 184; preparedness for change 41; professional learning 190; school culture 70–72; school organisation **279**; self-efficacy, Bandura **242**; teacher efficacy **239**; teamwork problems 150

Black and minority ethnic (BME or BAME) 251, 255, 262–265, 272

Business and Technology Education Council qualification (BTEC) 77

change 77–122; accountability 78, 93, **99**, 107, 136, 141, 146, 185; action learning *see* action learning sets; challenges, middle leaders 85; challenges, parents 22, 86; challenges, resources 89; challenges, school leaders 83; challenges, schools 89; challenges,

294

Index **295**

students 88; challenges, teachers 85, 91–96; first, order of 80; models of change 96; monitoring response 106; national policy change/s 81; preparedness 103, **115**; responding to change 79–81; second, order of 80; success 106; theories of change 94, 96–100, 139

classroom: assessment 4, 13, 23, **37**, 49, 77, 82–83, 88, 93, 106, 134, 147, 164, 175; leadership impact 23, 30–32, 82

collaboration 12, 18–19, 22, 26, 34, 46, 55, 59, 103, 111–112, **115**; distributed leadership 6, 13, 18, 34, 107, 123–129, 258; middle leadership 33, 85, 123–126, 130, 132–133, 135–138, 145, 147; teamwork 103, 124, 139, 141–143, 145–148, 150, 230, 288

Continuing Professional Development (CPD) 23, 137, 148, 156, 175, 181, 186; *see also* professional development

countries, studies in or participants from: Africa 253, 256, 261, 264, **276**; Australia 66, 85, 94, 101, 125, 129–131, 137, 163, 214; Belgium 54; Burma 260; Canada 18, 24, 66, 95, 97, 109, 231; China 54, 270; Colombia 66; England 77, 86, 89–90, 97, 111, 123, 132, 156, 164, 176, 178, 180, 182–185, 206–208, 213, 217, 229, 234, 262–263, 265; Finland 65, 83, 104, 106; Iceland 129; Ireland 129, 258–259; Netherlands 56; Scotland 55, 129, 168; Spain 229, 255; USA 218, 260, 264; Wales 82

culture 2, 4, 7, 12, 36, **38**, 46–76; academy 53; change 51; definition 47, 61; effectiveness 22, 25; expectations 57; iceberg model, Herman *50*; improvement 63; pressure cooker 21; school 52, 57, 64; students, view of 58, 61; symbols of 65; teachers, view of 52, 61; web model, Johnson et al 52

curriculum 2, 18, 22, 24, **27–28**, 67, 80, 84, 132, 139, 148, 167, 172, 179, 231, 258, 265, 286; auditing 17, 41–42; change 79–80, 97, 106, 113; departmental leadership **27–28**, 148–150, 207–208;

leadership 4, 17, **17**, 20, 77–78, 88, 131, 139, 148, 185, 217, 274, **279**; national policy 77–78, **177**

Department for Education (DfE) 2, 4, 123, 131, 176, 182, 185, 202–205, 207, 209, 214, 251–253, 262, 265–266; national policy 183, 262; NPQ 134, 183; NPQH 123, 131, 182, 184–185; teaching Standards 4, 161, **177**, 178

deputy headteachers 145, 207

development 13, 34, 50, *50*, 66–67, 86, 89, **99**, 102, 104–105, 113–114, 133–135, 156–193; approaches 13; coaching 164, 171–174; distributed leadership, of *see* distributed leadership; evaluation **28–29**, 185; induction, role of 176–178; leaders, of 22; mentoring 173–176; middle leaders **28–29**, 125–126, 134; *see also* middle leadership; planning *50*, 82, **99**; professional capital 232; professional development 4–5, 18, 23, 25, 133–135, 156–193; professional learning community 5, 105–106, 190; school vision 5, 41, 49–50, 100; senior leaders 18, 30; sustainability 85, 107–109; teachers 22, 25–26; teams 139–146; theories 139–147

educational policy 3, 21; changes of 77, 79–80, 87, 101, 108; early career teacher (ECT) 176, **177**; impact on schools 82, 90; teacher qualification 134, 182, 184–185

Education Endowment Foundation (EEF) 183

effectiveness 59, **71**, 107, 145–146; definition 60; ineffective/effective 59; obstacles 83, 112, 146, 191, 193–194, 259; senior leadership teams (SLTs) 136, 138, 144

English as an Additional Language (EAL) 259–260, **275–276**

Equity, Diversity and Inclusion (EDI) 251–279; definition 251–252; diversity 251–252; equality act 251, 253, 261, 280;

equity 252, 254, 257, 260, **279**; inclusion 261–262, 268, 289; LGBGT+ 267–268
ethos *see* culture

financial pressures 20, *50*, 53, 89–90, 111, 141, 179, 206, 208, 218, 260, 266, 285
Free School Meals (FSM) 5, 26, 62, 209, 286

General Certificate of Secondary Education (GCSE) 24, 77–78, 90, 205
goals *see* aims
governors 87, 110, 113, 206–207, 284–285, 289
Graduate Teacher Programme (GTP) 210

headteachers 4, 178; approaches 5, 13–20; dealing with change 4, 81–91; developing culture 34, 220; initiating change 77–79; leading 3, 6, 12, 14–20, 30, 32, 141; managing 124; practices **17**, **27**, 32; professional development 156–193; relationships with staff 33–34; styles 5, 7, 79, 114, **117**, 123, 147, 170
Higher Education Institution (HEI) 171
high-need schools 62–63, 107, 127, 202, 207–209, 213, 229, 235
home 15, 17, 56, **242**, 267, **278**; partnerships with school 91, 254

identity 6, 24, 52, 56, 58, 95, 169, 185, 254, 267; affected by change 92; attitudes 91, 96; headteachers 84, 167, **278**; teachers 96, 133, 160, 167, 174, 179
implementation 19, 78–79, 81, 163, 172–173, 185, 262; diagnosing challenges 90; monitoring development 78, 104, 106; monitoring success 82–83, 90, 132; whole school initiative/s 19, 163
improvement 30–32, 46, 59, 63, **115**; accountability 3–4, 6, 18, 20, 30, 35, 37, 79, 93, **99**, 106–107, 140, 146, 218; measuring 61–62, 64, 69, 187–188
Initial Teacher Training (ITT) 203, 218
initiation: change, of 60, 111
innovation 32, 63, **73**, 78–79, 83, 86, 95, 100, 109–110, 166, 171

inservice training, INSET *see* Continuing Professional Development, professional development

Key Stage (KS) 104, 124, 126, 132–133, 136, 204–205

leadership 1–9; approaches 5, 12–13, 15–16, 30, 125; authoritative 5, 287; characteristics 11, 16–17, **17**, 51, **117**, 145; concept 88, 90–91, 126, 288; decision-making 3, 5, 18, 36, **38**, **72–73**, 89, **98**, 125, 127, 138, 145–146, 229–230, 238, **242**, 255, 257–258, 260, 265, 274, 288–289; difference to management 124; distributed 4, 6, 13, 34, 107, 123–128, 139, 146–148, 258–259, 288; hero 125, 138–139, 147, 269; instructional 4–5, 12–14, 30, **37**, 125–126, **239**, **242**, 258, 267; learning centred 7, 11, 13, 30; middle 123–125, 131–132, 136–138; practices 11, 14–16, 18–19, 22, 30–31, 126, **277**, 289; strategies 36, 256; styles 5, **117**, 123, 147, 170, 230, 236, 288; transformational 4–6, 13, 32, 123, 127, 229–230, 236, 267, 285, 288
local authorities (LAs) 270
Local Education Authority (LEA) 3, 178

management: difference to leadership 34, 53, 124–126
middle leaders 123–150; concept 125; effectiveness 131–138; impact, 143–149; organisation 138–142
models: action research 165; cultural paradigm 46–49, *52*; experiential learning 160; functioning of a team 144; iceberg *50*; reflective teaching 161; school culture and effectiveness 59; teacher agency influences 233
Multi-Academy Trust (MAT) 4, 77, 183, 285

National Association of Headteachers (NAHT) 206, 210
National College for School Leadership (NCSL) 182, 184

National Health Service (NHS) 214
National Professional Qualification for Headteachers (NPQH) 182, 185
Nine pillars of greatness 6, 123

Organization for Economic Cooperation and Development (OECD) 125, 159, 210
Office for Standards in Education (Ofsted) 2, 5, 20, 26–27, 33, 101, 103, 108–110, 156, 158, 164, 186, 205, 213, 217–218, 286–287; characteristics of categorised schools 112–114; great schools 21–22, 87–88; inspection framework 78, 207
organisation: culture 47–51; effectiveness 26, 59–60, 71, 136, 145–146, 259; performance 12, **17**, 20, 25–26, 30, 37, 57, 60, 62, 69, 78, 102, 104, 141, 147–148, 231–232, 235–236, 238, **246**, 266, **275**

partnerships 184, 267, 270; parents 22, 113, 185; schools 4, 34, 88–89
pedagogy 2, 67, 101, 132, 173
Planning Preparation Assessment (PPA) 205
policies 3, 18, 30, 34, 70, 77, 81–82, 90, 180, 254; impact 81, 180; implementation 77, 81–83, 90; national 3, 7, 21, 24, 62, 77, 80, 90, 107, 233, 255, 285; school 41, 47, 73, 80, 82–83, 112, 258, 287
postgraduate teachers 204
power 3–5, 52–53, 55, 95, 107, 127–129, 131, 135, 138, 146, 164, 257, 264, 269, 274
pressures 4, **99**, 107, 111, 123, 211–212, 218; cooker 21; national policy 2–3, 24, 77, 80, 86; school context 4, 54, 58, 92–93, 136
primary schools 5, 47, 64, 77, 90, 111, 113, 134, 204, 210, 230, 234, 263, 266, 271, 285; case studies 4–5, 21–22, 46, 51–52, 63, 66–67, 86–88, 127–128, 135, 139, 207–208, 211, 213–217, 220, 259, 266, 286–287; research studies 14, 18, 82, 85, 125–126, 129–130, 132, 134, 137–138, 145, 206
professional development (PD) 5, 16, 22–23, 25, 41, 78, 85, 89, 105–106, 127, 133–135, 147, 156–193, 232; effective 96, 102, 132, 147, 180; evidence 18, 135, 179–180; impact 22, 108, 110, 146, 185, 187, **239**, **242**; INSET 148, 238, 273–274, 286–287; theories of 159–175
progress 12, 23, 26, **27–28**, 31, 35, 39–40, 54, 59, 102, 107, 109, 111, 149, 157, **177**, 180, 186, 256, 260, 286–287; action plans 143, 150; attainment 4, 14, 18, 21–**27**, **28–29**, 31–32, 35, 41, 60, 62–64, 107, 144, 228; 8 77–78; measuring 66, 77–78, 83, 132, 187–188, 227; monitoring **39**, **98–99**, 106–107, 232
Pupil Premium (PP) 22
Pupil Referral Unit (PRU) 215, 263
pupils/students 1, 5–6, 11–12, 14–17, 19, 21–22, 88, 212–213; assessment 20–21, 31, 82, 175; impact 14–16, 23, 31; views 58

Qualified Teacher Status (QTS) 23
quality assurance 183

recruitment 202–221, 228, 263, **275–276**; communicating about opportunities 205, 218–219; interviewing 218, 221–222; role of leaders 202, 205, 218–219; selecting 205–206
reflective practice 161–164; developing culture 162, 166; development 161; improving 164; performance 161, 163; policy 163; teaching 162
research xviii, xix, xxi, 2–3, 5–8, 11, 18, 23, 31, 34, 49–50, 52–54, 56, 58, 60–61, 66, 78, 81–83, 85–95, 97, 100–101, 105–106, 108, 124, 126, 129–139, 145, 157, 159, 164–167, 170, 172, 179–180, 185, 189, 205, 208–220, 228–231, 249–252, 256, 259–267, **277–278**; action research 31, 40, **115**, 161, 164–165, 182; evidence xviii, 6, 8, 63, 285; *see also* research; interviews 53, 58, 65, 94–95, 97, 126, 130, 176, 186, 206–207, 209, 214, 221, 229, 233, 256, 259, 266–267, 287; lesson study 23, 156, 171–173, 179; observations 23, 65, 159–160, 162, 186, 256, 259; qualitative 32, 164, 185, 188;

quantitative 18; questionnaires 19, 47, 53, 56, 66, 94, 130, 186, 192, 229, 231; studies 54, 58, 61, 63, 66, 81, 108, 126, 132, 138, 176, 207, 217, 234, 263, 266, 271; surveys **28–29**, 56, 186, 207, 213

retention 202, 206, 208–221; culture 205, 218–220, 233, 257, 259–261, 269–274, **278**; opportunities 220, 226, 236, 238, 252–254, 260, 263, 272, 284; roles in school 222, 263, 266–268, 272, 274

roles 141; leadership teams 19, 25, 53, 86, 102, 108, **117**, 125, 144, 184, 189, 232, 238, 284; responsibilities 141–143

secondary schools 13, 57, 62, 64, 77, 82, 89, 93, 125, 130, 132, 134, 137–138, 142, 170, 202, 209, 211–212, 230, 255; case studies 52, 77, 87, 90–91; research studies 13–14, **27–29**, 57–58, 61–64, 93, 109–110, 130–131, 138, 267

Senior Leadership Team (SLT) 19, 26, 33–34, **70**, 134, 136, 144–145; classroom practice 91, 123, 164, 173, 186; leadership responsibilities 19, 145; Senior Management Team (SMT) 127

self-efficacy 95, 127, 164–165, 226, 230–232, 237–238, **239–240**, 289; Bandura 230–231; teacher perception 232

Special Educational Needs and Disabilities (SEND) 4, 185, 211, 266; pupils with 266

standards 2, 22, 24–26, **38**, 42, 68, 123, 143, **177**; headteacher 4, 131, 252; leadership 20; Ofsted 21, 286–287; teaching 71, 77–78, 157–158, 161, 176, 266, 286

strategy *see* approaches and practices

success 11, 15–16, 18, 21, 23, 40, 55, 60–62, 66, 69, 81, **98–99**, 106–107, 112, **115**, 149, **177**, 181, 192, 236, 288; action learning sets 22–23, 25, 31; measurement 192–194, 237; monitoring 64–65, 106; research evidence **277–278**, 286; teams 141, 143

superheads 90–91

teachers: and change 85, 91–96; collaboration 171; delegation of responsibility 6, 125, 129; evaluation 192; leadership 85, 103; meeting management 40–42, 149; peers, relationship with 133, 166–167; professional development 104, 163, 178–181, 214; professional practice 157, 235; relationships: peers 133, 166–167; pupils/students, relationships with 133, 166–167

Teacher Workforce Model (TWM) 203

Teaching and Learning International Survey (TALIS) 210

Teaching Assistant (TA) 25–26, 32

teamwork 143; addressing issues 143–145; benefits 145; common obstacles 146; creating teams 139–140; developmental phases 139; effective/ineffective teams 143; member functions 141; theorising about teams 139

Universities Council for the Education of Teachers (UCET) 134, 183